THE ENGLISH LANGUAGE

VOLUME 2

THE ENGLISH LANGUAGE

VOLUME 2

ESSAYS BY LINGUISTS AND MEN OF LETTERS
1858–1964

SELECTED AND EDITED BY

W. F. BOLTON

Professor of English, University of Reading

AND

D. CRYSTAL

Lecturer in Linguistic Science, University of Reading

CAMBRIDGE

AT THE UNIVERSITY PRESS

1969

Published by the Syndics of the Cambridge University Press
Bentley House, 200 Euston Road, London N.W.1
American Branch: 32 East 57th Street, New York, N.Y.10022

Library of Congress Catalogue Card Number: 66–11030
Standard Book Numbers:
521 07325 1 clothbound
521 09545 x paperback

Printed in Great Britain
at the University Printing House, Cambridge
(Brooke Crutchley, University Printer)

CONTENTS

ACKNOWLEDGEMENTS

We are indebted to the following for permission to reproduce copyright material: Appleton-Century-Crofts, New York, for 'The Social Significance of Differences in Language Practice and the Obligation of the Schools' by C. C. Fries, from *American English Grammar*.—The Clarendon Press, Oxford, for 'The Value of Place-Name Study' from Eilert Ekwall's introduction to the fourth (1960) edition of his *Concise Oxford Dictionary of English Place-Names*; and for the following Society for Pure English tracts: 'The Society's Work', Tract XXI, by Robert Bridges, 'Needed Words', Tract XXXI, by Logan Pearsall Smith, and 'Slang', Tract LV, by Eric Partridge.—The English Universities Press Ltd and Thomas Y. Crowell, Co., New York, for 'Words' by Anthony Burgess, from his *Language Made Plain*.—A. M. Heath and Co. Ltd, Miss Sonia Brownell and Secker and Warburg Ltd and Harcourt, Brace and World, Inc. for 'Politics and the English Language' by George Orwell, from *Horizon*.—Alfred A. Knopf, Inc. for 'English or American?', reprinted, by permission of the publisher, from *The American Language*, fourth edition, by H. L. Mencken. Copyright, 1936 by Alfred A. Knopf, Inc., renewed, 1964.—Linguistic Society of America, Austin, Texas, for the following contributions to *Language*: 'English Verb Inflection', vol. 23, by Bernard Bloch, and 'A Multiply Ambiguous Adjectival Construction in English', vol. 36, by R. B. Lees.—D. Lloyd James for 'Broadcast English' by A. Lloyd James.—National Council of Teachers of English, USA, for 'The Lexicographer's Uneasy Chair' by James Sledd, from vol. 23 of *College English*.—Oxford University Press, New York, for 'The Interinanimation of Words' by I. A. Richards, from *The Philosophy of Rhetoric*.—The Public Trustee and The Society of Authors for 'A Plea for Speech Nationalisation' by George Bernard Shaw. Reprinted with permission of The Macmillan Company from the *Encyclopaedia of the Social Sciences*, edited by E. R. A. Seligman and Alvin Johnson, 'Language' by Edward Sapir, vol. IX, pp. 155–69. Copyright 1933 by the Macmillan Company, renewed 1961 by the Macmillan Company.—University of Michigan Press, Ann Arbor, for the introductory section from H. Kurath and R. I. McDavid's book, *The Pronunciation of English in the United States*.

We wish to thank all who assisted us in compiling this book, especially our colleagues; the Librarian and staff of Reading University Library; our proof-reader, Miss Janet A. Ashdown; Simon Fraser University, British Columbia, for a generous grant in the final stages of preparation; our wives; and the Syndics and those responsible for its production at the Cambridge University Press.

W.F.B.
D.C.

Reading
October 1968

INTRODUCTION

The twenty-two essays in this book illustrate both the internal and the external history of literary English prose since 1858; that is, they are examples of the structure of the language and of attitudes towards it over more than a century. The points of view are those of both men of letters and linguists, and they represent something of the development and changing nature of English language study in the light of the growth of linguistic science. The order of selections is chronological, but readers may find other arrangements which correspond to their own interests, such as the idea of a 'standard' English, spelling reform, neologisms, the American language, grammar, lexicography, morphology or syntax.

Men of letters have long been the most articulate members of the linguistic community and the most readable and influential writers, and they provide revealing manifestations of the importance of linguistic resources and linguistic theory for literary style. But for the history of linguistic science, men of letters supply very imperfect illustrations, showing sometimes its motivating concerns, sometimes its published conclusions, more often only the gulf between professional writers and professional students of language. It is not difficult to see why such a gulf should have developed, if we briefly trace the development of linguistic science as a specialized intellectual discipline. A historical survey also shows why any book dealing with English language in the twentieth century has to look to linguists rather than to men of letters for the greater part of its information.

At the end of the nineteenth century, the only systematic research into the nature of language was being carried on in Europe. This was the long-established field of 'comparative philology', the historical study of language, which was primarily concerned to ascertain the earliest states and prehistories of the major European languages. Consequently it had very little to say about the English language, or any other, in its modern state. Nor did the foundation of learned societies to study language, such as the Philological Society in Great Britain (founded in 1842), stimulate much organized research into modern English structure—apart, of course, from the pioneer work in lexicography (see Essay 5 of this book). It was not until the twentieth century was well under way that comments on the contemporary state of the language came more frequently from the linguist than the man of letters. Henry Sweet, whose work is represented in Essay 2, was a central influence on English language research, especially in phonetics, but he was very much an exception. The majority of linguists were preoccupied with matters of language history, and the ordinary user of language was on the whole quite satisfied with his traditional grammar books, in which English was largely described in terms originally devised and more appropriate for the analysis of Greek and Latin.

By the second decade of this century, the situation had changed. The work of Ferdinand de Saussure in Europe, and that of Edward Sapir (see Essay 10) among others in America, completely changed the orientation of linguistic study. The traditional historical view of language switched to a predominantly non-historical, or 'synchronic', view. Languages came under study in their modern states, regardless of their histories, and also in their own terms, regardless of the traditions suggested by classical language study. Speech was seen as more central to an understanding of the phenomenon of language than was writing. This was particularly the case in America, where the linguistic situation forced these priorities upon scholars. Here the stimulus for linguistic research was almost exclusively anthropological. In order to study the cultures of the dying American Indian tribes, it was necessary to master the tribal languages; and as none of these had ever been written down, the first thing which had to be done was to make an analysis of the tribe's speech. Detailed phonetic transcriptions were made, and both Sapir and Bloomfield did pioneer work in developing linguistic techniques to handle material of this kind. It was thus in such a climate that the scientific study of language—which is what Linguistics is—evolved. And while in these early days few scholars paid much attention to English, the theoretical principles and procedures which came out of the study of these languages were not long in being put to use in research on more familiar tongues. English, the native language of the majority of linguists, was used more frequently than any other language to illustrate theoretical points clearly, and accordingly benefited a great deal. It is now without doubt the most thoroughly studied language in the world, though much still remains to be discovered about it.

Early theoretical developments were the concept of the phoneme (the smallest contrastive unit of sound in a language) and, not long after, the analogous concept of the morpheme (the smallest contrastive grammatical unit): see Essays 10 and 17. Issues connected with the definition and application of these notions were argued at great length on both sides of the Atlantic. With the work of Bloomfield (see Essay 11), the major linguistic developments of the first thirty years of this century were presented in one volume, *Language* (1933), which proved to be the dominant influence on research for the next twenty years. His method for approaching the analysis of a language involved three main stages: first you studied the characteristics of the entire range of sounds which would be used (made a phonetic analysis); second, you grouped these sounds into contrastive units, distinguishing those sounds which could be used to make changes of meaning in utterances from those which could not (a phonological analysis); third, you made an analysis of the basic units of grammar (a morphological analysis). Afterwards, you went on to the rest of the language—to syntax (essentially, the way in which words and other grammatical units are arranged in sequences) and semantics (the study of linguistic meaning). The focus of attention was clearly on the first three aspects of language organization, however, and here it stayed until the late 1940s and early 1950s, when men like Fries (see Essay 15) began to explore the neglected area of syntax.

Linguistics, especially in its application to English language study, matured as an intellectual discipline during the post-war period in both Europe and America. Before the war, apart from the above developments, which were relatively slow in coming, and which were the work of a small number of scholars, there was little one could point to. A great deal of philological work continued to be done, naturally. Organized groups, such as the Society for Pure English (see Essay 7), produced numerous pamphlets, articles, and so on, but only a small number were of permanent importance, dealing with areas of English particularly neglected at that time (see, for example, Essay 14). Research into dialects and place-names (see Essay 12) proceeded rapidly, but in relative isolation from other developments. Some attempt was made to provide new methods of teaching English to foreigners. The most important advances were certainly the large-scale descriptive studies of English grammar by such men as Jespersen and Kruisinga.

The Second World War changed this situation, particularly in the field of foreign language teaching, where linguistic techniques had proved of value for the teaching of such esoteric languages as Arabic and Japanese. Immediately after, there was an influx of potential linguists, some already trained, into the universities; departments of Linguistics began to flourish; and, as a consequence, so did post-graduate research. Linguistics societies were inaugurated, and new journals began to appear. More widespread communication between European and American schools of thought took place. Applications of Linguistics to new fields were discovered, making use of recent technical developments, particularly in computers and acoustics. Linguists began writing introductory textbooks on their subject. As a result of all this ferment, the 1950s saw a spate of grammars on English, mainly applying traditional linguistic approaches to the language, but spending more time on the syntax than hitherto.

In the late 1950s, a number of scholars, dissatisfied with the traditional methodologies of language analysis, introduced a completely different approach, known as generative grammar (see Essay 19). This departed from the phonetics–phonology–morphology approach to language study, and began with syntax, which these linguists felt was the core of language. Theoretical developments since have largely been in connexion with the views of this school. There have of course been other theories of language put forward; for example, the 'tagmemic' view, associated primarily with the name of Kenneth Pike, or the theories developed by J. R. Firth; and the relative merits and demerits of these theories are of considerable interest at the present time. In addition, a great deal of valuable work has gone on not attached to any of the major schools of linguistic thought, such as in dialectology (see Essay 20).

Most linguists still use English as the main language of exemplification for their theoretical notions, and scholars' knowledge of this language is clearly in a state of flux at the moment. The subject of teaching English to foreigners is now an industry in itself, and a large number of other fringe areas have developed, such as stylistics, psycholinguistics and speech pathology. A great deal still remains to be done in the field of English Linguistics, of course. While the greater part of phonetics and morphology has been well studied, there remain many problems of syntax which have hardly been touched, and the whole field of the semantics of English (including the question of how English vocabulary is structured) awaits investigation. The lines of needed research for scholars over the next few years are clear, and an increasing number of people trained in the subject is appearing.

But the result of this rapid specialist development has its dangers too. As linguists study language in greater depth and with more precision, using specially devised theories, terminology and procedures, it is necessarily going to be the case that they leave the non-linguist further and further behind. The science of language, though much needed, has brought a gulf between the expert and Everyman's natural interest in his own language, and this is a gap which needs to be bridged. It is to be hoped that the objective precision of the linguist and the sensitive response of the man of letters will come closer together as the subject of Linguistics becomes more widely known and its aims more generally appreciated.

This brief history outlines the ideas that controlled the selection of texts for this book. Some (including a number of 'pivotal' papers) were excluded because they duplicated those already chosen; some were too technical or unrepresentative; for some there was simply no room. A number of these rejected essays are referred to in the study questions. Except where otherwise noted, the texts are those of the first edition, save that obvious errors have been silently corrected, bibliographical 'reading lists' and irrelevant cross-references have been omitted, and a few small matters of style like footnote conventions and the use of inverted commas in quotations have been standardized. Although the texts have been set in the same type and have a uniform system of headings other original typographical features have been preserved. Neither the introductory paragraphs nor the study questions are exhaustive. The reader may find them a useful way of relating the texts to one another, or he may prefer to follow his own interests, using the topical index. Editorial footnotes provide translations and some other clarifications where necessary.

I

CHARLES DICKENS
(1812–1870)

Dickens founded *Household Words* in 1850 when his fame as a novelist was already secure. In this contribution he brings together a substantial number of the facts and ideas about the history of the English language that were familiar to the reading public around the middle of the nineteenth century. He applies the facts and ideas, which are almost all about vocabulary alone, to standards of English style, especially among the great figures in English literature. He begins and ends with the cardinal criterion: intelligibility.

'Saxon-English'

(*Household Words*, vol. 18, 1858)

When a man has anything of his own to say, and is really in earnest that it should be understood, he does not usually make cavalry regiments of his sentences, and seek abroad for sesquipedalian words. We all know that an Englishman, if he will, is able to speak easily and clearly; also he can, if he please, write in such a manner as to send the common people to their dictionaries at least once in every page. Let him write Saxon, and the Saxons understand him; let him use Latin forms that have been long in use, and they will also understand him; but let him think proper to adopt Latin or Greek expressions which are new, or at all events new to the many, and they will be puzzled. We can all read with comfort the works of Thomas Fuller, Swift, Bunyan, Defoe, Franklin, and Cobbett; there, sense is clear, feeling is homely, and the writers take care that there shall be no misunderstanding. But in Robertson, Johnson, and Gibbon, one word in every three is an alien; and so an Englishman who happens to have, like Shakespeare, 'small Latin and less Greek,' is by no means quite at home in their society.

Two hundred years ago, Dr. Heylin remarked, 'Many think that they can never speak elegantly, nor write significantly, except they do it in a language of their own devising: as if they were ashamed of their mother tongue, and thought it not sufficiently curious to express their fancies. By means whereof, more French and Latin words have gained ground upon us since the middle of Queen Elizabeth's reign than were admitted by our ancestors, not only since the Norman, but the Roman conquest.' And Sir Thomas Browne, who was himself a great Latinist, says, 'If elegancy still proceedeth, and English pens maintain that stream we have of late observed to flow from many, we shall, within few years, be fain to learn Latin to understand English, and a work will prove of equal facility in either.'

Our language has gone through its changes. Spenser resisted affectations of Italian speech, and went out of his way to be Saxon. Our best authors, except Milton, have all been maintainers of Saxon: but the Latin taste, of which Heylin complained, which Milton supported, and which overran much of our literature in Queen Anne's time, after passing through various stages, is only in our own generation yielding before a restored love of books written in Saxon-English, which will conquer in time even the affectations of the ignorant, and the tardier literary perceptions of the man of science.

It must not, however, be supposed that the mere use of Saxon words can stand for a token of good writing; many a common word of Latin-English is known better than the corresponding Saxon. But if a man wishes to write for all, he must know how to use the speech of all, and he will come nearest all hearts with words that are familiar in every home, and find their way even into the prattle of the nursery.

During the last twenty or thirty years great attention has been paid by scholars, both in England and in Germany, to the youth of our language; its mother, its nurses, and its schools, have been looked up, and we know more than we did about its origin. We are beginning, in fact, to understand the History of the Language: and it may be worth while to take a rapid view of the facts now most commonly received.

Although we often speak of the Saxons or Anglo-Saxons as the invaders of Britain in the fifth century, yet it must not be forgotten that other tribes, such as the Jutes and Frieslanders, came over, too. Foremost, however, were the Angles and the Saxons, and these two names appear side by side in various ways; the Angles gave their name to the country, Engla-land; and the Saxon version of the gospels is headed, 'That Godspell on Englisc.' But, on the other hand, to this day the Welsh call the English language Saeson-aeg, or the Saxon speech; and the Scotch Highlanders call an Englishman, Sassenach. Some have maintained that a few of the tribes, and particularly the Jutes, were

Scandinavians; but it is admitted that the greater part of the invaders were men of Teutonic (or Dutch) race, who came over from the North of Germany, or the South of Denmark. In the widest sense, we may look on the terms German, Teutonic, and Dutch, as all meaning the same thing: and we may say that the same Teutonic race inhabits Europe from the Alps to the North Sea, between the Rhine upon the west, and the Elbe, or even the Vistula, upon the east. This race includes Austrians, Tyrolese, Northern Swiss, Bavarians, Prussians, Hanoverians, Hollanders, Flemings, and others: but when speaking without reference to politics, they are to be divided into High and Low Dutch; Dutch of the highlands of Southern Germany, and the Dutch of the low lands of Northern Germany. High Dutch happens to have become the polite dialect, the language of German literature; and Low Dutch, fallen into disrepute, is cultivated now in Holland only. But to Low Dutch belongs honour, as the parent of our modern English. Our very sailors who trade to Rotterdam or Hamburgh, cannot help being struck with the likeness of the two languages, and their conclusion is, that 'after all, Dutch is only a sort of broken English.' English, in truth, is a sort of broken Dutch. The Dutch skippers (that is, shippers) who trade to Liverpool or Whitehaven, have no great difficulty in understanding our own northern dialects. A Lancashire boy, who was sent to school at Hamburgh, happening to land on a very hot day, went up to some maid-servants who were drawing water at a fountain, and said, 'Will you give me a drink?' 'Wat sagt-en?' was the reply. 'Will you—give me—a drink?' he repeated. 'Ja, ja, du kanst drinken,' (Yea, yea, thou canst drink), was the ready answer. The broad Lancashire and the broad Dutch were soon at home together.

The Angles, the Saxons, and other Teutonic tribes, made sundry descents on the kingdom of Britain for about one hundred years, and at last conquered a large part of the country, driving the native Britons (whom they called the Welsh, or foreigners), to the fastnesses of Wales, to Cumberland, and the Strathclyde.

They held possession till the year one thousand and sixty-six; and as they adopted few Welsh words, it follows that a pure Teutonic was spoken in England for six hundred years. It is true that divers dialects of the same language were current in divers parts; and it seems that the Angles, who were settled in the north and east, spoke in a broader dialect than Saxons who lived in the south and south-west. To this day, therefore, the pronunciation common in the North of England remains broader and more open than that of the South. But probably the tribes could understand one another, as well as in our day a Yorkshireman can understand a Somersetshire peasant.

This language, commonly called the Anglo-Saxon, was cultivated with great diligence, especially from the time of King Alfred, who laboured hard to promote the cause of native literature. The laws were written in that language; and useful books were translated, in order that a love of learning might be fostered among the people. Some few Latin words were adopted; but in most cases the foreign terms were translated into the mother tongue; the Evangelium was the God-spell, that is, good-spell, or good-tiding; the Saviour was the Haelend, or Healer. In speaking of God, they called him not only the Ael-mihtig, or all-mighty, but likewise the All-walda, or all-wielder, and the Ael-craeftig, or all-skilful. For infinite, they said Un-ge-end-ed, that is, un-ended or unbounded; and consciousness was the in-witness.

We may thus see, that in Anglo-Saxon there was not only a power of making compound words, but a habit of translating Latin or Greek compounds into the corresponding Saxon; and the same principle was carried out in all the sciences, as far as the learning of the time extended. Astronomy was Star-craft; literature was Book-craft, and a literary man was a Book-man; botany was Herb-craft; magic was Witch-craft; and even yet, the labour of the hands is said to be used in a Hands-craft.

This Teutonic, or Anglo-Saxon language, prevailed for about six hundred years; but, when the Normans came over and subdued the country, they made great changes. Thenceforward, while Saxon was the language of the common people, French was spoken by their lords and masters. This French, which is a sort of corrupt Latin, was taught in the schools, spoken in the courts of justice, and used in the drawing up Acts of Parliament. And so, from the Conquest till the time of Henry the Third, there were two distinct languages in the country, both undergoing change in their own way; the Saxon losing the purity which it had in Alfred's days; the French of London failing to keep pace with the French of Paris. But the common people did not give up their own language; and they have retained for us some very pure fragments of it in our county dialects.

Thus, for about three hundred years, the two languages went side by side, though both were changing,—drawing closer to each other. The changes undergone by Saxon, are seen in the later portions of the Saxon Chronicle, which was a note-book kept through a long series of years, until the reign of Henry the Second, and also in poems of a later time. As for the French, Chaucer tells us that the French spoken in the neighbourhood of Stratford-le-Bow was no longer recognised at Paris: for, when describing the Prioress, in his Canterbury Tales, he says:—

> And French she spake ful fayre and fetisly
> After the schole of Stratford-atté-Bowe;
> The French of Paris was to hir unknowne.

Victors and vanquished were to speak one tongue; the groundwork of it and the grammar remained Saxon; but a large number of words, particularly of compound words, were French; for the custom of translating Latin into Saxon ceased. And thus, towards the end of these three hundred years, a language was formed, which was intelligible both to the gentry and the common people.

Dean Trench, in his valuable work on the Study of Words, has considered the relations of the Saxon and Norman occupants; and thinks, that from an intelligent study of the contributions which they have severally made to the English language, we might almost get at the main story of the country, even though we had lost our written records. He observes, that at one period there would exist duplicate terms for many things; but that when a word was often upon the lips of one race, while its equivalent was seldom employed by the other, the word frequently used would very probably be handed down, and its equivalent would be forgotten. In other cases, only one word may have existed; inasmuch as the thing which it represented was confined to one half of the nation, and remained strange to the other.

He also remarks that our words which denote dignity, state, or honour, are mostly derived from the Norman-French. Such words are, sovereign, sceptre, realm, chancellor, palace, &c., whence we may infer that the Normans were the ruling race. For the word king, which is an exception, he gives an ingenious explanation. On the other hand, the objects of nature, the affairs of daily life, the ties of domestic life, are denoted by Saxon terms. 'The palace and the castle may have come to us from the Norman, but to the Saxon we owe far dearer names,—the house, the roof, the home, the hearth. The instruments used in cultivating the earth, the flail, the plough, the sickle, the spade, are Saxon; so, too, the main products of the earth, as wheat, rye, oats, &c. And observe, that the names of almost all animals, so long as they are alive, are Saxon, but, when dressed and prepared for food, become Norman; a fact which we might have expected beforehand; for the Saxon hind had the labour of tending and feeding them, but only that they might appear at the table of his Norman lord. Thus ox, steer, cow, are Saxon, but beef, Norman; calf is Saxon, but veal, Norman; sheep is Saxon, but mutton, Norman; so it is severally with swine and pork, deer and venison, fowl and pullet. Bacon, the only flesh, which, perhaps, ever came within his reach, is the single exception.'

We may remember also the anecdote told about the order of the Garter, and the remark ascribed to King Edward the Third, 'Honi soit qui mal y pense,' a motto which still remains upon our coat of arms, and which, like Dieu et mon droit, is a daily memento that the ruling race formerly spoke in the French language. But we hear a different speech in the mouths of the commons under Wat Tyler and John Ball, with their popular outcry:—

When Adam dalf and Eva span,
Where was then the gentleman?

or as the Germans still have it in almost the same words:—

Als Adam grub und Eva spann,
Wo war da der Edelmann?

The best and most agreeable way of learning the state of the English language, as it existed during the latter part of the fourteenth century, is to read John Wycliffe's version of the New Testament, and Geoffrey Chaucer's Canterbury Tales. In these works the two streams combine, though perhaps not in equal proportions; for the writings of Wycliffe, being designed for the people, contain a larger proportion of Saxon words; and those of Chaucer, composed for readers who were not unacquainted with the French metrical romances, include a number of terms used in romance and chivalry; and, as we have seen, most of these terms were Norman. It is to be regretted that more attention is not paid by English readers to Wycliffe and Chaucer.

It unfortunately happens that Chaucer's English is just old enough to require the aid of a glossary, and yet not difficult enough to confer upon those who master it, credit as linguists. Many a person would not refuse to spend several hours upon a hundred lines of Ariosto or Tasso, who would grudge equal labour to a tale of Chaucer's; for, after all, Chaucer is only an Englishman, and we feel that we have a birth-right to consider ourselves English scholars. As reader of Italian, one can make some pretence of the accomplishments. But if any one caring to work at English, should desire to render his course of study easy, he would find it worth while to study with care Wycliffe's version of St. John's Gospel; he would then be prepared, in some measure, to go on with Chaucer's

Canterbury Tales; and, after reading two or three thousand lines, he would be surprised to find himself almost as much at home with the father of English poetry, as he can be with Shakespeare or with Milton. At the same time he may find it good suggestive work to compare the original of the Knight's Tale, or the Wife of Bath's Tale, with modernised versions of the same by Dryden and Pope.

In examining the words of Wycliffe and Chaucer, we find that most of them are either Saxon or French, and that a few are derived directly from Latin. Sometimes Wycliffe employs a Latin word, as Resurrection, at other times he translates it, the Agen-rysynge (or again-rising); so also the word Except appears as Out-taken, thus, Out-taken women and children, for Except women and children.

From the fourteenth century until the Reformation, the language received constant accessions of Latin words, particularly in works which treated of art or science, law or religion. For as the authors had all studied in Latin, they were apt to introduce school phrases whenever they attempted to convey their thoughts in English. And when, after the fall of Constantinople, and the consequent dispersion of the Greeks, old Greek literature released from the ban first set on it, began to attract notice in Western Europe, it became the fashion to imitate the languages of classical antiquity, and to regard Teutonic literature as barbarous. This influence was very strongly felt between the reigns of Queen Elizabeth and Charles the First.

The Reformation worked both ways: on the one hand it aroused a desire of translating the Bible into English, and the translators had a direct object in using words which the common people could understand; but, on the other hand, the religious disputes which ensued, caused many theological and scholastic terms, such as justification, sanctification, transubstantiation, consubstantiation, and others, to become part of our ordinary language.

Hence it is, that we find Latimer, Bishop Hall, and Bunyan, addressing themselves to the plain intelligence of the people; while Hooker and Jeremy Taylor, adopting a much more ambitious style, wrote for the educated classes in society.

Roger Ascham has, however, well observed, that a good writer must speak as the common people do, and think as wise men do; for so shall every man understand him, and the judgment of wise men approve him.

2

HENRY SWEET

(1845–1912)

Sweet was a pioneer student of the English language who did much to further knowledge of both its history and its living structure. (Henry Higgins, of Shaw's *Pygmalion*, is modelled on him in some measure.) In this essay he seeks to correct the exclusively retrospective orientation of linguistic science in his own day, and the mistakenly Latinate treatment of traditional descriptions of English grammar, by postulating a new analysis of the materials. He begins with the phonetic level and shows, among other things, the independence of phonetic and logical systems in language. From this he goes on to a broader consideration of the logical side and the relation between linguistic categories and natural categories, which he finds also to be independent. In his last section he proposes at length a classification of the parts of speech on purely formal (inflectional and positional) criteria. (The section on 'Logic and Language' is here omitted.)

'Words, Logic and Grammar'

(*Transactions of the Philological Society*, 1876)

Introduction

One of the most striking features of the history of linguistic science as compared with zoology, botany and the other so-called natural sciences, is its one-sidedly historical character. Philologists have hitherto chiefly confined their attention to the most ancient dead languages, valuing modern languages only in as far as they retain remnants of older linguistic formations—much as if zoology were to identify itself with palæontology, and refuse to trouble itself with the investigation of living species, except when it promised to throw light on the structure of extinct ones.

Philologists forget, however, that the history of language is not one of decay only, but also of reconstruction and regeneration. These processes are of equal, often more importance than those by which the older languages were formed, and, besides, often throw light on them.

They have further the great advantage of being perfectly accessible to the observer. Thus the growth of a language like English can be observed in a series of literary documents extending from the ninth century to the present day, affording examples of almost every linguistic formation.

But before history must come a knowledge of what now exists. We must learn to observe things as they are without regard to their origin, just as a zoologist must learn to describe accurately a horse, or any other animal. Nor would the mere statement that the modern horse is a descendant of a three-toed marsh quadruped be accepted as an exhaustive description. Still less would the zoologist be allowed to ignore the existing varieties of the *Equidæ* as being 'inorganic' modifications of the original type. Such, however, is the course pursued by most antiquarian philologists. When a modern language discards the cumbrous and ambiguous inflexions it has received from an earlier period, and substitutes regular and precise inflexions and agglutinations of its own, these formations are contemptuously dismissed as 'inorganic' by the philologist, who forgets that change, decay and reconstruction are the very life of language—language is 'inorganic' only when it stands still in its development.

The first requisite is a knowledge of phonetics, or the form of language. We must learn to regard language solely as consisting of groups of sounds, independently of the written symbols, which are always associated with all kinds of disturbing associations, chiefly historical. We must then consider language in its relation to thought, which necessitates some study of the relation of language to logic and psychology. Such investigations, if carried out consistently, will greatly modify our views, not only of English, but of language generally, and will bring us face to face with many of the ultimate problems of language, which have hitherto been rather shirked by philologists. Such problems are those which I propose to discuss in the present paper. I begin with the important question of sentence-, word- and syllable-division, beginning again with the purely formal, or phonetic criteria.

Sentence- and word-division

The first and most obvious is the organic necessity of taking breath—we are unable to utter more than a certain number of sounds in succession without renewing the stock of air in our lungs, which unavoidably necessitates a pause. Speech in its simplest form consists mainly of short questions and answers expressed in simply constructed phrases—in this case there is not merely a pause, but an absolute cessation of voice.

Within these 'breath-groups,' or phonetic sentences, there is no pause whatever. This is important to observe, as many people, misled by our ordinary word-division, imagine that they make a pause at the end of every word. But a very little observation will be enough to convince them that the words of a sentence run into one another exactly in the same way as the syllables of a word do. This coalescence is most readily observable in the stopped consonants, which, when sounded alone, or at the end of a sentence, end in a marked explosion of breath, which is sometimes called the 'organic recoil.' Now if we compare such a sentence as 'he took off his ha*t*' and 'he took his ha*t* off,' we see that this organic recoil is quite wanting in the second sentence, the *t* in 'hat off' being pronounced exactly as in the single word 'hatter.'

The second criterion is force or stress—the most important element in the synthesis of speech-sounds. We will now examine some simple sentences, writing them provisionally without division into words or syllables, and see what light is thrown on their structure by the degrees of force with which their elements are pronounced.[1] Let us take the sentences (kəmtəmorou) and (henrikeimhoumyestəde). It is at once evident that certain syllables are pronounced with greater force than others; marking force provisionally by the use of italics, we have therefore (*k*əmtə*m*orou) and (*h*enri*k*eim*h*oum*y*estəde), disregarding minuter shades of force for the present. We find, in short, that every sentence can be analyzed into smaller groups characterized by one predominant stress-syllable, round which the others group themselves. In our first sentence there are two such stress-groups, in the second four; and if we consider the meaning of these two sentences, we see that the number of stress-groups agrees exactly with that of the words they contain—a word is, phonetically speaking, a stress-group. It must now be observed that the stress, although it tells us how many words there are in a sentence, does not tell us where the words begin. Thus in our first sentence

[1] In the phonetic notation I have here used, the letters are employed as far as practicable in their original Roman values, arbitrary combinations being excluded as much as possible. Words and sentences written phonetically are enclosed in parentheses.

a	as in	f*a*ther.	əə	as in	b*ir*d, b*ur*n.	dh	as in	*th*en.
æ	,,	h*a*t.	i	,,	b*i*t.	zh	,,	rou*g*e.
ae	,,	h*ai*r.	iy	,,	b*ea*t.	q	,,	si*ng*.
ao	,,	n*ough*t.	o	,,	n*o*t.	c	,,	*ch*ur*ch*.
e	,,	b*e*t.	ou	,,	n*o*te.	j	,,	*j*u*dge*.
ei	,	b*ai*t.	u	,,	f*u*ll.	x	,,	si*x*.
ə	,,	b*u*t, fath*er*.	uw	,,	f*oo*l.			

there is nothing in the *sound* to enable us to assign the second syllable to the first or the second stress-group—there is, phonetically speaking, no more reason for the division (kəm təmorou) than for (kəmtə morou), although the *sense* shows clearly that the first is the only possible one. Word-division is really a very complex problem, involving many considerations, phonetic, logical and grammatical. We get so accustomed to our received word-division that we regard it as something self-evident. But when we have to deal with unwritten languages, we find it by no means so easy. Thus in Mr. Jenner's paper on the Cornish Language (Trans. 1873–4) it is stated that at the beginning of the last century Cornish was 'a most irregular jargon, the chief peculiarity of which was a striking uncertainty of the speakers as to where one word left off and another began.' I must confess to having encountered the same difficulty in my study of our own language.

It is evident that word-division implies *comparison*. As long as we confine ourselves to the examination of isolated sentences, we shall not advance one step further. But when we compare a variety of sentences in which the same sound-groups are repeated in different combinations, we are able first to distinguish between meaning and unmeaning sound-groups, and finally to eliminate a certain number of groups having an independent meaning and incapable of further division. The test of independent meaning is *isolation*, or the power of forming an independent sentence. We may, therefore, define a word as an ultimate, or indecomposible sentence. Thus the verb (kəm) pronounced with a falling tone is equivalent to the fuller sentence, 'I order you to come;' the adverb (əp) pronounced with a rising tone may signify 'shall we go up?' or may have some analogous meaning determined by the context. The same applies also to nouns, pronouns and adjectives. Sound-groups, which, although phonetically capable of isolation, are meaningless when so isolated, are not words.

But between these two extremes there is an intermediate class of sound-groups, which, although not capable of being isolated and forming sentences by themselves, are yet not utterly devoid of meaning, and can, therefore, be to a certain extent isolated in thought, if not in form. Thus, if we compare the three groups (mæn), (əmæn) and (dhəmæn), we see that the two prefixes have an unmistakable, though somewhat vague meaning of their own, which enables us to identify them at once in all other cases in which they are prefixed to nouns, and yet these two syllables would convey no meaning if pronounced alone. If, on the other hand, we attempt to analyze such a group as (diyvieit), we find that not only are its elements incapable of logical isolation, but that they fail to suggest any idea whatever. The last syllable is, of course, identical with the preterite of the verb 'eat,' but the association is felt to be purely fortuitous. But if we compare (de*n*ai), (de*p*ouz) and (de*p*raiv), we feel at once the meaning of deprivation and negation in the (de), just as we feel the generalizing and specializing meaning of the prefixes in (ə*m*æn) and (dhə*m*æn), although the syllables (nai), (pouz) and (praiv) have no meaning whatever by themselves. We are, therefore, obliged to regard (de*n*ai), etc., as ultimate, indecomposible words, in spite of the significance of the prefix, while in the case of (dhə*m*æn) and (ə*m*æn) it is, to some extent, an open question whether we have here one word or two words. It seems best to distinguish two classes of words, *full-words* and *half-words*, (mæn) being a full-word, (dhə) a half-word—that is, a word incapable of forming a sentence by itself, or of suggesting an independent meaning.

The next question is, how far do these logical distinctions correspond to the phonetic ones already laid down? The answer is simple enough. Full-words correspond to stress-groups, half-words to stressless syllables. If we wish to know how many full-words there are in a sentence, we only have to count the number of full stresses. Each full stress indicates a full-word, although it does not show where the word begins and ends.

It must be remarked that the test of being able to form a sentence by itself does not strictly apply to all words. The finite verb is an important exception. The third person (gouz), for instance, cannot form a sentence by itself; by the sentence-test, therefore, (gouz) is not a word; while (hiygouz) is. And yet it would be absurd to deny the title of word to (gouz) in such a sentence as (dhə*m*ængouz). We feel (gouz) to be a full-word, 1) because it has the full stress, 2) because of the analogy of the imperative (gou), which can stand alone, and 3) because of (hiygouz), which is felt to be a compound precisely analogous to (dhə*m*æn), etc.

There is, finally, an important phonetic element of word-division to be noticed. This is the fact that certain sounds and sound-combinations only occur in certain positions. Thus the sound (q) and the combinations (tl), (x), etc., never occur at the beginning of a sentence, and others, again, never occur finally. It is, therefore, clear that these sounds cannot begin or end any full-word.

Derivative syllables and inflexions

We must now consider the important question of the relation of half-words to derivative syllables and inflexions. It need scarcely be remarked that no absolutely definite line can be drawn between them, and that the distinctions made in practice are often purely conventional.

We must first consider an important distinction between full- and half-words, which clearly brings out the semi-inflexional character of the latter, viz. that full-words are position-free, half-words not. Compare the varying position of (gou) in such sentences as (gouəwei), (ailgou), (ailgouəwei), with the unvarying præ-position of (dhə) in (dhə*m*æn). The same fixity of position characterizes derivatives and inflexions also, but in a higher degree. Thus, although the position of (dhə) *before* its noun is fixed, the connexion is loose enough to allow an adjective to come between, as in (dhəgud*m*æn). Such 'incorporations' are quite exceptional with derivative syllables,[1] and still more so with inflexions.

Derivations may be either initial or final, inflexions are only final. This last is, of course, an arbitrary limitation, which, although convenient enough in treating of the old Aryan languages, in which the most general relations were generally expressed by suffixed syllables, does not apply to other languages, which indicate the same relations by means of prefixes. Even in the Aryan languages such formations as the augment and reduplication can only be conventionally separated from the postfixed inflexions. It is, however, undeniable that, in the Aryan languages at least, the end of words is more exposed to phonetic decay than the beginning, and consequently that that intimate fusing together of root and modifying syllable, which is felt to be something more advanced than mere derivation, and which we call inflexion, has a right to be considered rather as a 'final' than as an 'initial' phenomenon.

There are several important distinctions between half-words and derivatives. Half-words can be used everywhere where their meaning allows of it, thus (dhə) can be prefixed to all nouns. Such a derivative as (be), on the other hand, can only be prefixed to certain words without any apparent reason—we have (bekəm), but not (begou). Further, the root often has no independent existence; from (be*h*eiv), for instance, we cannot deduce a verb (heiv). Or else the connexion between the meaning of the simple root and that of the derivative is not evident, as in (kəm) and

[1] The Gothic *ga-u-laubjats* = 'Do ye-two believe?' with its incorporated interrogative particle *u*, is a case in point.

(bekəm). There are, of course, various degrees of obscuration of meaning; the prefix (be), for instance, is practically almost meaningless in the present English, while (mis) in (misteik), (misfaotyən), etc., has a perfectly clear meaning. But as a general rule the connexion between derivative syllable and root is logically very intimate, more so even than in inflexions. Sometimes the derivative syllable even takes the full-stress from the root, as in the German *ant-wort*, which never happens with half-words and inflexions.

Inflexions differ from derivative syllables, and agree with half-words in being of general, unrestricted application, and in always preserving a more or less definite general signification. Their main characteristic is phonetic variation and obscuration: derivative syllables are invariable in form, inflexions not. Compare the plural forms (hæts), (dogz), (men), (fiyt), so definite in meaning, and so divergent in form, with a group of (be)-derivatives, with their constancy of form and want of meaning. Inflexions often express the same idea in totally different ways, either from phonetic change, as in the Latin acc. plurals *ovēs*, *equōs*, and the Greek acc. singulars *híppon*, *ópa*, or from confusing the meanings of forms of independent origin, as in the Latin datives *populō* and *patrī*.

If we assume, as we seem to be justified in doing by historical evidence, that derivative syllables and inflexions have developed out of half-words, we may roughly describe a derivative syllable as a half-word which has lost its logical, an inflexional as one which has lost its phonetic independence.

Syllable-division

We may now turn to the important question of syllabification. The definition of a syllable is easy enough: it is a group of sounds containing a vowel, or, in some cases, a vowel-like consonant. To determine the number of syllables in a word, we have simply to count the number of vowels. The difficulty is to tell where the syllable begins. Here I am compelled to differ both from Mr. Bell and Mr. Ellis. Mr. Bell considers that the division into syllables is determined by the nature of the sounds which constitute the syllable, whereas I hold that syllabification has nothing to do with the sounds themselves, but depends entirely on the force with which we pronounce them. (It must be understood that I speak of the natural syllabification of spoken language, not of the artificial syllabification of the spelling-books.) Let us consider the syllabification of a natural, simple sentence, such as (teikəpdhətiykəp).

Here we at once feel that the first (k) belongs to the preceding syllable, that the syllabification is clearly (teik-əp), while the second (k) belongs to the following syllable, the division being (tiy-kəp), the consonant being the same in both cases. The difference is simply one of stress, the first (k) being pronounced with weak, the second with strong force. (We may for the present disregard the fact that the stress is in both cases secondary.) The influence of the syllable-stress in determining the meaning of words is so important that if we reverse that of (teikəp) by beginning the secondary stress not on the vowel, but on the preceding (k), the word becomes quite unintelligible, or rather, sounds like an Irish pronunciation of 'teacup.' Other examples of varying syllabification are (notətaol)[1] and (ətaolmæn), (ətæk) = 'attack' and (ətæk) = 'at Ack '(name of place). We see, in short, that a syllable is a vowel-group beginning with a certain degree of force, which decreases up to the end of the syllable, till a new stress marks the beginning of another syllable. This decrease of force is observable in monosyllables also: in (kæt), for instance, the (k) is much stronger than the (t)—we do not pronounce (kæt) or even (kæt), but only (kæt). Indeed, it may be stated as a general law that perfect uniformity of force is something exceptional: force is followed by weakness of stress, and uniform weakness, again, cannot be sustained, but requires force to relieve it. These principles are clearly shown in the accentuation of polysyllable words. If we carefully measure the degrees of force with which the different syllables of a word like (impenətrəbiliti) are pronounced, we shall find that every syllable has a different degree of force. Simple sentences, which are phonetically identical with polysyllabic words (or even in some cases with monosyllable ones), follow the same laws. They always have one predominant stress which dominates over the simple word-stress. The great distinction between words and sentences is that in the former the predominant stress is fixed and invariable, while in the latter it varies according to the principle of emphasis, which gives the strongest stress to the most important word.

Before leaving the subject of syllabification, I have only to warn against the error of imagining that the division into the syllables is ever made by any kind of pause—the truth is that there is no more break in (ətaol) than there is in (ətaolmæn), and the idea that we pause between (ət) and (aol) is simply due to the association of the graphic separation in 'at all.' Mr. Ellis considers that there is often a distinction made by omitting the 'glide' from vowel to consonant, or vice versa, but it seems to me that he is confusing *absence* of glide with mere *weakness* of glide.

[1] Generally, however, pronounced (notətaol), just as (əthoum) becomes (ətoum).

than in the case of inflexions and derivatives. Inflexions are only acknowledged when sanctioned by Latin Grammar. Such purely modern inflexions as the negative (ai*k*aant) from (ai*k*æn), where the (nt) = (not), although conventionally only a half-word, not a true inflexion, could not be written as an isolated word, are shirked by that convenient compromise the apostrophe ('): by writing 'can't,' we keep up the fiction of the divisibility of a monosyllable into two separate words.

All these considerations show the hopeless confusion into which orthography falls when it attempts to overstep its legitimate function—that of giving a faithful graphic representation of the sounds of the spoken language. The attempt to indicate simultaneously the formal and the logical side of language by the same alphabet—an alphabet, it may be remarked, which is barely capable of fulfilling its purely phonetic duties alone—is about as successful as most compromises, that is, instead of doing one thing properly, it does two things badly. If, for instance, it is convenient to denote a substantive by a capital letter in German, why should we not do so in English, and why should not the same principle be extended to the other parts of speech? Adjectives, for instance, might be written with a turned capital, verbs with an italic, adverbs with a turned italic. Again, in Latin it would be very convenient to have a series of marks to indicate the different cases, independently of their form, and would much facilitate the understanding of Latin. Others, again, think that the spelling of every word ought to give a brief epitome of its etymology and history. If carried out consistently, all this would postulate an entirely independent set of signs, which, for special purposes, would be written between the lines of ordinary phonetic writing, forming a sort of short-hand logical, grammatical or historical commentary, as the case might be. In the same way I should consider word-division simply as a logical commentary on the phonetic text; in short, I would abolish the ordinary word-division altogether.

But the abandonment of conventional word-division by no means postulates a return to the old system of writing each sentence without a break. On the contrary, it is clear that the great assistance afforded to the reader by presenting the letters in groups of moderate length was the one great reason for abandoning the original system of non-division. As we have seen, the most important element in the synthesis of speech-sounds is stress. I propose, therefore, to follow the analogy of musical notation, and divide our sentences into bars, making the beginning of each group of letters coincide with a full-stress. The accent-mark otherwise required to mark the full-stress would be available for the secondary stress, and the same mark, when placed before a letter-group or 'stress-group,' as we may call it, would indicate the emphatic sentence-stress. Thus with a single mark we should be able to indicate no less than four degrees of stress. We should, however, also require a mark to indicate absence of stress at the beginning of a sentence. If we added a sign for breath-taking, and two accents to indicate the rising and falling tones, we should be able to dispense entirely with the present unsatisfactory system of punctuation, etc., and to express clearly and precisely what they indicate only imperfectly and vaguely...

Structure of English

I now propose to say something about the structure of English, and the proper method of treating its grammar. I may state at once that I consider the conventional treatment of English to be both unscientific and unpractical, starting as it does with the assumption that English is an inflexional language like Latin or Greek. The time is still not very far distant when the grammar of all languages—however diverse their structure—was servilely modelled on that of Latin. It was assumed, for instance, that as Latin had five cases, English must necessarily have just as many and no more. In those days *man* was declined thus:

nom.	man.	acc.	man.
gen.	man's.	voc.	oh man!
dat.	to a man.	abl.	by a man.

After a time, however, when the historical and comparative study of language had opened people's eyes a little, they began to see that on this principle the number of cases in English might be indefinitely extended—in short that there might be as many cases as there were prepositions. The cases were, accordingly, cut down to three, nominative, genitive and accusative. As I shall show hereafter, it is very doubtful whether the so-called accusative of the pronouns has any right to be considered a case at all, and when we consider that the genitive inflexion can generally be replaced by the preposition *of*, we see to what narrow limits the English cases, or rather case, are confined. The verbal inflexions are hardly less limited. The only personal inflexion is the *s* of *he goes*, which is practically a superfluous archaism. The only other inflexions are those which form the preterite and the two participles. These, together with the plural of nouns, are the only essential inflexions of English. No wonder, then, that the historical philologist looks with contempt on

English as a language 'destitute of grammar.' Certainly it is so, if judged from a purely antiquarian point of view. That this point of view is inadequate to the requirements of English grammar is tacitly admitted by the grammarians, who, while refusing to allow that 'of a man' is a case, do not scruple to put 'I did love,' etc., on a level with the inflexional preterite. And yet most of them ignore the equally important formations of the emphatic and negative forms or moods, simply because such forms are not recognized in Latin grammar.

All this confusion and inconsistency arises from the fact being ignored that the history of language is not merely one of negative decay, but also of positive reconstruction. Every language has the right to be regarded as an actual, existing organism, not merely as the representative of earlier stages. The fact that English was an inflexional language two thousand years ago does not prove that it is so now. The only rational principle is to look at the language as it is now, and ask ourselves, How does this language express the relations of its words to one another? If we examine English on this principle, we shall have no hesitation in characterizing it roughly as an isolating language which is passing into the agglutinative stage, with a few traditional inflexions. Hence the value of English as a preparation for the study of language generally, when studied rationally: it enables us to watch many linguistic phenomena in the very process of formation, which in other languages can only be observed in a stereotyped condition. Another advantage of English for comparative purposes is the many-sidedness of its structure. In this respect it differs essentially from languages whose structure is primitive, not, like that of English, the result of casting off an effete inflexional system. In most agglutinative languages there is no distinction of meaning made by position, all grammatical relations being expressed by modifying syllables which have a fixed order, from which they never depart. English can, therefore, only be compared with such languages in as far as it is itself agglutinative, while in that part of its grammar which depends on position it can only be compared with 'isolating' languages, such as Chinese. Again, although English agglutination is mostly of a rudimentary type, it is in other cases extremely advanced. Who, for instance, in comparing the positive future (hiylgou) with the negative (hiywountgou), would be able to detect the root (wil), which comes out clearly in the emphatic future (hiywilgou)? In such forms there is as much obscuration of the formative elements as in the traditional inflexions. These observations show how difficult it is to draw the lines which separate the different stages of linguistic development—languages pass from the isolating to the agglutinative and inflexional stages by insensible degrees, and even during the fullest development of inflexion begin to lay the foundation of future agglutination.

One striking result of the English power of expressing grammatical relations by position is the freedom with which one part of speech may be converted into another. The (səndi) is a noun, (dhen) an adverb, but in (səndi iyvniq, ʌdhə[1] dhen steitəvə faeəz) they are both attribute-words. In the same way any part of speech may be made into a noun simply by prefixing an article or adjective.

Even groups of words may be treated in this way. Thus in the sentence (ʌdhə bukyu sentmiywəz nou yuws), (nou yuws) is simply equivalent to the adjective 'useless.' When we talk of (ʌdheëm ploiəzlaiə bilitifər injəri bil) the whole of the group except (bil) is nothing but a huge composite adjective. These groups may also be inflected like simple words, as in (ʌdhə mænai sao yestədeətdhə thiyətəz faadhə), where on all received principles of grammar (thiyətəz) ought to be parsed as the genitive of 'theatre.'

English, in common with the Romance languages, is often described as an 'analytical' language, as opposed to a 'synthetic' language, such as Latin. This term is meant to imply that the agglutinations of modern languages are deliberate substitutions for the older inflexions—the inflexions are supposed to be 'analyzed' into their simple elements. It is easy to see that this view is quite erroneous. If the characteristic agglutinations of modern English, for instance, were nothing but substitutes for inflexions, there would be exactly as many agglutinations as there originally were inflexions; but, as we see, we have in English combinations to which there is nothing corresponding in the older inflexional languages, while, on the other hand, many inflexional distinctions are entirely lost.

Cases

I propose now to examine some portions of English grammar more in detail, beginning with the cases of nouns and pronouns.

It is a curious fact, hitherto overlooked by grammarians and logicians, that the definition of the noun applies strictly only to the nominative case. The oblique cases are really attribute-words, and inflexion is practically nothing but a device for turning a noun into an adjective or adverb. This is perfectly clear as regards the genitive, and,

[1] ʌ indicates weak stress.

indeed, there is historical evidence to show that the genitive in the Aryan languages was originally identical with an adjective-ending, 'man's life' and 'human life' being expressed in the same way. It is also clear that 'noctem' in 'flet noctem' is a pure adverb of time. It is not so easy to see that the accusative in such sentences as 'he beats the boy' is also a sort of adverb, because the connexion between verb and object is so intimate as almost to form one simple idea, as in the case of noun-composition. But it is clear that if 'boy' in the compound noun 'boy-beating' is an attribute-word, it can very well be so also when 'beating' is thrown into the verbal form without any change of meaning.

Our difficulty in determining the meaning of the accusative has, as far as I know, never been pointed out hitherto, viz. that in many cases it has no meaning at all, but merely serves to connect a verb with a noun in various arbitrary ways. With such verbs as 'heat,' 'carry,' etc., the accusative unmistakably denotes the object of the action expressed by the verb, but with such verbs as 'see,' 'hear,' it is clearly a mere metaphor to talk of an 'object.' A man cannot be beaten without feeling it, but he can be seen without knowing anything about it, and in many cases there is no action or volition at all involved in seeing. And in such a sentence as 'he fears the man,' the relations are exactly reversed, the grammatical nominative being really the object affected, while the grammatical accusative represents the cause, but as he is conceived as a *passive* cause, the fiction of object can still be maintained. The meaninglessness of the accusative is further shown by the inconsistencies of its actual use in language. Thus Latin has 'rideo aliquem,' English 'laugh at,' while 'deride' has the accusative as in Latin. Compare also English 'see' with 'look at' and the divergent use of the dative and accusative in Greek and Latin. It is, indeed, often doubtful à priori whether any language in a given case will employ the accusative or not—we can only tell by observing the actual form. Now in English, in the noun at least, the only 'form' of the accusative is its position after the verb. As far as the form goes, then, 'king' in 'he became king,' 'he is king,' may be in the accusative. And, as a matter of fact, English people who have not been taught grammar, that is to say Latin grammar, in their first attempts to express themselves in such a language as German, *do* put 'king' in the accusative. They are naturally confirmed in this idea when they find that if they substitute for the noun a personal pronoun, which is supposed to have distinct forms for nominative and accusative, the accusative is used, and it is only the influence of ignorant grammarians that prevents such phrases as 'it is me' from being adopted into the written language, and acknowledged in the grammars. In Danish 'det er mig' is the *only* form known, and 'det er jeg' would be as wrong as 'c'est je' would be in French. Indeed, were it not for Latin grammar, we can easily imagine the grammarians proving that 'king' in 'he became king' could not possibly be anything but the accusative, the action of the verb 'become' passing on to the object 'king.' That there is really nothing extravagant in this view is shown by the Old English 'hé wearð tó cyninge (gehálgod)' and the German 'er ward zum könig.'

Further we have also a positional dative, as in 'he gave the man a book.' May not then the supposed accusative in 'he flattered the man,' 'it pleased the man,' be really a dative, as it certainly would be historically?[1] This view might again be supported by an examination of the corresponding pronoun forms, for 'him' is historically a dative, not an accusative, and so with the others also.

But the truth is that, whatever the history may be, the so-called accusative of the personal pronouns is functionally not a case at all, but a special form which may be indifferently nom., acc. or dat., as the case may be. The real difference between 'I' and 'me' is that 'I' is an inseparable prefix used to form finite verbs, while 'me' is an independent or absolute pronoun, which can be used without a verb to follow. These distinctions are carried out in vulgar English as strictly as in French, where the distinction between the conjoint 'je' and the absolute 'moi' is rigidly enforced. The difference between French and English is that French has also a true conjoint accusative 'me,' which, as in Basque, is incorporated into the verb. In vulgar English we hear not only 'it is me,' but also with the relative, as in 'him that's here' (ʌimdhəts iyə), where the polite language only tolerates 'he.' In the polite language we find such monstrosities as 'it will give my friend and I great pleasure'—the natural result of the artificial reaction against 'it is me.'

And now a few words about the terminology. It will be observed that I have throughout avoided the names 'possessive' and 'objective.' The distinctions implied are historical, and therefore the historical names should be retained. If the names of grammatical forms were to be changed whenever their meanings changed, we should have different names for every period and every language. It is much simpler to regard these terms as being what they really are, purely conventional names of forms whose meanings are often vague and sometimes nothing at all. Historically English nouns can only be said to have one case, the genitive. The unmodified base represents historically both nominative

[1] Old English, 'hé ólecte ðám menn' and 'hit lícode ðám menn.'

and accusative (possibly also dative in some cases), we may therefore call it the 'common' case. Pronouns have three cases, nominative, genitive, as in 'it is his,' and dative. The question whether 'his' in 'his book' is a genitive, or a possessive adjective, is really an idle one, for the genitive is in all cases functionally identical with an adjective. If we disregard history, and take position as the criterion of case, we are able to distinguish doubtfully a subject and object case, the former corresponding to the old nominative, the latter sometimes to the acc., sometimes to the dat.

Pronouns

Pronouns bear the closest analogy to proper names. They are nouns which, in themselves, only connote 'human being,' and in some cases sex also. When we hear that 'he is coming,' all we learn is that a male human being is coming, and we learn just as much from the proposition 'James is coming.' The main distinction is that pronouns are of general, proper names of special application, for, if the system of giving proper names were carried out perfectly, every one would have a name to himself, which would be shared by no one else. Pronouns are, therefore, even less significant than proper names: 'he' may refer in turn to each individual man there is, if the grammatical structure of the sentence allows it.

All pronouns are relative—they always refer to some noun. 'He' is quite as relative in signification as 'who' is, and the two are really identical in meaning, the distinction being purely formal, viz. that a sentence beginning with 'who' is always accompanied by another sentence containing some statement about the person to whom the pronoun refers, and until we have this sentence, we feel that the first sentence is formally incomplete. 'He' is, therefore, relative in meaning, 'who' in meaning and form also. 'He is here' does not really convey any more information than 'the man who is here,' but it can stand alone, whereas the other cannot.

Adjectives

Adjectives may be either special or general attribute-words. Special adjectives are 'bright,' 'blue,' etc., while such adjectives as 'this,' 'that,' which connote nothing but the attribute of existing in space, are general. Still more general are such adjectives as the definite article 'the,' which connotes nothing but the attribute of forming a member of a class, or something similar. Many of these general adjectives are at the same time pronouns when they stand alone, thus 'some' alone is equivalent to 'some human beings,' while in 'some men' it is simply an adjective, or, as it is sometimes absurdly called, an 'adjective pronoun.' Similarly in vulgar English 'them' by itself is a pronoun (ʌdhemdhəts on eint duwin nou wəək), but before a noun (dhem thiqz), it is a general (demonstrative) adjective.

The two articles are often so devoid of meaning as to amount practically to nothing more than prefixes for forming nouns, although this is not carried so far as in French and German, where the definite article may be said to have hardly any meaning at all, being not only prefixed, as in English, to the names of things which only occur singly, such as 'the sun,' 'the earth,' but also to proper names and the names of abstractions.

In 'a good man' 'a' belongs not to 'good,' but to 'man.' We have, therefore, here a case of incorporation, which is avoided in 'all the way,' 'so great a work,' etc. In 'a hundred men,' the 'a' belongs to the 'hundred,' forming with it a single attribute-word.

Verbs

The really characteristic feature of the English finite verb is its inability to stand alone without a pronominal prefix. Thus (gou), (rən), (flai), by themselves may be either nouns or verbs; if, for instance, the indefinite article is prefixed to any of them, it becomes a noun—(əgou), (ərən), (ə*f*lai), are all nouns. But (aigou), (wiyrən), (dheiflai) are verbs. With the help of other prefixes a great variety of verbal forms may be made without the slightest change of the primitive form. Thus (wiylgou) is future, (wiydgou) is conditional, (wiydidgou) is a form of the preterite, etc. If for the pronoun a noun is substituted, the verb is recognized solely by its position after the noun in its common case, thus in (dhə*men*rən) there is nothing but the fact of (rən) following the uninflected plural (dhə*men*) to show that it is a verb. Even when there is a noun preceding, the pronominal prefix is often used in common talk, especially among the uneducated; thus we often hear, instead of (ʌmai brədhəz kəmiq houmtə morou), (ʌmai brədhəhiyz kəmiq . . .). The tendency to employ a pronominal prefix is also strikingly illustrated by the impersonal verbs, such as (itreinz), (it*h*æpnz), etc., where the (it) is quite unmeaning.

These facts illustrate the peculiar complexity of English grammar, and the difficulty of attaining a just and adequate view of its characteristic features. In such a sentence as (ʌdhə men kəm), (kəm) is a verb mainly through its position, in (dhei*k*əm) because of the pronominal prefix, and in (hiy*k*əmz) both because of the prefix and of the inflexional (z).

It is important to observe that English has no infinitive, except from an historical point of view. (Kəm) by itself is, as we have seen, not necessarily a verb at all, still less an infinitive 'mood,' and it is certainly most in accordance with the instinct of those who speak English naturally to consider (kəm) simply as a base or common form of the verb, just as (mæn) is felt to be a common case.[1]

The term 'mood' is, of course, quite a misnomer as applied to the infinitive in any language, for the infinitive is nothing but a sort of nominal form of the verb. On the other hand, there are in English several forms of the verb which, on all sound analogy, ought to be included among the moods. These are the emphatic (ai*d*uwgou), the negative (ai*d*ountgou), the interrogative (duwaigou), the negative-interrogative (*d*ountaigou), the first of which is quite peculiar to English.

The inflected subjunctive is almost extinct in English. In form it is only in a few cases to be distinguished from the indicative, and its original meaning is so completely lost that English people have great difficulty in learning the proper use of the subjunctive in such languages as German and French, where it is still a living element of the language. We still employ it chiefly in a few stereotyped optative phrases, such as 'God save the Queen,' and mechanically after certain conjunctions. In the language of the vulgar it seems hardly to be used at all, and such constructions as 'if I *was* you'...seem to be gradually spreading even among the educated.

Prepositions

The combination of a preposition and its noun (or pronoun) is identical in meaning with an oblique case of a noun, that is to say, it is a compound attribute. The preposition itself is modified attributively by the noun, and the two together constitute an attribute of some other word. Thus in 'he stood by,' 'by' is an attribute-word modifying 'stood,' in 'be stood by the gate,' 'by' is modified by 'the gate,' which is virtually an adverb of 'by,' and the two together form a compound attribute of 'stood.' In this example the prepositional compound is equivalent to an

[1] The form (təgou), as in (ʌai wishtə gou), might be called the supine. It is not even historically an infinitive.

adverb, but it may also qualify a substantive, as in 'the church in the town,' which is equivalent to 'the town church,' or, in German, 'die städtische Kirche.'

Sentence-words

There are a variety of words which have the peculiarity of always forming a sentence by themselves; they might also be called isolated words. These words are: 1) the imperative mood of verbs, 'come!' for instance, being equivalent to 'I command, or ask you to come'; 2) the 'adverbs' *yes* and *no*, which are equivalent to affirmative and negative propositions; and 3) the interjections, many of which, as, for instance, *alas!* from the adjective *lassus*, are quite erroneously described as inarticulate imitative sounds, and which have as much right to be considered parts of speech as the imperatives of verbs.

Concluding remarks

It is of great importance to obtain a clear idea of the province of grammar as opposed to that of the dictionary—a subject on which considerable confusion of ideas prevails. The popular notion is that the business of a grammar is to explain *forms*, of a dictionary to explain *meanings*. But it is clear that the study of forms involves also a study of their meanings as well, and, indeed, the whole of syntax is nothing else but an investigation of the meanings of grammatical forms. The real distinction is that grammar deals with the general facts of language, lexicology with the special facts. Thus the fact that 'tree' becomes 'trees' when we speak of more than one tree, is a general one, for it applies, with certain restrictions, to nearly all other nouns as well; but the fact that the combination of sound that constitutes the sound-group 'tree' has the meaning we attach to it and no other, is an isolated one, and there is nothing in the sounds themselves or the way in which they are combined to necessitate one meaning more than another, while even if we were ignorant of the meaning of the word 'tree,' we should be able to recognize in 'trees' the meaning of 'plurality,' if we met with it in an unambiguous sentence. If we had a rationally constructed Universal Language, in which every letter in a word would be significant and combined according to definite laws, so that the connexion between form and meaning would be at once evident, there would be no dictionary at all—everything would be grammar, and the dictionary would be simply an alphabetical index to the grammar.

The simple question, then, that we have to ask ourselves in determining the scope of the grammar of any language is, how does this language indicate general meanings? The answer to this question is the grammar. If the language chiefly employs what are conventionally termed 'inflexions,' its grammar will be mainly an 'inflexional' one; if position, its grammar will be like that of Chinese, and, to a great extent, of English also, 'positional.' To assert that Chinese has 'no grammar,' or 'no grammar *properly speaking*,' as it is sometimes cautiously put, is simply an eccentric way of stating that it has no *inflexional* grammar.

An essential part of English grammar is *intonation*. An immense number of general ideas, both emotional and purely logical, are expressed in English by the rise and fall of the tones of the voice. The distinction between affirmation and interrogation, subject and predicate, doubt and certainty, etc., are all expressed either partly or entirely by intonation.

The following are, then, the essential elements of English grammar:

1 Phonology, or an account of the formation of the sounds of the language, their combinations, etc.

2 Phonetic Synthesis, comprising Quantity, Force or Stress, and Intonation. (Voice-timbre, Expression, etc., belong rather to Elocution, which is a special branch of Grammar.)

3 Word Position.

4 Parts of Speech, Inflexion, Agglutination, etc., (including all that is commonly understood as 'Grammar.')

The relation of form to meaning may, of course, be considered in various ways. The form may first be considered purely as form, as when we analyze the various degrees of quantity, the exact intervals of intonation, etc., and we may then either consider the various meanings attached to each form, or starting from the meaning alone, determine what forms are used to express it. In a full grammar all these arrangements must be represented, partially at least. The facts must also be so stated that due prominence is given to the really important elements. Archaisms and fossilized forms must be duly subordinated to the living means of expression.

The different *strata* of the formative elements must also be distinguished. Thus, while the combinations of noun and preposition would be treated at full under the same category as inflexion—'of man' and 'man's,' for instance, coming together—the traditional inflexions would also be grouped together separately, apart from the later agglutinations. Even merely *nascent* forms and tendencies would also be grouped together separately. It is, for instance, important to observe the tendency to indicate the singular of nouns by prefixes, leaving the plural unmodified; 'man,' for instance, means 'man in general,' or, in short, 'men,' while 'the man,' or 'a man,' has a definitely singular meaning. It is of course true that we can also say 'the men' in the plural, but it is at least conceivable that in a more advanced stage of English the use of the articles may be confined entirely to the singular, and in that case it is highly probable that the plural inflexions would be entirely lost, so that the distinction between singular and plural would be denoted entirely by prefixes. Compare the French singulars (əq[1] sha, lə sha) with the plural (de sha, le sha).

If English grammar were treated in this way, it would give the student just notions not only of the structure of his own language, but also of language generally, and a solid foundation would be laid for historical and comparative philology. The ordinary grammars, which ignore many of the most characteristic features entirely, and subordinate others to purely exceptional ones, not only give the student an entirely erroneous idea of the structure of English, but also train him to habits of erroneous and superficial observation, the evil results of which are seen every day both in scientific philology and in the practical acquisition of foreign languages.

[1] I use (q) to denote the French nasal: (əq sha) = 'un chat.'

3

FITZEDWARD HALL

(1825–1901)

Hall was born in New York State and went to Harvard. He travelled and taught in India, where he learned Sanskrit. In 1862 he came to England where he remained until his death, teaching, writing, and taking part in projects like the *Oxford English Dictionary*, the *Dialect Dictionary*, and the Early English Text Society publications. In this essay, a characteristic one about philological polemics, he studies the proscriptive school of linguistic criticism in the past and among his own contemporaries. He subjects their views to the test of linguistic history and of reason. Having shown that only professional students of language have the authority to judge it, he goes on to a study of the American politician, journalist and orator William Cullen Bryant. He concludes that 'the doings of American philologasters are, in truth, a curious study'.

'English Rational and Irrational'

(*The Nineteenth Century*, vol. 43, 1880)

Die Hauptsache überall die ist, die Erkenntniss von der Meinung zu unterscheiden.[1]
F. E. D. Schleiermacher

Peremptory and unreasoned pronouncements as to what is bad English are not the least of the minor pests which vex our enlightened age; and the bulk of them, as the better-informed are well aware, may be traced to persons who have given only very slight attention to verbal criticism. The effective disseminators of these pronouncements are, indeed, far from numerous. By these we mean, for the most part, those would-be philologists who collect waifs and strays of antipathies and prejudices, amplify the worthless hoard by their own whimseys, and, to the augmentation of vulgar error, digest the whole into essays and volumes. That, however, their utterances should be echoed unquestioningly by the demi-literate, and adopted as subordinate articles of the Philistine creed, is only what might be expected. Far more readily

[1] [*Die Hauptsache...unterscheiden* The main point among all this is to distinguish knowledge from opinion.]

than the contrary, whatever partakes of the nature of disparagement may calculate on popular acceptance. Account should be taken, also, that any seeming evidence of a man's superiority to his associates is, in general, a source of keen gratification to him. Of all that he claims as his own, nothing is likely to raise him higher in his own conceit than his fancied possession of knowledge to which, with the elegance implied in it, they are strangers. Then again, research, or even patient reflection, where the subject-matter lies deeper than the most obvious superficialities, is a characteristic of scholars, and, as being so, is entirely secure from appropriation by the half-educated and their favourite guides. All things considered, we may be thankful, and perhaps we ought to be surprised, that the conceit of omniscience, original and derived, touching propriety in English, is not more widely diffused than we find it to be.

Nevertheless, instinctive legislation concerning our language is too frequent and too obtrusive to be endured without occasional protest. Suspicion of its temerity can hardly occur to those who indulge in it deliberately. That they should see the matter in its true light, that they should surmise its utter presumptuousness, their complacent self-sufficiency renders all but impossible. Philology, as they rate it, is a thing light enough to serve as their mere avocation and pastime. In their own opinion, and by their tacit profession, they have read all that one needs to read, they are infallible in point of memory, and their taste and their judgment are past gainsaying. Their attitude is, in short, exactly that which conciliates most speedily the adhesion of the multitude. Acting on the maxim, that modesty is not a note of inspiration, they believe unwaveringly in themselves, they are visited by no doubts, they cautiously avoid dealing in alternatives; and none, sooner than such, are welcome to the unthinking and the timid, and may assure themselves of a host of disciples. To the ordinary mind there is something irresistibly attractive, and something which invites unstinted confidence, in the pretensions of a man who, conforming to a familiar practice, declares, for instance, that a given word or sense of a word had no existence before a defined date, or is not to be met with in the pages of any reputable writer. Only arrant sciolists, certainly, will venture on sweeping assertions of this stamp. It is, however, precisely these that are wholly at one with the vulgar mob of readers, characterised as it is, what with impotence and indolence, by a repugnance to all enunciations which bewilder by being limited or qualified. On these worse than blind dictators argument would, of course, be wasted. Still, it is not altogether hopeless that suggestions of their incapacity, for cause shown, may penetrate, and with good effect, to some whose reliance on their false lessons, if it continued unshaken, would promote the propagation of foolish and mischievous fancies.

In the case of a living language, not yet in its decline, interesting as its historical philology may be, its practical philology is of importance vastly greater. Of this the scope is, to discover and to record the best recent and present usage—in other terms, eligible precedents. Nor can a different view of its functions be accepted, unless one first postulates, consciously or unconsciously, principles which will bear no serious examination. The view specially alluded to is that of grammarians, lexicographers, and rhetoricians, of the autocratic type. Pronouncing, as they do, arbitrarily, or from a predilection for the obsolete, as to what is right and what is wrong, they ought, certainly, to produce credentials from heaven, or from some other exalted quarter, conclusive that their autocratism is authentic. In the meantime, all is not so smooth as it ought to be. If we are to believe themselves, they are virtually inspired; and, it being only injunctions that they have to do with, the hapless sceptic is constantly molested by doubts how to separate, therein, warrantable prescriptions from personal suggestions. But a language is never a finality, nor a fixture; and its course is beyond the staying or the controlling of speculators or theorists. Its prevailing features, at whatever period of its career, are impressed upon it, of necessity, by circumstances which constitute and distinguish that period. Depreciation of the former is, therefore, depreciation, inclusively, of the latter. For example, when modernisms are decried, as often happens, on the sole avowed ground of their being modernisms, it is silently taken for granted, that, in comparison with our forerunners, we have retrograded in good sense, or in good taste, or in having superfluous wants; for, if we have not, the expressions which satisfied them would satisfy us. It does not seem to occur to the rigid philological conservative, that every particular of what he idolises as classicism of phrase was once the very freshest of novelties, and so every word ever spoken, back to the primeval interjections or what not. If, as he contends, we do amiss when we innovate on what has been handed down to us, it behoves him to show what there is about us for which we should be denied a privilege enjoyed by all bygone generations. He is to show, also, and antecedently, that, after a certain course of development, a language need change no more, and that it differs from all things else, in not being relative, and subject to the law of mutation which reigns throughout nature. In fact, taken as a whole, speech, equally with the form of our coats and of our hats, is at no time otherwise than a precarious and fugitive fashion, a resultant of causes so inscrutable in their working that it looks much like the offspring of caprice; and, while we can but blindly appreciate its true antecedents, its future fortunes wholly transcend our divination. However, from the point of view of practice, all that imports most of us, respecting it, is, to ascertain what English is accredited by the best contemporary writers, and to govern ourselves accordingly. Adepts will, in exigency, go further than this; but let no one believe lightly that he belongs to their select brotherhood.

That which we have here set forth being, on the face of it, barely in advance of the axiomatic, it is curious to observe the inconsiderateness in which even men usually most circumspect are seen to allow themselves. Thus, Lord Macaulay[1] speaks of Bunyan as affording a sample of 'the old unpolluted English language,' and tells us 'how rich that language is in its own proper wealth, and how little it has been improved by all that it has borrowed.' Prudently enough, the thesis of what constitutes the unpollutedness of Bunyan's English is left unattempted. And is not that pleonastic property, its being 'rich in its *own proper* wealth,'[2] just as predicable of our present English as it is of Bunyan's? And has 'borrowed' English been a peculiarity of the last two or three centuries? On the assumption, as a starting-point, that the English of a certain age was a gift direct from the skies, and so pure and perfect as not to admit, save to its harm, of alteration or addition, Lord Macaulay's eulogy is reconcilable with right reason. But it is not that he delivered himself ambiguously. His error is fundamental. If it had been said of Bunyan, that, looking to all his circumstances, he utilised a simple style of English with most unexpected felicity, quite enough would have been said. To Lord Macaulay the English of the Bible, as of those older writers who recall it to mind, was powerfully attractive. And we are not obliged to suppose that it was so adventitiously, that is to say, owing to those early associations whose bias few outgrow. Tried by the severest canons of taste, it is found to merit praise which cannot easily be exaggerated. For who can deny its exquisite concinnity with its subject-matters, or be insensible to the charm of its unconstrained and rhythmical fluency? Still, for the general purposes of us moderns, it would, indisputably, prove most meagre and insufficient.

[1] In his *Essays* (7th ed.), vol. I, pp. 423, 424.

[2] Another pleonasm of Lord Macaulay's is such as an irresolute man would hardly hazard: 'He *walked on foot*, bareheaded,' &c. *History, &c.* (10th ed.), vol. I, p. 557.

The history of English, from the days of those happy ventures whose fruits, no more than slightly modified, we see in the authorised version of the Bible, is the history of what Lord Macaulay would have called its pollution. Previously to the later years of Henry the Eighth, so inadequate was our tongue for most purposes other than social communication, that the more learned Englishmen who aspired to make a mark in literature were, with few reservations, fain to content themselves with Latin. Such quasi-vernacular phenomena as are associated with the names of Bishop Pecock, Lord Berners, and a few others, are noteworthy, over and above their unseasonableness, simply as having been too daringly tentative to induce imitation. While revolting, from their ungainly novelty, to the educated with whom their appearance was contemporaneous, probably they were well-nigh unintelligible to all except the educated. Our older poetry apart, from the works of Sir John Mandeville, Wicliffe, Sir John Fortescue, Sir Thomas Malory, Tyndale, and Sir Thomas More, with the *Paston Letters*, one may derive a very fair idea of the speech of our forefathers, as exhibited in what were its most acceptable forms, down to near the middle of the sixteenth century. But the outburst of intellectual vigour and activity which concurred with the Reformation and the introduction of printing could not but tell on our language advantageously. To Sir Thomas Elyot we are indebted for the first resolute attempt that proved successful, towards its enrichment and its improvement throughout. In contrast to his predecessors who had experimented to the same end, Elyot was a man of consummate tact. Besides this, he presented himself just when the public temper was attuned to the propounding of innovations. The authority which attached to his diction, in the eyes of the generation next succeeding his own, is exemplified by a rugged couplet of Richarde Eden, himself, at least in prose, and for his age, no indifferent literary practitioner. In deprecation of censure at the hands of purists, he says:—

> I have not for every worde asked counsayle
> Of eloquent Eliot or Sir Thomas Moore [*sic*].

As to the good writers who, in uninterrupted series, connect his day with our own, it is enough here to glance at the nature of their services which have brought English to be what it is. The art was very soon discovered of framing sentences not unreasonably protracted; and, by degrees, involution and complexity—though most translators, and those who leaned to foreign modes, were slow in disusing them—came to be looked upon as questionable merits. But, from the first, the want of an ampler vocabulary was practically acknowledged, and steps were taken to supply it. Latin, French, and Italian are the chief sources which were deemed available for this object; and, as short words are better than long words of equivalent import, it is to be regretted that our dialects were not freely laid under contribution. The preference given to Latinistic importations increased steadily for something like a century, after it had set in with force, above all among ecclesiastics and those whose style they influenced. Though it never reached the exorbitant pitch which was gravely advocated by Henry Cockeram, it surely neared the limits of the conceivably endurable in Milton, Sir Thomas Browne, and Henry More. That, in the meanwhile, the tradition of English such as the run of men could follow understandingly did not disappear from books altogether, we have to thank, in a great measure, the humbler divines. With the Restoration, a new phase of our language was developed. Foremost among its representatives are, not to name others, Sir William Temple, Tillotson, Dryden, Jeremy Collier, Shaftesbury, Defoe, Addison, Steele, Swift, Bolingbroke, Pope, Berkeley, Middleton, Fielding, and Richardson. And then came Dr. Johnson, with his monotonously balanced periods and his superficial reminders of the Caroline divines. We say superficial; for, while classical polysyllables were, to them, often little more than aids to mere grandiloquence, they served, in his use, to mark genuine distinctions and refinements. Successful imitators he could, in the nature of things, have but few. His sonorousness and the structure of his cadences may easily be mimicked; but his style, in its distinctive essence, is a faithful reflex of his mental idiosyncrasy, and, until we shall see his second self, can be only counterfeited, not reproduced. The short-sighted idea was, in his day, rapidly gaining ground, and with injurious practical effect, that our language had attained a form from which to deviate must be to deteriorate. This, though not at all intentionally, he contributed directly to counteract. Yet, quite independently of his undesigned philological liberalism, there were causes at work, even before his death, operating to break the uneasy shackles by which the expression of thought had so long been hampered among us, and promoting the advent of the more cosmopolitan English of the last seventy years, the English of Bentham, Southey, Coleridge, Landor, Mr. J. S. Mill, Bishop Thirlwall, Cardinal Newman, Mr. Swinburne, and Mr. John Morley.

As long ago as 1557, Sir John Cheke was persuaded that English could dispense perfectly well with further accessions from without.

Not only so, but he deemed that such accessions, if realised, would entail something very portentous. He predicted, with reference to our language, that, 'if we take not heed bi tiim, ever borowing and never payeng, she shall be fain to keep her house as bankrupt.' How the borrowing here could possibly be compensated by the paying, he can hardly have troubled himself to inquire. Just as little did antiquity warrant him from writing nonsense, as it warranted many a wiser man. Like Lord Macaulay, Cheke must have entertained the notion, that our language, at a certain point in time, shared the nature of a revelation, and that a self-sufficing revelation. Alternative to this absurd position is the superstition, equally absurd, which magnifies the wisdom of our ancestors into inerrancy, and supposes that they foresaw what must be good for us better than we ourselves see it. To the one or to the other we must, perforce, trace the long-lived lament—for it comes to this—so worthy of its fatuous origin, that our speech has grown, grows, and bids fair to go on growing.

The unreason which we have thus stripped to its nakedness is, of course, ordinarily so disguised, that, until closely scrutinised, it looks more or less plausible. A dogmatiser in the province of philology is almost certain to be a good deal in the clouds. Instead of intelligent and intelligible convictions, he has scarcely more than tenacious partialities. These he would justify, if he could; and, in his inability to establish them on grounds of plain sense, the device, alike most obvious and most imposing, to which he is wont to resort as a preliminary, is a vague appeal, with magisterial air, to something beyond average apprehension. Having thus thrown dust into the eyes of the unwary, he ventures whatever first occurs to him that seems to subserve the argument from analogy. This done, he retires with a metaphorical bow; the silent salute being designed to signify that your submission is anticipated, at the peril of your being accounted no more sagacious than you should be. The procedure here sketched shall be illustrated by an extract from the *Edinburgh Review*:[1]—

We cannot admit the authority of usage, when it is clearly opposed to the very principles of language. There is, we fear, ample authority, amongst writers of the present day, for the use of the word *supplement*, not as a noun substantive, which is its proper meaning, but as a verb active, in the sense of 'to supply what is deficient,' 'to complete.' We have seen it used, of late years, by prelates and judges, who ought to have abhorred such a solecism; nay, we will even confess, so infectious has it become, that it has, once or twice, crept, notwithstanding

[1] Vol. 120, p. 42 (1864).

our utmost vigilance, into these pages. *Supplement* is, by its form, the 'thing added or supplied,' not the 'act of supplying' it. You might just as well say, that, instead of appending another page to your book, you intend to *appendix* it.

From a writer who openly denies the authority of usage we ought not to be astonished at any shallowness or at any sophistry. And, when such a person preludes about 'the very principles of language,' it is odds that his acquaintance with those principles is not of much the same scientific stamp as was that of Ephraim Jenkinson with cosmogony and Ocellus Lucanus. According to what we have just transcribed, as to 'the word *supplement*,' 'a noun substantive...is its proper meaning.' It may be that we are not to complain of this, however, unless we would at once lower ourselves in the estimation of the reviewer, and would be thought to demand impossibilities. For we are admonished, in the next page but one after that from which we have quoted: 'If a man writes in a way which cannot be misunderstood by a reader of common candour and intelligence, he has done all, as regards clearness, that can be expected of him. To attempt more is to ask of language more than language can perform.' Assuredly, this is no improvement on the maxim of Quintilian: *Non ut intelligere possit, sed ne omnino possit non intelligere curandum.*[1] To proceed, *supplement*, as a verb, is asserted to be a solecism; and what is meant for a reason is brought forward to substantiate the assertion. We are directed to mark the signification which alone is deducible from the substantive *supplement*, on account of its form. Restricting ourselves to English, we reply that *achievement* denotes both 'act of achieving' and 'thing achieved;' and similarly twofold in meaning are *acquirement*, *allotment*, *assignment*, *attainment*, and *averment*, to go no further. On the other hand, *abasement* is not 'thing abased;' and in the same class with it are *abetment*, *abridgment*, *adjustment*, *adornment*, *allurement*, *amazement*, *amusement*, *appointment*, *arraignment*, *arrangement*, *assessment*, *astonishment*, and so on to weariness. The termination *-ment* supplies a variety of senses; and even the Latin termination *-mentum* supplies two. *Supplementum*, and with strict regularity, is either 'thing supplied' or 'act of supplying;' and convention would have broken no squares in decreeing that *supplement* should bear the second of these imports as well as the first. And all this might, surely, be discovered without much of what the critic calls, at p. 56, '*high* literary *acumen*.' It would have sufficed us, indeed, to enunciate the indisputable fact, that, in English, the significatory relation between a

[1] [*Non ut...curandum* You must take care, not that your work can be understood, but that it can by no means be misunderstood (Quintilian, *Instit. Orat.* VIII. 2. 24).]

substantive and its corresponding verb, whether they have the same form or not, and whichever of them preceded the other, is, to a very great extent, arbitrary. *Supplement*, as a verb, and meaning what it does, is, consequently, not a shade more irregular, viewed etymologically or in any other way, than *augment*, *ornament*, *torment*, or the Scotch *implement*, or the obsolete *detriment*, 'injure.' Again, the adduction of the verb *appendix*, with intent to discredit the verb *supplement*, is peculiarly unfortunate. We have often seen the phrase 'to *climax* an argument;' and who, after having heard a few times 'to *appendix* a book,' would revolt against it, any more than against 'to *index* it,' or against 'to *catalogue* a library'?

By way of pointing the lesson, how futile it may be, save as furnishing material for history, to comment on expressions of recent emergence or comparative rarity, we shall specify some words which, in the centuries when our language was undergoing most rapid transformation, were designated for their novelty, if not also with disapproval or ridicule. Sir Thomas Elyot, in 1531, condemned, by implication, *industry*, *magnanimity*, *maturity*, and *modesty*; and shortly afterwards he proposed *crudity* and *lassitude*. Nicolas Udall, in 1542, while using, explained, *clime*, *geography*, *parasite*, *pedagogue*, *prorogation*, and *stratagem*. And we are to add *fountain*, which Bishop Bale, too, in 1550, would not risk without a definition tacked to it. Thomas Langley, in 1546, introduced *circus*, *labyrinth*, and *obelisk*, with interpretations which show that, in his judgment, they were then entire strangers. Writing in 1577, Richarde Willes frowned on *despicable*, *destructive*, *homicide*, *imbibed*, *obsequious*, *ponderous*, *portentous*, and *prodigious*. These words, he says, 'cannot be excused, in my opinion, for smellyng to much of the Latine.' Among words which Dr. William Fulke, in 1583, scouted as 'affected novelties of termes, such as neither English nor Christian ears ever heard in the Christian tongue,' are *gratis*, *neophyte*, *paraclete*, *prepuce*, *scandal*; and he thought no better of *advent*, *evangelise*, *sandal*, *scandalise*, and *schism*. Reginald Scot, in the year following, gave, as specimens of 'mysticall termes of art,' 'termes of the art alcumystical, devised of purpose to bring credit to cousenage,' the substantives *induration*, *ingot*, *mollification*, *termination*, *test*, and the verbs *cement*, *imbibe*, *incorporate*, and *sublime*. Robert Parke, in 1588, defined, when he used, the word *hurricane*, or, as he writes it, *uracan*. George Puttenham, in 1589, named, as new-comers, *compendious*, *declination*, *delineation*, *dimension*, *figurative*, *function*, *harmonical*, *idiom*, *impression*, *indignity*, *inveigle*, *method*, *methodical*, *metrical*, *numerous*, *obscure*, *penetrable*, *penetrate*, *placation*, *prolix*, *refining, savage, scientific, significative*, &c. &c. Sir John Smythe, also in 1589, reclaimed against *beleaguer*. Ben Jonson, in 1601, derided *clumsy, conscious, damp, inflate, puffy, reciprocal, retrograde*, and *strenuous*. Dekker, Chettle, and Haughton, in *Patient Grissil*, published two years later, levelled their wit at *accoutrements, adulatory, capricious, compliment, conglutinate, fastidious, misprision, project*; and Chapman, in 1606, saw something to amuse in *collaterally, condole, endeared*, and *model*. Among expressions which Philemon Holland, in 1609, held it necessary to elucidate for his readers, are included *aborigines, cataract, cylinder, father-in-law, hemisphere, sectary*; and, in 1629, on using *myriad*, he expounded it in a marginal annotation. *Holocaust, rational*, and *tunic* stand in the list of terms for avoiding which King James's revisers of the Bible plume themselves on having 'shunned the obscurity of the Papists.' Edward Leigh, in 1639, found *avarice, coadjutor, dominical, impudicity, paraclete*, and *prevaricate* unendurable. Dr. Peter Heylin, criticising the phraseology of the Romish version of the Bible, enumerates, as among its 'words utterly unknown to any English reader, unlesse well-grounded and instructed in the learned languages,' *acquisition, advent, host, presence, proposition, victim*. The date of this remark is 1656, at which time its author, giving proof of a memory as often treacherous as faithful, did not hesitate to apply the epithets 'uncouth and unusuall' to *abstruse, acquiesce, adequate, adoption, adventitious, alleviate, amphibious, animadvert, antagonist, asperse, causality, chirography, commensurate, compensate, complacence, complicate, concede, concrete, confraternity, culpability, depredation, despondence, desponding, destination, dual, embryo, emerge, emergent, emolument, eradicate, erudition, evacuate, excogitate, excoriate, exuberancy, fortuitously, germinate, gestation, gust, hectic, hibernal, horizontal, hypothesis, identity, imminent, impede, impetuosity, impurity, inaudible, inauspicious, incantation, incurious, inflame, initiation, inquietude, intense, interfere, intersect, intrinsic, irritate, iteration, luminary, luxuriancy, magnetic, meliorate, metamorphosis, minatory, mode, morass, narrator, nave, nonsense, noxiousness, nude, oblique, occult, ocular, odium, offertory, omen, onerous, operate, opine, organical, placable, ponderous, portentous, precarious, preponderate, prevarication, radiant, rancidity, reciprocate, reduction, refulgent, relax, repertory, respond, retention, reverberation, salubrious, scheme, scintillation, sedulous, series, sterile, stimulate, stipulate, stricture, supinely, susceptible, symbol, synopsis, system, temerity, temporalities, tendency, treatment, trepidation, unison, vacuity, valediction, veniality, veteran, vigil, virile*. But we must desist. As every wide and observant reader is fully aware, not only do strictures of this description bestrew our literature most freely, from the days of Heylin to our own, but that fanciful and very subjective critic has had an army of followers as unadvised as himself.

Executive faculty and judicial we usually look to find each by itself. Proficiency in an art and proficiency in its related science seldom offer themselves to view conjoined in one person. Be his use of his native language ever so irreproachable, a man is not consequently a philologist. From a mere instinct of conservatism, superficially cultivated, he may avoid very much that rationally offends. If, however, he would judge language critically, he must habituate himself to that industry of observation and that heedfulness of statement which are essential in the exact sciences, and by recourse to which, sound philology assimilates to those sciences so closely. These remarks we shall illustrate very briefly.

Archbishop Whately, after assigning the character of 'unfortunate' to Locke's 'encomium upon Aristotle,' goes on to say:—

> He praises him for the '*invention* of syllogisms,' to which he certainly had no more claim than...Harvey to the praise of having *made the blood circulate*.... And the utility of this invention consists, according to him, in the great service done against 'those who were not ashamed to deny anything;' a service which never could have been performed, had syllogisms been an *invention* of Aristotle's; for what sophist could ever have consented to *restrict himself to one particular kind of arguments dictated by his opponent?*[1]

Apparently, His Grace must have had peculiar notions as to what is meant by '*Invention* of the Cross' in the Prayer-book. Before criticising the English of one of our older writers, he ought, surely, to have acquainted himself with the language of that writer's age; and, had he construed Locke as Locke was construed by his contemporaries, there would not have been a vestige of foundation for the animadversion here remarked on. If *invention* had, in Locke's day, something of ambiguity about it, the same kind of defect, only heightened, unquestionably attached to *discovery*, senses of which, then familiar to the learned, were 'exploration,' 'examination,' 'exhibition,' 'exposure,' 'disclosure,' &c.

Sir James Fitzjames Stephen suffers himself to be moved from his philosophic equanimity by what he is pleased to call 'the hideous adjective *educational*, and its even more hideous substantive *educationist*.'[2]

Now, are *additional*, *conditional*, *congregational*, *constitutional*, *devotional*, *discretional*, *emotional*, *fractional*, *functional*, *intentional*, *national*, *occasional*, *professional*, *proportional*, *provisional*, *rational*, *sectional*, *sensational*, *sessional*, *traditional*, and *transitional* 'hideous'? And are *abolitionist*, *excursionist*, *opinionist*, *oppositionist*, *protectionist*, and *religionist* 'even more

[1] *Elements of Logic*, book I, § I, footnote. [2] *Essays by a Barrister*, p. 191.

hideous'? *Educational* was in print as long ago as 1652; it was used by Mrs. Mary Knowles, in a colloquy with Dr. Johnson, and, as far as is known, escaped rebuke; and it enjoyed the sanction of Edmund Burke. It has age in its favour, then, besides analogy; and its respectability and utility, being attested by good modern usage, stand in need of no vindication. As to *educationist*, not only is it a regular formation, and euphonious enough, but it dispenses us, as *educational* does, from the necessity of a long periphrasis. But this, and much more that we might urge pertinently, must be all but superfluous to any one who troubles himself to reflect a little. For the rest, it is at least somewhat singular that Mr. Justice Stephen, with his judicial turn of mind, should proffer unsubstantiated disparagement as a substitute for argumentation. His mere pleasure that *educational* should be 'hideous,' and that *educationist* should be 'even more hideous,' is hardly likely to be accepted as an irreversible ruling.

That, in a province of investigation where keenly perceptive critics like Archbishop Whately and Sir James Fitzjames Stephen have strayed from the right road, men of no more than average prudence should go well-nigh utterly astray, can occasion no surprise. In former generations, self-important, and generally useless, and popularly pernicious speculators, of this calibre, abounded more in Scotland than in England; and, of very late years, they have had a whole legion of imitators and copyists in the United States. Their vagaries we have, at present, no great inclination to expatiate on. However, among the American followers of misguiding Britons, there has been one whose quixotic attempt to set our language on what he took to be its legs we purpose to appreciate briefly. We refer to the late Mr. William Cullen Bryant.[1] The home-reputation of this gentleman has, in Great Britain, only the faintest of echoes to such as have read his poem bearing the impossible title of *Thanatopsis*;[2] for, in America, and above all in New York,

[1] This article, substantially as now given, was in the hands of the editor several months before Mr. Bryant's death.

[2] *Thanatopsia* or *Thanatopsy* is correct. Compare *autopsy*. *Thanatopsis*, like the naturalists' *cereopsis* and *coreopsis*, is just as indefensible a formation as *telegram*, which Mr. Bryant would not hear of even in his newspaper. *Synopsis* is right; but a large number of the Greek-derived technicalities in *-is*, coined by English scientists, as *biogenesis*, &c., are quite illegitimate, and as bad as δυστύχη or θεοδόξα would be. Every philologist, not still in his novitiate, knows the reason. [δυστύχη for δυστυχία 'misfortune'; θεοδόξα (an actual form, not, as Hall thinks, impossible, meaning 'glory of God': Didymus Alexandrinus, *Exp. in Ps.* 18. 2) for θεοδοξία 'appearance of divinity'.]

Mr. J. C. Pickett, an American, imitating Mr. Bryant's impossibility, has entitled one of his poems '*Thermopsis*: The Hot Weather.'

People who make new words would often do well to submit their coinages to

Mr. Bryant is, in reminiscence, a power of formidable magnitude. Provided that fulness of years confers sagacity, he must have constituted a rather troublesome argument to all good Democrats, considering that, at the ripe age of eighty-three, and as a recent seceder from their ranks, he was still editing a Republican newspaper, and with considerable vigour. Reformed himself, he would have reformed others, and, as we shall see, in more things than one. The political party with which he was originally identified is, notoriously, that which embraces among its adherents nearly the whole of the most lawless, turbulent, and illiterate elements of the American citizenry; people whose leading aim, it would seem, is, first to establish a general social equality, and Heaven alone knows what by and by. After parting company with these levellers, Mr. Bryant did not, however, make a halt at the conviction that the instinctive wisdom of the rabble is unequal to the task of managing the State to the best advantage. He also came to believe that the practice of right English was a matter in which his countrymen required lessoning. With intentions which had, no question, a laudable motive, he would have promoted the diffusion of that practice; but the method by which he essayed to achieve his object was, as far as in him lay, that of a rigid absolutist. No one connected, as a writer, with his journal was to act on his own notions as to what was English, unless, as respected a long list of words and phrases, those notions tallied with such as were held by his chief.[1]

Mr. Bryant is not always by any means desirably clear; but still we think we do not err in understanding that he proscribes outright the substantives *aspirant*, *authoress*, *humbug*, *interment*, *item*, *nominee*, *oration*, *poetess*, *proximity*, *raid*, *rough*, *seaboard*, *telegram*,[2] *vicinity*; the adjectives *jubilant* and *talented*; the verbs *base*, *collide*, *commence*, *inter*, *jeopardise*,

scholars. Mr. A. J. Ellis, in one of his works, treats of *homonyms* and also of 'heteric *polynyms*.' See *A Plea for Phonetic Spelling* (ed. 1848), pp. 173–6. Of course, he can have no notion that the second constituent of *homonym* is from ὄνυμα (ὄνομα). [ὄνυμα, ὄνομα 'name'].

The objection to *synonym* and *homonym*, as ordinarily employed, we have set forth elsewhere. Mr. Ellis's *homonyms* and *polynyms* (*polyonyms*) we would call *homophones* and *homographs*. The first are identical to the ear only; the second, identical to the eye.

[1] See, for the details which follow, Mr. W. Fraser Rae's *Columbia and Canada* (1877), pp. 56-8.

[2] The prohibitory mandate runs thus: '*telegrams*, for *despatches*.' But a *despatch* may be of many sorts besides *telegraphic*. Indistinctness, it thus appears, is recommended in preference to neoterism.

With similar want of precision, Mr. Bryant has: '*nominee*, for *candidate*;' '*raid*, for *attack*;' '*state*, for *say*.'

locate, *notice*, *repudiate*, *state*,[1] *taboo*; the adverb *subsequently*; and phrases like *is being done*, with *prior to*,[2] *take action*, *the deceased*, *try an experiment*, *we are mistaken in*,[3] *which man*,[4] *would seem*.[5] Add the familiar *artiste*, *cortége*, *début*, *dépôt*, *employé*, *en route*, *rôle*, *tapis*, *viâ*. The title *Rev.* is to be allowed, if ushered in by the definite article; but *Esq.* and *Hon.* are not to be borne with on any terms.

But, before going further, we wish to note a fact of literary history, make a few quotations, and propose a query or two. Some years ago, then, Mr. Bryant put forth a moderate-sized volume called *Letters of a Traveller*. Its contents are, manifestly, the result of great care and elaboration. And, in that volume, we find the author practically neglectful of the following articles from his list of *evitanda*: '*call attention*, for *direct attention*;' '*claimed* for, *asserted*;' '*co-temporary*, for *contemporary*;' '*numerous*, as applied to any noun save a noun of multitude;' '*past two weeks*, for *last two weeks*, and all similar expressions relating to a definite time;' '*quite*, prefixed to *good*, *large*, &c.;'[6] '*talent*, for *talents* or *ability*;' '*tariff*, for *rates of fare* or *schedule of rates*;' '*those who*, for *those persons who*;' '*wharves*, for *wharfs*.'

Among Americanisms which Mr. Bryant forbids are '*bogus*;' '*donate*;' '*loafer*;' '*loan* or *loaned*, for *lend* or *lent*;' '*on yesterday*;' '*over* his signature;' '*posted*, for *informed*;' '*primaries*, for *primary meetings*;' '*section*, for *district* or *region*.' None of these peculiarities are seen in his *Letters*, where, however, we find, and uncondemned by his later criticism:

At evening we arrived at Canada—p. 45. And at p. 16.

I look upon the introduction of manufactures *at* the South as an event of the most favourable promise for that part of the country—p. 349.

[1] If *locate*, *repudiate*, and *state* are unendurable, are *location*, *repudiation*, and *statement* to be dismissed along with them? And may one no longer '*repudiate* a wife'? Further, *disinter*, *disinterment*, *misstate*, and *unnoticed* should go out with *inter*, *interment*, *state*, and *notice*.

[2] Perhaps Mr. Bryant would ignore this phrase only when used adverbially; his substitute, 'before,' being ambiguous. But even the adverbial *prior to* is supported by respectable authority.

[3] We are instructed to say *we mistake in*, as if the other were not far better.

[4] Interrogatively, also? And may we not say 'I do not know *which* man you allude to'? We are left quite in the dark here.

[5] Put 'seems,' enjoins Mr. Bryant. Not to speak of the almost incredible contempt here shown for the sanction of the best writers, a man must be musing who does not at once feel the difference between *seems* and *would seem*.

[6] This wording would apply to such an expression as 'not *quite large* enough.' But *quite large*, unqualified by a negative, is, in many contexts, good English, as even Mr. Bryant ought to have recollected.

Back of the bluffs extends a fine agricultural region—p. 58. At pp. 250, 273, 285, 321, 329, 389, also.

If the new tariff obliges them to sell it for *considerable* less, they will still make money—pp. 318, 319.

I went on deck, and saw one of the Faro Island ponies, which had *given out* during the night, stretched dead upon the deck—p. 423.

We passed through a well-cultivated country, interspersed with towns which had an appearance of activity and *thrift*—p. 201. And at pp. 321, 329, also.

We meet, besides, with *dry-goods merchant*; *dutiable*; *floor*, for *pave*; *molasses*, for *treacle*; *parlour*, for *drawing-room*; *sidewalk*, for *pavement*; *spool*, for *reel*. Mr. Bryant also improves the *railroad-car* of his countrymen into *railway-waggon*.

Even in what precedes, we have ample data from which to construct an estimate of Mr. Bryant as a verbal critic. His decisions as to admissible English are attributable to what our forefathers now and then grandly called opsimathy, 'late culture;' and Cicero's reminder, ὀψιμαθεῖς *quam sint insolentes non ignoras*,[1] can only by accident not have been forestalled by Solomon. We have seen, from his register of unlawful expressions, that, in drawing it up, he must have had in his contemplation, with others, his former self, as exhibited in his *Letters*. And we have further seen that his *Letters* contain very strange things which his register passes by unnoticed. Did he suppose these Americanisms to be good English? That he would have disallowed, in the currently written columns of a newspaper, words and phrases which he would have allowed in a volume destined for more leisurely perusal, and for greater duration, than the issues of the *New York Evening Post*, is not to be presumed.

But we have not yet done with his category of exclusion. He lays under ban: '*action*, for *proceeding*;' '*aggregate*, for *altogether* or *total*;' '*average*, for *ordinary*;' '*beat*, for *defeat*;' '*conclusion*, for *close* or *end*;'[2] '*couple*, for *two*;'[3] '*decade*, for *ten years*;' '*decease*, as a verb;' '*endorse*, for *approve*;' '*graduates*, for *is graduated*;' '*issue*, for *question* or *subject*;' '*leniency*, for *lenity*;' '*majority*, relating to places or circumstances, for *most*;' '*materially*, for *largely* or *greatly*;'[4] '*partially*, for *partly*;' '*portion*, for *part*;' '*progress*,[5] for *advance* or *growth*;' '*realised*, for *obtained*;'

[1] [ὀψιμαθεῖς *quam*... *ignoras* You are aware how arrogant they are who come late to learning (misquoted from Cicero, *Ad Fam.* IX. 20. 2).]

[2] Why not, then, restrict *conclude* to the sense of 'infer'?

[3] Yet he saw, somewhere, 'a *pair* of mango trees'! *Letters*, &c., p. 374.

[4] Would he have demurred to *material*, in 'a *material* difference'?

[5] On the verb *progress* he is silent.

'*spending*, for *passing*;' '*start*, for *begin* or *establish*;' '*the United States*, as a singular noun.'[1] Nor, if he could help it, were his fellow-citizens to speak of *greenbacks*, but *treasury-notes*, or of the *fall* of the year, or of a *freshet*; and yet he himself used the provincial *slut*, for *bitch*, with the Scotticisms *winded*, for *wound*, and *sparse*. The austerity of taste which would have effaced *Brother Jonathan* and *John Bull* could not, of course, permit that a negro should ever be called a *darkey*. And there is to be no toleration of 'Wall-street slang generally: *bulls*, *bears*,[2] *long*, *short*, *flat*, *corner*, *tight*, *moribund*, *comatose*, &c.' In the interest of something undeclared, and not easy of conjecture, *afterwards* is never to show itself, but the quaint and not over-euphonious *afterward*. As to '*banquet*, for *dinner* or *supper*,' '*indebtedness*, for *debt*,' and '*lengthy*, for *long*,' who ever misuses them thus? Here, however, as often elsewhere, it may be that Mr. Bryant, with his bewildering obscurity of drift, meant to interdict words absolutely, and did not trouble himself about exactness of definition. But, for brevity, we must leave unsaid much that we should like to say.

Of Mr. Bryant's own ventures in English, to the end undisclaimed, we shall presently give some specimens, supplementary to those produced already. On his practical authority, as will be seen, or as would be seen from vouchers for which we have no room, the following passage, in spite of what will strike English readers as its singularities, ought to be accepted as quite faultless:—

I am from America, where my home is *at* the North; and I *would* like to know why so many Englishmen dislike me on that account. For some time, my circumstances have been better *with every year*; and I have laid by thousands *after* thousands annually. So, having a good sum of money *beforehand*, enough not to *give out* soon, I have come to *make* England a visit. Before my late voyage, I had never been on *the main ocean*; and it *took me with surprise*. *At* morning and evening, I could not but observe the appearance of *the brine*, which, *to* inspection,

[1] Why, then, did Mr. Bryant, in his *Letters*, &c., p. 335, write 'Bellows Falls *is*'?

In the sequel, we shall try some points of Mr. Bryant's fastidiousness by the standard of Lord Macaulay. With reference to one particular of idiom, however, he contrasts to advantage with that celebrated stylist. '*Eight dollars* a month *is* the common rate.' (*Letters*, &c., p. 137.) Lord Macaulay has: '*Four shillings* a week, therefore, *were*, according to Petty's calculation, fair agricultural wages.' (*History*, &c., chapter iii.) '*Ten thousand pounds* sterling *were* sent for outfit.' (Ibid. chapter x.) And so often. Yet Lord Macaulay is not consistent. 'The ambassador told his master that *six thousand guineas was* the smallest gratification that could be offered to so important a minister.' (Ibid. chapter vi.) And who does not prefer *was* here, appealing, in its defence, to Coleridge's dictum about 'the inward and metaphysic grammar resisting successfully the tyranny of formal grammar'?

[2] Can Mr. Bryant really have supposed financial *bulls* and *bears* to be peculiar to Wall-street, New York?

appeared to be tinged *of* a peculiar colour. I am *much subject* to sea-sickness; and I *took* a severe attack. But the ship-surgeon's supply of remedies *were* all at my disposal; and he *put me by the danger* of being weakened. I landed at Queenstown in due time, and *afterward* proceeded *on* the railroad. I was glad to find myself in a *railway-waggon* once more, though I *took* an unpleasant jolting, and though my travelling companions were very disagreeable *individuals*; these *parties* being a *pair* of squalid *females* and two equally unwelcome *personages* of the male sex. I was at Dublin a week, and *each day* was more interested. The lower Irish are curious for *the* costume. The number of them enjoying *thrift*, though wasteful, is, as compared with Americans, very *few*. Your climate is trying; but I have already *began* to *take a seasoning*. During a week as a visitor *to* Malvern, I every day *ascended a steep declivity* near by there. The orchards of *the apple and pear* in your western counties excited my admiration. Here in London, I was not satisfied with *either the hotels* I tried at first; and I shall not remain long where I am now. They are *flooring* the *sidewalks* on *either side* of the street; and the din is incessant. Day after day *have* passed, and there are no signs of its discontinuance. Besides this, just *back of* me is a *house of religious worship*, where, by the by, I have *attended at* church several times. Its rector is, I judge, a *considerable* able and energetic man. He has a good *record*, I am told, and preaches *to* acceptance; and I hear that his parishioners held a meeting the other day, *to* his honour, and voted him a testimonial. But I have arrived *to* the conclusion that his constant bell-ringing is too much for me. Consequently, as I am of *that* nature that I love quiet, I keep *without* my lodgings as much as possible. But I have not inclination *to the telling of* any more of my discomforts.

In contrast to this, we offer a paragraph wholly inadmissible, because of the expressions in it which are italicised, to the pages of Mr. Bryant's daily journal:—

Here is a *telegram* from London. Its *items* are *numerous* enough; and some few of them are worth *noticing*. The *progress* of the Turco-Russian contest is very slow. The Russians have *beaten* the Turks again; but we are not to *base* hopes of immediate peace on the fact. The *aggregate* loss of the Turks was only two thousand men; and this cannot cripple them *materially*. It *would seem* that *we are mistaken in* supposing that the Conservatives purpose intervention. Several of their leading men *repudiate* the idea. The Liberals are, of course, *jubilant*. Their desire to see the war brought to a *conclusion* will probably be *realised* before very long. *Attention* has again been *called* to the continued imprisonment of certain Fenians; and the result has been the release of a *couple* of them. During the *past* week, two well-known *authoresses*, one of them a *poetess*, have died. Neither of them was *interred* in Westminster Abbey. It is *stated* that the panic about hydrophobia is decreasing. General Grant intends to *spend* several months in the south of Europe. That he is a man of only *average* ability as a statesman, or even of less, may be *quite* true; but he showed true genius as a soldier. *Experiments have been tried* with the telephone, first in London, and *afterwards* at Dover. The *majority* of them were successful. In London and its *vicinity*, snow has scarcely been seen this winter. The moon has been *partially* eclipsed. Just *subsequently to* the eclipse, the wind was unusually high. Bull Ram Ghoose has made his appearance as an *aspirant* to the throne of Choochoo; but the *proximity* of powerful tribes favourable to its present occupant threatens to defeat his ambition.[1]

What Mr. Bryant believed to be English, the excerpts from his *Letters*, here following, bear speaking evidence. Nine-tenths, at least, of the sentences which we marked for extraction must, however, be omitted.

These are all curious for *the* costume—p. 53.

They tell you very quietly, that everybody who comes to live there must *take a seasoning*—p. 60.

They are, in fact, becoming better *with every year*—p. 107.[2]

Turning out of the main road, we began to *ascend* a steep green *declivity*—p. 157. And at p. 332.

In the afternoon I *attended at* one of the churches—p. 179.

By my side was a square-built, fresh-coloured *personage*, who had travelled in America, and whose accent was almost English—p. 203.

He carried it to a large pond near his house, the *longest diameter* of which is about a mile—p. 250.

Five years ago, the *number was very few*—p. 259.

Among them I saw a face or two quite *familiar in* Wall-street—p. 277.

A single stroke of the paddle, given by the man at the prow, *put us safely by* the seeming danger—p. 281.

It is about ten miles from *either the hotels* to the summit—pp. 332, 333.

The vast extent of the mountain-region... *took me with surprise and astonishment*—p. 333.

[1] Among recent writers of note, no one, perhaps, has been more fastidious than Lord Macaulay. And yet, in turning over some of his pages, we have fallen in with proof that even he, if living, would have had to mend his ways, in order to pass muster as a penny-a-liner on the staff of the *New York Evening Post*. For, by his use of *afterwards, aggregate, aspirant, average, banquet, beat, call attention to, commence, conclusion, graduate, inter, interment, issue, materially, nominee, notice, numerous, oration, partially, portion, progress, quite, raid, realise, spend, state, subsequently, talent, tariff, those who, try an experiment, vicinity*, and *would seem*, he has infringed Mr. Bryant's dictates; and he has also '*above* seventy,' '*above* five thousand men,' '*above* a year,' &c., in which phrases, according to that gentleman, *above*, for *more than*, is bad English.

Lord Macaulay uses freely both *try an experiment* and *make an experiment*, and in one and the same sense; but he has the former at least twice as often as the latter. The truth is, that there is little or nothing to choose between them. *Try an experiment* is almost an instance of what, in Latin grammar, is known as the cognate accusative, of which we have a fair number of samples in older English.

[2] This Germanism is becoming very common in the United States. Compare *mit jedem Jahre, mit jedem Tage, mit jedem Augenblicke*, &c. Another Germanism often heard there is 'what for a,' *was für ein*.

Commonly the dead are piled, without coffins, one above *the* other, in the trenches—p. 366.

I saw a group of children, of different ages, all *quite* pretty—p. 379.

Here are broad woods, large orchards of *the* apple and pear—p. 430.

A fine piece of old Etruscan wall...built of enormous uncemented *parallelograms* of stone—p. 439.

We find, moreover, such old words as *depasture*, *disfurnish*, *minsters*, and *haunt* as a verb neuter; together with 'a dense *umbrage* of leaves,' and 'the leaves grow *sere*.' *Emigrants* is, from fear of a most useful modernism, made to do duty for *immigrants*. *Impend* is often preferred where good taste would dictate *hang*; and we have 'looms from which two unfinished mats were *depending*.'[1] Yet Mr. Bryant cashiers, as intolerable Latinisms, *inter*, *jubilant*, *oration*, *proximity*, *repudiate*, *subsequently*, and *vicinity*. But we ought not to wonder at any judgment, or at any crotchet, how eccentric soever, as regards the English language, from a man who *ascends* a *declivity*; who meets with a pond of at least three *diameters* of different lengths, and a wall built of *parallelograms*, figures of only two dimensions; and who can write: 'To use a phrase very common in England, they are the most *extraordinary* pictures I ever saw.'[2]

As lately as 1873, Mr. Bryant brought out a volume entitled *Orations and Addresses*, of his own composition. To give all desirable completeness to our body of evidence as to what this gentleman, afterwards so severe a censor of the language of others, was then capable of, in the way of sinning against good English, we remit the curious to pp. 3, 45, 50, 70, 99, 104, 112, 163, 164, 168, 169, 191, 202, 228, 247, 275, 371, 391 of the volume in question, where will be found 'of *that* nature that,' 'a public dinner *to* his honour,' 'conclusions *to* which he arrived,' '*booked* for a pleasantry,' 'written *to* such acceptance,' 'with no enemy to lay the axe *at* its root,' &c. &c.

The violations of idiomatic propriety, with the occasional bad grammar and vulgarity, observable in the passages referred to, speak abundantly for themselves. In particular, it is, we apprehend, a writer's appropriate choice of prepositions, quite as much as anything else, that evidences conclusively his genuine familiarity with the tongue he is using; and herein the punctilious Mr. Bryant failed most egregiously. It is instructive, also, to see, in the case of many things which, eventually, he would not suffer in his newspaper, how soon before he was unconvinced of their disreputableness. In the volume under notice,

[1] *Letters*, &c., p. 292.

[2] *Letters*, &c., p. 165.

though he employs *afterward* twelve times, he employs *afterwards*, which he later came to turn his back on, eight times. *Parties*, when not technical for *persons*, at last was ostracised, and with reason; but, at p. 116, Mr. Washington Irving and the lady he would have married are spoken of as 'both *parties*.' Further, at p. 320, he has 'for nearly half a century *past*;' at p. 186, *poetess*; at p. 357, the substantive *progress*; at p. 70, the verb *state*; at p. 159, 'years had been *spent*;' at pp. 221, 223, *tariff*; at p. 326, *telegram*; at p. 116, *try an experiment*. 'His party-*record*,' exemplifying an American innovation which he subsequently repudiated, occurs at p. 282. Indeed, the very title of his book contains a word which was forbidden to his contributors, *orations*. How any literary assistant of his could have obeyed the law laid down for him, if he had taken this book as the subject of a review, passes our conjecture. But enough of this, if not more than enough.

Here, it must be admitted, is a rather startling portrait of a verbal critic, as outlined by himself. Who can now question, that, in the function which he arrogated, the artist had vastly more to learn than to teach? Not only Germans, Hollanders, Danes, Russians, Italians, Hungarians, Greeks, and Finns, but divers Hindus, Parsees, and Japanese, distinctly better versed than Mr. Bryant in the employment of the English language, have, from first to last, crossed our path. Fully regardful of the claims to venerable memory which may be urged in behalf of a high-minded, energetic, and altogether estimable man, who lived to weather more than four-score winters, we submit for consideration whether he has not exhibited himself as a very novice in the management of our mother-tongue. To speak within compass, his qualifications to pose as an Aristarchus were, for the most part, barely, if at all, short of ludicrous. Living, as he did, among a people among whom, in the case of all but a very few writers and speakers, our language is daily becoming more and more depraved,[1] he is not to be

[1] While preparing this paper, we have chanced to run through *Edgar Huntly*, by Charles Brockden Brown, an American novelist of the end of the last century and beginning of this. *Edgar Huntly* was finished and published in 1799. Despite its occasional oddities and inaccuracies of expression, it seldom reminds one of its author's nationality. Whoever compares it with Mr. Bryant's *Letters*, the English of which is not much worse than that of ninety-nine out of every hundred of his college-bred compatriots, will very soon become aware to what degree the art of writing our language has declined among educated Americans.

According to Mr. C. A. Bristed, 'the admitted classics' of American literature, 'such as Irving and *Bryant*, for example, use language in which the most fastidious would be puzzled to detect any deviation from the purest English models.'—*Cambridge Essays* (1855), p. 62.

refused praise for having exerted himself, according to his lights and opportunities, to prevent the diffusion of unquestionable inaccuracies and vulgarisms; for of these there are, in his catalogue of unpermitted expressions, many, not remarked on in this paper, which every one would do well to avoid. But why, it is obvious to ask, did he pass by scores of such things, including a large number of Americanisms, which contributors to his journal must have been just as likely to trespass into as into those which he has particularised? Was it, as his silence and his own practice lead us to infer, because they had his approval? Be this as it may, he is seen to have stigmatised an abundance of forms and modes of speech against which there is no rational objection whatever, as must be clear to all who know what is, in England, deemed unexceptionable English.

And whence did he derive his opinions as regarded impure English? We have no hesitation in hazarding a surmise on this point. The consensus as to words and uses of words, to be discovered by perusing the best English writers of this century, can have counted, in his estimation, as only most unimportant. On the other hand, unless we suppose as possible an amount of consentaneous whimsicality bordering on a miracle, the unweighed judgments of the criticasters whose noxious sway we set out with deploring, were, to him, so many laws, and laws precluded from all reversal. Nor was he peculiar, in this respect, among Americans. He was simply an exponent of an enormous class of them. Independence of determination touching what is good English, or bad, founded on observation of the usage of the most creditable modern authors, they, with rare exceptions, apparently acknowledge to be beyond their competence. To the decisions of sundry Englishmen and Scotchmen, mainly shallow pretenders, whom they are pleased to take for deep philologists, they defer, however, with uninquiring submission. These decisions are reissued and countersigned among them, with amplifications, in books, and magazines, and newspapers, by persons who, for no more solid reason than their positiveness in asserting, are recognised as of authority; and misconceptions of the grossest and most absurd cast are thus obtruded upon all who can read. Something of this kind of result is seen in England; but, in the United States, the evil of which we speak is far more conspicuous. So influential there are the lessons of prejudice and caprice, inculcated by indigenous teachers, that, for instance, *afterwards*, instead of *afterward*, is usually accounted an error quite unpardonable. As to imperfects passive, like *is being built*,[1] to say that they have been reprobated as seemingly on a plane with moral turpitude, is not to exaggerate facts. Again, Professor William C. Fowler, in his *English Grammar*, rules that *any manner of means, demoralise, first-rate, fogy, full swing, goings-on, humbug, on to, out of sorts, snooze, to stave off*, &c. &c., are Americanisms. The doings of American philologasters are, in truth, a curious study. On the aversion, entertained by so many Americans who affect immaculate English, to reputable words of recent introduction, or, where the words are old, to current senses of them which lack, or are thought to lack, the countenance of long prescription, we forbear to dilate. Yet we may note, that, as a type of the rest, Mr. Bryant, while he disdained certain of these words and senses, patronised still more, probably from being unaware of their comparative novelty. Nor shall we dwell on other salient features of the misplaced precisianism of Americans, of which the greater share is to be attributed, where not to ignorance, at least to misappreciation, of those precedents of usage which Englishmen are content to abide by. And, as these characteristics of unwisdom and bad taste have been illustrated sufficiently, so, it will be granted, we have given a full measure of attention to Mr. Bryant and his fantastic and parcel-learned ambition to render æsthetic aid and comfort, in the province of speech, to the upward or to the downward career of the American ochlocracy.

Common-sense, if duly exercised, would, assuredly, avail to put an end to false philology. In every ancient language whose literature has reached us, we can clearly mark an era when, in the combined articles of expressiveness, perspicuity, and other qualities of excellence, it was eminently at its best. This era we call classical; and locutions which belong to a posterior era we are taught to look upon with a certain contempt; as if Tacitus, and even St. Augustine and the first Pope Gregory, among the later developments with which they abound, did not offer, in many a normal derivative, and in many a terse and pregnant phrase, genuine improvements on Ciceronian circumlocution and diffuseness. Nevertheless, not to award the palm of merit to the

[1] Lord Macaulay, we are informed by his biographer, Mr. Trevelyan, reproved, as solecistic, 'the tea *is being made*.' Yet, at different dates, beginning with 1826, he himself, in familiar letters, did not scruple at 'while it *is being read*,' 'all the *Edinburgh Reviews are being bound*,' 'measures *are being taken*.' See *Life*, &c. (1st ed.), vol. I, pp. 140, 354; vol. II, p. 124, footnote.

That imperfects passive were creeping into use upwards of a hundred years ago, is now ascertained. James Harris, the philologist, wrote, in 1779, 'Sir Guy Carlton *was*...*being examined*;' and his wife wrote, ten years earlier, 'there *is* a good opera...now *being acted*.'

Roman writers who flourished just before and during the reign of Augustus, would be preposterous. With the strictest propriety, we may speak of the golden age of Latin; only it is for a reason which forbids that we should speak of a golden age of English. Latin has a finished history; whereas it may still be early, twenty centuries hence, to tell how English rose, culminated, and gradually parted with its identity. And yet there are many, at this day, as there probably have been from time out of mind, so unthinking as to bewail the decadence of our mother-tongue. It has likewise been, and it still is, the express wish of these visionaries, with Dean Swift as their spokesman, 'to settle our language, and put it into a state of continuance.'[1] Heedless that new discoveries, inventions, and speculations, converse with foreign nations and their literary productions, and various other causes tending to modify human speech, have always been working changes in English, our linguistic conservatives unconsciously demand, for the realisation of their insensate chimera of fixity, that the course of nature should be suspended, and, withal, that the mind of man should be reduced to complete stagnation. Page after page might be filled with absurdities conceived in the same spirit as that of these rhymes of Robert Gould,[2] dated in the year 1687:—

> Our language is at best; and it will fail,
> As th' inundation of French words prevail.
> Let Waller be our standard: all beyond,
> Tho' spoke at court, is foppery and fond.

To turn to dreamers of another species, not a whit behind Gould, on the score of irrationality, is Gilbert Wakefield, with his idolatry, whatever its consequences, of analogy and grammar. These being in his contemplation, not in their real character, as things in perpetual flux, but as though they possessed the constancy of space, or of the folly of the wise, he thus delivers himself:[3] 'It is, certainly, high time for our unconstructed and solecistic style to be modelled by the rectitude of their immutable and applicable standard, which, sooner or later, must be called in to our assistance, and will then essentially impair the beauties and diminish the utilities of our noblest writers, in prose and verse, to future generations.' Jupiter forbid that we should ever give ourselves to the worship of Wakefield's false gods, and incur the

[1] If we may believe Lord Macaulay, the consummation here wished for has been attained; for, referring to the seventeenth century, he speaks of it as a time 'long after our speech had been fixed.' *Essays* (7th ed.), vol. I, p. 405.

[2] Prefixed to Fairfax's *Godfrey of Bulloigne*.

[3] See his *Memoirs*, vol. II, p. 231.

retribution for it which is so frigidly presaged! Nor shall we; but, to the very end, we shall do as countless generations have done before us. When it shall come to be at all patent, that the English nation, whether from luxury, neglect of mental culture, or any other moral or intellectual cancer, has entered on the downhill road to barbarism, or to some like calamity, the day will have arrived, and not till then, to view the later fortunes of our speech with misgiving. In the meantime, despondents and small critics would evince a discretion beyond expectation, by the modesty of silence, and by being satisfied with following, instead of aiming to lead. To the small critics, moreover, it cannot be too often reiterated, that what Dr. Johnson[1] frivolously speaks of as 'the more airy and elegant studies of philology and criticism,' are not things on which, without long and patient preparation, it is otherwise than rash to trust one's self as a legislator. They may rest assured, that we of the nineteenth century, who have worked our way to so much that is good, have shaped our English to a fashion which harmonises, and more fitly than any other fashion of it could harmonise, with the grand total of our complex environment. In the vigour and intrepidity which signalise our time, there is something wholly alien to an apprehensive and emasculate finicalness of expression. Having ceased largely to think as our fathers thought, we can no longer, with justice to the change which has passed on us, write as they wrote. For the rest, given in combination those disciplines which, as a whole, alone deserve to be entitled education, one will hardly select the most appropriate vesture for one's ideas, if one makes it a subject of harassing inquisition. And, on the part of the world at large, we shall not, it is likely, see in it anything better than reminders of the pharisaic tithe-paying and slight of matters much weightier, as the fruit of deferring to the conceits and the counsels of a piddling and nibbling philology.

[1] In the *Idler*, No. 91.

4

WALT WHITMAN

(1819–1892)

Whitman was born in New York and began work at the age of eleven. He spent most of his life in journalism. He published his first book of poetry in 1855, in which he struck a new note of personal and national independence, expressed in a verse-form equally free. In this essay, written towards the end of his life, he employs a characteristically aggressive term to denote the whole American contribution to the English language. He goes on to show the role that a 'radical' science like philology can have in elucidating this contribution.

'Slang in America'

(*The North American Review*, vol. 141, 1885)

Viewed freely, the English language is the accretion and growth of every dialect, race, and range of time, and is the culling and composition of all. From this point of view, it stands for Language in the largest sense, and is really the greatest of studies. It involves so much; is indeed a sort of universal absorber, combiner, and conqueror. The scope of its etymologies is the scope not only of man and civilization, but the history of Nature in all departments, and of the organic Universe, brought up to date; for all are comprehended in words, and their backgrounds. This is when words become vitalized, and stand for things, as they unerringly and very soon come to do, in the mind that enters on their study with fitting spirit, grasp, and appreciation.

Slang, profoundly considered is the lawless germinal element, below all words and sentences, and behind all poetry, and proves a certain freedom and perennial rankness and protestantism in speech. As the United States inherit by far their most precious possession—the language they talk and write—from the Old World, under and out of its feudal institutes, I will allow myself to borrow a simile even of those forms farthest removed from American Democracy. Considering Language then as some mighty potentate, into the majestic audience-hall of the monarch ever enters a personage like one of Shakspere's clowns, and takes position there, and plays a part even in the stateliest ceremonies. Such is Slang, or indirection, an attempt of common humanity to escape from bald literalism, and express itself illimitably, which in highest walks produces poets and poems, and doubtless in pre-historic times gave the start to, and perfected, the whole immense tangle of the old mythologies. For, curious as it may appear, it is strictly the same impulse-source, the same thing. Slang, too, is the wholesome fermentation or eructation of those processes eternally active in language, by which froth and specks are thrown up, mostly to pass away; though occasionally to settle and permanently crystallize.

To make it plainer, it is certain that many of the oldest and solidest words we use, were originally generated from the daring and license of slang. In the processes of word-formation, myriads die, but here and there the attempt attracts superior meanings, becomes valuable and indispensable, and lives forever. Thus the term *right* means literally only straight. *Wrong* primarily meant twisted, distorted. *Integrity* meant, oneness. *Spirit* meant breath, or flame. A *supercilious* person was one who raised his eyebrows. To *insult* was to leap against. If you *influenced* a man, you but flowed into him. The Hebrew word which is translated prophesy meant to bubble up and pour forth as a fountain. The enthusiast bubbles up with the Spirit of God within him, and it pours forth from him like a fountain. The word prophecy is misunderstood. Many suppose that it is limited to mere prediction; that is but the lesser portion of prophecy. The greater work is to reveal God. Every true religious enthusiast is a prophet.

Language, be it remembered, is not an abstract construction of the learned, or of dictionary-makers, but is something arising out of the work, needs, ties, joys, affections, tastes, of long generations of humanity, and has its bases broad and low, close to the ground. Its final decisions are made by the masses, people nearest the concrete, having most to do with actual land and sea. It impermeates all, the Past as well as the present, and is the grandest triumph of the human intellect. 'Those mighty works of art,' says Addington Symonds, 'which we call languages, in the construction of which whole peoples unconsciously co-operated, the forms of which were determined not by individual genius, but by the instincts of successive generations, acting to one end, inherent in the nature of the race—those poems of pure thought and fancy, cadenced not in words, but in living imagery, fountain-heads of inspiration, mirrors of the mind of nascent nations, which we call Mythologies—these surely are more marvellous in their infantine spontaneity than any more mature production of the races which evolved them. Yet we are utterly ignorant of their embryology; the true science of Origins is yet in its cradle.'

Daring as it is to say so, in the growth of Language it is certain that the retrospect of slang from the start would be the recalling from their nebulous conditions of all that is poetical in the stores of human utterance. Moreover, the honest delving, as of late years, by the German and British workers in comparative philology has pierced and dispersed many of the falsest bubbles of centuries; and will disperse many more. It was long recorded that in Scandinavian mythology the heroes in the Norse Paradise drank out of the skulls of their slain enemies. Later investigation proves the word taken for skulls to mean *horns* of beasts slain in the hunt. And what reader had not been exercised over the traces of that feudal custom, by which *seigneurs* warmed their feet in the bowels of serfs, the abdomen being opened for the purpose? It now is made to appear that the serf was only required to submit his unharmed abdomen as a foot cushion while his lord supped, and was required to chafe the legs of the seigneur with his hands.

It is in embryons and childhood, and among the illiterate, we always find the groundwork and start, of this great science, and its noblest products. What a relief most people have in speaking of a man not by his true and formal name, with a 'Mister' to it, but by some odd or homely appellative. The propensity to approach a meaning not directly and squarely, but by circuitous styles of expression seems indeed a born quality of the common people every where, evidenced by nick-names and the inveterate determination of the masses to bestow sub-titles, sometimes ridiculous, sometimes very apt. Always among the soldiers during the Secession War, one heard of 'Little Mac' (Gen. McClellan), or of 'Uncle Billy' (Gen. Sherman). 'The old man' was, of course, very common. Among the rank and file, both armies, it was very general to speak of the different States they came from by their slang names. Those from Maine were called Foxes; New Hampshire, Granite Boys; Massachusetts, Bay Staters; Vermont, Green Mountain Boys; Rhode Island, Gun Flints; Connecticut, Wooden Nutmegs; New York, Knickerbockers; New Jersey, Clam Catchers; Pennsylvania, Logher Heads; Delaware, Muskrats; Maryland, Claw Thumpers; Virginia, Beagles; North Carolina, Tar Boilers; South Carolina, Weasels; Georgia, Buzzards; Louisiana, Creoles; Alabama, Lizzards; Kentucky, Corn Crackers; Ohio, Buckeyes; Michigan, Wolverines; Indiana, Hoosiers; Illinois, Suckers; Missouri, Pukes; Mississippi, Tad

Poles; Florida, Fly up the Creeks; Wisconsin, Badgers; Iowa, Hawkeyes; Oregon, Hard Cases. Indeed I am not sure but slang names have more than once made Presidents. 'Old Hickory,' (Gen. Jackson) is one case in point. 'Tippecanoe, and Tyler too,' another.

I find the same rule in the people's conversations everywhere. I heard this among the men of the city horse-cars, where the conductor is often called a 'snatcher' (i.e. because his characteristic duty is to constantly pull or snatch the bell-strap, to stop or go on.) Two young fellows are having a friendly talk, amid which, says 1st Conductor, 'What did you do before you was a snatcher?' Answer of 2d Conductor, 'Nailed.' (Translation of answer: 'I worked as carpenter.') What is a 'boom'? says one editor to another. 'Esteemed contemporary,' says the other, 'a boom is a bulge.' 'Barefoot whiskey' is the Tennessee name for the undiluted stimulant. In the slang of the New York common restaurant waiters a plate of ham and beans is known as 'stars and stripes,' codfish balls as 'sleeve-buttons,' and hash as 'mystery.'

The Western States of the Union are, however, as may be supposed the special areas of slang, not only in conversation, but in names of localities, towns, rivers, &c. A late Oregon traveler says:

> On your way to Olympia by rail, you cross a river called the Shookum-Chuck; your train stops at places named Newaukum, Tumwater, and Toutle; and if you seek further you will hear of whole counties labelled Wahkiakum, or Snohomish, or Kitsar, or Klikatat; and Cowlitz, Hookium, and Nenolelops greet and offend you. They complain in Olympia that Washington Territory gets but little immigration; but what wonder? What man, having the whole American continent to choose from, would willingly date his letters from the county of Snohomish or bring up his children in the city of Nenolelops? The village of Tumwater is, as I am ready to bear witness, very pretty indeed; but surely an emigrant would think twice before he established himself either there or at Toutle. Seattle is sufficiently barbarous; Stelicoom is no better; and I suspect that the Northern Pacific Railroad terminus has been fixed at Tacoma because it is one of the few places on Puget Sound whose name does not inspire horror.

Then a Nevada paper chronicles the departure of a mining party from Reno: 'The toughest set of roosters that ever shook the dust of any town left Reno yesterday for the new mining district of Cornucopia. They came here from Virginia. Among the crowd were four New-York cock-fighters, two Chicago murderers, three Baltimore bruisers, one Philadelphia prize-fighter, four San Francisco hoodlums, three Virginia beats, two Union Pacific roughs, and two check guerrillas.' Among the far-west newspapers, have been, or are, *The*

Fairplay (Colorado) *Flume*, *The Solid Muldoon*, of Ouray, *The Tombstone Epitaph*, of Nevada, *The Jimplecute*, of Texas, and *The Bazoo*, of Missouri. Shirttail Bend, Whiskey Flat, Puppytown, Wild Yankee Ranch, Squaw Flat, Rawhide Ranch, Loafer's Ravine, Squitch Gulch, Toenail Lake are a few of the names of places in Butte county, Cal.

Perhaps indeed no place or term gives more luxuriant illustrations of the fermentation processes I have mentioned, and their froth and specks than our Mississippi and Pacific coast regions, at the present day. Hasty and grotesque as are some of the names, others are of an appropriateness and originality unsurpassable. This applies to the Indian words, which are often perfect. Oklahoma is proposed in Congress for the name of one of our new Territories. Hog-eye, Lick-skillet, Rake-pocket and Steal-easy are the names of some Texan towns. Miss Bremer found among the aborigines the following names: *Men's*, Horn-point; Round-Wind; Stand-and-look-out; The-Cloud-that-goes-aside; Iron-toe; Seek-the-sun; Iron-flash; Red-bottle; White-spindle; Black-dog; Two-feathers-of-honor; Gray-grass; Bushy-tail; Thunder-face; Go-on-the-burning-sod; Spirits-of-the-dead. *Women's*, Keep-the-fire; Spiritual-woman; Second-daughter-of-the-house; Blue-bird.

Certainly philologists have not given enough attention to this element and its results, which, I repeat, can probably be found working every where to-day, amid modern conditions, with as much life and activity as in far-back Greece or India, under pre-historic ones. Then the wit—the rich flashes of humor and genius and poetry—darting out often from a gang of laborers, railroad-men, miners, drivers or boatmen! How often have I hovered at the edge of a crowd of them, to hear their repartees and impromptus! You get more real fun from half an hour with them than from the books of all 'the American humorists.'

The science of language has large and close analogies in geological science, with its ceaseless evolution, its fossils, and its numberless submerged layers and hidden strata, the infinite go-before of the present. Or, perhaps Language is more like some vast living body, or perennial body of bodies. And slang not only brings the first feeders of it, but is afterward the start of fancy, imagination and humor, breathing into its nostrils the breath of life.

5

J. A. H. MURRAY

(1837–1915)

The *New English Dictionary on Historical Principles*, also known as Murray's Dictionary, after the name of its chief editor, is the most comprehensive source of information about the history of our vocabulary that we have, and its information about contemporary forms and meanings is surpassed only by the recent *Webster's Third New International Dictionary* (see Essay 21). Material began to be collected as early as 1857 by a number of scholars, under the auspices of the Philological Society, but systematic compilation did not take place until 1878; publication of the Dictionary took forty-four years, from 1884 to 1928. A corrected edition and supplement was brought out in 1933, when the title was changed to the *Oxford English Dictionary* (or *OED*), and a second supplement is in preparation. In the Introduction, Murray presents the principles on which the Dictionary was based.

'General Explanations'

(*A New English Dictionary on Historical Principles*, vol. I, 1888)

The vocabulary

The Vocabulary of a widely-diffused and highly-cultivated living language is not a fixed quantity circumscribed by definite limits. That vast aggregate of words and phrases which constitutes the Vocabulary of English-speaking men presents, to the mind that endeavours to grasp it as a definite whole, the aspect of one of those nebulous masses familiar to the astronomer, in which a clear and unmistakable nucleus shades off on all sides, through zones of decreasing brightness, to a dim marginal film that seems to end nowhere, but to lose itself imperceptibly in the surrounding darkness. In its constitution it may be compared to one of those natural groups of the zoologist or botanist, wherein typical species forming the characteristic nucleus of the order, are linked on every side to other species, in which the typical character is less and less distinctly apparent, till it fades away in an outer fringe of aberrant forms, which merge imperceptibly in various surrounding orders, and whose own position is ambiguous and uncertain. For the convenience of classification, the naturalist may draw the line, which bounds a class or order, outside or inside of a particular form; but Nature has drawn it nowhere. So the English Vocabulary contains a nucleus or central mass of many thousand words whose 'Anglicity' is unquestioned; some of

them only literary, some of them only colloquial, the great majority at once literary and colloquial,—they are the *Common Words* of the language. But they are linked on every side with other words which are less and less entitled to this appellation, and which pertain ever more and more distinctly to the domain of local dialect, of the slang and cant of 'sets' and classes, of the peculiar technicalities of trades and processes, of the scientific terminology common to all civilized nations, of the actual languages of other lands and peoples. And there is absolutely no defining line in any direction: the circle of the English language has a well-defined centre but no discernible circumference.[1] Yet practical

[1] The above diagram will explain itself, as an attempt to express to the eye the aspect in which the Vocabulary is here presented, and also some of the relations of its elements typical and aberrant. The centre is occupied by the 'common' words, in which literary and colloquial usage meet. 'Scientific' and 'foreign' words enter the common language mainly through literature; 'slang' words ascend through colloquial use; the 'technical' terms of crafts and processes, and the 'dialect' words, blend with the common language both in speech and literature. Slang also touches on one side the technical terminology of trades and occupations, as in 'nautical slang,' 'Public School slang,' 'the slang of the Stock Exchange,' and on another passes into true dialect. Dialects similarly pass into foreign languages. Scientific terminology passes on one side into purely foreign words,

utility has some bounds, and a Dictionary has definite limits: the lexicographer must, like the naturalist, 'draw the line somewhere', in each diverging direction. He must include all the 'Common Words' of literature and conversation, and such of the scientific, technical, slang, dialectal, and foreign words as are passing into common use, and approach the position or standing of 'common words', well knowing that the line which he draws will not satisfy all his critics. For to every man the domain of 'common words' widens out in the direction of his own reading, research, business, provincial or foreign residence, and contracts in the direction with which he has no practical connexion: no one man's English is *all* English. The lexicographer must be satisfied to exhibit the greater part of the vocabulary of *each* one, which will be immensely more than the whole vocabulary of *any* one.

In addition to, and behind, the common vocabulary, in all its diverging lines, lies an infinite number of *Proper* or merely *denotative* names, outside the province of lexicography, yet touching it in thousands of points, at which these names, and still more the adjectives and verbs formed upon them, acquire more or less of connotative value. Here also limits more or less arbitrary must be assumed.

The Language presents yet another undefined frontier, when it is viewed in relation to *time*. The living vocabulary is no more permanent in its constitution than definite in its extent. It is not to-day what it was a century ago, still less what it will be a century hence. Its constituent elements are in a state of slow but incessant dissolution and renovation. 'Old words' are ever becoming obsolete and dying out: 'new words' are continually pressing in. And the death of a word is not an event of which the date can be readily determined. It is a vanishing process, extending over a lengthened period, of which contemporaries never see the end. Our own words never become obsolete: it is always the words of our grandfathers that have died with them. Even after we cease to use a word, the memory of it survives, and the word itself survives as a possibility; it is only when no one is left to whom its use is still possible, that the word is wholly dead. Hence, there are many words of which it is doubtful whether they are still to be considered as part of the living language; they are alive to some speakers, and dead to others. And, on the other hand, there are many claimants to admission into the recognized vocabulary (where some of them will certainly one day be

on another it blends with the technical vocabulary of art and manufactures. It is not possible to fix the point at which the 'English Language' stops, along any of these diverging lines.

received), that are already current coin with some speakers and writers, and not yet 'good English', or even not English at all, to others.

If we treat the division of words into current and obsolete as a subordinate one, and extend our idea of the Language so as to include all that has been English from the beginning, or from any particular epoch, we enter upon a department of the subject, of which, from the nature of the case, our exhibition must be imperfect. For the vocabulary of past times is known to us solely from its preservation in written records; the extent of our knowledge of it depends entirely upon the completeness of the records, and the completeness of our acquaintance with them. And the farther back we go, the more imperfect are the records, the smaller is the fragment of the actual vocabulary that we can recover.

Subject to the conditions which thus encompass every attempt to construct a complete English Dictionary, the present work aims at exhibiting the history and signification of the English words now in use, or known to have been in use since the middle of the twelfth century. This date has been adopted as the only natural halting-place, short of going back to the beginning, so as to include the entire Old English or 'Anglo-Saxon' Vocabulary. To do this would have involved the inclusion of an immense number of words, not merely long obsolete but also having obsolete inflexions, and thus requiring, if dealt with at all, a treatment different from that adapted to the words which survived the twelfth century. For not only was the stream of English literature then reduced to the tiniest thread (the slender annals of the Old English or Anglo-Saxon Chronicle being for nearly a century its sole representative), but the vast majority of the ancient words that were destined not to live into modern English, comprising the entire scientific, philosophical, and poetical vocabulary of Old English, had already disappeared, and the old inflexional and grammatical system had been levelled to one so essentially modern as to require no special treatment in the Dictionary. Hence we exclude all words that had become obsolete by 1150. But to words actually included this date has no application; their history is exhibited from their first appearance, however early.

Within these chronological limits, it is the aim of the Dictionary to deal with all the common words of speech and literature, and with all words which approach these in character; the limits being extended farther in the domain of science and philosophy, which naturally passes into that of literature, than in that of slang or cant, which touches the colloquial. In scientific and technical terminology, the aim has been to include *all words English in form*, except those of which an explanation would be unintelligible to any but the specialist; and such words, not English in form, as either are in general use, like *Hippopotamus, Geranium, Aluminium, Focus, Stratum, Bronchitis*, or belong to the more familiar language of science, as *Mammalia, Lepidoptera, Invertebrata.*

Down to the Fifteenth Century the language existed only in dialects, all of which had a literary standing: during this period, therefore, words and forms of all dialects are admitted on an equal footing into the Dictionary. Dialectal words and forms which occur since 1500 are not admitted, except when they continue the history of a word or sense once in general use, illustrate the history of a literary word, or have themselves a certain literary currency, as is the case with many modern Scottish words. It is true that the dialectal words are mostly genuine English, and that they are an essential part of the contents of a *Lexicon totius Anglicitatis*;[1] but the work of collecting them has not yet been completed; and, even when they shall have been collected, the phonetic variety in which they exist in different localities, and the want of any fixed written forms round which to group the variations, will require a method of treatment different from that applicable to the words of the literary language, which have an accepted uniform spelling and an approximately uniform pronunciation.

Classification of the vocabulary

For the purposes of treatment in this Dictionary, words and phrases are classed as: 1) Main Words, 2) Subordinate Words, 3) Combinations. MAIN WORDS comprise i) all single words, radical or derivative (e.g. *Ant, Amphitheatrically*), ii) all those compound words (and phrases) which, from their meaning, history, or importance, claim to be treated in separate articles (e.g. *Afternoon, Almighty, Almsman, Air-pump, Aitch-bone, Ale-house, Forget-me-not, Adam's apple, All fours*). The articles in which these are treated constitute the *Main Articles.* SUBORDINATE WORDS include variant and obsolete forms of Main Words, and such words of bad formation, doubtful existence, or alleged use, as it is deemed proper, on any ground, to record. The *Main* and *Subordinate* Words are arranged in a single alphabetic series, the former being printed in a larger, the latter in a smaller type. COMBINATIONS, when so simple as either to require no explanation, or to be capable of being

[1] [*Lexicon totius Anglicitatis* complete lexicon of English.]

briefly explained in connexion with their cognates, are dealt with under the Main Words which form their first element, their treatment forming the concluding part of the Main Article.

MAIN WORDS

Every Main Word is treated, once for all, under its modern current or most usual spelling; or, if obsolete, under the most typical of its latest spellings; the form or spelling thus chosen being considered the *Main Form* of the word.

Occasionally a form or spelling of an obsolete word has been assumed, which is not actually found in the quotations adduced, but is in accordance with the usual analogies of the language, as seen in kindred words. Thus *Annoyously* is given as the Main Form, on the analogy of *annoy*, *annoyous*, although only *anoyously* has actually been found.

All other important forms of each word, current or obsolete, are entered in their alphabetical order, as *Subordinate Words*, and are there concisely referred to the *Main Form* under which they are treated.

When a word which is historically one has different grammatical relations, it is treated as one word only, and the different relations are indicated by the division of the article into sections (marked A, B, C). This refers especially to substantives used also *attributively* (or *adjectively*), as in 'an ounce of *gold*, a *gold* watch, *gold*-coloured scales'; to adjectives used *substantively* or *pronominally*, as in 'the *catholic* church, a good *catholic*; *that* book, *that* is mine, the words *that* he spoke'; to adjectives used adverbially, as in 'the *according* voice of national wisdom', 'he acted *according* to orders'; to adverbs, prepositions, and conjunctions, originally the same word, as ABOUT, AFTER, SINCE, AS; and of course *à fortiori*[1] to verbs used *transitively* and *intransitively*, as 'to abide battle, to abide at home,' which, in some dictionaries, are reckoned as two distinct words.

In this Dictionary, *transitive* and *intransitive* seldom appear even as leading divisions of a verb, but, in accordance with the actual history of the word, in most cases only as varying and often temporary constructions, subordinate to the different senses, and liable to pass one into the other in the development of the language. Thus a verb at one time intransitive finally takes a simple object, through the phonetic decay of a dative or genitive ending, or the elision of a preposition, and is accounted transitive, without any change either in form or meaning (e.g. ANSWER); and a verb used transitively, likewise without change

[1] [*à fortiori* all the more.]

of meaning and form at length becomes intransitive, through the regular modern English suppression of the reflexive pronoun (e.g. Ezek. xx. 22 I *withdrew* mine hand; Mark iii. 7 Jesus *withdrew* himself to the sea; *Revised Version*, Jesus *withdrew* to the sea). The history of ANSWER or WITHDRAW would be misrepresented by splitting them each into two words, or even by classifying their senses in a manner which would conceal these historical relations.

But verbs uniform in their stems with substantives or adjectives, as LAND, to LAND, DRY, to DRY, ABSTRACT, to ABSTRACT, are, of course, distinct words; as are adjectives and adverbs which, through 'levelling' of terminations, have become identical in form, though originally distinct, as ALIKE *a.*, ALIKE *adv.*; and substantives and adjectives which have always been identical in form, but were of separate introduction into the language, and have separate histories, as ANIMAL *sb.*, ANIMAL *a.* Where a word originally one has been, in the course of its history, split into two, whether with distinction of sense, as ALSO, AS, or merely as synonyms, as ANT, EMMET, APPRENTICE, PRENTICE, both modern forms are treated as separate words, and there is a reference from one article to the other. Where two original words of identical or similar form have coalesced into one, the modern word is treated as one or two, according to practical utility. When they are treated as two words, these come, of course, immediately together: see ALLAY, ALLOW, AMICE.

The treatment of a Main Word comprises:—I THE IDENTIFICATION, II THE MORPHOLOGY, III THE SIGNIFICATION, IV THE ILLUSTRATIVE QUOTATIONS.

I THE IDENTIFICATION INCLUDES:

1 The *Main Form*, i.e. the usual or typical spelling, as already described. (In certain cases where two spellings are in current use, both are given in the Main Form, as ANALYSE -YZE, CHEMISTRY CHYMISTRY, INFLECTION INFLEXION.) Words believed to be *obsolete* are distinguished by prefixing †; *non-naturalized* or *partially-naturalized* words, by ||.

In the case of rare words, especially those adopted or formed from Latin equivalents, it is often difficult to say whether they are or are not obsolete. They are permanent possibilities, rarely needed, but capable of being used whenever they are needed, rather than actually discarded terms. To these and other words, of which the obsoleteness is doubtful, the † is not prefixed.

As to their citizenship in the language, words may be classed as *Naturals*, *Denizens*, *Aliens*, and *Casuals*. NATURALS include all *native* words like *father*, and all fully *naturalized* words like *street*, *rose*, *knapsack*, *gas*, *parasol*. DENIZENS are words fully naturalized as to use, but not as to *form*, *inflexion*, or *pronunciation*, as *aide-de-camp, locus, carte-de-visite, table d'hôte.* ALIENS are names of foreign objects, titles, etc., which we require often to use, and for which we have no native equivalents, as *shah, geyser, cicerone, targum, backsheesh, sepoy.* CASUALS are foreign words of the same class, not in habitual use, which for special and temporary purposes occur in books of foreign travel, letters of foreign correspondents, and the like. There are no fixed limits between these classes, and the constant tendency is for words to pass upwards from the last to the first. But, while casuals and aliens from barbarous languages are readily and quickly naturalized, words from French and the learned languages, especially Latin, which are assumed to be known to all the polite, are often kept in the position of denizens for centuries: we still treat *phenomenon* as Greek, *genus* as Latin, *aide-de-camp* as French. The words marked with || in the Dictionary comprise *Denizens* and *Aliens*, and such *Casuals* as approach, or formerly approached, the position of these. Opinions will differ as to the claims of some that are included and some that are excluded, and also as to the line dividing *Denizens* from *Naturals*, and the position assigned to some words on either side of it. If we are to distinguish these classes at all, a line must be drawn somewhere.

2 (Within parentheses) the *Pronunciation* or symbolization of the actual existing form of the word, as explained hereafter. A recognized difference of pronunciation is also shown, with occasional notes on the diversity. Of Obsolete Words usually no pronunciation is given, but the place of the stress or accent, when ascertained, is indicated by a 'turned period' after the stress-vowel, as **Alfe·res, A·nredly**. In partially naturalized words two pronunciations are often given, viz. the native (or what passes for the native), and one conformed more or less to English analogies; in actual use many intermediate varieties may be heard, cf. *rendez-vous, envelope, environs, prestige, chignon, recitative, Koran, caviare,* and the like.

3 The *Grammatical Designation*, i.e. the Part of Speech, or subdivision of the same, as *pers. pron., vbl. sb.* See the list of Abbreviations. All words having no Grammatical Designation are *substantives*; the letters *sb.* are employed only where required to avoid ambiguity.

4 In words of more or less specific use, the *Specification*, as *Mus.* (in Music), *Bot.* (in Botany), etc.

5 The *Status*, where there is any peculiarity, as *Obs.* (obsolete), *arch.* (archaic or obsolescent), *colloq.* (colloquial), *dial.* (now dialectal, though formerly in general use: words exclusively dialectal are not inserted, except on special grounds). Here also is added, when applicable, the epithet *rare*, with $^{-1}$, or $^{-0}$, indicating that only *one*, or *no* actual instance of the use of the word is known to us. Words apparently employed only *for the nonce*, are, when inserted in the Dictionary, marked *nonce-wd.*

6 The principal earlier *Forms* or Spellings, with their chronological range indicated by the unit figure of the century, thus 3–6 = 13th to 16th cent.; 1 standing for all centuries down to 1100.

These figures also correspond broadly to distinct periods of the language; viz. 1 *Old English* or 'Anglo-Saxon'; 2 (12th c.) *Old English Transition* ('semi-Saxon'); 3 (13th c.) *Early Middle English*; 4 (14th c.) *Late Middle English*; 5 (15th c.) *Middle English Transition*; 6 (16th c.) *Early Modern* or Tudor *English*; 7 (17th c.) *Middle Modern English*; 8, 9 (18th and 19th c.) *Current English.*

7 The *Inflexions*, i.e. plural of substantives, and principal parts of verbs, when other than the ordinary *-s*, *-ed.*

II The Morphology or *Form-History* [within heavy square brackets] includes:—1) the *Derivation*, or *Etymology*, showing the actual origin of the word, when ascertained. 2) The *Subsequent Form-history* in English, when this presents special features, as phonetic change, contraction, corruption, perversion by popular etymology or erroneous association. 3) *Miscellaneous facts* as to the history of the word, its age, obsolescence, revival, refashioning, change of pronunciation, confusion with other words.

In the light of *historical* Etymology, an English word is (1) The extant formal representative, or direct phonetic descendant, of an earlier word; that is to say, it is the earlier word itself, in a later or more recent form, as it has been unconsciously changed in the mouths of the successive generations that have used it. For example, Acre (now really $\bar{e}^{i}$·kəɹ), formerly *aker*, is the extant form of Old English *æcer*, this the later form of prehistoric *æcr*, the special English form of *acr*, *akr*, this of West Germanic *akra*, this, through earlier *akra-z*, of Original Teutonic *akro-z*, this of original Aryan or Indo-European *agro-s*; and *agros*, *akroz*, *akraz*, *akra*, *akr*, *æcr*, *æcer*, *aker*, *āker*, *ācre* ($\bar{e}^{i}$·kəɹ), are all merely successive and temporary forms of one and the same word, as employed during successive periods. The word has never died; no year, no day probably, has passed without its being uttered by many: but this constant use has so worn it down and modified its form, that we commonly look upon *acre* as a distinct word from *agros*, with which it is connected by many intermediate forms, of which only a few have been discriminated in writing, while the finer and more intimately connecting links have never been written. This *phonetic descent* is symbolized by (:—); thus Acre:— OE. *æcer*:—O.Teut. **akro-z*.

If not the extant formal representative of an original Teutonic word, an English word has been (2) *adopted* (a.), or (3) *adapted* (ad.), from some foreign language; i.e. it is a word once foreign, but now, without or with intentional change of form, used as English; or it has been (4) *formed* on or from (f.) native or foreign elements, or from a combination of them. *Adoption* is essentially a popular process, at work whenever the speakers of one language come into contact with the speakers of another, from whom they acquire foreign things, or foreign ideas, with their foreign names. It has prevailed in English at all periods from the earliest to the latest times: *inch*, *pound*, *street*, *rose*, *cat*, *prison*, *algebra*, *antic*, *orange*, *tobacco*, *tea*, *canoe*, *focus*, *meerschaum*, are adopted words. *Adaptation* is essentially a learned or literary process; it consists in adapting a foreign word to the 'analogies of the language', and so depriving it of its foreign termination. Examples are Latin or Greek words reduced to their stem form, or receiving recognized English endings. Latin words which lived on in Gaul there underwent regular phonetic changes, whereby they at length became 'French'; in this living French form they were adopted in Middle English; but in more recent times numerous Latin words have been taken into English directly, yet modified, in their terminations, in the same way as if they had lived on in French and been thence adopted into English.[1] Such

[1] The French words adopted before 1400 were generally taken from the Anglo-French, or French spoken for several centuries in England, where they had undergone further phonetic change. It was in strict conformity with linguistic facts that Chaucer told of his *Prioresse*:

> Frenssh she spak ful faire and fetisly,
> After the scole of Stratford at-te Bowe,
> For frenssh of Parys was to hire vnknowe:

for the Anglo-French dialect of the 14th century was distinct not only from Parisian, but from all dialects of continental French. In its origin a mixture of various Norman and other Northern French dialects, afterwards mixed with and greatly modified by Angevin, Parisian, Poitevin, and other elements, and more and more exposed to the overpowering influence of literary French, it had yet received, on this side the Channel, a distinct and independent development, following, in its phonology especially, English and not continental tendencies. As the natural speech of the higher and educated classes, it died out in the 14th century; but it maintained a kind of artificial existence for a longer period, and was used (in an increasingly debased form) for writing law-reports down to the 17th century, in which stage it still influenced the spelling of English words. Its forms survive in many of our terminations: *armour*, *colour*, *glorious*, *gracious*, *envious*, *perilous*, *arrival*, *espousal*, *language*, *enjoy*, *benefit*, *gaoler*, *caitif*, are the actual Anglo-French forms, as distinct from those of continental Old and Modern French. As a rule, it may be assumed that the original form of every Middle English word of French origin was *identical* with the Anglo-French form; and that, where a gap appears between the earliest known English form of a word and its Old French equivalent, that gap would be filled up by the recovery of the Anglo-French and earliest English form. It was not until the 15th century, and chiefly at the hands of Caxton, that continental French forms and spellings began directly to influence our language.

English words originate in an *adaptation* of the Latin original, not in an adoption of its French (or other Romance) extant representative. *Formation* consists in the combination of existing words or parts of words with each other, or with *living formatives*, i.e. syllables which no longer exist as separate words, but yet have an appreciable *signification* which they impart to the new product. Formation is the chief natural process by which the vocabulary of a language is increased: it is both popular and learned; in its popular application, it gives such words as *black-bird, shep-herd, work-er, high-ness, grand-ly, a-swim, be-moan, after-noon*; in learned application, such as *con-caten-ation, mono-petal-ous, chloro-phyl, tele-phone*; in a mixture of the two, such as *acknowledge-ment, lion-ize, starv-ation, betroth-al.*

Much of the terminology of modern science is identical, or as nearly so as the forms of the languages permit, in English and French, in English, French, and German, or sometimes even in most of the European languages. It would often be as difficult as useless to ascertain in which language a particular scientific term first appeared in print, this being, linguistically, a mere accident: the word was accepted as common property from the beginning. In such cases, *modern formation* (mod. f.) is employed to intimate that it is uncertain in what modern language, English or continental, the word was first used; it may indeed have occurred first in some modern Latin work, either of English or foreign authorship.

Phonetic descent (:—), *adoption* (a.), *adaptation* (ad.), word-*formation* (f.) are usually combined under the term *derivation*; but, until we know in which of them, singly or in combination, a word has originated, we do not know its Etymology.

In this Dictionary, words originally native are traced to their earliest known English, and, when possible, to their earliest Teutonic form, authenticated and illustrated by the cognate words in other Teutonic languages and dialects; those of foreign origin are referred to the foreign word or elements whence they were immediately adopted or formed. In certain cases these foreign words, especially the French, are themselves traced to their antecedent forms or component elements; but these antecedents are considered only with a view to the clearer comprehension of the history and use of the word in English. To trace the remoter history of these words, and determine their Aryan or other 'roots,' is no part of their English history.

Of many words it has to be stated that their origin is either doubtful or altogether unknown. In such cases the historical facts are given, as far as they go, and their bearing occasionally indicated. But *conjectural etymologies* are rarely referred to, except to point out their agreement or disagreement with the historical facts; for these, and the full discussion which they require, the reader is referred to special treatises on etymology.

III THE SIGNIFICATION (*Sematology*). Some words have only one invariable signification; but most words that have been used for any length of time in a language have acquired a long and sometimes intricate series of significations, as the primitive sense has been gradually extended to include allied or associated ideas, or transferred boldly to figurative and analogical uses. This happens to a greater extent with *relational* words, as prepositions (cf. *About*, *After*, *Against*, *And*, *Anent*) than with *notional* words, as verbs and nouns; of these, also, it affects verbs and adjectives more than substantives; of substantives, it influences those which express actions, qualities, and mental conceptions (cf. *Account*), more than those which name, and are, as it were, fixed to material objects. Yet even these latter have often acquired many different senses. Thus, *Board* names a material object; yet compare: a thin *board*, a frugal *board*, a card-*board*, *board* and lodgings, passengers on *board*, to fall over *board*, to sit at the council *board*, a *board* school, the *Board* of Trade, to tread the *boards*, a sea-*board* parish. The order in which these senses were developed is one of the most important facts in the history of the word; to discover and exhibit it are among the most difficult duties of a dictionary which aims at giving this history. If the historical record were complete, that is, if we possessed written examples of all the uses of each word from the beginning, the simple exhibition of these would display a rational or logical development. The historical record is not complete enough to do this, but it is usually sufficient to enable us to infer the actual order. In exhibiting this in the Dictionary, that sense is placed first which was actually the earliest in the language: the others follow in the order in which they appear to have arisen. As however, the development often proceeded in *many* branching lines, sometimes parallel, often divergent, it is evident that it cannot be adequately represented in a single linear series. Hence, while the senses are numbered straight on 1, 2, 3, &c., they are also grouped under branches marked I, II, III, &c., in each of which the historical order begins afresh. Subdivisions of the senses, varieties of construction, &c., are marked **a**, **b**, **c**, &c.; subdivisions of these, which rarely occur, (*a*.), (*b*.), (*c*.), &c. So far for words of which the senses have been developed in English itself. But in adopted or adapted words which had already acquired various significations in the language (e.g. Latin) from which they were taken, it often happens that the order in which the senses appeared in English does not agree with the natural order in which they were developed in the original language. The English order is in fact accidental. For it was not in the primary sense that the word was first taken into English, but in a figurative, transferred, or specialized use, as an ecclesiastical, legal, grammatical, or medical term, which perhaps took root in our language, and here received a development of its own. Subsequently, however, familiarity with the Latin language and literature sometimes led to a fresh adoption of the word in the primary sense, or to a sudden extension of English usage, so as to include the primary sense, which thus appears as of quite late origin in English. In such a case it is not possible to make the historical order of the senses in English agree with the logical order in which they arose in Latin or other previous language; and every such word must be treated in the way which seems best suited to exhibit the facts of its own history and use. Instances of such words are afforded by ADVENT, AGONY, ANNUNCIATION, APPEND.

Obsolete Senses, like obsolete words, have † prefixed, so as to be at once distinguished from those now in use. Under ¶ are included *Catachrestic* and erroneous uses, confusions, and the like.

To a great extent the *explanations* of the meanings have been framed anew upon a study of all the quotations for each word collected for this work, of which those printed form only a small part. But the labours of other scholars in this, the most successfully cultivated department of English lexicography, have not been neglected. In particular, the explanations of Dr. Johnson and of his editor Archdeacon Todd have often been adopted unchanged (within inverted commas and marked J. or T.), as have those of N. Bailey, and other early lexicographers, to whom it is only right to give credit for original work which has become the common property of all their successors.

IV THE QUOTATIONS illustrate the forms and uses of the word, showing the age of the word generally, and of its various senses particularly; the earliest and, in obsolete words or senses, the latest, known instances of its occurrence being always quoted. Except in special cases, where the letters of the Greek alphabet, α, β, γ, &c. are used to separate parallel forms, the illustration of the *forms* is subordinated to that of the *senses*: the quotations illustrating each sense immediately follow the explanation. They are arranged chronologically, so as to give about one for each century, though various considerations often render a larger number necessary. The original spelling is retained, as an essential part of the history of the language. But merely graphical or typographical devices, such as contractions, erratic presence of capitals, and (in seventeenth-century books) employment of italics to emphasize words, phrases, or whole passages, are not reproduced; and simple blunders, which would mislead the reader, are tacitly corrected. The recent use of italics, to indicate a doubt about the status of a word, is retained as being often of historical importance.

As to letters, the Old and Middle English 'thorn' (þ = *th*) and Old English 'divided *d*' or 'the' (ð; usually only a variant of 'þ', though sometimes distinguished, as in the KEY TO PRONUNCIATION) are retained; also ME. 'open-tailed *g*', or 'yea' (ȝ = *y* initially, *gh* finally). In Old English, the letter *g* had the form 'ȝ, *ȝ*' (a peculiar British development of the Roman G). Besides the original sound in *g*o, *g*ild, this letter had also (at least in later Old English) a fricative sound as in German ta*g*, or Irish lou*gh* (or both), and a palatalized sound, approximately = *y* in *y*e, *y*es. After the Norman Conquest the modern forms 'g, *g*', were introduced (from French) for the sound in *g*o, and the new sound in *g*in*g*er; but the OE. form (in process of time slightly modified) was retained for the sounds in lou*gh*, *y*es, till the introduction of Printing. In printing Old English, modern scholars sometimes reproduce the contemporary 'ȝ, *ȝ*' (as is done by Sievers, in his *Angelsächsische Grammatik*), but more commonly substitute modern 'g, *g*'. The adoption of either course exclusively in this work would have broken the historical continuity of the forms; in the one case, we should have had the same word appearing in the eleventh century as 'ȝold', and in the twelfth century as 'gold'; in the other, the same word written in the eleventh century 'ge' and in twelfth century 'ȝe'. To avoid this, both forms are here used in Old English, in accordance with the Middle English distinction in their use; thus, 'gold', 'ȝe', 'dæȝ'. The reader will understand that 'g' and 'ȝ' represent the same Old English letter, and that the distinction made between them is purely editorial (though certainly corresponding to a distinction of sound in OE.). For ME. the form 'ȝ' commonly used in reprints is employed, so that OE. 'ȝe' becomes ME. 'ȝe', modern 'ye'; OE. 'ȝenóȝ, ȝenóh', ME. 'ynoȝ, inouȝ', mod. 'enough'.

It is to be distinctly borne in mind that the quotations are not merely examples of the fully developed use of the word or special sense under which they are cited: they have also to illustrate its origin, its gradual separation from allied words or senses, or even, by negative evidence, its non-existence at the given date. It would often have been desirable to annotate the quotations, explaining the purpose for which they are adduced; but the exigencies of space render this impossible, and they are therefore left to speak for themselves. Some help has been offered by enclosing within [...] quotations given for what may be called subsidiary purposes.

The need to keep the Dictionary within practicable limits has also rendered it necessary to give only a minimum of quotations selected from the material available, and to make those given as brief as possible. It is to be observed that in their abridged form they simply illustrate the word, phrase, or construction, for which they are given, and do not necessarily express the sentiments of their authors, though in no case have they been intentionally curtailed in such a way as to misrepresent their original meaning. This, however, may always be ascertained, and the full context recovered, by help of the *exact reference* to author, work, and passage, which it is a special feature of this work to give. Here also the utmost conciseness has been indispensable; the exact date renders the surnames only of authors in most cases sufficient; the titles of books are so abbreviated as to be recognizable by those who know them, or to be adequate for the purpose of reference to a library or bibliographical catalogue. This is all that is now attempted; but a list, hereafter to be given, of all the authors and works quoted, with the editions read, and the Readers who extracted them for the Dictionary will give the full title of each work and form of abbreviation used, as well as indicate the mode of reference to each. Meanwhile, it may be stated that, in order to make the latter as simple as possible, an approximately uniform value has been given to different forms of numerals. Thus, in all works, Roman Capitals (IV.) stand for *volume*; small capitals (IV.) for *book*, *part*, or other larger division; lower-case letters (iv.) for *chapter* or its equivalent; and Arabic numerals (42) for *page*. Other divisions, as *marginal section*—the most useful of references, since it is not dependent on the paging of a particular edition—are indicated by special marks. In the Essayists of the 18th c. (*Spectator*, &c.), of which the editions are innumerable, the reference ¶ is to the paragraphs of each essay or number, counted for this purpose. In *Poetry*, the reference IV. iv. 42 means *act*, *scene*, *line*; or *canto*, *stanza*, *line*, (rarely *book*, *canto*, *stanza*,) as the work may be divided. In *Shakspere* (where the reading is that of the First Folio, 1623) the lines of the Globe edition are referred to. In dramatic works, or other long poems, of which the lines are not numbered, the Arabic numerals mean the *page* of the edition quoted. Single poems are, whenever possible, cited by *name* and *line*; in Chaucer's *Canterbury Tales*, every edition of which has its own order and numbering, the only useful mode of reference was to number the lines of each piece, tale, or prologue, separately. As neither MSS. nor editions agree as to the junction of the *Canon's Yeoman's Prologue* and *Tale*, the two have been reckoned as one piece. *Melibœus* and the *Parson's Tale* are referred to by the versicles as divided in the Six-text edition, but numbered separately. In many works, both prose and verse, the only available reference has been to the *volume* and *page* of a *specified edition*, which is thus indicated, 'Wks. 1802, III. 178'.

Wherever practicable, a work is dated and quoted from its first edition: if the reference is to a later edition (as has been often unavoidable), the date of this is added (within parentheses) to the reference.[1] It is necessary to be precise on this point; for later editions often change the spelling: hence a quotation from them is valid for the use of the word, but not for its spelling, at the date assigned. It is hoped that reasonable accuracy has been attained in dates and references: in the former, absolute accuracy is in many cases impossible, and, for the purposes of this work, not essential; in the latter, errors are inevitable in the work of so many years and so many readers.

SUBORDINATE WORDS

Under this head are here included:—1) (and mainly) *Obsolete* and *variant forms* of words, when these are so far removed in spelling as not to come closely before or after the regular form, or readily to suggest it. These words are concisely referred to the Main Form to which they belong, with an explanatory synonym, when the latter is itself obsolete; as **Almucantar**, **-urie**, obs. ff. (i.e. obsolete forms of) ALMACANTUR; **Abugge**, obs. w. and s.w. f. (= obsolete western and south-western

[1] In the case of some well-known and often-quoted works, where the reference is always to a standard edition or modern literal reprint, it has not been thought necessary to insert the date of it. This omission occurs in the case of nearly all the publications printed by the Early English Text and other similar Societies, the reprints of Mr. Arber, and the following among other works:—*Ancren Riwle* (ed. 1853), Bellenden, *Livy* (ed. 1821), Ld. Berners, *Froissart* (ed. 1812), Burke, *Works* (ed. 1808), Fabyan, *Chronicle* (ed. 1811), Gower, *Confessio Amantis* (ed. 1857), Hall, *Chronicle* (ed. 1809), Holinshed, *Chronicle* (ed. 1587), Holland, *Pliny* (ed. 1634), Johnson, *Works* (ed. 1787), Luttrell, *Brief Relation* (ed. 1857), Maundevile, *Travels* (ed. 1839), Sir T. More, *Works* (ed. 1557), Palsgrave, *Eclaircissement de la Langue Française* (ed. 1852), Pecock, *Repressor* (ed. 1860), Raleigh, *History of the World* (ed. 1736), Robert of Brunne, *Chronicle* (ed. 1825), Robert of Gloucester, *Chronicle* (ed. 1824), Shaftesbury, *Characteristics* (ed. 1737), Shoreham, *Poems* (ed. 1849), Adam Smith, *Wealth of Nations* (ed. 1869), Southey, *Works* (ed. 1853), Stanley, *History of Philosophy* (ed. 1701), Stewart, *Chronicle of Scotland* (ed. 1856), Topsell, *History of Four-footed Beasts* (ed. 1673), *History of Serpents* (ed. 1653), Trevisa, *Higden's Polychronicon* (Rolls Series).

form of) ABYE *v.*; **Almoise, -moyse,** var. (= variant of) ALMOSE, *Obs.* alms. To economize space variant forms which differ from the regular form only in the doubling of a single consonant or the converse, as *Appert* for APERT, *Aple* for APPLE, or in the interchange of *u*, *v* or *i*, *j*, are not usually inserted. 2) *Irregular* or *Peculiar inflexions* of Main Words. 3) *Alleged words* of bad or doubtful formation, or doubtful existence, and spurious or erroneous forms found in Dictionaries, or cited from single passages in authors, but having little or no claim to recognition as genuine constituents of the English vocabulary: their character is pointed out, and their history briefly given.

COMBINATIONS

Under this term are included all collocations of simple words in which the separate spelling of each word is retained, whether they are formally connected by the hyphen, or virtually by the unity of their signification. The formal union and the actual by no means coincide; not only is the use of the hyphen a matter of indifference in an immense number of cases, but in many where it is habitually used, the combination implies no unity of signification; while others, in which there is a distinct unity or specialization of meaning, are not hyphened. The primary use of the hyphen is *grammatical*: it implies either that the syntactic relation between two words is closer than if they stood side by side without it, or that the relation is a *less usual* one than that which would at first sight suggest itself to us, if we saw the two words standing unconnected. Thus, in the three sentences, '*After consideration* had been given to the proposal, it was duly accepted,' '*After consideration* the proposal was accepted,' '*After-consideration* had shown him his mistake,' we have *first* no immediate syntactic relation between *after* (conjunctive adverb) and *consideration*; *secondly*, the relation of preposition and object; *thirdly*, the relation of attribute and substantive, closer than the first, less usual than the second (since *after* is more commonly a preposition than an adjective). But *after-consideration* is not really a single word, any more than *subsequent consideration*, *fuller consideration*; the hyphen being merely a convenient help to the sense, which would be clearly expressed in speech by the different phrase-accentuation of *a·fter considera··tion* and *a··fter considera·-tion*. And as this 'help to the sense' is not always equally necessary, nor its need equally appreciated in the same place, it is impossible that its use should be uniform. Nevertheless *after-consideration*, as used above, is on the way to become a single word, which *reconsideration* (chiefly because *re-* is not a separate word, but also because we have *reconsider*) is reckoned to be; and indeed *close grammatical relation* constantly accompanies close union of sense, so that in many combinations the hyphen becomes an expression of this unification of sense. When this unification and specialization has proceeded so far that we no longer analyze the combination into its elements, but take it in as a whole, as in *blackberry*, *postman*, *newspaper*, pronouncing it in speech with a single accent, the hyphen is usually omitted, and the fully developed compound is written as a single word. But as this also is a question of degree, there are necessarily many compounds as to which usage has not yet determined whether they are to be written with the hyphen or as single words. Many specialized combinations, indeed, are often not even hyphened: especially is this the case with *descriptive names*, formed of a substantive preceded by an adjective or possessive case, or followed by a phrase, as *Aaron's Rod*, *All fours*, *Blue John*, *Jack by the hedge*, *Jack in a box*, *Jew's harp*, *Sea Anemone*, *Sea Horse*.

There is thus considerable difficulty in determining to what extent combinations are matters for the lexicographer, and to what extent they are merely grammatical. While no attempt is made fully to solve this difficulty, combinations formal and virtual are, for practical purposes, divided into three classes: *First*, those in which each word retains its full meaning, the relation between them falling under one or other of the ordinary grammatical categories. Of these, specimens merely are given, at the end of each Article, which are printed in *italics*, and illustrated collectively by a few quotations. *Second*: Combinations of which the signification is somewhat specialized, but still capable of being briefly explained in a few words, in connexion with their cognates. These also are concisely treated at the end of the Main Article, where they are printed in **small Clarendon** type in an alphabetical series, and illustrated by quotations arranged in the same order. When these are very numerous the word illustrated is distinguished in the quotation by prefixing *, in order that it may catch the eye more readily. *Third*: Combinations which attain in specialization of sense to the position of full compounds or which are used in various senses, or have a long history, and thus require to be dealt with more at large. These are enumerated (in SMALL CAPITALS) at the end of the Main Article, and thence referred to their alphabetical place, where they are treated in all respects as Main Words.

All Compounds and Combinations of interest or importance will thus be found either in their alphabetical order, or under the word which constitutes their first element. But phrases are treated under their leading word, as *on account of*, under ACCOUNT; and specific names, like *Sea Anemone*, *Black Alder*, under their generic names ANEMONE, ALDER, etc. *Sea Anemone* is considered (linguistically) as a kind of *Anemone*, but *Adam's Needle* not as a kind of *Needle*, nor *Mouse-ear* as a kind of *Ear*.

Pronunciation

The pronunciation is the actual living form or forms of a word, that is, *the word itself*, of which the current spelling is only a symbolization—generally, indeed, only the traditionally-preserved symbolization of an earlier form, sometimes imperfect to begin with, still oftener corrupted in its passage to our time. This living form is the *latest fact* in the form-history of the word, the starting-point of all investigations into its previous history, the only fact in its form-history to which the lexicographer can personally witness. For all his statements as to its previous history are only reproductions of the evidence of former witnesses, or deductions drawn from earlier modes of symbolizing the forms of the word then current, checked and regulated by the ascertained laws and principles of phonology. To register the current pronunciation is therefore essential, in a dictionary which deals with the language on historical principles. It would be manifestly absurd, for example, to trace the form-history of the first numeral from the Old Teutonic *ain*, through the Old English *án*, to the Middle English *oan*, *on*, *oon*, *one*, and to stop short at the last of these, without recognizing the modern English wvn, which represents a greater change within the last three and a half centuries than had previously taken place in 1500 years. The fact that the *written* history, as embodied in the spelling, accidentally stops short at the Middle English *one*, makes it all the more necessary to give the modern history and current form of the living word, since of these no hint is otherwise conveyed.

But the living word is *sound* cognizable by the ear, and must therefore be itself symbolized in order to reach the understanding through the eye. The most that can be done is to provide a careful and consistent means of representing it, in which the symbols should agree with the actual values of letters used either in the earlier or later stages of the language. For historical purposes the earlier values of letters are the more convenient; and accordingly, the symbols here adopted are the Roman letters, in most cases retaining the values which they had when first employed to write English; to these are added such modifications and amplifications as are required by the phonetic changes and discriminations which distinguish a modern from an ancient language. The reference of the symbols to a permanent standard, such as the *Visible Speech* of Mr. A. Melville Bell, will be made elsewhere: in the following table they are merely illustrated by words which exemplify the sounds.

As a general principle, each simple sound is represented by a single symbol. In choosing additional symbols, regard has been had to former usage or analogy; thus 'æ' was the Old English symbol for *a* in *at*, 'ǫ' the Icelandic for *o* in n*o*t; ə (reversed e) is used for a sound most commonly written *e*, as in *e*rr, ev*e*r; ɒ (reversed *a*) for a sound expressed by *a* in Sanskrit and Oriental languages, as in *Chandarnagar* or *Chundernugger*. In the consonants, ɹ (reversed r) is used for the vocalized retracted *r* in he*r*; 'þ' and 'ð' are taken from Old English, with their powers discriminated; ʃ (*sh*), ʒ (*zh*), and ŋ (*ng*) from the Phonotypy of Messrs. Pitman and Ellis.

In the *Vowels*, *ordinary* (or *short*) quantity is unmarked; *long* quantity is marked by (¯); *medial* quantity, when distinguished, by (ˋ); obscure quality by (ˇ). In modern English speech, vowels are regularly obscured in syllables that have neither primary nor subordinate stress, especially in those that follow the main stress; they then approach, or fall into, the sound of the mid-mixed vowel or ə. But, in syllabic or rhetorical pronunciation, or in singing, the original vowels are more or less heard; by writing these with the mark of obscuration, we are enabled to indicate at once the theoretical and the actual pronunciation. The vowel in p*a*ss, comm*a*nd, variously identified by different speakers with *a* in m*a*n, and *a* in f*a*ther, is symbolized by the avowedly ambiguous a. Similarly, the doubtful length of the *o* in *o*ff, s*o*ft, l*o*st (by some made *short* as in g*o*t, by some *long* as in C*o*rfe, by others *medial*), is indicated by ǫ̀. In cases where sounds are identified by some English speakers, and distinguished by others, it has been thought best to mark the distinction, which may be disregarded by those to whom it is unknown; thus, the sounds in f*i*r and f*u*r are discriminated by the majority of orthoepists, though commonly identified by natives of the south of England, to whom our fə̄ɹ and fɒ̄ɹ will thus indicate the same sound. So ǫ and *ǫ*, in w*a*tch, Sc*o*tch, are identified by many.

The generally recognized *Diphthongs* in *by*, *boy*, *bow*, *few*, *pure*, are expressed by əi, oi, ɑu, i*ū*, iū; and the diphthong in *ay* (yes) by ai (when distinguished from that in *eye*, əi). After *r*, the simple *u*, u, take the place of i*ū*, iū; which is also the usage of many speakers after *l*, as in l*ieu*, l*u*nar, l*u*re, where others make, or try to make, a diphthong. This doubtful diphthong we write ^{i}*ū*, ^{i}ū, as l^{i}*ū*, l^{i}ū^{ə}ɹ. The half-sized ^{i}, ^{u}, are also used to express the second element in the imperfect or doubtful diphthongs in f*a*te, n*o*te (fē^{i}t, nō^{u}t), which many orthoepists treat only as long *ē*, *ō*; the half-sized ^{ə} is similarly used to express the non recognized vowel-element developed between ī, ē, o, ū, and ɹ or r, as in p*ier*, p*are*, p*ore*, p*oor*, we*ary* (pī^{ə}ɹ, wī^{ə}·ri).

Syllables are not divided; but, when two vowels come together and do not make a diphthong, they are separated by the break (ˌ), which in this case divides two syllables. The break is not written between the two vowels in groups such as *-ial*, *-ian*, in *pictor-ial*, *Fen-ian*, which are pronounced either in two syllables, or (familiarly) in one. It is written between t and ʃ, d and ʒ, in compounds like *knightship* (nəitˌʃip), where the two consonants do not form a consonantal diphthong, as tʃ and dʒ ordinarily do, as in *pitcher*, *lodging* (pi·tʃəɹ, lǫ·dʒiŋ). Also in words like *antacid*, *antambulacral* (æːntˌæ·sid, æːntˌæmbiulēⁱ·krăl) where the first syllable is *ant-*, not *an-*. And it is used in combinations and long words with two accents, to separate the two accentual groups into which the word naturally falls, as in *plano-convex*, *agamogenesis* (plēⁱːnoˌkǫ·nveks, æːgămoˌdʒe·nĭsis).

The main *Stress* or *Syllabic Accent* is indicated by a 'turned period' (·) after the vowel, whether long or short (not after the consonant at the end of the syllable); subordinate stress is marked (ː), only where it attains to the strength of secondary accent, in long words and compounds, as *cry:stalliza·tion*, *a·fter-wi:tted*; the ordinary subordinate stress, as in the first syllable of *telesco·pic*, *antece·dent*, which is not more than tertiary, is not marked, being sufficiently indicated by the clearness of the vowel (telĭskǫ·pik, æntĭsī·dĕnt). In loose combinations, of which both elements have a main accent, the stronger stress is occasionally indicated by (··) as in *a··fter-cou·nsel*.

6

GEORGE BERNARD SHAW

(1856–1950)

Shaw, born in Dublin, came to London as a young man and commenced a career as a speaker and writer on music, drama, and Fabian socialism; later he began to write the plays which made him famous. This letter, written after he had met the phoneticians Henry Sweet and Alexander Ellis, is a reply to 'Spelling Reform and Phonetic Spelling' (*Morning Leader*, 10 August 1901) by William Archer, the man with whom Shaw had collaborated on his first play ten years earlier. Shaw's interest in phonetics never dwindled, and in his will he left money for the creation of a new alphabet.

'A Plea for Speech Nationalisation'

(*Morning Leader*, 16 August 1901)

TO THE EDITOR OF 'THE MORNING LEADER'

SIR,—I have not read Professor Brander Matthews's article on this subject; and I am for the moment out of reach of a bookstall; but the 'Study and Stage' essay of my friend Mr. William Archer on the subject provokes me to add a couple of thousand words or so.

Mr. Archer throws over the Columbian snob to whose belated ignorance spelling reform is 'hopelessly, unspeakably, sickeningly vulgar.' And he throws the established orthography after him. But he insists on the need for a conventional spelling, and declares that it must not be a phonetic spelling. Yet I may take it, I think, that he does not want a Chinese ideography, or a hieroglyphic system. What, then, does he want? At one point in his article he suggests a spelling of the language as it would sound if it were declaimed poetically, and with the obscure vowels pronounced like the letters that are used haphazard to represent them in our conventional orthography. Thus the obscure vowel in absurd would be pronounced like a in cab, that in enough or peculiar like e in be. But this would be a phonetic spelling just as much as Mr. Sweet's Romic, though it would represent, not the sounds that we utter, but the sounds that Mr. Archer thinks he hears in his mind's ear when he reads poetry, or, to use his own phrase, 'the ideal sonorities of the language.'

Further on, Mr. Archer says that what he wants to reform is not conventional spelling, but a number of needless and absurd anomalies of convention. By this I understand him to mean that it is a needless and absurd anomaly to spell telegram telegram and programme programme. So it is; but how would Mr. Archer propose to reform the anomaly? Apparently, not by spelling programme program, because that would be choosing the phonetic principle, which he denounces as 'noxious.' He would therefore spell telegram telegramme, and so remove the anomaly without phonetic noxiousness. He would spell off 'ough' and trite 'tright,' Lumley 'Lolmondeley,' and Holborn 'Hockburn.' Or rather he would do nothing of the sort, but would write another 'Study and Stage' article, confessing that Voltaire's are not the only principles that 'lead to disintegration and chaos when pushed to their logical conclusion.' Besides, if so, why push them? I am quite ready to let Mr. Archer off if he will let off Voltaire.

The fact is, you must either let our spelling alone or else reform it phonetically. No sane person now proposes to reform it 'etymologically'; and once the etymological aberration is outlived, nothing remains to be spelt except sound. Our alphabet *is* a phonetic one as far as it goes; and our established spelling is phonetic spelling, partly out of date, and partly corrupted by an ignorant academic attempt to make it etymological. Discard the etymologic blunder, and you cannot predicate either rationality or anomaly for our spelling except in reference to phonetic propriety and consistency. Rule out phonetics, and 'programme' remains neither an irrational spelling nor an anomalous one: it is simply a French spelling; and the sole objection to it is that in English it is unphonetic; and leads the people who have never heard it pronounced to say programmy, and the people who have never seen it written to write program, and be humiliated and snubbed by the empty uppish, a class ably represented by the Columbian University bounder quoted by Professor Brander Matthews.

And, now, what harm does our spelling do to literature? Among other things, it so obscures the history of the language as to make even a literary expert like Mr. Archer commit himself in print to the undownliveable statement (if only he really meant it) that the English language has hardly drifted since Shakespear's time because it has been anchored to the rock of a conventional spelling. As a matter of fact, Shakespear's English is a dead language. No living man can speak it or write it. He can imitate it just as Milton and Landor imitated Latin poetry; and people with a literary turn can understand it without difficulty. Mr. Archer has, no doubt, become so accustomed to it that it no longer strikes him as archaic; but let him ask a policeman the way to Hanwell in the best Elizabethan he can muster, and that policeman will probably see that he arrives there. And we need not go back so far as Shakespear. No metropolitan Englishman can now write or speak eighteenth century English, though Irish and Scotch writers still use modified Augustan. Early nineteenth century English is equally obsolete to young men. No journalist under forty could write anything like one of the 'Sketches by Boz.'

All this Mr. Archer, of course, knows as well as I do. Then what does he mean by saying that the language has not changed? Probably nothing more than that most of the words in Shakespear's vocabulary are still in use, a statement which, applied to so short a period of time as nine or ten generations, is not worth making. Words last a long time; and the highest literary expression changes slowly from one great master to another; but vernacular locutions change very rapidly: for example, the 'whoreson knaves' of the sixteenth century become, in the paragraphs of modest police-court reporters, the —— ——s of the nineteenth. Our conventional spelling has not hindered any of these changes: they would have occurred at the same rate if the English language had been spelt all the time on the Weller principle, 'according to the taste and fancy of the speller.' All that the conventional spelling has done is to conceal the one change that a phonetic spelling might have checked: namely, the changes in pronunciation, including the waves of debasement that produced the half rural cockney of Sam Weller, and the modern metropolitan cockney of Drinkwater in 'Captain Brassbound's Conversion.' At all events, here alone was the establishment and maintenance of a standard humanly possible; for the influence of the printed word over pronunciation can hardly be exaggerated. The moment the masses learnt to read, they stopped saying 'werry' for 'very,' and 'inwalable' for 'invaluable.' Just so far as our spelling was phonetic, it helped and corrected them. But just so far as it was unphonetic, it misled them; and before Mr. Archer is an old man he will be ridiculed as a fogey unless he yields to the overwhelming currency of modern mispronunciations founded on the phonetic suggestions of our half phonetic spelling. If we, the literary men, will not spell as we pronounce, the world will end by pronouncing as we spell. For instance, we spelt obleege oblige, to show that we were French scholars; and now we are forced to say oblige. If Archer were spelt Arjoricher, the familiar name 'William Ought-jer' would be unknown in London. Beauchamp's Pills would never be deemed worth a guinea a box. We cannot prevent people from interpreting our spelling phonetically: there is no other way of interpreting it for people whose vocabulary is not literary, nor even always printable. What does Mr. Archer himself do when he comes upon the name of a Russian statesman in print? He pronounces it as the spelling suggests, just as his great-great grandfather pronounced the name of Handel. And, like his ancestor, he pronounces it wrongly. But as everybody else in England, except perhaps the diplomatic staff, does the same, his wrong pronunciation becomes the standard one; and an Englishman pronouncing the Russian name properly becomes as insufferable and unintelligible as if he were to talk about Hendel. In vain will Mr. Archer urge his readers to act like logical Scotchmen, and, recognising the fact that our spelling is not perfectly phonetic, refrain from drawing phonetic inferences from it. We cannot draw any other inferences from it: if we want to use the word and are not on speaking terms with anybody who knows how to pronounce it, we *must* pronounce it as it is spelt or misspelt, as the case may be. Refuse to teach the Board School legions your pronunciation, and they will force theirs on you by mere force of numbers. And serve you right!

And here I come to the real question which has extracted this long letter from me—the question of the nationalisation of the existing class monopoly of orthodox English speech. The only English schools now worth counting are the schools under the Education Department: the only important universities are the Polytechnics. From them we are turning out hosts of young men about ten times as full of primary and secondary instruction as Mr. Archer was when he graduated at Edinburgh, Mr. Walkley when he graduated at Oxford, or as I am to this day. They are a new race; and Mr. H. G. Wells is probably right in anticipating that they will finally become the dominant force in our social organisation. But they speak, not of the sun and moon, but of the san and mə-oon (I use the inverted e for that obscure vowel which offends Mr. Archer in 'absurd.') Tea and coffee they call tə-ee and corfee. Now san for sun does not matter; for though Gladstone would have scorned it, to-day it has become the received Oxford-West-end pronunciation. But the young man who says mə-oon and tə-ee, or in a political conference calls himself a delegite, or perhaps a dyollagite, will find these solecisms obstructing his way through life more than three or four sentences of imprisonment would obstruct a peer's. Yet, if matters are left as they are, he will undoubtedly triumph in the long run, and force the smart people to say 'mə-oon' and 'delegite,' as he has already forced them to say 'dahn tahn' for down town (which is rather pretty), and 'ow now' for 'oh no' (which is detestable). But he himself does not want to be let alone. He already takes the greatest pains to speak well by the fatal process of imitation, and succeeds mostly only in adding affectation to mispronunciation. Why will not Mr. Archer let him be taught in the only possible way, by instruction in the phonetic alphabet, and by having a standard pronunciation suggested to him on every printed page? Mr. Archer supposes that practical phonetics are impossibly complex and difficult. That is a novice's notion. The subtle differences of which Mr. Archer is thinking do not trouble experts at all: there may be six-and-thirty ways of saying 'get' (and 'every single one of them is right'), just as there may be six-and-thirty ways of saying 'git' (and every single one of them is wrong); but that does not in the slightest degree complicate the simple process of teaching a child to say get instead of git. I put it to friend William, does he seriously suppose that when a Frenchman goes to the Reader of Phonetics at Oxford to be taught to pronounce English, Mr. Sweet has any difficulty in teaching him? He does not even require a special type for his reading lessons: ordinary type can be made to suffice when the vowels are eked out by turning e and c upside down occasionally. In short, the supposed complication does not exist. Mr. Archer may dream of a script that would distinguish between the voice and speech of Miss Ellen Terry and the voice and speech of Mrs. Patrick Campbell; but nobody proposes to go into such subtleties in a board school classroom. What is proposed, and what is perfectly feasible, is a script which shall distinguish between the correctness of speech common to both these ladies, and the quaint slavey lingo of Miss Louie Frecar.

I am convinced that such instruction would be popular. Once, years ago, I was asked to go down to the docks and give a few young dock laborers a lecture on elocution to refine the oratory of the 'New Unionism' of that period. They probably expected me to spout Shakespear to them. Instead, I discoursed on *their* phonetic alphabet. They were sufficiently amused to tell me I ought to be 'a quick-change artist'; but they were also keenly interested, because they were quite aware that there was a difference for the worse between their pronunciation and, say, Mr. Archer's; but the nature of that difference—which they earnestly desired to remove—was a mystery to them.

I need not repeat familiar arguments about the waste of teachers' time, and the difficulties thrown in the way of English children learning to read their own language; or the fact that nobody without a *visual* memory for words ever succeeds in spelling conventionally, however highly educated he or she may be; or the barrier placed between England and France by both nations using their printing presses to conceal their language from one another; or the drifting away of colonial and American speech from English for want of a common standard; or the moral mischief of encouraging stupid habits and inventing bad excuses for persisting in them, and so on.

But I do beg Mr. Archer and my contemporaries generally either to let this subject alone or at least take the trouble to acquaint themselves with the latest lights on it. It is really shocking to see a paper like 'The Morning Leader' beginning the century as the vehicle of the University Conservatisms of the sixties. No doubt the subject is painfully associated in the minds of most middle-aged journalists with early unsuccessful attempts to master the thoroughly bad system of shorthand which was so ably pushed commercially by the late Sir Isaac Pitman, and with the Tonic Sol Fa notation, the Decimal system, the cabbage and rice stage of vegetarianism, and even with Robert Owen's New Moral World, all of which got quaintly mixed up with Spelling Reform in the last century. But now that a Readership of Phonetics has been established at Oxford, and the subject has been worked at throughout Europe by scholars of a very different stamp to Sir Isaac, all that is *vieux jeu*.[1] Spelling Reform may not matter to Mr. Archer, who speaks correctly without knowing anything about phonetics, just as Mr. Walkley wrote grammatically long before I taught him to distinguish prepositions from adverbs; but to the enormous majority of their fellow-townsmen, persistence in our spelling means that worst of handicaps in life, the Board School alphabet of I, Bə-ee, Sə-ee, Də-ee, Ǝee, Af, Jə-ee, Hyche, Aw, Ji, Ki, Yoll, Am, An, Ow, Pə-ee, Kə-oo, Awr, Ass, Tə-ee, Yə-oo, Və-ee, Dabblyəoo, Ax, Waw, Zad.

G. BERNARD SHAW

[1] [*vieux jeu* an old game, i.e. something outmoded.]

7

ROBERT BRIDGES

(1844–1930)

Bridges—poet, critic, and playwright—became Poet Laureate in 1913, and in the same year helped found the Society for Pure English along with other literary men and linguistic scholars. The First World War delayed its work, and the first tract appeared in 1919. Bridges accepted the scientific view of language but gave it a literary and educational bias.

'The Society's Work'

(Society for Pure English, Tract XXI, 1925)

This twenty-first Tract begins a new Series. No. XX will be an Index-number to the preceding Tracts and will appear in due course. We had not foreseen the call for an Index, but in future we shall respect its conveniences by continuous pagination: in other matters also we may profit by experience and hope to meet the wishes and needs of our readers better from the practical knowledge which their continued support has brought us.

The present Tract will be devoted to what we think the most urgent needs of the Society, *viz.*

1 A full and definite statement of our motives and aims.
2 An explanation of the means by which we hope to attain success, and
3 Practical suggestions concerning the sort of work which our widely scattered members can do to aid the movement.

In all these matters we think that we have learned a good deal, and the independent approval of our policy by the representatives of the various branches of literature, philologists, grammarians, authors, and journalists, has encouraged our confidence.

We are disseminating this Tract outside our membership, in order to solicit the notice of those to whose co-operation we look for assistance. We beg them to take this considered advertisement as a direct appeal to join us individually and contribute useful matter to our Journal.

The primary distinction of our Society is that, as its title implies, it is purely *linguistic*, not *literary* in the usual sense of that word. Though language invades every corner of literature, encountering with style and diction as well as with idiom, grammar, definition, and logical construction, we have no immediate concern with the moral, philosophical, or personal interests which occupy most of the attention of students in schools of literature. It may be useful to explain and repeat here that the word *pure* in our title does not mean *Teutonic*, as William Barnes would have intended it: it was deliberately adopted as an assertive protest against that misappropriation of the term which would condemn our historic practice.

Motives and aims

Two primary considerations called our Society into being.

1 The English language is spreading all over the world. This is a condition over which we have no control. It is a substantial imperious fact that entails a vast responsibility and imposes on our humanity the duty to do what we can to make our current speech as good a means as possible for the intercommunication of ideas.

That we did not of our own will or intention put ourselves in this predicament cannot excuse our neglect; nor in the exposure and trial that our language has to face can we honestly sustain our native pride in it, if, shutting our eyes to its defects, we refuse to accommodate it to the obvious needs of perspicuity and logical precision which are the essential virtues of any cultured speech.

In certain respects the English language is in its present condition inferior to some of its rivals as a convenient carrier of thought; and it would be a disgrace to us if we made no effort to bring it up to the mark. The qualities which have given it advantage in competition are due to its having been during its evolution subjected to sudden violent changes of environment, irruptions or interruptions so disconnected that they must rank scientifically as external accidents. While it took much wealth from these unconformable trials, it carries many scars, and it is natural that some of its imperfections should be so closely correlated with its history as to be irremediable. But not a few of its defects —whether due to the rudeness or embarrassment of our native instinct, or to the chance that the overruling dialect was not the one that in certain particulars had attained the best solution—are still corrigible, and indeed some have their cure ready to hand in existing dialects. Again, there are those abundant absurdities common to all receptive languages that can be corrected more efficiently by intelligent criticism than by unguided practice; since in practice they are never discarded until their existence has become intolerable.

This general statement will suffice here; but the scientific attention which we owe to the details cannot but awaken an intelligent appreciation of the whole problem and educate us to a more delicate sense for the elementary proprieties against which our present practice offends. Here is a wide subject for analysis and construction.

2 The second consideration is this: we are inheritors of what may claim to be the finest living literature in the world. Now the history of languages shows that there is danger lest our speech should grow out of touch with that literature, and losing, as it were, its capital, and living from hand to mouth, fall from its nobility and gradually dissociate itself from apparent continuity with its great legacy, so that to an average Briton our Elizabethan literature would come to be as much an obsolete language as Middle English is to us now, or as Homer or Æschylus to a modern Greek. This danger is much increased by the widespread and haphazard distribution of English speakers all over the world exposed to all manner of unrelated environments. It would seem that no other language can ever have had its central force so dissipated—and even this does not exhaust the description of our special peril, because there is furthermore this most obnoxious condition, namely, that wherever our countrymen are settled abroad there are alongside of them communities of other-speaking races, who, maintaining among themselves their native speech, learn yet enough of ours to mutilate it, and establishing among themselves all kinds of blundering corruptions, through habitual intercourse infect therewith the neighbouring English. We can see this menace without any guess as to what may come of it, and in the United States, where it is most evident, it is natural that despair should encourage a blind optimism, expressed—as I redd[1] it in the *New York Times*—in some such jaunty phrase as this, that *the old Lady may be trusted to take care of herself*. But, whatever sort of speech might naturally arise, it is extremely unlikely that the unknown accidental linguistic profits would outbalance the calculable loss.

Both the above motives were set forth in our first tracts. We have given examples of indisputable defects, and of apparent lines of decay,

[1] I venture this spelling, long advocated by Henry Bradley and others, for the perfect of *read* and *spread*, like the use of *lead led*, *breed bred*, *speed sped*, &c., the added *d* being the common sign of the perfect tense.

and we have explained our principles, conservative and democratic, whereby we hold that concerted action would be effective for good. But is reform feasible?

Is reform feasible?

The two motives given above are sufficiently strong to impel us to promote conscious reform, but we have to give a reasonable answer to those who assert that the undertaking to bridle living speech and guide it in any particular direction is a Quixotic project. Those who think thus urge that language is made and developed in the mouths of those who speak it, not at all by committees of learned academies. It is a living force which proceeds on its way quite out of reach of conscious control: and if this refractoriness to central control is a property of all languages, it must be greatly intensified in English owing to the dispersion of the speakers.

This objection is inherited from a generation who rightfully held it as sound impeccable truth. It was of course well known to us, and a hundred years ago we might have thought it insuperable: but in the last century conditions have so changed that it is no longer true, for we are now in possession of full means for doing this thing which was previously impossible.

Our Society was inaugurated not in ignorance of this difficulty, but because we realized that we are possessed of means to overcome it. It is well that all those engaged in the work should be strengthened in their confidence by a full comprehension of the situation, which, as we see it, is as follows.

SCIENCE

First of all is the present condition of the science of language. A hundred years ago Philology was in its cradle, but now, though first origins of speech may still be in dispute, the knowledge of the resultant languages if not complete is so proficient, the phonetic laws that govern them are so scientifically understood, that there is no fear of educated linguists fighting blindly against nature, or seeking to impose scholastic pedantries by authority. On the other hand they are so well acquainted with the overruling forces and tendencies that they are in a position to make use of these powerful influences to empower their action. This is only a part of the general conviction that we may see growing up in all departments of science, especially in biology, namely, that man's mind is coming to emancipate itself from the material trend of blind natural evolution, and acquiring power to determine his future course consciously towards his spiritual perfection: nor will it be denied that on the unfathomed and trackless Ocean of Life mankind is making a little progress in the art of navigation.

In our particular department there is a homely detail of great practical value, that is, the possession of the *Oxford Dictionary*: for that compendium of historic learning puts at every student's disposal the facts that must govern our procedure.

JOURNALISM

Secondly: The fact that language develops in the common talk of the people is as true as ever, but it is a truth that is nowadays much qualified by the fact that every one now reads; indeed most people read more than they speak, and this, especially in the growth of journalism, has created a new factor; for our speech is now actually more subjected to our eyes than to our ears. Well-wishers, who were yet sceptical as to the sanity of our project, would often say 'But what will you do with the newspapers?' thinking that they had propounded the insurmountable obstacle. Our reply was 'What could we do *without* the newspapers?' We look to the newspapers with confidence as our most strenuous and effective helpmates. There is no line to be drawn between authors and journalists—many of our best authors began as journalists,—and there are very few of our best writers who do not write in the newspapers. With scanty exceptions our journalists are nowadays educated men, who aim at excellence, and if their particular conditions do not allow them time to consider carefully all that they write, and their habit of hasty performance and the necessity for writing often against inclination must encourage carelessness, they are none the less anxious to do well. It is natural, therefore, that we should receive from them, as we have received, both thanks and support. One of the chief difficulties that all who write our language must feel is the perpetual uncertainty as to what is better or worse, correct or incorrect, right or wrong in idiom and grammar. Now all these questions are questions of particular detail; the examples of how we propose to treat such things may be seen in the Tracts, and the resolution of them will be more useful to those who write hastily than to those who have leisure to consider.

Looking then actually to the journalists to make our first fighting rank, we hope in every Editor soon to find a captain. For instance—in all printing houses it is needful to fix rules for the compositors. This is done to ensure uniformity in doubtful usages and to prevent loss of time in deciding the many minor questions of spelling and grammar with which the loose practice of writers worries a conscientious printer. For mere economy of routine, therefore, most printing houses have set rules, in the devising whereof there may be much searching of heart; as was found in the Oxford University Press, when the late Mr. Hart took the best counsel's opinion in drawing up his regulations, which for all his care have since his time been in part superseded. Editors, as reasonable human beings, welcome any trustworthy guidance and, so long as their practice is grateful to the public, they would be very glad to amend and extend their rules in the right direction. In one or two instances, these suggestions proposed in our Tracts have already been received and have replaced older usage. Progress on this line is very strictly limited by public opinion because readers are offended by the slightest change in what they consider to be established orthography. A man who has spent all his morning in studying the politics of the world—National Finance, German Reparations, Unemployment, Bolshevist Propaganda, International Disarmament, The Yellow Peril, The Kenya Problem, Weir Houses, Singapore Base, Indian Disaffection, Cairo Murders,—will rise up with no fact so deeply bitten into his soul as that he has encountered a split infinitive or seen the word *judgment*, spelt without its first *e*; and no editor, however strongly he may be convinced of the reasonableness of some particular change, will venture to adopt it in the face of this punctilious irritability of his customers' prejudices. No swift advance therefore can be looked for here until the confidence of the public is won, and they become a party in the adventure. Hence to the journalists, as distinct from the Editors, we must first look for practical assistance, to habituate their readers with more liberal ideas, and win their bias in favour of good sense.

The spelling of English is such a vexed question, and its present condition is held by so many to be the incommodity which cries loudest for reform, that in proclaiming the aims of our Society we thought it necessary to state that it was not our main object, and that we should deal with it only incidentally and in minor detail. It will be well to formulate here our opinion on this subject.

We consider the present Victorian spelling to be defensible only upon the grounds that established its convention, namely, it is more convenient for printers and for readers that the same word should always be spelt in the same way than that any particular words should be spelt reasonably or correctly. It was the printers who determined what that spelling should be; they promoted general convenience, but there was nothing scientific in their product, except this,—that they took the dictionaries for guides, and those word-books were compiled by men who had more or less expert knowledge. The result, however, is an uncompromising tyranny; those who reverence it have to learn that it has no divine right, and if they obstinately uphold its usurpation they are playing into the hands of the revolutionists, who would cast it off altogether and substitute the worse tyranny of a questionable phonetic system.[1]

Our position here is that we recognize the value of our traditional literary spelling, but we do wish to have it conveniently reformed and simplified on scientific principles: we believe that all that is desirable can be done by gradual change and that it is actually the wish of practical authors and journalists to adopt better spellings of words that needlessly offend. We have no doubt that if such unexceptionable minor changes were introduced by those whose example and taste are respected, the public would then quickly appreciate and adopt the new spellings, and thereby coming to take a more sensible view of the situation would assist instead of obstructing further reasonable reforms. The convenience of readers is the commanding condition of reform, and that will be best met if the gradual changes, which we advise, were simultaneously adopted in the printing houses: a few first simple ventures would clear the way for scientific procedure.

The prejudice, however, in favour of what a man's eyes are accustomed to, and the vulgar assumption that whatever is new or strange is wrong or foolish, have to be eased in every possible way. The reproduction of old books with their contemporary spelling serves this purpose, and the dated records of all the obsolete spellings of common words in the *Oxford Dictionary* may be studied with advantage, for they show that almost every old word has at different times been spelt in every conceivable way: while this demonstrates the convenience of a fixed form, it certainly should overcome the purely conservative objection to the adoption of more convenient and correct forms than those which happen to be in fashion at present.

It should also be realized that, since the only cause for the existing prejudice is the habit of the eye, any widely adopted change which had reason and analogy on its side would very quickly win over the prejudice to its own favour. For instance, if by a miracle the word *have* should suddenly appear in all journals and books as *hav* without its final *e*, then in ten days no one would believe that he had been accustomed to

[1] The crying need for phonetics in elementary education is another matter.

see it spelt differently, and if the old *have* should venture to raise its head again it would be resented by him and redd as we pronounce *slave*, *shave*, *crave*, *knave*, *save*, *wave*, *deprave*, &c. We think it not too much to hope that we may influence public opinion to tolerate and approve of such reasonable reforms.

COMPULSORY EDUCATION

Thirdly, there is compulsory State Education. Though it is impossible that every child should be schooled well and rightly, yet that all children are schooled provides a machinery which can be and is used to counteract what was assumed to be the uncontrolable natural trend and growth of language; in fact this national schooling cannot exist without affecting speech very strongly: and that is the whole point of it here. The results are not always such as we should wish, yet there is a balance of advantage. There is no more baffling problem than that of education. There are not enough good teachers, and never can be: then the teachers need to be taught, and who is to instruct their teachers? Now popular opinion is sound in dreading above all things the tyranny of professional authority, and being unable to estimate the wisdom of any imposed legislation would rebel against a heaven-sent Board. So we come down to the vicious circle which is the bedrock fact of the situation, namely, that nothing much can be done to guide public practice until public opinion is enlightened enough to appreciate it: and for that reason we instituted a democratic procedure. Scrupulous attention to the quality of the elementary text-books provided by commercial competition appears to be the first practical step, and we invite correspondence and criticism on this subject.

TELEPHONE AND BROADCASTING

Fourthly, the common use of the telephone, and with much greater effect the later invention of broadcasting speech by wireless, have revolutionized the whole problem. We cannot yet tell exactly how broadcasting will affect speech, but some results seem inevitable. It must, we think, encourage a stricter standardization than otherwise would have been possible or might have seemed desirable; also a clearer and more distinct articulation of syllables than is generally practised: and this points to its making a differentiation of dialects on the scientific basis of their acoustical merits, which implies the utilitarian recognition of an *æsthetic* standard which has hitherto been scouted as a vain fancy of educated taste. The slipshod pronunciations fashionable in Southern

English, against which we have sometimes protested, will have their actual defects exposed: indeed we hear that this has already been recognized.

FASHION

Fifthly and lastly: the force of example and fashion which, as well as the force of education, used to be denied or at least grossly underestimated by the phonetic scientists, will be much increased by the unlimited extension of the speaker's audience. Those who on theoretic axioms denied that the future development of our speech could be affected by teaching were the first to complain that the ubiquitous schoolmaster was indiscriminately annihilating the local dialects. The fact is that example and fashion are the most powerful agents; and the recognition of their power should lead to the better exercise of it.

These then are the new conditions, and taken together it cannot be denied that they offer a machinery that has never existed before for the control of the evolution of speech. They are in any case the means on which we rely. It would be a disgrace to us to make no use of them: the methods which we propose are our attempt to make a good use of them.

How the Society should work

Our first and most essential tenet was to have a popular not an academic constitution; to proceed, that is, by inquiry and discussion rather than by authority. No success can be looked for without the goodwill of the public, whose goodwill can only be won by reasonable persuasion. Principles must be demonstrated to common sense and their application logically displayed. It happens that at the present time both literary and scientific opinion are well disposed; they are strong allies: we do not undervalue them, but on the other hand there is a considerable section of the public which would be alienated by any assumption of superior guidance in these matters and will even react against it. Since literary tradition is of its nature pedantic there is much good sense in this obstinate revolt; it may even be held that average literary practice is as liable to censure as common talk is, and since the talk is always living while the literary phraseology is often dead, when these two come to fight it out between them, the vulgar talk must win: as has been seen again and again when eminent writers, men too of enlightened mind and liberal principles, have fulminated against the use of popular terms that were new in their time; since those very terms which they denounced as intolerable vulgarities have won general acceptance, and are now spoken and written without suspicion of reproach.

We offered then from the first an open court where new and doubtful matters might be argued, promising to guarantee as far as possible the scientific facts and weigh pros and cons in any disputed question, being convinced that the better diffusion of right knowledge would dispel prejudice and assure favour for the best solutions. The Tracts hitherto published dealing with a good many points of various importance will show how far we have fulfilled our intention. The effect has been a wider welcome from all classes than our modest output really deserved; and this good reception, even where disfavour might have been predicted, was no doubt due to a feeling of want on the part of the public, as well as to the temper of our performance. We certainly owed much to the confidence that was rightly felt in the late Dr. Henry Bradley's learning and good sense. We can no longer, alas, rely on that; our small company has been lamentably depleted also by other serious losses, but we shall not lack for competent coadjutors.

We have always recognized that the sound and solid influence that we hope to establish can grow up but slowly, and we are sorry to think how we must have disappointed the more enthusiastic of our members by the first scrappy foundations that we have been able to lay: but we are very grateful to them for their enthusiasm; the mere gathering together of those who understand and are ready to fight is the indispensable preliminary to concerted action. In one respect our friends have not yet come up to our expectations, for if our Tracts are, as we wished, to be an Open Court for the intercommunication of outlying members *it is necessary that they should contribute their quota of correspondence*. Their own interest in the Tracts would be increased if their special problems were discussed in them; the variety of subjects would enrich the funds of our knowledge and extend its survey. We will later make some suggestions for their better collaboration.

The sort of work that scientific methods may look to accomplish was seen last year, when a single observation suddenly changed the whole aspect of what may be called the Anglo-American controversy: that problem promises to be no longer controversial.

When I was a boy there was a foolish prejudice in England against 'Americanisms' in diction or spelling. The universal attitude of Englishmen of all classes towards American practice was indeed not only foolish but ill-mannered and offensively contemptuous. It naturally enough provoked a similar retaliant feeling in America towards our English habits; whereupon twenty years ago, when we had learned on our side to behave somewhat more reasonably, the true American patriot was reviling our ways of speech as heartily as ever we had ridiculed theirs. They asserted the linguistic superiority of the American habit; and though scientific knowledge has gradually mitigated this conflict, there is still a section of patriotic Americans who repudiate the slightest appearance of British influence, claiming that the form of English that has grown up in their country should have free play to develop independently of English literature or general British tradition. They are fond of their differences and wish to increase them.

Now it was recently observed (by Professor Craigie) that in the *O.E.D.* the later examples of some obsolete words or special senses of words were all derived from American writers. It followed thence that a Dictionary which took its quotations only from American writers would probably show a continuous use of those words in American practice.

Examination also revealed American writers to be of two classes—those, that is, who affected English style, and those who wrote naturally in the style of their own talk; it even appeared that there were some American authors who wrote, consciously or unconsciously, now in one style and now in the other.

The desideratum is plainly a Dictionary which shall exhibit the unbroken tradition of American writers by drawing its examples from them: a study that promises satisfactory settlement of the disputes that caused estrangement. The removal of the whole question from the field of prejudice to that of scientific inquiry must establish the historical continuity; whence two results should follow: first, that all such 'Americanisms' as are shown to be due to a tradition more conservative than our own will not only be honourably accredited but may even be re-established in our common speech; secondly, the convenience of taking our primary educational models from the older literature will be evident. This is, in our opinion, a matter of first importance, since, according to our creed, the healthy development of the language can only be secured by familiarity with its historic forms. If the people are grounded in the older literature they can be trusted to develop it reasonably: on the other hand if they have no better groundwork than the chance corruptions prevalent in their district, what they may ultimately make of them is inconceivable. Development based on corruption can end only in confusion.

Retrospect of past publications

As for the work which we have already done, though it has not come up to our wishes either in amount or in punctuality of supply, we are willing to be judged by it. For the purpose of our present appeal it will be convenient that the reader should have a selected analytical summary.

SUMMARY

Certain Tracts deal at some length with particular subjects.

II. The paper 'on English homophones' exhibits to the eye the conditions of this nuisance, shows the utilitarian and æsthetic objections, the self-destructive property of the homophone, and the necessity for distinctive pronunciation of words that in the fashionable dialect of Southern English are needlessly assimilated.—IV, 'on the Pronunciation of English words from the Latin', is a historical account of the rules which prescribe the traditional pronunciation of all such words, and disposes of the scholastic pedantry which has shown a tendency to invalidate the tradition.—V, 'on the Englishing of French words', is by an American who supports our contentions, and in the same Tract there is criticism of an author whose poems are an object lesson of what is desirable or possible in the resuscitation of dialectal words.—VII and XIII contain a valuable contribution to the history of 'English words in French'. The detail into which this is led by the author's research may seem beyond the practical purposes of our Society, but together with VIII, 'What is pure French?' it is instructive in comparing how another language deals with one of our own problems.—IX, 'The language of Anatomy', takes that special subject to illustrate the relation of æsthetic speech to scientific terminology, and strongly opposes a wrong practice which was threatening our Medical Schools.—XVI is a paper by Professor Jespersen on 'the relation of logic to grammar', especially in English. In other Tracts special grammatical questions are dealt with, e.g. *Inversions: Use of hyphens: Split Infinitive: Preposition at end of sentence: Use of subjunctive: Position of adverbs: Shall and will, and should and would:* XVII discusses the origin, history, and meaning of the words *Romantic, Originality, Creative,* and *Genius,* and—XIX '*The Middle Age*' and *Medieval.* A lesser treatment in other Tracts deals with the words *British, Britisher, Great Britain, Pictorial, Picturesque, Grotesque, Fascist,* &c.: and many words to which some present abuse calls attention, such as *Morale, Timbre, Respective, Implicit, Practically, Literally, Infinite, Alright, Laches, Allelomorph,* &c., &c.

This short digest will indicate the kind of fare which we have provided and shall continue to provide.

The action of members

All that is expected of those who wish to promote the objects of the Society is that they should master and advocate its principles, as these are expounded in our Tracts, and contribute their example by practically observing them in detail, whether in speaking, writing, or teaching. If a sufficient number of individuals do that, then the general practice will be affected for good in the manner which we have proposed, because they will *ipso facto* become a sort of linguistic school whose example will be observed and followed.

Local organization

We have had letters from various members overseas desiring to establish local centres of the Society: at present our only centres are the branch houses of the Oxford University Press in Canada, Australia, New Zealand, India, South Africa, &c., and it is well that the publishing house should be recognized as the place where the Tracts can be procured and information about the Society obtained, but it would be of great assistance if in any of these places we could also have, as we have in the United States, an Agent who would undertake to enrol local members, collect their subscriptions, and report to the Secretary in England. He would have to make a voluntary gift of some trouble and time, but he could recoup himself for his actual expenses in stationery, postage, &c., by an account debited against the sum of the subscriptions which he transmitted quarterly to the Secretary in Oxford. We should be very glad to hear of volunteers who would undertake this work.

Beyond this first step we do not at present advise any special organization: we rather recommend that existing opportunities should be persistently exploited: for instance, in any place, wherever there are enough persons interested in our work to form anything in the way of a linguistic club, there will generally be some sort of literary club or Society already in being: advantage should be taken of such an organization to persuade it to favour and adopt our principles.

Since literary Academies are as a rule in need of practical schemes for useful work and are apt both in their methods and products to be desultory, ill-directed, and disappointingly ineffective, their members, who are honestly anxious to serve the cause of literature, would surely welcome such a programme as the conscientious prosecution of our aims offers to them. They may, therefore, be invited to work with us; and if they would supply our Tracts with the substance of their special local experience it would give satisfaction to all parties.

Any such local club as we have supposed should subscribe for our Tracts and keep copies of them on their table. Their organization, whatever it might be, would be of great use and would not interfere with our liberty.

Special work can be found anywhere in observation of local habits or peculiarities; these are always of interest and frequently valuable. A competent tabulation of any group would make good matter for Correspondence in the Tracts: it would provoke comparative inquiry in other quarters and mutually affect practice.

Again, determined effort should be made to interest the Editors of newspapers in our work. This opportunity is everywhere present, nor is there any field in which more important results can be expected. Nothing but ignorance interferes with our progress in this direction, and the spreading of the scientific knowledge which we preach should be the chief work of our members. The more Editors of newspapers and weekly journals that can be recruited to serve in our campaign the better. We hope that this present Tract may be found useful in explaining what our principles are.

Text-books

We have had a good many letters also from Teachers complaining of the Text-books which they have to use in their Schools; and it is evident that we are here in face of an all-important question: it is too big to be broached parenthetically,—meanwhile we invite correspondence on the subject.

R.B.

CHILSWELL, *May 1925*

8

A. LLOYD JAMES

(1884–1943)

Lloyd James was a lecturer and later Professor of Phonetics in the University of London. He had a special interest in the application of phonetic science, and—in addition to being Secretary to the BBC Advisory Committee on Spoken English—was Phonetic Adviser to the Linguaphone Institute and Adviser on Radio Telephone Speech to the Royal Air Force. In this introduction, he weighs the considerations that enter into a definition of 'standard' pronunciation.

'Broadcast English'

(BBC Pamphlet, 1926)

General considerations

The language that had its birth in these islands, and was for centuries confined to them, is now more widely spread over the world than any other language; and its history is an epitome of the nation's history. We who speak it, however, are but little concerned with its past; we are responsible, though unconsciously, for its present, and we steadfastly refuse to contemplate its future. In our study of the growth of the Empire we forget that this territorial expansion of our language sowed the seeds of its disintegration. In our review of the social advancement of the nineteenth century, we forget that compulsory education and universal reading have begun to break up our historic dialects, and given to the printed word a degree of authority that it never possessed before. In our outlook upon the future we cherish the delusion that our language will remain as we know it now, the optimistic even seeing in it a future world-language.

It requires a peculiar refinement of the historical sense to see history in our every-day life, and an exercise of the imagination to see in broadcasting a feature of our national life that may have a permanent influence upon our language. It is not improbable that this general dissemination of the spoken word may tend to counteract the disintegrating influences that have hitherto always disturbed the unity of a language when that language has, through the political expansion of a nation, become scattered over an area larger than that which gave it birth.

Styles of speech

But however indifferent we are to language as a whole, most of us are far from indifferent to our own speech. On the contrary, it is nowadays considered essential that those who aspire to be regarded as cultured and educated should pay a due regard to the conventions that govern cultured and educated speech. It would appear that this interest in the niceties of our language is more alive now than ever before, and it has been suggested that broadcasting is in some way responsible for this quickening.

We now have a certain type, or rather a carefully chosen band of types of English, broadcast over the length and breadth of our country, so that, although many listeners hear daily a type of speech with which they are familiar, and which they habitually use, many others hear a type that is different from that which they usually hear and use. This in itself is enough to ensure abundant criticism: the man who is familiar with the broadcast pronunciation will be inclined to criticise any discrepancy between it and his own. The man who realises that the pronunciation of the loud-speaker is not his own, and not one that he hears about him in his every-day life, may resent the fact that an alien dialect is inflicted upon him. The one may accuse the broadcast speaker of ignorance or affectation: the other may make a general condemnation of the unfamiliar speech, calling it cockney, or Manchester, or Oxford. There are, for instance, current in modern English many ways of saying the word 'dance': they can all be divided into two main classes, viz.:

1 Those that use the short vowel of 'Dan'.
2 Those that use the long vowel of 'darn'.

Speakers who use the first variety often accuse the others of being cockney: those who use the second accuse the others of being provincial. Criticism does not end here, for those members of either group whose precise shade of vowel sound is not to the satisfaction of other members of the same class may be called affected, or uneducated.

The Englishman claims many birthrights, not the least of which is his right to speak his own language as, subject to the good-will of his friends, it pleases him to do; perhaps next in importance must be ranked his right to think whatever he pleases of any style of speech that is different from his own. Every man is a law unto himself in this matter, having one standard of conduct and one alone—that which he and his fellows invariably do, this being, for that reason, the right thing as far as it concerns him. He dresses like his fellows, and any conspicuous variation in the colour or shape of a garment is usually ridiculed: the style associated with one class, or with one occasion, is not deemed fitting in another class, or upon a different occasion. The kilt is as conspicuous in Piccadilly as the silk hat upon the moors: there are, however, occasions when a black tie is considered suitable by all classes. What is true of dress is in some degree true of speech, for both are governed by local convention and public taste, with a necessary reverence for historical tradition and the original purpose for which they were designed.

Affectation and pedantry are to be found wherever language is spoken; they are not confined to any one local or class variety of speech. The indiscriminate use of *h*, for instance, among some uneducated speakers is a pretension to superiority that may merely amuse us. Such pronunciations as *nevaa*, *faa*, *waaliss*, for *never*, *fire*, *wireless*, will appear an offensive affectation to those who are unacquainted with the class variant of which these pronunciations are so characteristic a feature.

Perhaps it may help us to view this question of taste in language in its proper setting if we realise that it is the same, in its fundamental principle, all the world over. Even in the primitive communities of Africa there are dialects, and it is often a matter of grave concern, when the language has to be written for the first time, and books have to be printed, which particular dialect shall be chosen. The speakers of all but the chosen one will resist the attempt to force upon them and their children a fashion of speech which is not that of their tribe, of their fathers, of the heroes of their legend.

Local pride and prejudice in speech, therefore, are not confined to the more civilised communities; it would appear, however, that the higher a community climbs in the social scale, the greater is the degree of uniformity in the speech. Wherever language is spoken, there is present in the minds of the speakers the notion that there is a 'right way' of speaking it, and the larger the community using the given language, the greater the number of 'right ways.' Every district will have its 'right way'—not that the speakers of that district will think of it as a 'right way'; they merely conform to the local way. Every social class will have its 'right way,' so much so that a man's social class will be more evident from the fashion of his speech than from any other fashion he adopts. So it is with English, and since English is, geographically, the most widely spread language in the world, it follows that the problems common to all languages are more acute here than they are elsewhere. It needs but little imagination to realise that when oral communication with all parts of the English-speaking world becomes, through the wireless medium, a daily event, there will have to be a greater degree of toleration shown towards the language of the loud-speaker than is at present shown by some of its critics. But though we may say that 'correct' and 'right' are not proper terms to use in these questions of pronunciation, yet there are exceptions; for where the different considerations of propriety, instead of conflicting, all lead to the same conclusion (and that is not uncommon), we may conveniently use the terms right and wrong.

The question of a *standard pronunciation* is bound to arise wherever language is spoken. English has a further question, arising from the absence of any recognised authority in its pronunciation. This is the question of *alternative pronunciations*. The two questions are intricately connected, but we may for convenience examine them separately.

I. IS THERE A STANDARD DIALECT OF ENGLISH?

The listener who writes to the B.B.C. asking why the London announcer pronounces 'daance' for 'dance' is, in reality, protesting against having an alien fashion of speech thrust upon him. The listener who complains that the London announcers are obviously affected is registering, in all probability, his protest against having thrust upon him the fashion of speech peculiar to a class of society, to a locality, or to a type of character, with which he is not in daily touch. Both critics imply that there is a 'better way' of speaking than that adopted by the announcers. The listener who writes to ask the 'correct way' of pronouncing a word quite evidently assumes that there *is* a 'correct way.' In all these queries and criticisms there is implied the idea of a standard pronunciation. We have a standard yard, a standard pound weight, a standard sovereign, and a standard pint. The yard does not vary from Aberdeen to Plymouth, and the pint pot contains as much in Mayfair as in Bethnal Green. Unfortunately speech is not capable of rigid measurement, and there is no standard of pronunciation. Pronunciation varies from district to district, from class to class, from character to character, in proportion to the local, social, or moral difference that separates them. Certain general observations may be made upon this aspect of the question without going into details, *e.g.*:—

1 There are district variants of speech in every social class, and class variants in every district.

2 Local variants become increasingly unlike one another as we descend the social scale.

3 They become more alike as we ascend.

4 The greater mobility of educated people tends towards the elimination of some of their local peculiarities.

5 The general spread of education tends to bring about the unification of the social variants in all districts.

6 Out of the broad band that comprises all district and class variants, there is emerging a considerably narrower band of variants that have a very great measure of similarity.

7 This narrow band of types has more features in common with Southern English than with Northern English.

8 Those who speak any one variety of the narrow band are recognised as educated speakers throughout the country. They may broadcast without fear of adverse intelligent criticism.

There may be other conclusions, but it is quite evident that we are not entitled to conclude that there is *one* standard pronunciation, *one* and *only one* right way of speaking English. There are varieties that are acceptable throughout the country, and others that are not.

II. ALTERNATIVE PRONUNCIATIONS

Germany has attempted to lay down certain principles to be followed by actors in the countries where German is spoken: it is obviously desirable that two members of the same cast should, unless it is expressly desired that they should not, speak the same variety of German. The Conservatoire in Paris, with the support of the National Theatres and the State Opera, exercises a control over the style of pronunciation to be used on the stage. In both these countries there is a 'right way,' or at any rate a very powerful tradition.

In Great Britain there is no such officially inspired authoritative tradition, and consequently our language is particularly rich in alternative pronunciations of equal authority. The B.B.C. has no desire to accept or to dictate any standard of pronunciation other than the current usage of educated speakers. But where there is diversity of opinion among works of reference, and diversity of practice among educated speakers, it is evident that no solution of doubtful questions can be attained that will meet with universal approval. The function of the Advisory Committee on Spoken English is to suggest to the Corporation, for the use of announcers, solutions that shall be in accordance with one accepted usage.

With the question of a standard language, this question of alternative pronunciations is involved, and the relationship between the two questions is best understood by reference to particular cases. Is *dance* to have the long vowel or the short vowel? Speakers of the Northern acceptable varieties favour the short vowel, while Southerners favour the long. Both pronunciations must stand: both are common among educated speakers. It is probable that the Southern variety will prevail, merely because it is the Southern variety, and is current in the metropolis. There is no standard dialect, but here, as in all communities, the educated speech of the capital starts with a heavy handicap in its favour.

Is *laboratory* to have the accent on the first syllable or on the second? Here there is no question of district variants: the two pronunciations are heard in all parts of the country. This is a question of alternative pronunciations, and, since most of the work of the Advisory Committee is concerned with alternative pronunciations, it will be well to examine very briefly the causes that give rise to these alternatives in our language.

Visual and spoken language

To begin with, it must be borne in mind that the language of a modern civilised community embraces the *spoken* or *oral* language, and the *written* or *visual* language. The visual language is generally an attempt to represent by means of visible symbols the sounds of the spoken language. Since it is impossible to make sounds visible, it follows that the relationship between the sounds and the symbols must be a conventional one; furthermore, since the same set of symbols has to serve for all the local and class variants of any given tongue, there will be a variety of conventions. Observance of these conventions is what is known as correct spelling; and, as a general rule, it may be stated that the greater the degree of uniformity prevailing in the conventions of any language, the simpler is its spelling, which is but another way of saying that the language is highly *phonetic*.

The arts of reading and writing are, in essence, nothing more than the understanding and the observance, respectively, of the conventional relationships that exist in language between the sounds used in the spoken language and the symbols used in the written language to represent these sounds. The conventions are necessary because sound and sight are fundamentally different; no system of symbols can ever represent speech adequately or accurately.

Visual languages are of two main kinds, viz.—

1 Those in which no attempt is made to represent the sounds—Chinese.

2 Those in which some such attempt is made—English, Greek, Sanskrit.

Languages of the first class require a separate sign for every word; reading and writing are not possible until the beginner has learned some hundreds of signs. It takes a Chinese student many years to learn the thousands of characters he requires in order to read a newspaper.

In languages of the second class an attempt is made to represent the pronunciation by means of letters, each of which is supposed to have a certain value when translated into sound. There are usually more sounds than letters, with the result that the ideal of one sound per letter is seldom attained—unless indeed this happy state prevails in Korean. The same letter may have several values: *e.g.* the letter 's' stands for the 's' sound in *picks*, for the 'z' sound in *pigs*, and for the 'zh' sound in *measure*. The same sound may be represented in many ways; *e.g.* the 'f' sound is represented by 'f' in *feel*, by 'ph' in *philosophy*, and by 'gh' in *laugh*. A single letter may stand for one or more groups of sounds; thus the letter 'x' represents the sounds 'ks' in *six*, and the sounds 'gz' in *exist*. A single sound may require a group of letters, and the same group of letters may represent several sounds: *e.g.* the two letters 'th' represent one sound in *thick*, another sound in *then*, and yet another sound in *thyme*.

These discrepancies arise from the very simple fact that a language may have more sounds than letters. English uses the Roman alphabet, with certain additions, and has twenty-six letters to do duty for its sounds. Our language comprises at least thirty main essential sounds, for which symbols are indispensable. Unless a language is fortunate enough to have an alphabet that can provide one letter per sound, then there is bound to be established a conventional relationship between some sounds and some symbols. In time the conventions are observed differently by different districts, and variant pronunciations will begin to arise.

No system of symbols, then, can represent a system of sounds without a series of conventions; and it follows, therefore, that the ideally phonetic language does not exist. This truth must have been realised very early, for, although written language starts as an avowed attempt to reproduce the spoken language, it soon abandons the effort, and tends more and more as time goes on to persist unchanged, ceasing to register the very considerable ravages made by time upon the spoken idiom. The havoc wrought upon the sounds of our language before our own time is accepted complacently, but we are all inclined to resist vigorously the inroads that are being made in our own day.

We are thus faced with the additional anomaly that the visual language is not really a picture of the language as it is now, but rather of the language as it was when the visual language began to become popular. In the case of English, we possess in our visual language a picture of what our pronunciation was, in its main features, in the century that immediately succeeded the introduction of printing.[1] The further removed we are in time from the date of the popularisation of our visual system, the greater will be the discrepancy between the spoken and the written languages. Tibetan orthography was fixed in the seventh century, and is still current as then fixed, so that a word which appears written as *dbyus* is pronounced 'ü.' In our own time the word written *plough* is now spoken as *plow*, *rough* is spoken as *ruff*, *cough* as *coff*. What we now see as *dough*, we speak as *dō*, having to make a new word to represent a pronunciation that the letters 'dough' once represented. The new word is *duff*. Sound and symbol are by their very nature irreconcilable, and their very nature serves to make them still more irreconcilable as time progresses. Sounds are vague and ethereal things that cannot be crystallised: they arise, in language, from muscular habits of the organs of speech, and change from generation to generation with a constancy in which some scholars have professed to see the regularity of natural law. The inevitable law of spoken language is change, because sound is sound, and because the impression of sound upon the mind is not as enduring as the impression of sight. The equally inevitable law of written language is persistence, because the eye has become accustomed to see, and the hand to make, certain signs in certain orders, and the mind has become accustomed to read them silently with little or no reference to the sounds they were intended to represent. Any alteration of the existing visual language will disturb the smooth working of two processes, reading and writing, that have taken

[1] In English, the main features of our spelling became fixed in the sixteenth century, so that the far-reaching changes in our pronunciation which took place during the next three centuries are, of course, unrecorded in our orthography. Wyld, *Historical Study of the Mother Tongue*, p. 15.

years to bring to perfection. It is conceivable that the two processes would be more easily acquired if there were some attempt to reconsider the conventional relationships existing between sound and symbol; it is possible that if no such reconsideration ever takes place, the discrepancy between spoken and written language will increase with time until the conventions are so numerous that there will be one convention pei word, as in modern Chinese. As against this, it is not surprising that there is now a steadily increasing tendency to make the visual language a standard, and to pronounce words, not according to their later acquired pronunciation, but according to their traditional spelling. Whereas the writing was originally designed to represent the sounds, we are now trying to make the sounds conform to the symbols. Thus there has come about a strange inversion of the original processes.

This discrepancy between sound and symbol, then, is a fertile cause of uncertainty in pronunciation. The letters 'ei' have one sound in *eight* and another in *receive*. Therefore we may expect uncertainty as to their value in unfamiliar words, e.g. *inveigle*. It is unnecessary to multiply examples, for many of the alternative pronunciations recorded in English dictionaries are examples of this uncertain relationship between sound and symbol.

Foreign words

Into this chaos of conflicting relationships there must be thrown, according to some, a further convention, namely, a relationship between the value of the symbol in the modern language and the value it had in a classical language. *Cinema* derives from a Greek word that began with the 'k' sound, therefore, it is alleged, the English word must have the 'k' sound.

The number of people who are familiar with the original phonetic values of these letters is small; and there is often uncertainty as to what these original values really were. In view of the complicated nature of the already existing relationship between sound and symbol in English, it would appear advisable not to add a further complication by this consideration of ancient values. But so long as this consideration is regarded as desirable, it will be a fertile source of alternative pronunciations.

To some extent the same is true of modern foreign languages from which our vocabulary continues to enrich itself. What is to be done with the countless words that come to us from these sources? Are we to keep the foreign pronunciation? Or are we to read the words as though they were English words? This question bristles with difficulties, and little can be said about it here, beyond registering the view that the question is not one to be dismissed in the summary way that is not uncommon. In early days such words were read as English words. French was read as though it were English, and the matter ended there. But since we have begun to learn French and to speak it with some attempt at giving our effort a French sound, it is thought desirable to give French words as near an approximation to their French pronunciation as possible. The approximation is often a poor one, because French sounds are not English sounds, and because the rhythm and accent of French are alien to English. So it comes about that however laudable our intention to preserve the French pronunciation, the result is a collection of those already existing English sounds that most nearly approximate to the French. The only French sound in the average English pronunciation of the word *restaurant* is the 's,' which is the same in English and French. In the case of other languages less familiar than French, there is usually less attempt to reproduce the native pronunciation, especially when that attempt involves the production of sounds which are usually considered difficult. Most people are aware that the initial consonant in the name *Wagner* sounds like an English 'v,' and most of us pronounce it as such, because there is a 'v' sound in English. *Bach* is less fortunate, for his name contains a sound that English people have forgotten for some centuries how to make; he is therefore frequently called *Baak*. The further afield we travel, the more hopeless becomes the attempt to reproduce the native pronunciation, and he would be a bold man who would recommend that we should adopt the initial sound that the Arab uses in the word *Koran*, or the initial click that the Zulu uses in *Cetewayo*. A language will seldom accept or embody either sounds or rhythms or accents that are alien to those which are its historical heritage. Isolated speakers may use these exotic sounds, but the bulk of the people will reject them.

Position of stress

There must also be noticed another source of alternative pronunciations with which the Advisory Committee is very much concerned. This is the nature and position of the stress or accent in modern English. Concerning the nature of this stress, little is known beyond the fact that its function is to give prominence to certain syllables; these syllables tend in connected speech to recur at regular intervals of time, this regularity constituting that essential feature of our language, its rhythm. This prominence, which is popularly believed to be due to loudness, may owe its origin to other sources. For example, the syllable may be made prominent by its tone, by its length, or by the quality of the vowel sound it contains. What is important to remember is that any question concerning stress *may* be concerned with length or vowel quality.

As to the position of the stress, English offers an example almost unique in the world of languages, for there is no known principle that governs the incidence of stress. The words *photograph*, *photographer*, *photographic*, have the stress on the first, second and third syllables respectively. Some words, e.g. *convict*, *increase*, are nouns if the stress falls on the first syllable, and verbs if it falls on the second syllable. We are all agreed as to where the stress falls in many words, e.g. *agree*, *belong*, *prominent*, *independent*. But there is no uniformity with regard to *magazine*, *apologise*, which differ in the North and South, or with *laboratory*, *peremptory*, *gyratory*, *applicable*, *indisputable*, and hundreds of others. There would appear to be a popular tendency to place the stress in long words as near to the beginning as possible, with the result that the remaining syllables suffer by the distortion or loss of their vowel sounds. The only disadvantage of this tendency is that the resultant distortion or loss of unstressed vowel sounds frequently brings into awkward contact numbers of consonants, and leads, especially in broadcast speech, to confusion and unintelligibility. *Laboratory* when broadcast with the stress on the first syllable is liable to be heard by a listener as *lavatory*; it is therefore desirable, at any rate in broadcast speech, to avoid throwing the stress too far back. Against this tendency to throw back the stress as far as possible, there is also another principle which is active in determining the accent of polysyllables; that is, the utilitarian principle of keeping the original accent of the root on all its derivatives. This latter principle seems now in favour, driving out older pronunciations, but as it cannot be always observed it will have to win its victories word by word, in the general rub: thus *indispútable* is winning from *indísputable*, because of *dispute*. For an example of anomalies, compare *omniscience* and *omnipotent* with *omnipresence*.

Relationship between stress and sound

There remains finally to be mentioned the relationship between the stress and the quality of the vowel sound in English. This may best be understood by considering an example. The vowel in the word *man*, as the word is said usually, possesses a certain acoustic quality and a certain length; if the word is placed in a position where it does not carry what we know as the stress, e.g. *postman*, the quality and length of the vowel are altered. The stressed vowel is different from the unstressed vowel: indeed, as we have said, this difference of itself may constitute no small part of the nature of the English stress. This difference is not due to any carelessness of speech; it is an inevitable consequence of that very peculiar feature of our language known as the stress or accent. Any attempt to pronounce English, giving to the unstressed vowels the exact quality they possess when stressed, results in a pronunciation that is not recognisable as English. The degree of difference between stressed and unstressed vowels varies in different parts of the country: there is usually less difference in Yorkshire than in London, with the result that, or possibly because of the fact that, the rhythm of Yorkshire English is different from that of London English. It is impossible to say which is cause and which is effect.

This modification of the vowel sound of unstressed syllables is a source of much anxiety to those who are concerned with speech. Most of us agree that the final vowels of *singer*, *actor*, *banana*, are the same in sound, although they are differently represented in writing. Some speakers rhyme *palace* with *Paris*, *audible* with *laudable*; others make a difference, being guided by a recollection of the appearance of the words. Speakers who hear unstressed vowels that differ from their own are inclined to be very critical, asking, for example, why *wireless orchestra* is pronounced *wireliss orchistra*.

The unstressed vowels in English are working out their own destiny, and it is impossible to predict what the future has in store. One has only to compare the havoc wrought upon unstressed vowels in other languages, *e.g.* French, to realise that in a language that has a strong stress the quality of the stressed vowel is but little guide to the quality of the same vowel when it is unstressed. The Advisory Committee believes that this distortion should be as little as is consistent with the rhythm of Southern English.

Conclusion

It will be seen that the question of making any decisions upon English pronunciation is not one to be investigated without much thought. The considerations that have been outlined in this introduction are, so to speak, the academic or scholastic background of the problem, and with these the average educated speaker of the language is rightly not much concerned. But they are the considerations that are ever present in the minds of those who are responsible for the pronunciations recorded in out standard dictionaries.

But dictionaries disagree among themselves, some offering alternatives that others ignore, some giving first choice to one alternative, some to another. If the B.B.C. quotes one standard dictionary, the critic quotes another, and there is no end to argument.

Moreover, dictionaries grow out of date: the Oxford English Dictionary has been some forty years in the making, and its early volumes already need revision. New words appear that are not recorded in the early volumes; new pronunciations of old words arise, and gain so great a measure of currency that they must be admitted into our speech. For it must not be forgotten that a pronunciation is not bound to be 'right' merely because it appears in a dictionary: it appears in the dictionary because it *was* 'right' in the view of the lexicographer at the time when he made his dictionary.

Most of the words that follow[1] admit of more pronunciations than one; they are all words that have caused difficulty to announcers, or words that have given rise to criticism from listeners. The Advisory Committee on Spoken English has discussed each word on its merit, and it recommends that announcers should use the pronunciations set out below. It is not suggested that these pronunciations are the only 'right' ones, and it is not suggested that any special degree of authority attaches to these recommendations. They are recommendations made primarily for the benefit of announcers, to secure some measure of uniformity in the pronunciation of broadcast English, and to provide announcers with some degree of protection against the criticism to which they are, from the nature of their work, peculiarly liable.

The representation in print of pronunciation is always a difficult matter; it is easy when a complicated phonetic alphabet is employed, but such an alphabet requires special types, and is, moreover, difficult to read. But unless a phonetic alphabet is employed, there must be a lack of consistency and indeed of accuracy. The pronunciations set out below are indicated as simply as possible, and the original spelling is interfered with as little as possible.

The only general convention that has been observed is that the doubling of a vowel letter indicates a long vowel sound, while the

[1] [See extract from the Advisory Committee's list, question 5 on p. 308.]

doubling of a consonant letter indicates that the previous vowel sound is short.

The long 'o' sound, as in *no,* is represented by ō; the sign ˘ is used to denote a short vowel when the doubling of the following consonant is not convenient. The position of the stress is indicated by the mark ʹ over the stressed syllable.

Where the pronunciation can be shown by a note of explanation, this has been done.

9

LOGAN PEARSALL SMITH

(1865–1949)

Pearsall Smith was primarily a literary scholar and critic, but with a strong interest in the history and present state of the English language. He played a prominent role in the Society for Pure English (see Essay 7), and in the present tract he addresses himself to clarifying one of the most controversial themes that the Society was founded to discuss—the changing nature of vocabulary in a living language. He takes the view that there are deficiencies in the language's vocabulary which have to be made good, and suggests various means whereby remedies might be obtained.

'Needed Words'

(Society for Pure English, Tract XXXI, 1928)

Language, Walter Bagehot wrote, 'was shaped and fashioned into its present state by common ordinary men and women using it for common and ordinary purposes. They wanted a carving-knife, not a razor or lancet.' This inadequacy of language for the finer purposes of thought has been felt since the time of Aristotle who often noted the want of terms to express his meaning, and who would sometimes coin them as the need arose. Words, indeed, for the ordinary purposes of life are seldom lacking; our most pressing needs are somehow satisfied; new inventions and conveniences, new developments in political and social life find their popular denominations, and at least twenty or thirty new terms are added to our familiar vocabulary every year.

But if the provision of common carving-knives is perhaps adequate, the finer razors and lancets required for the more delicate operations of the mind are often lacking, and language is thus always lagging behind the development of thought. This is, however, a large subject; every form of speech has its deficiencies as well as its happy inventions, and I must confine myself to a few of the deficiencies in our English vocabulary which are obvious, and to certain others of a less obvious kind which various of our writers have noticed, and to the methods which have been suggested, and sometimes successfully carried out, to remedy these deficiencies and fill up these gaps.

Drastic proposals for grammatical changes—the provision, for instance, for a neutral pronoun like *thon* for 'he or she'—are outside the scope of this paper; for such proposals, however beneficial from an ideal point of view, are impracticable at present, and our Society has wisely confined its activities to reforms which have some chance of succeeding. Among the practicable improvements of our speech mentioned in our original prospectus was the suggestion by our members of new terms to supply our needs as they arise.

The most obvious way of becoming aware of these needs is by noting the foreign words, and especially the French words, which we are forced to borrow to fill up the gaps in our current vocabulary. These terms, which we print in italics and try to pronounce as foreign words, are regarded by our linguistic purists as contaminations of our speech, and we are exhorted to avoid their use. But the attempt to put a ban upon such foreign words and deport them as undesirable aliens always fails; we cannot do without them, since they fill certain gaps in our means of expression for which we possess no convenient native terms.

When we classify these foreign makeshifts, we find that a large number of them belong to a special class of words in which the vocabularies of all languages are lacking in a sufficient variety of terms. These words are words descriptive of ways of feeling; there are more ways of feeling, as Spinoza noted, possible to human beings than the human vocabulary can describe.[1] 'Language', as Dr. Johnson said, 'is scanty, and inadequate to express the nice gradations and mixtures of our feelings.' Many, therefore, of the foreign words which we are forced to borrow are words like *blasé*, *ennui*, *malaise*, *Schadenfreude* and *Weltschmerz*, which describe various ways of feeling.[2]

Closely allied to the names of emotional states are words which describe ways of thought and attitudes of mind: *état d'âme*, for instance, *naïveté*, *distrait*, *Weltanschauung*; and the word *Zeitgeist* to describe the collective way of thinking of a special period.[3]

[1] Spinoza remarks, for instance, that, although we have the word *commiseratio* (pity) for pain arising from another's hurt, he knew of no word for the feeling of pleasure arising from another's good. *Ethics*, III, xxii.

[2] Other words of this kind are *ému*, *froissé*, *nonchalance*, *joie de vivre*, *sangfroid*, *abandon*, *mauvaise honte*, *amour-propre*, *Schwärmerei*, and *Sehnsucht*. *Esprit de corps*, *moral* describe collective ways of feeling and moral attitudes for which we have no English names.

[3] Lord Morley quotes a remark of Dugald Stewart on the richness of French terms to describe delicate shades of mind and feeling: *esprit juste*, for instance, *esprit étendu*,

The almost infinite variety of human relations needs, like the variety of ways of feeling, more terms to describe it adequately than our vocabulary—or indeed the vocabulary of any language—can supply; and among the terms of this class which we are forced to borrow from France may be mentioned *employé*, *protégé*, *fiancé* and *liaison*.[1]

We are forced to eke out our vocabulary of social intercourse with many French words,[2] and to borrow from French many of the theatrical[3] and literary[4] terms we want; and the need for additions to our vocabulary of political and social questions also forces us to borrow many words from France,[5] and in various other departments of our vocabulary we are compelled—or at least we find it convenient—to make use of French words like *élan*, *éclat*, *débâcle*, *milieu*, *nuance*, *provenance*, &c.

Obvious gaps like these have been noted at various times by English writers and critics. Thus John Evelyn, for instance, remarked that we had no equivalents in English for the French words *naïveté*, *ennui*, *bizarre*, *concert*, *émotion*, *defer*, *effort*.[6]

Writing in 1756 Lord Chesterfield pointed out another deficiency in our language; we had no single word, he said, in our language to express the meaning of the French word *mœurs*. 'Manners', he said, did not express enough, while 'morals' said too much.

The general meaning of *mœurs* was, according to Lord Chesterfield, 'a general exterior decency, fitness, and propriety of conduct in the common intercourse of life.'[7] Cicero, he says, had made use of the word *decorum* in this sense, and Chesterfield suggested that *decorum* should be added to our English vocabulary to express this meaning. *Decorum* was, as a matter of fact, already established as an English word

esprit fin, *esprit délié*, *esprit de lumière*; and compares this variety of descriptive words with the colloquial use of our overworked word 'clever'. *Studies in Literature* (1891), p. 80.

[1] *Clientèle*, *personnel*, *cortège* are other words of this class for which we have no available English equivalents.

[2] *Coterie*, *élite*, *fête*, *salon*, *savoir faire*, *comme il faut*, *double entente*, &c.

[3] *Début*, *dénouement*, *rôle*, *répertoire*, *claque*, *matinée*, *mis-en-scène*, *pièce de résistance*, *succès d'estime*, &c.

[4] *Cauterie*, *exposé*, *réchauffé*, *résumé*, *pensée*, &c.

[5] *Coup d'état*, *lèse-majesté*, *entente*, *rapprochement*, *pourparler*, *laissez-faire*, *sabotage*, &c.

[6] Of these words *concert* has now become an English word, *ennui*, *naïveté*, *bizarre* are half-naturalized among us. *Defer* and *effort* are found much earlier than Evelyn's date, though his note seems to show that they were not then in common use. *Emotion* in its modern sense seems to become current in the eighteenth century.

[7] *The World*, no. 189.

when Chesterfield wrote; there is, however, another meaning of the French word *mœurs* which we are unable to express in a single term. *Mœurs* signifies in French not only propriety of behaviour; it is used also of the ways of living, usages, customs, and prejudices of a particular person or class or epoch; *autres temps, autres mœurs*, is a phrase whose meaning could not be succinctly expressed in English, and the gap in our language which Lord Chesterfield noted has never been filled up.[1]

The existence of a convenient foreign word for which we have no native equivalent is not the only way in which a gap in our own language becomes apparent. Several of our writers have become aware of these deficiencies in their attempts to give a lucid expression to their thoughts. Thus Wordsworth, for instance, in the famous preface to the second edition of the *Lyrical Ballads*, noted the limitation of our word *poetry* to metrical composition and the absence of a general term to describe works which have the character of poetry, although they are not written in verse.[2] Wordsworth remarked that he used the word *poetry* as opposed to *prose* against his own judgement, and that much confusion had been introduced into criticism by the false contradistinction between Poetry and Prose, the only strict antithesis to Prose being metre. Coleridge also called attention to this difficulty; the writings of Plato and Jeremy Taylor furnish, he says, undeniable proofs 'that poetry of the highest kind may exist without metre'; and the first chapter of Isaiah, he added, was poetry in the most emphatic sense.[3] 'Poetry', he says elsewhere, 'is not the proper antithesis to prose, but to science. Poetry is opposed to science, and prose to metre. The proper and immediate object of science is the acquirement, or communication, of truth; the proper and immediate object of poetry is the communication of immediate pleasure.'[4]

Coleridge[5] suggested that this deficiency in our language—this absence of a word for *poetry* not restricted to metrical composition—might be supplied by reviving the old word *poesy* as a generic or common term for that quality in works which, although they are not

[1] The word *folkways* is sometimes used by American anthropologists to describe the customs and usages of a race or epoch.

[2] Here again foreign usage is more convenient than our own. *Gedicht* in German can be used of a prose composition, and Goethe called Daphnis and Chloe a *Gedicht*. The French *poésie* can be used of works like Fénelon's *Télémaque*, or Chateaubriand's *Les Martyrs*.

[3] *Biographia Literaria*, chapter xiv.

[4] *Shakespeare, Notes and Lectures* (1875), p. 1.

[5] 'Essay on Taste', in *Miscellanies, Aesthetic and Literary* (1911), p. 44.

metrical compositions, are poetical in character and appeal to the imagination and the aesthetic sense.[1]

Another restriction and limitation in our aesthetic terms has been noted by Mr. A. C. Bradley—the restricted use of the word Beauty, which, he remarks, is commonly used of only certain kinds of beautiful qualities, as when we say a thing is pretty but not beautiful, or that it is beautiful but not sublime. We possess no word in our ordinary language, he adds, which means 'whatever gives aesthetic satisfaction', and yet that idea *must* have a name in Aesthetics.[2]

The need for another word of this kind, a word to name a general quality and group together the objects which possess it, was noted by that acute critic Walter Bagehot, when he said, 'There should be a word in the language of literary art to express what the word "picturesque" expresses for the fine arts. *Picturesque* means fit to put into a picture; we want a word *literatesque*, "fit to be put into a book".'[3] We are all aware, as Bagehot suggests, of characters or incidents which seem as peculiarly fitted for literary treatment as certain aspects of nature seem made, as it were, to be painted; and, as he points out, a word to describe these characters and incidents would be a most useful addition to our vocabulary of literary criticism.

That narrowness of the meaning of certain words which we have noted in words like *Poetry* and *Beauty*, which impedes our power of expression, is sometimes due to the limitation and degradation of a word which possessed, in the earlier use, a wider signification. An instance of this is the way in which the word *curiosity* has become limited and degraded in our modern usage. *Curiosity* meant in former times the desire to learn, a feeling of interest that led to inquiry; and it was in this sense that Dr. Johnson used it when he wrote, 'Curiosity is, in great and generous minds, the first passion and the last.' From this to the current use of the word, 'inquisitiveness, in reference to trifles on matters which do not concern one', the change is great, and the loss of the word's old meaning has left a gap in our language to which Matthew Arnold called attention in his *Essays in Criticism*. 'It is noticeable,' he says, 'that the word *curiosity*, which in other languages is used in a good sense, to mean, as a high and fine quality of man's nature, just

[1] The older usage of the word *poesy* (which is now nothing more than an archaic synonym for *poetry*) authorizes Coleridge's suggestion. Bacon uses the word *poesy* both for works in prose and works in verse, and Sir Philip Sidney says 'It is not ryming and versing, that maketh Poesy. One may be a Poet without versing, and a versifier without Poetry'.

[2] A. C. Bradley, *Oxford Lectures on Poetry* (1920), p. 39.

[3] Walter Bagehot, *Literary Studies* (1891), vol. II, p. 341.

this disinterested love of a free play of the mind on all subjects, for its own sake,—it is noticeable, I say, that this word has in our language no sense of the kind, no sense but a rather bad and disparaging one.'[1]

It was pointed out in the original prospectus of our Society that our authors had in former times done much to fill up the gaps in our vocabulary, and supply the need for new words as these needs arose. They did this in various ways, the most obvious of which was the borrowing and nationalization of useful terms from the classical languages, or from Italian or French. Our earlier writers, down to the middle of the seventeenth century, seem to have had no scruples about appropriating and giving English forms to all the foreign words they wanted; and although purists would now and then protest against these importations, such protests seem to have had little or no effect. But when, after the linguistic freedom which prevailed to the end of the Elizabethan age, ideals of correctness began to influence the character of our language, much of the old reactive force was lost, and it became more difficult to appropriate and make use of foreign terms,—or at least to give them English shapes and sounds. John Evelyn, as we have seen, noted our need for a number of foreign words; and writing to Sir Peter Wyche, who was chairman of a committee appointed by the newly-formed Royal Society to consider the improvement of the English tongue, he gives a list of French and Italian words for which we have no equivalents, and adds, 'Let us therefore, (as the Romans did the Greek) make as many of these do homage as are like to prove good citizens.'[2] Most of the French terms which Evelyn mentions have been added to our English vocabulary, which has been also enriched by a large number of Italian words connected with the arts, like *concert*, *opera*, *balustrade*, *corridor*, &c., which are first found in Evelyn's writings, and were apparently his importations from abroad.

Dryden was conscious of the need of foreign terms and boldly expressed his purpose of importing them. 'If sounding words,' he wrote in the dedication of his *Aeneis*, 'are not of our growth and manufacture, who shall hinder me to import them from a foreign country? I carry not out the treasure of the nation, which is never to return; but what I bring from Italy, I spend in England: here it remains, and here it circulates; for, if the coin be good, it will pass from one hand to another. I trade both with the living and the dead, for the

[1] The adjective *curious* has undergone the same degradation. With reference to persons it now means either 'odd' or 'prying', has lost its old meaning, 'eager to learn'.

[2] Evelyn's *Memoirs* (1819), vol. II, p. 152—letter of 20 June 1665.

enrichment of our native language. We have enough in England to supply our necessity; but, if we will have things of magnificence and splendour, we must get them by commerce.... If I find any elegant word in a classic author, I propose it to be naturalized, by using it myself; and, if the public approves of it, the bill passes.'

To the licence he allows himself in the appropriation of foreign words, Dryden adds, however, certain necessary cautions; every man could not distinguish between pedantry and poetry, and every man, therefore, was not fit to innovate; a poet must first be certain whether the word he would introduce is a beautiful word, and then that it will agree with the English idiom. On this point he should take the advice of judicious friends; and lastly he says, 'since no man is infallible, let him use this license very sparingly; for if too many foreign words are poured in upon us, it looks as if they were designed not to assist the natives, but to conquer them.'

There have been since Dryden no importers of foreign words with so liberal a conception of the profit of this kind of commerce; but Carlyle made familiar to us a few German words, and Coleridge introduced or made popular several terms of the Kantian philosophy.

Our ability to assimilate foreign words has been steadily decreasing since the time of Evelyn and Dryden; and, as we have seen, almost all the French words we are forced to use, and for which we have no equivalents, keep their foreign shapes and accents and remain as italicized foreigners in our midst. There are two main causes for this weakening of our assimilative powers. We make the acquaintance, in the first place, of these foreign words for the most part by the eye, rather than by the ear; we read them, but, as we do not hear them spoken, they keep their clear-cut alien forms, and seldom undergo that transformation which would assimilate them to our customary ways of speech. The second reason why we seldom naturalize our foreign borrowings has been more than once mentioned in the Tracts of this Society, the false ideal of correctness, namely, which regards the foreign forms of borrowed words as the right forms, and which impedes their assimilation. This perverted kind of purism is extremely aggressive, and often leads to protests, more angry than enlightened, in the public papers.[1]

[1] A protest of this kind was made, for instance, against the suggestion of Mr. Bridges (Tract III, p. 11) that we might do well to English the very useful word *timbre* as 'tamber'. The first time 'tamber' appeared in one of the weekly journals a distinguished man of letters wrote at once to denounce it; he hated it, he said, and all those with whom he had discussed it felt just as he did about it. *The Nation and Athenaeum* (13 March 1926).

Another great difficulty in the way of naturalizing the foreign terms we need is the conservatism of type-setters and proof-readers, to whom any kind of change is abhorrent, and against whom authors and editors fight, it would seem, in vain.[1]

The naturalization of foreign terms is not, however, the only, or the most important means by which men of letters have enriched our vocabulary. Many of our great writers of the past have possessed a plastic power over language, a genius for word-creation which they freely employed to fill up gaps in our language and supply needs of our own which no foreign term could meet. The commonest form of word-creation is what is called derivation, the addition, that is, of suffixes or prefixes to words already existing in the language. Thus, for instance, abstract words like *colonization*, *diplomacy*, *electioneering*, and the adjectives *financial* and *colonial* are first found in the speeches or writings of Burke, who made many useful additions to our political vocabulary. Jeremy Bentham was another great coiner of words; a few of the additions he made to our vocabulary will be found in Professor Graham Wallas's contribution to this Tract. The word-creating activities of various English writers have been described in various handbooks on the English language, and I need not enlarge upon them here. There are, however, two words, *scientist* and *sensuous*, which deserve a special mention, as they are especially relevant to our subject. *Scientist* is of interest as a deliberate and successful creation made to fill a consciously-felt gap in the language, to provide one of that class of comprehensive and collective terms which, as we shall see, are often wanting in our vocabulary.

Whewell, in writing his *Philosophy of Inductive Sciences*, remarked, 'We need very much a name to describe a cultivator of science in general. I should incline to call him a Scientist,' and thus by this happy suggestion he added a most useful term to the vocabulary of thought.

The word *sensuous* is of interest for another reason, as it seems to have been created by Milton to fill a gap caused by that degradation of an older word which, as we have seen, has limited the meaning of the words *curiosity* and *curious*. When Milton describes poetry as being

[1] In 1923 our Society published (Tract XIII) a list of the most current alien words, with suggestions of the way in which they should be printed as English words. This list, printed on a card to be hung up in compositors' rooms, was sent to the leading English journals, whose editors unanimously welcomed it, and said they would instruct their compositors to follow its directions. These instructions, however, have had little or no effect; italicized words and foreign spellings and accents still abound in the very journals whose editors had agreed to conform to our Society's suggestions.

'simple, sensuous, and passionate' he apparently coined the word *sensuous* as an alternative to the old word *sensual*, which, though possessing at first no evil meaning, had come, in the course of time, to imply something base or vicious,[1] and thus, as Sir Walter Raleigh has said, 'gave the English people an opportunity of reconsidering those headlong moral preoccupations which had already ruined the meaning of the word "sensual" for the gentler uses of the poet.'

Scientist and *sensuous* are words formed by derivation; another process of word-formation is that of making compound words, the joining together of two or more separate words to make a third. This is a favourite method of the poets, who have enriched the language with many beautiful compound epithets; and a certain number of current formations of this kind would appear to have been added to the language by various of our authors.

By far the greater number of compound words in English have, in recent times, been created by men of science out of Greek and Latin elements. This use of foreign elements to make the composite words of our scientific vocabulary would seem to have weakened our power of compounding words out of our own resources. English compounds, however correctly formed and however useful, seem uncouth to us at first, and meet with almost universal disapprobation; a word like *aviator* is accepted without question, while *airman* was disliked at first, and only succeeded in establishing itself owing to the persistent use of the word in *The Times*. Such words, as was pointed out in the prospectus of our Society, need to be used for some little time before we can overcome our dislike to them; while compounds of Greek and Latin origin, however cumbrous and unsuitable they may be, are accepted almost without question.

This power of forming native compounds, which has become more or less atrophied in our standard English, is still active in popular and dialect speech, and compounds from these sources like *makeweight*, *shortcoming*, *bedrock*, often make their way from popular speech into the standard language. This process has sometimes been assisted by men of letters, notably by Sir Walter Scott and Carlyle, who have made available and current several compounds of this kind.

Popular and dialect speech abounds not only in compound words; it is a treasure-house also of ancient terms which have become obsolete in

[1] Keats uses the word with the old and innocent signification in his *Ode on a Grecian Urn*,

Ye soft pipes, play on;
Not to the sensual ear—

the standard language; and along with these old words there are found many new terms coined in the ever-active mint of the popular vernacular. A number of these, which have been added to our standard vocabulary, are enumerated in Tract III of our Society's publications. Among these words of popular formation a very large number are monosyllables—words like *beach*, *bleak*, *blight*, *fad*, *fun*, *fog*, *freak*, *glen*, *nag*, *pet*, *shunt*, *skid*, *swamp*, *thud* and many others. With some of these we are familiar from their use by famous authors, as *lilt* and *croon* from Burns' poems, *daft* from Scott's novels, and *snob* from Thackeray's appropriation of this word of popular origin.

The fact that at least four monosyllables of popular derivation, the words *snob*, *coke*, *tram*, and *lunch*, have been added to the European vocabulary, shows what the value can be of monosyllables of this kind, and suggests a freer use of these penny-pieces of popular coinage which abound in vast numbers in our popular speech. Closely allied to this adoption of monosyllables from popular speech is another kind of word-creation which has been seldom made use of, but which has been strikingly successful when it has been tried. This is the deliberate and arbitrary choice of some unoccupied sound, generally a monosyllable, to describe a phenomenon for which we possess no name. Paracelsus is believed to have added the words *sylph*, *gnome* and *zinc*—words with no ascertainable etymology—to the vocabularies of Europe, and the most famous and brilliantly successful of all these creations is the word *gas*, arbitrarily formed by the Dutch chemist, Van Helmont—a creation which did much to make the science of chemistry possible. Another example of an arbitrary formation of this kind is the word *kodak*, which has been recently added to the European vocabulary.[1]

Men of letters have helped to enrich our language and fill up its gaps in yet another way, by reviving and giving renewed currency (as Coleridge attempted with the word 'poesy') to words which have

[1] It is possible that when the principles of nomenclature come to be better understood, this method of naming, this arbitrary choice of unoccupied sounds, and especially of monosyllables, will be more freely employed to provide us with useful terms to fill up the gaps in our vocabulary. There are thousands of these unoccupied sounds which might be taken over for this purpose; and indeed, from an ideal standpoint, the use we make of our monosyllabic sounds is somewhat wasteful and capricious. Some of them are made to bear the weight of many significations, while others are not made use of at all, and lie idle, like bits of unstamped coin, in the treasury of our speech. The efficiency of these arbitrarily-chosen sounds is generally as great as is the difficulty of giving currency to them, and it is generally the accident of the notoriety of some personal name, or of some happy combination of initial letters, which establishes them in the language. Thus the electrical terms *Ohm*, *Watt* and *Volt* are derived from personal names. Sounds more or less arbitrarily chosen, like *gas*, are of rarer occurrence.

fallen out of use. How much our vocabulary owes to the restoration of half-forgotten words by the writers of the Romantic School is familiar to us all, and it is not necessary to give a list of all these revivals.

One of the most useful and happiest of these restorations should not, however, go unmentioned—Coleridge's revival of Milton's word 'sensuous', which had apparently not been used since Milton's time, till it struck the attention of Coleridge, who deliberately re-introduced it to express, as he says, in one word what belongs to the senses or the recipient or more passive faculties of the soul.

In addition to reviving obsolete words, it is also possible to restore to a word, whose significance has been blunted, the finer edge of its original meaning; and Coleridge claimed to have performed a service of this kind with reference to the words *intuition* and *intuitive*.

Mr. Fowler, in his *Modern English Usage*, has pointed out a way by means of which many writers have assisted, and all writers can assist, the lucidity and expressiveness of our language. This method is called Differentiation, and consists in giving deliberate help to that natural process of language which is always tending to give different meanings to two words or synonyms which have at first the same significance. Words of this kind are apt to become differentiated, to assert for themselves separate spheres of expression from which others are excluded, until two words which could originally be used indifferently come to have clearly-discriminated meanings. Such discriminations are, however, tentative at first; they only become definite by being adopted in speaking and writing; and, as Mr. Fowler says, 'It is the business of all who care for the language to do their part towards helping serviceable ones through the dangerous incomplete stage to that in which they are of real value.'[1]

The naturalization or translation of needed foreign words, the creation of new words or the recovery and revival of old ones, the authorization of vivid words of popular creation, the reclamation of old meanings, and the establishment of new discriminations—these, then, are the methods by which men of letters have helped in the past to enrich our language, and make it a better carrier of thought, a more adequate medium of expression. It is a misfortune for our speech that precisely in this present age, when the need for new words is most pressing, when

[1] Mr. Fowler, under the heading *Differentiation*, gives a most interesting list of differentiations which are attempting to establish themselves and which should be encouraged, and of other differentiations which might be established with profit to the language. Each of these incipient or possible differentiations is also discussed under separate headings.

not only new inventions are being made almost daily, but new movements in thought, politics, art and social life are constantly arising, and mankind is becoming increasingly aware of new and rich fields of experience, our men of letters, unlike their predecessors, are no longer attempting to fulfil their necessary function of providing for these needs. The task of word-creation has been almost completely left to the very men who are in many ways least fitted to fulfil it, to the men of science, who have evolved a special system of nomenclature of their own. This system, though suitable to their own special needs, is most unfortunate in its effect on the vocabulary of our spoken and written speech. The subject of scientific nomenclature lies outside the scope of my paper; Mr. Bridges has discussed it with reference to the science of Anatomy in Tract IX of our publications, and it only remains for me to point out how the creation of this vocabulary of science, and the immense influx of scientific terms into our current speech, has injured its creative powers and imposed upon us a false ideal of verbal excellence.

The main object of scientific nomenclature is accurate description, and to achieve this extreme and recondite differentiation of objects and processes, scientists have had recourse to those long cumbrous compounds of Greek and Latin elements which are most convenient for their purpose. This habit of compounding words out of classical elements has not only weakened, as I have said, our powers of native composition, and given us a certain distaste for native compounds, but it has also, I think, given prevalence to a false ideal of nomenclature, to the notion, namely, that the name of an object or idea should contain within itself its meaning. The truth is, as the late Dr. Bradley pointed out,[1] that, when a thing to be denoted is familiar, what we require is an *identifying* and not a *descriptive* word for it. Words which attempt to describe and explain their meanings must of necessity be multisyllabic and cumbrous, while words which are simple designations are almost always brief and easy to pronounce, and can be readily added to the current vocabulary. This notion that a word should contain its meaning is a great hindrance to the always most difficult process of word-creation, and it should be realized that the best words never contain their definition; that they are labels and not explanations, or at most do no more than evoke some single and striking aspect or quality of the object they denote.

This great increase of the ugly, lifeless, mechanical vocabulary of science—the fact that most of our new words are bad words—has

[1] S.P.E. Tract III, p. 19.

contributed no doubt to our instinctive dislike to innovation, and the reluctance of our men of letters to meddle in this business. We run the danger of being involved in a kind of vicious circle; the fewer good new words there are, the fewer will be created, until word-coinage, being only performed by the makers of spurious coin, will come to be regarded as a kind of counterfeiting.

And yet, as I have said, the need for new words has seldom been more pressing, and twenty or thirty new terms are every year added to our current speech. That these should be vivid and expressive words, English in shape and sound, and formed according to the traditions of the language is a thing that we should all desire.

The importance of this task, and the duty of men of letters to fulfil it has been felt in other countries, especially in Germany, where many convenient terms have been deliberately created and added to the vocabulary by well-known German writers. Fénelon, in his famous letter to the French Academy, suggested that the Academy should undertake this task, and his wise advice is worth quoting.

> Un terme nous manque, nous en sentons le besoin; choisissez un son doux et éloigné de toute équivoque, qui s'accomode à notre langue, et qui soit commode pour abréger le discours. Chacun en sent d'abord la commodité: quatre ou cinque personnes le hasardent modestement en conversation familière, d'autres le répètent par le goût de la nouveauté; le voilà à la mode. C'est ainsi qu'un sentier qu'on ouvre dans un champ devient bientôt le chemin le plus battu, quand l'ancien chemin se trouve raboteux et moins court.[1]

The first thing for those who wish to increase the expressiveness of the language, is, as Fénelon suggests, to become fully conscious of its needs and requirements. If a word fails us to express something we are anxious to express, and after a careful search we are unable to find a fitting term, we should first of all make a note of that deficiency. These deficiencies will be of various kinds, according to the subjects which

[1] [*Un terme nous manque...court* We lack a term; we feel the need of one. Choose a pleasant sound, with no trace of ambiguity about it, which adapts itself to our language, and which is an easy way of making our speech more concise. Each individual first of all sees an opportunity for it; four or five people risk using it unassumingly in informal conversation; others repeat it because of its taste of novelty; and there it is in fashion. In this way a footpath newly begun across a field soon becomes the most well-trodden, when the old road is found to be uneven and not so short.]

Sainte-Beuve notes with regret that Fénelon's advice was not followed by the Academy. The democracy of words, like other forms of French democracy, like, he said, to be guided; but the Academy, by its pedantic conservatism, and its refusal to supply the needs which were continually arising, and must be satisfied, was allowing to fall from its hands the linguistic sceptre which the nation had conferred upon it. *Nouveaux Lundis*, vol. VI, p. 396.

principally interest us; but, judging by the deficiencies which various writers have noted in our speech, and by the terms which we are forced to borrow from other languages, it would seem that our modern vocabulary, with all its richness of expressive and descriptive terms, is still in many ways inadequate for our needs.

Of all the finer tools of thought the ones which are most useful, but most often lacking, are names of a comprehensive kind to describe things which possess some common property—abstract terms of wide classification which will enable us to think of the whole set of objects which possess certain qualities in common. Thus, as we have seen, comprehensive terms which will include everything that produces a poetical, or an aesthetic effect, are lacking in our language; and, until the word 'scientist' was deliberately created, we had no general term to describe all those who were devoting themselves to the study of the various sciences. A word, for instance, as the late Dr. Bradley pointed out in one of our Tracts,[1] is still lacking, in English at least, that can correctly be used as a general designation for a member of the healing profession, since the names physician and doctor do not include surgeons; the old word *leech*, which our ancestors possessed, has been lost to our language, owing to the use for the bloodsucking animal with the same name.

To describe without deprecation those intellectual members of the community who are ridiculed in America by the appellation of 'highbrows', we are forced to use the unassimilated Russian word *intelligentsia*; but the absence in our vocabulary of terms of this comprehensive kind is made evident in a striking manner by the fact that we possess no inclusive denominations for the citizens of the British Empire or of the United States of America. Another and most serious deficiency of this kind may be noted. Perhaps the most fundamental antagonism in modern political thought—the divergence of ideals which radically divides us into classes opposed to each other, is the antagonism between the ideal of 'qualitative' or 'quantitative' civilization; between those who would subordinate everything to the ideal of intensive culture, and those who are willing, for the sake of spreading education and enlightenment, to sacrifice, if necessary, their rarer and more exquisite manifestations. But for divergence of ideals we possess no available designation; the forces, thus fundamentally opposed, are armies which fight each other without battle-cries or names.

The supply of words to describe ways of thought and feeling is

[1] Tract IV, p. 33.

inadequate, as we have seen, in every language; that there are many gaps in this department of our English vocabulary is shown by the way we have to eke it out with words borrowed from the French. This poverty may be attributed perhaps to a certain practical and moralistic quality of the English mind, which tends to judge emotions more by their consequences than by their qualities, and to give them imputing rather than designating names. If we compare, for instance, the shades of meaning between our word 'malice' and the French *malice*, our 'intoxication' and the French *ivresse*, it will be seen how much fairer the French terms are in their power of naming things without suggesting disapproval. Even words which are used at first to describe the finer ways of thought or feeling are apt, as we have seen with regard to the word 'curiosity', to become narrowed and degraded in their meaning.[1] One of the greatest needs therefore of our vocabulary is a set of terms to describe ways of feelings and attitudes of mind by their intrinsic qualities; we need to 'de-moralize' our vocabulary of sentiments and emotions, to free it from moral implications, and enrich it with disinterested words which will do justice to our emotions by denoting their real nature,—what they are as we feel them—rather than their possible consequences of a disadvantageous kind.

Once a deficiency in the language has been noted—the need for a new tool of thought, of a new term to express some necessary meaning—the existing vocabulary should be first explored to see if a term cannot be found which may be made to serve this purpose. We may discover perhaps an old word which has fallen out of use, but which may be profitably revived; or there may be one of a pair of synonyms which can be differentiated and appropriated to this necessary meaning. Or a writer may find among the great treasure-house of dialectal words a happy and vivid expression which he may adopt and authorize by his usage.[2] But if no word of native formation is at hand, he may find a

[1] Another instance of this kind is the word *sentimental*, which was employed, when it first appeared in the eighteenth century, with reference to a refined and elevated way of feeling, but which we can no longer use, as the French, who borrowed it from us, can use it, in a neutral or laudatory sense—as when Barrès, for instance, writes of a *sentimentalité très—fine* [very refined sentimentality], or the poet Albert Samain describes the nightingale as

L'oiseau sentimental,
L'oiseau, triste et divin, que les ombres suscitent.

[That sentimental bird, That bird, sad and divine, that the shades create.]

[2] The following quotation, in which use is made of a popular word, apparently of Irish origin, the word *fetch*, meaning the apparition, double or wraith of a living person, will serve as an instance of the happy adoption of a dialect word. 'One great advantage of

term in some foreign language which expresses the required meaning, and to which he can give an English shape and spelling.[1]

If, however, no native term presents itself, and no foreign word that he can adopt and naturalize for his purpose, our writer in search of a word should ask himself whether it may not be possible to coin himself the term he needs. Word-coinage is, after all, no crime; many of our greatest writers in the past have greatly enriched the language by their new formations; it is possible that he may possess, like them, the word-creating faculty; his suggestions can do no harm, and if they happen to win acceptance, they may prove to be a real benefit to the language. The creation of a new and needed word is, after all, much more than a mere linguistic innovation; by giving precision to the meaning it expresses, it adds emphasis and importance to that meaning, and increases its value for us and its power.

We all hate new words; I myself hate them as much as anybody. And yet new words are often needed; not only names for new phenomena, but finer tools for the more delicate discrimination of our thoughts and feelings. It is only by a more liberal attitude on the part of writers of good books and their readers, that these wants can be supplied. Good writers should experiment with language, and their readers should try to overcome their blind hatred of linguistic innovation, and attempt to judge these experiments on their merits. If they are vivid and expressive terms, which supply some deficiency in our speech, we should welcome them into our vocabulary, and do our best, as Fénelon suggested, to make them current and acceptable. For new words, as Ben Jonson

writing over other professions is that it keeps the wits keen and the sensibilities alive. But later on a terrible temptation assails the writer. He begins to write from the semi-conscious mechanical part of his mind. A kind of ghost, or fetch, guards his pen when he sits down to write. His style improves at first and the pen travels nine times as fast. But it is not the man himself who is writing; the fetch cannot learn anything new, no fresh wind of life ever visits his imagination. The author becomes a marvellous old hurdy-gurdy, his habitual rhythms dominating his emotions, whatever his subject. There are many of them, aren't there—grinding away, grinding away? Look out when that time comes.' Desmond MacCarthy in the *New Statesman* (15 Oct. 1927).

[1] Most French and Italian words can be easily naturalized, often with little or no change in their spelling. Words like *rôle*, *régime*, *débâcle*, only need to drop their accents; *nuance*, *garage*, *provenance*, &c., require no more than to be pronounced as English words. Others, however, are more recalcitrant to assimilation: *ennui* has been familiar to us for more than two hundred years, but still wears its foreign garb, and a more recent borrowing, the useful word *milieu*, seems equally intractable. Although we have assimilated a few German compound words like *Kindergarten* and *Meerschaum*, such compounds seem as a rule incapable of assimilation. They have been, however, sometimes translated; thus *einseitig* became 'one-sided', and *Zeitgeist* appears as 'Time-spirit' in Carlyle's writings. 'World-outlook' has been recently suggested for *Weltanschauung*.

pointed out, are 'somewhat hard before they be softened with use. A man coins not a new word without some peril and less fruit; for if it happen to be received, the praise is but moderate; if refused, the scorn is assured. Yet', Ben Jonson adds (and I cannot end this paper with a more appropriate quotation), 'we must adventure; for things at first hard and rough, are by use made tender and gentle. It is an honest error that is committed, following great chiefs.'

10

EDWARD SAPIR

(1884–1939)

Sapir was Professor of Anthropology and General Linguistics at Yale. His work on language displays great attention to detail, with a wealth of comparative information from different languages (especially those of the American Indians); but he was also aware of unifying principles and patterns underlying the raw linguistic material he had accumulated, and he formulated a number of fundamental theoretical notions, many of which are outlined in the present article. Sapir himself did relatively little work on English as such, but his ideas have since been a stimulus to many English-language specialists. His book, *Language*, written in 1921, remains one of the best introductions to the subject.

'Language'

(*Encyclopedia of the Social Sciences*, vol. IX, 1933)

The gift of speech and a well ordered language are characteristic of every known group of human beings. No tribe has ever been found which is without language and all statements to the contrary may be dismissed as mere folklore. There seems to be no warrant whatever for the statement which is sometimes made that there are certain peoples whose vocabulary is so limited that they cannot get on without the supplementary use of gesture, so that intelligible communication between members of such a group becomes impossible in the dark. The truth of the matter is that language is an essentially perfect means of expression and communication among every known people. Of all aspects of culture it is a fair guess that language was the first to receive a highly developed form and that its essential perfection is a prerequisite to the development of culture as a whole.

There are some general characteristics which apply to all languages, living or extinct, written or unwritten. In the first place language is primarily a system of phonetic symbols for the expression of communicable thought and feeling. In other words, the symbols of language are differentiated products of the vocal behavior which is associated with the larynx of the higher mammals. As a mere matter of theory it is conceivable that something like a linguistic structure could have been evolved out of gesture or other forms of bodily behavior. The fact that at an advanced stage in the history of the human race writing emerged in close imitation of the patterns of spoken language proves that language as a purely instrumental and logical device is not dependent on the use of articulate sounds. Nevertheless, the actual history of man and a wealth of anthropological evidence indicate with overwhelming certainty that phonetic language takes precedence over all other kinds of communicative symbolism, which are by comparison either substitutive, like writing, or merely supplementary, like the gesture accompanying speech. The speech apparatus which is used in the articulation of language is the same for all known peoples. It consists of the larynx, with its delicately adjustable glottal chords, the nose, the tongue, the hard and soft palate, the teeth and the lips. While the original impulses leading to speech may be thought of as localized in the larynx, the finer phonetic articulations are due chiefly to the muscular activity of the tongue, an organ whose primary function has of course nothing whatever to do with sound production but which in actual speech behavior is indispensable for the development of emotionally expressive sound into what we call language. It is so indispensable in fact that one of the most common terms for language or speech is 'tongue.' Language is thus not a simple biological function even as regards the simple matter of sound production, for primary laryngeal patterns of behavior have had to be completely overhauled by the interference of lingual, labial and nasal modifications before a 'speech organ' was ready for work. Perhaps it is because this speech organ is a diffused and secondary network of physiological activities which do not correspond to the primary functions of the organs involved that language has been enabled to free itself from direct bodily expressiveness.

Not only are all languages phonetic in character; they are also 'phonemic.' Between the articulation of the voice into the phonetic sequence, which is immediately audible as a mere sensation, and the complicated patterning of phonetic sequences into such symbolically significant entities as words, phrases and sentences there is a very interesting process of phonetic selection and generalization which is easily overlooked but which is crucial for the development of the specifically symbolic aspect of language. Language is not merely articulated sound; its significant structure is dependent upon the unconscious selection of a fixed number of 'phonetic stations,' or sound units. These are in actual behavior individually modifiable; but the essential point is that through the unconscious selection of sounds as phonemes definite psychological barriers are erected between various phonetic stations, so that speech ceases to be an expressive flow of sound and becomes a symbolic composition with limited materials or units. The analogy with musical theory seems quite fair. Even the most resplendent and dynamic symphony is built up of tangibly distinct musical entities or notes which in the physical world flow into each other in an indefinite continuum but which in the world of aesthetic composition and appreciation are definitely bounded off against each other, so that they may enter into an intricate mathematics of significant relationships. The phonemes of a language are in principle a distinct system peculiar to the given language, and its words must be made up, in unconscious theory if not always in actualized behavior, of these phonemes. Languages differ very widely in their phonemic structure. But whatever the details of these structures may be, the important fact remains that there is no known language which has not a perfectly definite phonemic system. The difference between a sound and a phoneme can be illustrated by a simple example in English. If the word matter is pronounced in a slovenly fashion, as in the phrase 'What's the matter?' the *t* sound, not being pronounced with the full energy required to bring out its proper physical characteristics, tends to slip into a *d*. Nevertheless, this phonetic *d* will not be felt as a functional *d* but as a variety of *t* of a particular type of expressiveness. Obviously the functional relation between the proper *t* sound of such a word as matter and its *d* variant is quite other than the relation of the *t* of such a word as town and the *d* of down. In every known language it is possible to distinguish merely phonetic variations, whether expressive or not, from symbolically functional ones of a phonemic order.

In all known languages phonemes are built up into distinct and arbitrary sequences which are at once recognized by the speakers as meaningful symbols of reference. In English, for instance, the sequence *g* plus *o* in the word go is an unanalyzable unit and the meaning attaching to the symbol cannot be derived by relating to each other values which might be imputed to the *g* and to the *o* independently. In other words, while the mechanical functional units of language are phonemes, the true units of language as symbolism are conventional groupings of such phonemes. The size of these units and the laws of their mechanical structure vary widely in the different languages and their limiting conditions may be said to constitute the phonemic mechanics, or phonology, of a particular language. But the fundamental theory of sound symbolism remains the same everywhere. The formal behavior of the irreducible symbol also varies within wide limits in the languages of the world. Such a unit may be either a complete word, as in the English example already given, or a significant element, like the suffix *ness* of goodness. Between the meaningful and unanalyzable word or word element and the integrated meaning of continuous discourse lies the whole complicated field of the formal procedures which are intuitively employed by the speakers of a language in order to build up aesthetically and functionally satisfying symbol sequences out of the theoretically isolable units. These procedures constitute grammar, which may be defined as the sum total of formal economies intuitively recognized by the speakers of a language. There seem to be no types of cultural patterns which vary more surprisingly and with a greater exuberance of detail than the morphologies of the known languages. In spite of endless differences of detail, however, it may justly be said that all grammars have the same degree of fixity. One language may be more complex or difficult grammatically than another, but there is no meaning whatever in the statement which is sometimes made that one language is more grammatical, or form bound, than another. Our rationalizations of the structure of our own language lead to a self-consciousness of speech and of academic discipline which are of course interesting psychological and social phenomena in themselves but have very little to do with the question of form in language.

Besides these general formal characteristics language has certain psychological qualities which make it peculiarly important for the student of social science. In the first place, language is felt to be a perfect symbolic system, in a perfectly homogeneous medium, for the handling of all references and meanings that a given culture is capable of, whether these be in the form of actual communications or in that of such ideal substitutes of communication as thinking. The content of every culture is expressible in its language and there are no linguistic materials whether as to content or form which are not felt to symbolize actual meanings, whatever may be the attitude of those who belong to other cultures. New cultural experiences frequently make it necessary to enlarge the resources of a language, but such enlargement is never an arbitrary addition to the materials and forms already present; it is merely a further application of principles already in use and in many cases little more than a metaphorical extension of old terms and meanings. It is highly important to realize that once the form of a language is established it can discover meanings for its speakers which are not simply traceable to the given quality of experience itself but must be explained to a large extent as the projection of potential meanings into the raw material of experience. If a man who has never seen more than a single elephant in the course of his life nevertheless speaks without the slightest hesitation of ten elephants or a million elephants or a herd of elephants or of elephants walking two by two or three by three or of generations of elephants, it is obvious that language has the power to analyze experience into theoretically dissociable elements and to create that world of the potential intergrading with the actual which enables human beings to transcend the immediately given in their individual experiences and to join in a larger common understanding. This common understanding constitutes culture, which cannot be adequately defined by a description of those more colorful patterns of behavior in society which lie open to observation. Language is heuristic, not merely in the simple sense which this example suggests but in the much more far reaching sense that its forms predetermine for us certain modes of observation and interpretation. This means of course that as our scientific experience grows we must learn to fight the implications of language. 'The grass waves in the wind' is shown by its linguistic form to be a member of the same relational class of experiences as 'The man works in the house.' As an interim solution of the problem of expressing the experience referred to in this sentence it is clear that the language has proved useful, for it has made significant use of certain symbols of conceptual relation, such as agency and location. If we feel the sentence to be poetic or metaphorical, it is largely because other more complex types of experience with their appropriate symbolisms of reference enable us to reinterpret the situation and to say, for instance, 'The grass is waved by the wind' or 'The wind causes the grass to wave.' The point is that no matter how sophisticated our modes of interpretation become, we never really get beyond the projection and continuous transfer of relations suggested by the forms of our speech. After all, to say that 'Friction causes such and such a result' is not very different from saying that 'The grass waves in the wind.' Language is at one and the same time helping and retarding us in our exploration of experience, and the details of these processes of help and hindrance are deposited in the subtler meanings of different cultures.

A further psychological characteristic of language is the fact that while it may be looked upon as a symbolic system which reports or refers to or otherwise substitutes for direct experience, it does not as a matter of actual behavior stand apart from or run parallel to direct experience but completely interpenetrates with it. This is indicated by the widespread feeling, particularly among primitive people, of that virtual identity or close correspondence of word and thing which leads to the magic of spells. On our own level it is generally difficult to make a complete divorce between objective reality and our linguistic symbols of reference to it; and things, qualities and events are on the whole felt to be what they are called. For the normal person every experience, real or potential, is saturated with verbalism. This explains why so many lovers of nature, for instance, do not feel that they are truly in touch with it until they have mastered the names of a great many flowers and trees, as though the primary world of reality were a verbal one and as though one could not get close to nature unless one first mastered the terminology which somehow magically expresses it. It is this constant interplay between language and experience which removes language from the cold status of such purely and simply symbolic systems as mathematical symbolism or flag signaling. This interpenetration is not only an intimate associative fact; it is also a contextual one. It is important to realize that language may not only refer to experience or even mold, interpret and discover experience but that it also substitutes for it in the sense that in those sequences of interpersonal behavior which form the greater part of our daily lives speech and action supplement each other and do each other's work in a web of unbroken pattern. If one says to me 'Lend me a dollar,' I may hand over the money without a word or I may give it with an accompanying 'Here it is' or I may say 'I haven't got it. I'll give it to you tomorrow.' Each of these responses is structurally equivalent, if one thinks of the larger behavior pattern. It is clear that if language is in its analyzed form a symbolic system of reference it is far from being merely that if we consider the psychological part that it plays in continuous behavior. The reason for this almost unique position of intimacy which language holds among all known symbolisms is probably the fact that it is learned in the earliest years of childhood.

It is because it is learned early and piecemeal, in constant association with the color and the requirements of actual contexts, that language in spite of its quasi-mathematical form is rarely a purely referential organization. It tends to be so only in scientific discourse, and even there it may be seriously doubted whether the ideal of pure reference is ever attained by language. Ordinary speech is directly expressive and the purely formal patterns of sounds, words, grammatical forms, phrases and sentences are always to be thought of as compounded with intended or unintended symbolisms of expression, if they are to be understood fully from the standpoint of behavior. The choice of words in a particular context may convey the opposite of what they mean on the surface. The same external message is differently interpreted according to whether the speaker has this or that psychological status in his personal relations, or whether such primary expressions as those of affection or anger or fear may inform the spoken words with a significance which completely transcends their normal value. On the whole, however, there is no danger that the expressive character of language will be overlooked. It is too obvious a fact to call for much emphasis. What is often overlooked and is, as a matter of fact, not altogether easy to understand is that the quasi-mathematical patterns, as we have called them, of the grammarian's language, unreal as these are in a contextual sense, have nevertheless a tremendous intuitional vitality; and that these patterns, never divorced in experience from the expressive ones, are nevertheless easily separated from them by the normal individual. The fact that almost any word or phrase can be made to take on an infinite variety of meanings seems to indicate that in all language behavior there are intertwined in enormously complex patterns isolable patterns of two distinct orders. These may be roughly defined as patterns of reference and patterns of expression.

That language is a perfect symbolism of experience, that in the actual contexts of behavior it cannot be divorced from action and that it is the carrier of an infinitely nuanced expressiveness are universally valid psychological facts. There is a fourth general psychological peculiarity which applies more particularly to the languages of sophisticated peoples. This is the fact that the referential form systems which are actualized in language behavior do not need speech in its literal sense in order to preserve their substantial integrity. The history of writing is in essence the long attempt to develop an independent symbolism on the basis of graphic representation, followed by the slow and begrudging realization that spoken language is a more powerful symbolism than any graphic one can possibly be and that true progress in the art of writing lay in the virtual abandonment of the principle with which it originally started. Effective systems of writing, whether alphabetic or not, are more or less exact transfers of speech. The original language system may maintain itself in other and remoter transfers, one of the best examples of these being the Morse telegraph code. It is a very interesting fact that the principle of linguistic transfer is not entirely absent even among the unlettered peoples of the world. Some at least of the drum signal and horn signal systems of the west African natives are in principle transfers of the organizations of speech, often in minute phonetic detail.

Many attempts have been made to unravel the origin of language but most of these are hardly more than exercises of the speculative imagination. Linguists as a whole have lost interest in the problem and this for two reasons. In the first place, it has come to be realized that there exist no truly primitive languages in a psychological sense, that modern researches in archaeology have indefinitely extended the time of man's cultural past and that it is therefore vain to go much beyond the perspective opened up by the study of actual languages. In the second place, our knowledge of psychology, particularly of the symbolic processes in general, is not felt to be sound enough or far reaching enough to help materially with the problem of the emergence of speech. It is probable that the origin of language is not a problem that can be solved out of the resources of linguistics alone but that it is essentially a particular case of a much wider problem of the genesis of symbolic behavior and of the specialization of such behavior in the laryngeal region, which may be presumed to have had only expressive functions to begin with. Perhaps a close study of the behavior of very young children under controlled conditions may provide some valuable hints, but it seems dangerous to reason from such experiments to the behavior of precultural man. It is more likely that the kinds of studies which are now in progress of the behavior of the higher apes will help supply some idea of the genesis of speech.

The most popular earlier theories were the interjectional and onomatopoetic theories. The former derived speech from involuntary cries of an expressive nature, while the latter maintained that the words of actual language are conventionalized forms of imitation of the sounds of nature. Both of these theories suffer from two fatal defects. While it is true that both interjectional and onomatopoetic elements are found in most languages, they are always relatively unimportant and tend to contrast somewhat with the more normal materials of language. The very fact that they are constantly being formed anew seems to indicate that they belong rather to the directly expressive layer of speech which intercrosses with the main level of referential symbolism. The second difficulty is even more serious. The essential problem of the origin of speech is not to attempt to discover the kinds of vocal elements which constitute the historical nucleus of language. It is rather to point out how vocal articulations of any sort could become dissociated from their original expressive value. About all that can be said at present is that while speech as a finished organization is a distinctly human achievement, its roots probably lie in the power of the higher apes to solve specific problems by abstracting general forms or schemata from the details of given situations; that the habit of interpreting certain selected elements in a situation as signs of a desired total one gradually led in early man to a dim feeling for symbolism; and that in the long run and for reasons which can hardly be guessed at the elements of experience which were most often interpreted in a symbolic sense came to be the largely useless or supplementary vocal behavior that must have often attended significant action. According to this point of view language is not so much directly developed out of vocal expression as it is an actualization in terms of vocal expression of the tendency to master reality, not by direct and ad hoc handling of its elements but by the reduction of experience to familiar forms. Vocal expression is only superficially the same as language. The tendency to derive speech from emotional expression has not led to anything tangible in the way of scientific theory and the attempt must now be made to see in language the slowly evolved product of a peculiar technique or tendency which may be called the symbolic one, and to see the relatively meaningless or incomplete part as a sign of the whole. Language then is what it is essentially not because of its admirable expressive power but in spite of it. Speech as behavior is a wonderfully complex blend of two pattern systems, the symbolic and the expressive, neither of which could have developed to its present perfection without the interference of the other.

It is difficult to see adequately the functions of language, because it is so deeply rooted in the whole of human behavior that it may be suspected that there is little in the functional side of our conscious behavior in which language does not play its part. The primary function of language is generally said to be communication. There can be no quarrel with this so long as it is distinctly understood that there may be effective communication without overt speech and that language is highly relevant to situations which are not obviously of a communicative sort. To say that thought, which is hardly possible in any sustained sense without the symbolic organization brought by language, is that form of communication in which the speaker and the person addressed are identified in one person is not far from begging the question. The autistic speech of children seems to show that the purely communicative aspect of language has been exaggerated. It is best to admit that language is primarily a vocal actualization of the tendency to see reality symbolically, that it is precisely this quality which renders it a fit instrument for communication and that it is in the actual give and take of social intercourse that it has been complicated and refined into the form in which it is known today. Besides the very general function which language fulfils in the spheres of thought, communication and expression which are implicit in its very nature there may be pointed out a number of special derivatives of these which are of particular interest to students of society.

Language is a great force of socialization, probably the greatest that exists. By this is meant not merely the obvious fact that significant social intercourse is hardly possible without language but that the mere fact of a common speech serves as a peculiarly potent symbol of the social solidarity of those who speak the language. The psychological significance of this goes far beyond the association of particular languages with nationalities, political entities or smaller local groups. In between the recognized dialect or language as a whole and the individualized speech of a given individual lies a kind of linguistic unit which is not often discussed by the linguist but which is of the greatest importance to social psychology. This is the subform of a language which is current among a group of people who are held together by ties of common interest. Such a group may be a family, the undergraduates of a college, a labor union, the underworld in a large city, the members of a club, a group of four or five friends who hold together through life in spite of differences of professional interest, and untold thousands of other kinds of groups. Each of these tends to develop peculiarities of speech which have the symbolic function of somehow distinguishing the group from the larger group into which its members might be too completely absorbed. The complete absence of linguistic indices of such small groups is obscurely felt as a defect or sign of emotional poverty. Within the confines of a particular family, for instance, the name Georgy, having once been mispronounced Doody in childhood, may take on the latter form forever after; and this unofficial pronunciation of a familiar name as applied to a particular person becomes a very important symbol indeed of the solidarity of a particular family and of the continuance of the sentiment that keeps its members together. A stranger cannot lightly take on the privilege of saying Doody if the members of the family feel that he is not entitled to go beyond the degree of familiarity symbolized by the use of Georgy or George. Again, no one is entitled to say 'trig' or 'math' who has not gone through certain familiar and painful experiences as a high school or undergraduate student. The use of such words at once declares the speaker a member of an unorganized but psychologically real group. A self-made mathematician has hardly the right to use the word 'math' in referring to his own interests because the student overtones of the word do not properly apply to him. The extraordinary importance of minute linguistic differences for the symbolization of psychologically real as contrasted with politically or sociologically official groups is intuitively felt by most people. 'He talks like us' is equivalent to saying 'He is one of us.'

There is another important sense in which language is a socializer beyond its literal use as a means of communication. This is in the establishment of rapport between the members of a physical group, such as a house party. It is not what is said that matters so much as that something is said. Particularly where cultural understandings of an intimate sort are somewhat lacking among the members of a physical group it is felt to be important that the lack be made good by a constant supply of small talk. This caressing or reassuring quality of speech in general, even where no one has anything of moment to communicate, reminds us how much more language is than a mere technique of communication. Nothing better shows how completely the life of man as an animal made over by culture is dominated by the verbal substitutes for the physical world.

The use of language in cultural accumulation and historical transmission is obvious and important. This applies not only to sophisticated levels but to primitive ones as well. A great deal of the cultural stock in trade of a primitive society is presented in a more or less well defined linguistic form. Proverbs, medicine formulae, standardized prayers, folk tales, standardized speeches, song texts, genealogies, are some of the more overt forms which language takes as a culture preserving instrument. The pragmatic ideal of education, which aims to reduce the influence of standardized lore to a minimum and to get the individual to educate himself through as direct a contact as possible with the facts of his environment, is certainly not realized among the primitives, who are often as word bound as the humanistic tradition itself. Few cultures perhaps have gone to the length of the classical Chinese culture or of rabbinical Jewish culture in making the word do duty for the thing or the personal experience as the ultimate unit of reality. Modern civilization as a whole, with its schools, its libraries and its endless stores of knowledge, opinion and sentiment stored up in verbalized form, would be unthinkable without language made eternal as document. On the whole, we probably tend to exaggerate the differences between 'high' and 'low' cultures or saturated and emergent cultures in the matter of traditionally conserved verbal authority. The enormous differences that seem to exist are rather differences in the outward form and content of the cultures themselves than in the psychological relation which obtains between the individual and his culture.

In spite of the fact that language acts as a socializing and uniformizing force it is at the same time the most potent single known factor for the growth of individuality. The fundamental quality of one's voice, the phonetic patterns of speech, the speed and relative smoothness of articulation, the length and build of the sentences, the character and range of the vocabulary, the stylistic consistency of the words used, the readiness with which words respond to the requirements of the social environment, in particular the suitability of one's language to the language habits of the person addressed—all these are so many complex indicators of the personality. 'Actions speak louder than words' may be an excellent maxim from the pragmatic point of view but betrays little insight into the nature of speech. The language habits of people are by no means irrelevant as unconscious indicators of the more important traits of their personalities, and the folk is psychologically wiser than the adage in paying a great deal of attention willingly or not to the psychological significance of a man's language. The normal person is never convinced by the mere content of speech but is very sensitive to many of the implications of language behavior, however feebly (if at all) these may have been consciously analyzed. All in all, it is not too much to say that one of the really important functions of language is to be constantly declaring to society the psychological place held by all of its members. Besides this more general type of personality expression or fulfilment there is to be kept in mind the important role which language plays as a substitutive means of expression for those individuals who have a greater than normal difficulty in adjusting themselves to the environment in terms of primary action patterns. Even in the most primitive cultures the strategic word is likely to be more powerful than the direct blow. It is unwise to speak too blithely of 'mere' words, for to do so may be to imperil the value and perhaps the very existence of civilization and personality.

The languages of the world may be classified either structurally or genetically. An adequate structural analysis is an intricate matter and no classification seems to have been suggested which does justice to the bewildering variety of known forms. It is useful to recognize three distinct criteria of classification: the relative degree of synthesis or elaboration of the words of the language; the degree to which the various parts of a word are welded together; and the extent to which the fundamental relational concepts of the language are directly expressed as such. As regards synthesis languages range all the way from the isolating type, in which the single word is essentially unanalyzable, to the type represented by many American Indian languages, in which the single word is functionally often the equivalent of a sentence with many concrete references that would in most languages require the use of a number of words. Four stages of synthesis may be conveniently recognized; the isolating type, the weakly synthetic type, the fully synthetic type and the polysynthetic type. The classical example of the first type is Chinese, which does not allow the words of the language to be modified by internal changes or the addition of prefixed or suffixed elements to express such concepts as those of number, tense, mode, case relation and the like. This seems to be one of the more uncommon types of language and is best represented by a number of languages in eastern Asia. Besides Chinese itself Siamese, Burmese, modern Tibetan, Annamite and Khmer, or Cambodian, may be given as examples. The older view, which regarded such languages as representing a peculiarly primitive stage in the evolution of language, may now be dismissed as antiquated. All evidence points to the contrary hypothesis that such languages are the logically extreme analytic developments of more synthetic languages which because of processes of phonetic disintegration have had to reexpress by analytical means combinations of ideas originally expressed within the framework of the single word. The weakly synthetic type of language is best represented by the most familiar modern languages of Europe, such as English, French, Spanish, Italian, German, Dutch and Danish. Such languages modify words to some extent but have only a moderate formal elaboration of the word. The plural formations of English and French, for instance, are relatively simple and the tense and modal systems of all the languages of this type tend to use analytic methods as supplementary to the older synthetic one. The third group of languages is represented by such languages as Arabic and earlier Indo-European languages, like Sanskrit, Latin and Greek. These are all languages of great formal complexity, in which classificatory ideas, such as sex gender, number, case relations, tense and mood, are expressed with considerable nicety and in a great variety of ways. Because of the rich formal implications of the single word the sentence tends not to be so highly energized and ordered as in the first mentioned types. Lastly, the polysynthetic languages add to the formal complexity of the treatment of fundamental relational ideas the power to arrange a number of logically distinct, concrete ideas into an ordered whole within the confines of a single word. Eskimo and Algonquin are classical examples of this type.

From the standpoint of the mechanical cohesiveness with which the elements of words are united languages may be conveniently grouped into four types. The first of these, in which there is no such process of combination, is the isolating type already referred to. To the second group of languages belong all those in which the word can be adequately analyzed into a mechanical sum of elements, each of which has its more or less clearly established meaning and each of which is regularly used in all other words into which the associated notion enters. These are the so-called agglutinative languages. The majority of languages seem to use the agglutinative technique, which has the great advantage of combining logical analysis with economy of means. The Altaic languages, of which Turkish is a good example, and the Bantu languages of Africa are agglutinative in form. In the third type, the so-called inflective languages, the degree of union between the radical element or stem of the word and the modifying prefixes or suffixes is greater than in the agglutinative languages, so that it becomes difficult in many cases to isolate the stem and set it off against the accreted elements. More important than this, however, is the fact that there is less of a one to one correspondence between the linguistic element and the notion referred to than in the agglutinative languages. In Latin, for instance, the notion of plurality is expressed in a great variety of ways which seem to have little phonetic connection with each other. For example, the final vowel or diphthong of *equi* (horses), *dona* (gifts), *mensae* (tables) and the final vowel and consonant of *hostes* (enemies) are functionally equivalent elements the distribution of which is dependent on purely formal and historical factors that have no logical relevance. Furthermore in the verb the notion of plurality is quite differently expressed, as in the last two consonants of *amant* (they love). It used to be fashionable to contrast in a favorable sense the 'chemical' qualities of such inflective languages as Latin and Greek with the soberly mechanical quality of such languages as Turkish. But these evaluations may now be dismissed as antiquated and subjective. They were obviously due to the fact that scholars who wrote in English, French and German were not above rationalizing the linguistic structures with which they were most familiar into a position of ideal advantage. As an offshoot of the inflective languages may be considered a fourth group, those in which the processes of welding, due to the operation of complex phonetic laws, have gone so far as to result in the creation of patterns of internal change of the nuclear elements of speech. Such familiar English examples as the words sing, sang, sung, song will serve to give some idea of the nature of these structures, which may be termed symbolistic. The kinds of internal change which may be recognized are changes in vocalic quality, changes in consonants, changes in quantity, various types of reduplication or repetition, changes in stress accent and, as in Chinese and many African languages, changes in pitch. The classical example of this type of language is Arabic, in which as in the other Semitic languages nuclear meanings are expressed by sequences of consonants, which have, however, to be connected by significant vowels whose sequence patterns establish fixed functions independent of the meanings conveyed by the consonantal framework.

Elaboration and technique of word analysis are perhaps of less logical and psychological significance than the selection and treatment of fundamental relational concepts for grammatical treatment. It would be very difficult, however, to devise a satisfactory conceptual classification of languages because of the extraordinary diversity of the concepts and classifications of ideas which are illustrated in linguistic form. In the Indo-European and Semitic languages, for instance, noun classification on the basis of gender is a vital principle of structure; but in most of the other languages of the world this principle is absent, although other methods of noun classification are found. Again, tense or case relations may be formally important in one language, for example, Latin, but of relatively little grammatical importance in another, although the logical references implied by such forms must naturally be taken care of in the economy of the language, as, for instance, by the use of specific words within the framework of the sentence. Perhaps the most fundamental conceptual basis of classification is that of the expression of fundamental syntactic relations as such versus their expression in necessary combination with notions of a concrete order. In Latin, for example, the notion of the subject of a predicate is never purely expressed in a formal sense, because there is no distinctive symbol for this relation. It is impossible to render it without at the same time defining the number and gender of the subject of the sentence. There are languages, however, in which syntactic relations are expressed purely, without admixture of implications of a non-relational sort. We may speak therefore of pure relational languages as contrasted with mixed relational languages. Most of the languages with which we are familiar belong to the latter category. It goes without saying that such a conceptual classification has no direct relation to the other two types of classification which we have mentioned.

The genetic classification of languages is one which attempts to arrange the languages of the world in groups and subgroups in accordance with the main lines of historical connection, which can be worked out on the basis either of documentary evidence or of a careful comparison of the languages studied. Because of the far reaching effect of slow phonetic changes and of other causes languages which were originally nothing but dialects of the same form of speech have diverged so widely that it is not apparent that they are but specialized developments of a single prototype. An enormous amount of work has been done in the genetic classification and subclassification of the languages of the world, but very many problems still await research and solution. At the present time it is known definitely that there are certain very large linguistic groups, or families, as they are often called, the members of which may, roughly speaking, be looked upon as lineally descended from languages which can be theoretically reconstructed in their main phonetic and structural outlines. It is obvious, however, that languages may so diverge as to leave little trace of their original relationship. It is therefore very dangerous to assume that languages are not at last analysis divergent members of a single genetic group merely because the evidence is negative. The only contrast that is legitimate is between languages known to be historically related and languages not known to be so related. Languages known to be related cannot be legitimately contrasted with languages known not to be related.

Because of the fact that languages have differentiated at different rates and because of the important effects of cultural diffusion, which have brought it about that strategically placed languages, such as Arabic, Latin and English, have spread over large parts of the earth at the expense of others, very varied conditions are found to prevail in regard to the distribution of linguistic families. In Europe, for instance, there are only two linguistic families of importance represented today, the Indo-European languages and the Ugro-Finnic languages, of which Finnish and Hungarian are examples. The Basque dialects of southern France and northern Spain are the survivors of another and apparently isolated group. On the other hand, in aboriginal America the linguistic differentiation is extreme and a surprisingly large number of essentially unrelated linguistic families must be recognized. Some of the families occupy very small areas, while others, such as the Algonquin and the Athabaskan languages of North America, are spread over a large territory. The technique of establishing linguistic families and of working out the precise relationship of the languages included in these families is too difficult to be gone into here. It suffices to say that random word comparisons are of little importance. Experience shows that very precise phonetic relations can be worked out between the languages of a group and that on the whole fundamental morphological features tend to preserve themselves over exceedingly long periods of time. Thus modern Lithuanian is in structure, vocabulary and, to a large extent, even phonemic pattern very much the kind of a language which must be assumed as the prototype for the Indo-European languages as a whole. In spite of the fact that structural classifications are in theory unrelated to genetic ones and in spite of the fact that languages can be shown to have influenced each other, not only in phonetics and vocabulary but also to an appreciable extent in structure, it is not often found that the languages of a genetic group exhibit utterly irreconcilable structures. Thus even English, which is one of the least conservative of Indo-European languages, has many far reaching points of structure in common with as remote a language as Sanskrit in contrast, say, to Basque or Finnish. Again, different as are Assyrian, modern Arabic and the Semitic languages of Abyssinia they exhibit numerous points of resemblance in phonetics, vocabulary and structure which set them off at once from, say, Turkish or the Negro languages of the Nile headwaters.

The complete rationale of linguistic change, involving as it does many of the most complex processes of psychology and sociology, has not yet been satisfactorily worked out, but there are a number of general processes that emerge with sufficient clarity. For practical purposes inherent changes may be distinguished from changes due to contact with other linguistic communities. There can be no hard line of division between these two groups of changes because every individual's language is a distinct psychological entity in itself, so that all inherent changes are likely at last analysis to be peculiarly remote or subtle forms of change due to contact. The distinction, however, has great practical value, all the more so as there is a tendency among anthropologists and sociologists to operate far too hastily with wholesale linguistic changes due to external ethnic and cultural influences. The enormous amount of study that has been lavished on the history of particular languages and groups of languages shows very clearly that the most powerful differentiating factors are not outside influences, as ordinarily understood, but rather the very slow but powerful unconscious changes in certain directions which seem to be implicit in the phonemic systems and morphologies of the languages themselves. These 'drifts' are powerfully conditioned by unconscious formal feelings and are made necessary by the inability of human beings to actualize ideal patterns in a permanently set fashion.

Linguistic changes may be analyzed into phonetic changes, changes in form and changes in vocabulary. Of these the phonetic changes seem to be the most important and the most removed from direct observation. The factors which lead to these phonetic changes are probably exceedingly complex and no doubt include the operation of obscure symbolisms which define the relation of various age groups to one another. Not all phonetic changes, however, can be explained in terms of social symbolism. It seems that many of them are due to the operation of unconscious economies in actualizing sounds or combinations of sounds. The most impressive thing about internal phonetic change is its high degree of regularity. It is this regularity, whatever its ultimate cause, that is more responsible than any other single factor for the enviable degree of exactness which linguistics has attained as a historical discipline. Changes in grammatical form often follow in the wake of destructive phonetic changes. In many cases it can be seen how irregularities produced by the disintegrating effect of phonetic change are ironed out by the analogical spread of more regular forms. The cumulative effect of these corrective changes is quite sensibly to modify the structure of the language in many details and sometimes even in its fundamental features. Changes in vocabulary are due to a great variety of causes, most of which are of a cultural rather than of a strictly linguistic nature. The too frequent use of a word, for instance, may reduce it to a commonplace term, so that it needs to be replaced by a new word. On the other hand, changes of attitude may make certain words with their traditional overtones of meaning unacceptable to the younger generation, so that they tend to become obsolete. Probably the most important single source of change in vocabulary is the creation of new words on analogies which have spread from a few specific words.

Of the linguistic changes due to the more obvious types of contact the one which seems to have played the most important part in the history of language is the 'borrowing' of words across linguistic frontiers. This borrowing naturally goes hand in hand with cultural diffusion. An analysis of the provenience of the words of a given language is frequently an important index of the direction of cultural influence. Our English vocabulary, for instance, is very richly stratified in a cultural sense. The various layers of early Latin, mediaeval French, humanistic Latin and Greek and modern French borrowings constitute a fairly accurate gauge of the time, extent and nature of the various foreign cultural influences which have helped to mold English civilization. The notable lack of German loan words in English until a very recent period, as contrasted with the large number of Italian words which were adopted at the time of the Renaissance and later, is again a historically significant fact. By the diffusion of culturally important words, such as those referring to art, literature, the church, military affairs, sport and business, there have grown up important transnational vocabularies which do something to combat the isolating effect of the large number of languages which are still spoken in the modern world. Such borrowings have taken place in all directions, but the number of truly important source languages is surprisingly small. Among the more important of them are Chinese, which has saturated the vocabularies of Korean, Japanese and Annamite; Sanskrit, whose influence on the cultural vocabulary of central Asia, India and Indo-China has been enormous; Arabic, Greek, Latin and French. English, Spanish and Italian have also been of great importance as agencies of cultural transmission, but their influence seems less far reaching than that of the languages mentioned above. The cultural influence of a language is not always in direct proportion to its intrinsic literary interest or to the cultural place which its speakers have held in the history of the world. For example, while Hebrew is the carrier of a peculiarly significant culture, actually it has not had as important an influence on other languages of Asia as Aramaic, a sister language of the Semitic stock.

The phonetic influence exerted by a foreign language may be very considerable, and there is a great deal of evidence to show that dialectic peculiarities have often originated as a result of the unconscious transfer of phonetic habits from the language in which one was brought up to that which has been adopted later in life. Apart, however, from such complete changes in speech is the remarkable fact that distinctive phonetic features tend to be distributed over wide areas regardless of the vocabularies and structures of the languages involved. One of the most striking examples of this type of distribution is found among the Indian languages of the Pacific coast of California, Oregon, Washington,

British Columbia and southern Alaska. Here are a large number of absolutely distinct languages, belonging to a number of genetically unrelated stocks, so far as we are able to tell, which nevertheless have many important and distinctive phonetic features in common. An analogous fact is the distribution of certain peculiar phonetic features in both the Slavic languages and the Ugro-Finnic languages, which are unrelated to them. Such processes of phonetic diffusion must be due to the influence exerted by bilingual speakers, who act as unconscious agents for the spread of phonetic habits over wide areas. Primitive man is not isolated, and bilingualism is probably as important a factor in the contact of primitive groups as it is on more sophisticated levels.

Opinions differ as to the importance of the purely morphological influence exerted by one language on another in contrast with the more external types of phonetic and lexical influence. Undoubtedly such influences must be taken into account, but so far they have not been shown to operate on any great scale. In spite of the centuries of contact, for instance, between Semitic and Indo-European languages we know of no language which is definitely a blend of the structures of these two stocks. Similarly, while Japanese is flooded with Chinese loan words, there seems to be no structural influence of the latter on the former. A type of influence which is neither one of vocabulary nor of linguistic form, in the ordinary sense of the word, and to which insufficient attention has so far been called, is that of meaning pattern. It is a remarkable fact of modern European culture, for instance, that while the actual terms used for certain ideas vary enormously from language to language, the range of significance of these equivalent terms tends to be very similar, so that to a large extent the vocabulary of one language tends to be a psychological and cultural translation of the vocabulary of another. A simple example of this sort would be the translation of such terms as Your Excellency to equivalent but etymologically unrelated terms in Russian. Another instance of this kind would be the interesting parallelism in nomenclature between the kinship terms of affinity in English, French and German. Such terms as *mother-in-law*, *belle-mère* and *Schwiegermutter* are not, strictly speaking, equivalent either as to etymology or literal meaning but they are patterned in exactly the same manner. Thus *mother-in-law* and *father-in-law* are parallel in nomenclature to *belle-mère* and *beau-père* and to *Schwiegermutter* and *Schwiegervater*. These terms clearly illustrate the diffusion of a lexical pattern which in turn probably expresses a growing feeling of the sentimental equivalence of blood relatives and relatives by marriage.

The importance of language as a whole for the definition, expression and transmission of culture is undoubted. The relevance of linguistic details, in both content and form, for the profounder understanding of culture is also clear. It does not follow, however, that there is a simple correspondence between the form of a language and the form of the culture of those who speak it. The tendency to see linguistic categories as directly expressive of overt cultural outlines, which seems to have come into fashion among certain sociologists and anthropologists, should be resisted as in no way warranted by the actual facts. There is no general correlation between cultural type and linguistic structure. So far as can be seen, isolating or agglutinative or inflective types of speech are possible on any level of civilization. Nor does the presence or absence of grammatical gender, for example, seem to have any relevance for the understanding of the social organization or religion or folklore of the associated peoples. If there were any such parallelism as has sometimes been maintained, it would be quite impossible to understand the rapidity with which culture diffuses in spite of profound linguistic differences between the borrowing and giving communities. The cultural significance of linguistic form, in other words, lies on a much more submerged level than on the overt one of definite cultural pattern. It is only very rarely, as a matter of fact, that it can be pointed out how a cultural trait has had some influence on the fundamental structure of a language. To a certain extent this lack of correspondence may be due to the fact that linguistic changes do not proceed at the same rate as most cultural changes, which are on the whole far more rapid. Short of yielding to another language which takes its place, linguistic organization, largely because it is unconscious, tends to maintain itself indefinitely and does not allow its fundamental formal categories to be seriously influenced by changing cultural needs. If the forms of culture and language were then in complete correspondence with one another, the nature of the processes making for linguistic and cultural changes respectively would soon bring about a lack of necessary correspondence. This is exactly what is found to be the case. Logically it is indefensible that the masculine, feminine and neuter genders of German and Russian should be allowed to continue their sway in the modern world; but any intellectualist attempt to weed out these unnecessary genders would obviously be fruitless, for the normal speaker does not actually feel the clash which the logician requires.

It is another matter when we pass from general form to the detailed content of a language. Vocabulary is a very sensitive index of the culture of a people and changes of meaning, loss of old words, the creation and borrowing of new ones are all dependent on the history of culture itself. Languages differ widely in the nature of their vocabularies. Distinctions which seem inevitable to us may be utterly ignored in languages which reflect an entirely different type of culture, while these in turn insist on distinctions which are all but unintelligible to us. Such differences of vocabulary go far beyond the names of cultural objects, such as arrow point, coat of armor or gunboat. They apply just as well to the mental world. It would be difficult in some languages, for instance, to express the distinction which we feel between 'to kill' and 'to murder' for the simple reason that the underlying legal philosophy which determines our use of these words does not seem natural to all societies. Abstract terms, which are so necessary to our thinking, may be infrequent in a language whose speakers formulate their behavior on more pragmatic lines. On the other hand, the question of the presence or absence of abstract nouns may be bound up with the fundamental form of the language; and there exist a large number of primitive languages whose structure allows of the very ready creation and use of abstract nouns of quality or action.

There are many language patterns of a special sort which are of interest to the social scientist. One of these is the tendency to create tabus for certain words or names. A very widespread custom among primitive peoples, for instance, is the tabu which is placed not only on the use of the name of a person recently deceased but of any word that is etymologically connected in the feeling of the speakers with such a name. This means that ideas have often to be expressed by circumlocutions or that terms must be borrowed from neighboring dialects. Sometimes certain names or words are too holy to be pronounced except under very special conditions, and curious patterns of behavior develop which are designed to prevent one from making use of such interdicted terms. An example of this is the Jewish custom of pronouncing the Hebrew name for God, not as Yahwe or Jehovah but as Adonai, My Lord. Such customs seem strange to us but equally strange to many primitive communities would be our extraordinary reluctance to pronounce obscene words under normal social conditions. Another class of special linguistic phenomena is the use of esoteric language devices, such as passwords or technical terminologies for ceremonial attitudes or practises. Among the Eskimo, for example, the medicine man has a peculiar vocabulary which is not understood by those who are not members of his guild. Special dialectic forms or otherwise peculiar linguistic patterns are common among primitive peoples for the texts of songs. Sometimes, as in Melanesia, such song texts are due to the influence of neighboring dialects. This is strangely analogous to the practise among ourselves of singing songs in Italian, French or German rather than in English, and it is likely that the historical processes which have led to the parallel custom are of a similar nature. Thieves' jargons and secret languages of children may also be mentioned. These lead over into special sign and gesture languages, many of which are based directly on spoken or written speech; they seem to exist on many levels of culture. The sign language of the Plains Indians of North America arose in response to the need for some medium of communication between tribes speaking mutually unintelligible languages. Within the Christian church may be noted the elaboration of gesture languages by orders of monks vowed to silence. Not only a language or a terminology but the mere external form in which it is written may become important as a symbol of sentimental or social distinction. Thus Croatian and Serbian are essentially the same language but they are presented in very different outward forms, the former being written in Latin characters, the latter in the Cyrillic character of the Greek Orthodox church. This external difference, associated with a difference of religion, has of course the important function of preventing people who speak closely related languages or dialects but who wish for reasons of sentiment not to confound themselves in a larger unity from becoming too keenly aware of how much they actually resemble each other.

The relation of language to nationalism and internationalism presents a number of interesting sociological problems. Anthropology makes a rigid distinction between ethnic units based on race, on culture and on language. It points out that these do not need to coincide in the least—that they do not, as a matter of fact, often coincide in reality. But with the increased emphasis on nationalism in modern times the question of the symbolic meaning of race and language has taken on a new significance and, whatever the scientist may say, the layman is ever inclined to see culture, language and race as but different facets of a single social unity, which he tends in turn to identify with such a political entity as England or France or Germany. To point out, as the anthropologist easily can, that cultural distributions and nationalities override language and race groups does not end the matter for the sociologist, because he feels that the concept of nation or nationality must be integrally imaged by the non-analytical person as carrying with it the connotation, real or supposed, of both race and language. From this standpoint it really makes little difference whether history and anthropology support the popular identification of nationality, language and race. The important thing to hold on to is that a particular language tends to become the fitting expression of a self-conscious nationality and that such a group will construct for itself in spite of all that the physical anthropologist can do a race to which is to be attributed the mystic power of creating a language and a culture as twin expressions of its psychic peculiarities.

So far as language and race are concerned, it is true that the major races of man have tended in the past to be set off against each other by important differences of language. There is less point to this, however, than might be imagined, because the linguistic differentiations within any given race are just as far reaching as those which can be pointed out across racial lines, yet they do not at all correspond to subracial units. Even the major races are not always clearly sundered by language. This is notably the case with the Malayo-Polynesian languages, which are spoken by peoples as racially distinct as the Malays, the Polynesians and the Negroes of Melanesia. Not one of the great languages of modern man follows racial lines. French, for example, is spoken by a highly mixed population, which is largely Nordic in the north, Alpine in the center and Mediterranean in the south, each of these subraces being liberally represented in the rest of Europe.

While language differences have always been important symbols of cultural difference, it is only in comparatively recent times, with the exaggerated development of the ideal of the sovereign nation and with the resulting eagerness to discover linguistic symbols for this ideal of sovereignty, that language differences have taken on an implication of antagonism. In ancient Rome and all through mediaeval Europe there were plenty of cultural differences running side by side with linguistic ones, and the political status of Roman citizen or the fact of adherence to the Roman Catholic church was of vastly greater significance as a symbol of the individual's place in the world than the language or dialect which he happened to speak. It is probably altogether incorrect to maintain that language differences are responsible for national antagonisms. It would seem to be much more reasonable to suppose that a political and national unit, once definitely formed, uses a prevailing language as a symbol of its identity, whence gradually emerges the peculiarly modern feeling that every language should properly be the expression of a distinctive nationality. In earlier times there seems to have been little systematic attempt to impose the language of a conquering people on the subject people, although it happened frequently as a result of the processes implicit in the spread of culture that such a conqueror's language was gradually taken over by the dispossessed population. Witness the spread of the Romance languages and of the modern Arabic dialects. On the other hand, it seems to have happened about as frequently that the conquering group was culturally and linguistically absorbed and that their own language disappeared without necessary danger to their privileged status. Thus foreign dynasties in China have always submitted to the superior culture of the Chinese and have taken on their language. In the same way the Moslem Moguls of India, while true to their religion, which was adopted by millions in northern India, made one of the Hindu vernaculars the basis of the great literary language of Moslem India, Hindustani. Definitely repressive attitudes toward the languages and dialects of subject peoples seem to be distinctive only of European political policy in comparatively recent times. The attempt of czarist Russia to stamp out Polish by forbidding its teaching in the schools and the similarly repressive policy of contemporary Italy in its attempt to wipe out German from the territory recently acquired from Austria are illuminating examples of the heightened emphasis on language as a symbol of political allegiance in the modern world.

To match these repressive measures there is the oft repeated attempt of minority groups to erect their language into the status of a fully accredited medium of cultural and literary expression. Many of these restored or semimanufactured languages have come in on the wave of resistance to exterior political or cultural hostility. Such are the Gaelic of Ireland, the Lithuanian of a recently created republic and the Hebrew of the Zionists. In other cases such languages have come in more peacefully because of a sentimental interest in local culture. Such are the modern Provençal of southern France, the Plattdeutsch of northern Germany, Frisian and the Norwegian *landsmaal*. It is doubtful whether these persistent attempts to make true culture languages of local dialects that have long ceased to be of primary literary importance can succeed in the long run. The failure of modern Provençal to hold its own and the very dubious success of Gaelic make it seem probable that following the recent tendency to resurrect minor languages will come a renewed leveling of speech more suitably expressing the internationalism which is slowly emerging.

The logical necessity of an international language in modern times is in strange contrast to the indifference and even opposition with which most people consider its possibility. The attempts so far made to solve this problem, of which Esperanto has probably had the greatest measure of practical success, have not affected more than a very small proportion of the people whose international interests and needs might have led to a desire for a simple and uniform means of international expression, at least for certain purposes. It is in the less important countries of Europe, such as Czechoslovakia, that Esperanto has been moderately successful, and for obvious reasons. The opposition to an international language has little logic or psychology in its favor. The supposed artificiality of such a language as Esperanto or of any of the equivalent languages that have been proposed has been absurdly exaggerated, for in sober truth there is practically nothing in these languages that is not taken from the common stock of words and forms which have gradually developed in Europe. Such an international language could of course have only the status of a secondary form of speech for distinctly limited purposes. Thus considered the learning of a constructed international language offers no further psychological problem than the learning of any other language which is acquired after childhood through the medium of books and with the conscious application of grammatical rules. The lack of interest in the international language problem in spite of the manifest need for one is an excellent example of how little logic or intellectual necessity has to do with the acquirement of language habits. Even the acquiring of the barest smattering of a foreign national language is imaginatively equivalent to some measure of identification with a people or a culture. The purely instrumental value of such knowledge is frequently nil. Any consciously constructed international language has to deal with the great difficulty of not being felt to represent a distinctive people or culture. Hence the learning of it is of very little symbolic significance for the average person, who remains blind to the fact that such a language, easy and regular as it inevitably must be, would solve many of his educational and practical difficulties at a single blow. The future alone will tell whether the logical advantages and theoretical necessity of an international language can overcome the largely symbolic opposition which it has to meet. In any event it is at least conceivable that one of the great national languages of modern times, such as English or Spanish or Russian, may in due course find itself in the position of a de facto international language without any conscious attempt having been made to put it there.

II

LEONARD BLOOMFIELD

(1887–1949)

Bloomfield, Professor of Germanic Philology at Chicago, is often referred to as the major linguistic synthesizer of this century. Certainly it is the case that his main publication, *Language* (1933), attempts to survey all theoretical developments in the field up until that time and to present a coherent procedure for the analysis of language. His influence on scholars of the late 1930s and 1940s was substantial, and frequent mention is still made of a 'bloomfieldian' school of thought. He displays a similar range of interest to that of Sapir, and pays a great deal of attention to the history and comparison of language forms. He illustrates his theoretical points frequently from English, but the present paper seems to be the only instance of his taking some aspect of English for separate publication.

'The Structure of Learnèd Words'

(*A Commemorative Volume*, 1933)

The English vocabulary consists of three great types of words; the boundaries, to be sure, are not absolute. *Foreign* words are characterized by phonetic or phonologic peculiarities; they are isolated or else occur in very small morphologic sets; some of the nouns have a foreign plural. Examples are *mirage*, *intelligentsia*, *jiu-jitsu*, *alumnus* (*alumni*), *alumna* (*alumnae*). The rest of the vocabulary divides itself into a *normal* ('native') and a *learnèd* (semi-foreign) type. For instance:

Normal: *sing* (*sang*, *sung*), *song*, *singer*, *songster*.

Learnèd: *conceive*, *deceive*, *perceive*, *receive*.

To a large extent, these two types of words are made up of different constituents; normal roots combine with normal affixes, learnèd roots with learnèd affixes. The learnèd type uses more prefixes (*con-*, *de-*, *per-*, *re-*, etc.) than the normal; many learnèd words accent another than the radical syllable (*cóncept* beside *conceptual*, *invocátion* beside *invoke*). These and many other differences enable us to recognize learnèd affixes even in the cases where they are added to a normal root (*re-shape*, *right-eous*).

The historic origin of the learnèd vocabulary is familiar enough.[1] In the centuries after the Norman Conquest the language received many French loan-words. Among these were many *mots savants*,[2] Latin forms which the French had taken from books and incorporated into their speech with certain phonetic and structural modifications, much as ordinary loan-words are incorporated. Thus, by ordinary (spoken) tradition, Latin *fragile* became Old French *fraile*; but the Latin word was known to the French from books, whence they took it, in the reading-pronunciation of their time, as *fragile*. Both forms were borrowed by English: *frail*, *fragile*. Along with the borrowing of French *mots savants*, the English acquired the habit of making them up: English writers and speakers use Latin words (which they find in books). These words are re-shaped in accordance with the habit of the French *mots savants* and in accordance with the English phonetic development since the Norman borrowings. In fact, owing to the great number of these learnèd words, we are able to make new combinations of French and Latin-French elements (*mutinous*, *dutiable*, *eventual*, *fragmentary*).[3]

The outlines of this historical development have been fairly well traced, but a detailed study will be possible only when we have a systematic description. We need first an exact account of the present-day habits; then we must gather the evidence for past times, including not only the earlier occurrences of words (as listed, say, in the *New English Dictionary*), but also the evidence as to their phonetic shape, including, especially, the place of accent; finally, we shall need a description of the French speech that was brought to England.

The first step, then, is to describe the present-day forms. Although this description has not been made, we can gather some idea of what it will contain.

The present mass of English learnèd words does not entirely coincide with the words that the historian recognizes as borrowings; thus, the words *chair* and *cheer*, which, historically, are loans from French, are today normal words, showing none of the learnèd peculiarities. The grouping of English learnèd words into morphologic sets will perhaps often disagree with that of French or Latin. For instance, a descriptive analysis of present-day English will perhaps show (I do not know whether it will) that *atom* (*atomic*, *atomize*, older *atomy*) contains a root *at-* with a suffix *-om*, although the Latin (originally Greek) structure

[1] See, of course, O. Jespersen, *Growth and Structure of the English Language* (4th ed. London and New York, 1929), pp. 84–153.

[2] [*mots savants* learnèd words.]

[3] Jespersen, *Growth and Structure*, p. 123.

implied a root *-tom* 'cut' with a prefix *a-* 'not.' If this should prove true, then *atom* would not belong to the root-group of *microtomy, appendectomy, tonsilectomy*. The grouping of learnèd words will be difficult, because the meanings are largely abstract and vague. In a set like *conceive, deceive, perceive, receive* this is offset by the phonetic steadiness of the form *-ceive*, but, as the phonetic shape of the learnèd morphemes, especially of the roots, is subject to great fluctuation, this criterion also will be hard to apply.

The learnèd words, formed almost at will, often are carried along with little oral tradition; hence there may be great variety in their phonetic shape, especially as to accent; thus we have *hospítable* beside *hóspitable, revócable* beside *révocable, addréss* beside *áddress* (noun; the verb is always *addréss*), *ration* with [ej] or with [ɛ] in the first syllable.[1] A speaker may base his form on an imperfect hearing or on an imperfect observation of the printed symbols, so that he says, for instance, *portentious* instead of *portentous* (compare *pretentious, contentious*); thus, *morphodite* has become conventional, in sub-standard speech, for *hermaphrodite*. This merges with analogic creation on half-understood models, as in *normalcy* for *normality* (compare, perhaps, *bankrupt: bankruptcy, captain: captaincy, chaplain: chaplaincy*); a businessman wants to say *pneumogate* for 'travel by air' (compare *pneumatic* and *navigate*, where the compounding form of the first word would be *pneumato-* and the meaning 'travel' attaches not to the suffix-group *-igate*, but to the root *nav-* 'ship'). Further, we have to reckon with the fact that a complicated morphologic system leads to many smaller analogic modifications; some of these are furthered by spelling-pronunciation. Thus, *experiment* with [ij] in the second syllable (sub-standard) may be due to *experience* as well as to a false equation between spelling and spoken form. For *finality* we have forms with [i] and with [aj] in the first

[1] I transcribe according to Central-Western American (Chicago) pronunciation, using the following symbols:

[aj] as in *time* [tajm]	[ǰ] as in *jam* [ǰɛm]
[aw] as in *cow* [kaw]	[l̩] as in *kettle* [ketl̩]
[ɑ] as in *hot* [hɑt]	[n̩] as in *button* [botn̩]
[č] as in *chin* [čin]	[o] as in *son, sun* [son]
[e] as in *ten* [ten]	[ow] as in *go* [gow]
[ej] as in *say* [sej]	[r̩] as in *fir, fur* [fr̩]
[ɛ] as in *hat* [hɛt]	[š] as in *shin* [šin]
[i] as in *pin* [pin]	[u] as in *put* [put]
[ij] as in *see* [sij]	[uw] as in *moon* [muwn]
[j] as in *yes* [jes]	[ž] as in *measure* [mežr̩]

['] indicates stress accent on the following syllabic, as in *believe* [be'lijv].

syllable; compare, for the latter, *final* and the frequent use of the letter *i* for the sound [aj]. On the side of meaning the situation is much the same: striking departures from tradition are known as *malapropisms*, but there are also ordinary analogic developments, as in the case of *transpire* 'to leak out' (of news), and then merely 'to happen.'[1]

To illustrate the variability of learnèd roots, we may survey the group of *-ceive*:

1 *conceive, deceive, perceive, receive*
conceivable (*inconceivable*), *receivable*
2 *accept, except*
cóncept, pércept, précept
acceptable (*acceptabílity*)
perceptible (*perceptibílity, imperceptible, imperceptibility*)
contraceptive, deceptive (*deceptívity*), *inceptive, perceptive* (*perceptívity*), *receptive* (*receptívity*)
acceptance
acceptátion
conceptual (*conceptualize*), *perceptual*
preceptor (*preceptórial*)
conception, contraception (*contraceptional*), *deception, exception* (*exceptional*), *inception, perception, reception*
3 *incipient* (*incipience, incipiency*), *percipient, recipient*
4 *conceit, deceit, receipt*
5 *seize* (*seizure*).

The alternation of vowels in learnèd words consists largely in a distinction of two grades, diphthongal[2] (D) and monophthongal (M), as in the following examples:

D [ij]: M [e]: *sequence: consecutive*
D [ej]: M [ɛ]: *profane: profanity*
D [aj]: M [i]: *finite: infinity*
D [juw]: M [o]: *produce: productive*
D [ow]: M [ɑ]: *cone: conic*
D [aw]: M [o]: *abound: abundant.*

Both grades occur with various weakenings in unstressed position. Thus we have *finality* with D [fajn-] and with M [fin-]; *saline* with suffix D [-ajn] and M [-in]. There are various degrees of weakening, as *finality* with [fen-] or [fn̩-].

[1] Jespersen, *Growth and Structure*, p. 121.

[2] For the history, see K. Luick, *Historische Grammatik der englischen Sprache* (Leipzig, 1913 ff.), pp. 439–69.

Irregular alternations of vowels are fairly frequent. Beside D [sijv] in *receive*, M [sept] in *receptive*, we have seen also M [sip] in *recipient*. The suffix D [-ijk] in *antique*, *oblique* has M [ikw] in *antiquity*, *obliquity*. A vowel may lose syllabic value; thus, syllabic [er, r̥] appears in *refer*, *reference*, *differ*, *differential*, but non-syllabic [r] in *different*, *difference* [difrent, difrens]. Most important in this respect is the treatment of [ij] before vowels; in *curious* it may drop its [i] or keep it, so that the word has either two or three syllables; similarly, the [j] of [ij] is kept or dropped in *religiosity*; in *opinion* the [i] is dropped; in *religious* the entire [ij] is dropped.

These features are determined by the constituents of the form. Thus, the suffix *-ious* demands D [ej, ow] in the preceding syllable, as in *capacious*, *ferocious*, but in the alternation of [aj—i] it demands M [i], as in *religious*, *delicious* (*delight*), *vicious* (*vice*). The suffix *-ity* demands M in the preceding (stressed) syllable: *capacity*, *ferocity*, *brevity* (*brief*); of irregularities we may mention *scarce*: *scarcity* with D before *-ity*, and *clear*: *clarity* with alternation of D [ij] and M [ɛ].

The most regular consonant alternation is the coalescence of dentals with the [ij, j] of such suffixes as *-ion*, *-ial*, *-ious* (*opinion*, *perennial*, *curious*); here [t, s] with [ij, j] gives [š]: *delight*: *delicious*, *vice*: *vicious*. With the [j] of *-ion* [d, z] give [ž]: *erode*: *erosion*, *fuse*: *fusion*. Before these and certain other suffixes [k] is replaced by [s] and [g] by [ǰ]: *public*: *publicity*, *theologue*: *theology*, and antevocalic [ij, j] coalesces with these sounds to [š, ǰ]: *optic*: *optician*, *theologue*: *theologian*. The coalescence of [t, d, s, z] with the [j] of suffixes like *-ue*, *-ure*, *-ule*, *-une*, gives [č, ǰ, š, ž]: *percept*: *perceptual*, *grade*: *gradual*, *sense*: *sensual*, *please*: *pleasure*, but there are also unaltered forms, with [tj] and so on, and the two are variously distributed: mostly (but not always) the unaltered variants are over-formal and semi-educated. The suffix *-ity* demands retention of [ij, j]: *religious* [-ǰos] but *religiosity* [-ǰi'jasitij], *artificial* [-šl̥] but *artificiality* [-š'jɛlitij], *precious* [-šos] but *preciosity* [-ši'jasitij]; *fatuous* has [č] rather than [tj], but *fatuity* has [tj] rather than [č]. At the beginning of a root, as in *produce*, *reduce*, *duke*, the coalescence is not made (in Chicago pronunciation, at least), hence *educate*, which has [j], cannot be grouped with the root [djuwk], but must be analyzed with a root [ed-]. This analysis happens to agree with the structure of the word in Latin, but it is the analysis, not the Latin structure, which makes the spelling-pronunciation with [dj] unpleasing to our ears.

There are many irregular alternations of consonants, such as [gn] with [n] in *benignity*: *benign*, *dignity*: *condign*, *deign*. Voiced consonants alternate with unvoiced in certain forms: *anxious: anxiety*; beside *equate* we have *equation* with [š] or with [ž]. Especially, initial [s] is replaced by [z] after prefixes in certain forms: *sessions: possession*, *assume: presume*, *consent: resent*. Many roots have one or more alternant forms in which [t] is added, and this addition is made with various irregularities; thus, beside [sijv] *receive*, [sip] *recipient*, we have seen [sept] *receptive* and [sijt] *receipt*. Some roots appear in extremely deviant alternants whose classification offers difficulty, such as [sijz] *seize* beside [sijv]; historically these are due to the divergence of genuine French words from French *mots savants*, as *frail: fragile*. In the same way, we owe some irregularities to the circumstance that native English words have been drawn, through phonetic resemblance, into a learnèd group; thus, *flow* (native) is grouped with *fluent* (Latin).

The place of stress is determined by suffixes. One variety of *-y* (including the combination *-it-y*) demands stress on the third-last syllable: *rémedy*, *vorácity*; contrast *cóntroversy* with another variety of the *-y* suffix. Forms with suffix 'zero'—that is, absence of a suffix—in certain cases accent the prefix: *convíct* (verb): *cónvict* (noun).[1] In some forms the prefix has a D vowel: *prótest* [ow], *rébate* [ij]; in others it has an M vowel: *próduct* [a], *récord* [e].

Some affixes are accompanied by other peculiarities. When *-ity* is added to adjectives in *-ac-ious* and *-oc-ious*, the *-ious* is dropped: *capacious: capacity*, *ferocious: ferocity*; in other cases such as *-u-ous*, there are forms with loss of *-ous*, such as *vacuous: vacuity*, and others which keep *-ous*, such as *sinuous: sinuosity*; in the group *-it-ous* both suffixes are dropped: *fortuitous: fortuity*.

A systematic description of English morphology is desirable for its own sake, as a statement of facts. Without it, moreover, our historical account will fall short of what is attainable in the way of completeness and precision. Aside from these theoretical benefits, however, a systematic description of this kind, in the hands of the teacher (and perhaps even of the advanced student) would greatly help the foreign learner of English.

[1] K. H. Collitz in *Englische Studien*, 43 (1911), p. 252.

12

EILERT EKWALL
(1877–1964)

Ekwall was a Swedish scholar, Professor of English at the University of Lund, who concentrated on the study of English place-names. His dictionary of place-names begins with a long introduction in which he gives a general view of his subject. In the course of this he presents an estimate of its value, notably in the contribution it can make to disciplines other than philology.

'The Value of Place-Name Study'

(*The Concise Oxford Dictionary of English Place-Names*, 1936; the text is from the fourth edition, 1960)

The study of place-names is of value in itself, inasmuch as the meaning and history of English place-names must offer a good deal of interest to English people. Place-names form a part of the vocabulary and deserve as much attention as other words. But incidentally they give valuable information of a particular kind.

1 Place-names embody important material for the history of England. The various elements in the English place-nomenclature (British, Scandinavian, &c.) testify to changes in the population of the British Isles, and place-names often supplement the meagre data of recorded history. They give hints as to the districts where a British population preserved its language for a comparatively long time. Names such as WALTON, BIRKBY (from *Bretabýr* 'village of the Britons') indicate places where Britons dwelt in independent settlements, after the Anglo-Saxon immigration. A systematic study of various types of place-names will, it may be hoped, give some information on the history of Anglo-Saxon settlements and the distribution of the population at various periods. It has been shown that place-names in *-ing* (READING and the like) are very old, and probably belong to the period of the early settlements of Anglo-Saxons in England. These names, where they occur frequently, indicate early Anglo-Saxon communities. These and other names consisting of or containing folk-names

give a hint as to the importance of the tribe and family in early Anglo-Saxon times. Names such as DENGE, EASTRY, LYMINGE, STURRY, which contain an Old English *gē* corresponding to German *Gau*, tell us that Kent was, at an early period, divided into districts called *gē*, which would be analogous to the German *Gau*'s.

The Scandinavian place-names in England are really the chief source for our knowledge of the Scandinavian settlements. They tell us what parts of England were most thickly populated by Scandinavians. They tell us that the Scandinavian population in the east of England was on the whole Danish, that in the north-west chiefly Norwegian. But some names (as HULME, FLIXTON, URMSTON) prove that there was once a Danish colony in South-East Lancashire.

2 Place-names have something to tell us about Anglo-Saxon religion and belief before the conversion to Christianity. Though the Christian religion was introduced about 150 years after the immigration into England, there had been time for many places to get names referring to heathen worship. Names such as WOODNESBOROUGH, WEDNESBURY, WEDNESFIELD, WANSDYKE denoted places where *Woden* was worshipped or that were associated with him. THUNDERFIELD, THUNDER(S)LEY, probably THURSLEY in Surrey, must have been places where *Þunor* had a temple, and TUESLEY, TYSOE record places dedicated to the worship of *Tīw* (*Tīg*). FROYLE, FREEFOLK and others may contain the name of the goddess *Frīg* (*Frēo*). GRIM'S DITCH contains *Grīm*, a byname of Woden. Many names such as HARROW, WEEDON, WILLEY contain a word which meant a heathen temple (OE *hearg*, *wēoh*).

Numerous names throw some light on the belief in supernatural beings of a lower order, elves, sprites, goblins. Such are GRIMLEY, SHINCLIFFE, SHOBROOKE, SHUCKBURGH, THURSFORD, probably HASCOMBE, HESCOMBE. Interesting is *Nikerpoll* in an Assize Roll of 1263, which contains Old English *nicor* 'water monster'. The pool was at Pershore. DRAKELOW is probably a reminiscence of a myth according to which the mound in question was inhabited by a dragon. Names like HOLYWELL, HOLY OAKES tell us of holy wells or trees; FRITWELL, ELWELL of wishing-wells.

3 Some place-names indicate familiarity with old heroic sagas in various parts of England. *Grendles mere* 931 Birch, Cart. Sax. 677, *Grendeles pytt* 739 ib. 1331, found in boundaries of Ham in Wilts and Crediton, show that the Grendel episode in Beowulf was known in Devon and Wilts, perhaps even that it was localized to definite places in these counties. The name WAYLAND SMITH'S CAVE (OE *Welandes*

smiððe 955 ib. 908) shows that the Weland saga was popular in Wilts in the Old English time. There is a good deal of probability that some place-names in WADE- contain the name of the mythical hero Wade. *Hnæf* in *Hnæfes scylf* 973–4 ib. 1307 (in bounds of Crondall) and in NASEBY may well refer, not to an Anglo-Saxon *Hnæf*, but to the hero of Finnsburg. WITHINGTON in Gloucestershire (*Wudiandun* 737) may possibly have got its name from the *Widia* of heroic saga.

But it is obvious that the greatest caution must be exercised in the interpretation of names like these. In most cases, places were no doubt named from actual persons, not from heroes of popular legends and sagas. But it is quite possible that people were named from legendary heroes sometimes, and in that case names testify to familiarity with the sagas in question.

4 Place-names give important information on antiquities. Names such as STRATFORD, STRETTON contain Old English *strǣt* 'Roman road', and speak of a Roman road running past or through the place. Such names give help in determining the line of Roman roads and often even tell of such roads that are now unknown. Names containing words for 'fort', 'Roman station', sometimes prove that an old fort must have once existed at a place where there are now no traces of it. The name ECCLES and names in ECCLES- indicate that there was an old church in the place, probably one of British origin. On FAWLER see dictionary.

Some place-names give information on early architecture or building-material. BERECHURCH, BRADKIRK, FELKIRK mean 'church made of boards or planks'. On the other hand WHITCHURCH, literally 'white church', in reality seems to mean 'stone church'. VOWCHURCH is 'multicoloured church', and must refer to some decoration. HORNCHURCH is 'church with horns or hornlike gables'. STONEHOUSE is self-explanatory, it is a rare name. SHINGLE HALL and THATCHAM seem to have been named from the material of their roofs. LOFTHOUSE, fairly common in Yorkshire, refers to a house with an upper story. On BELCHAMP see dictionary.

Names in *-bridge*, of course, indicate the existence of an early bridge, but they sometimes give a hint as to the material or nature of the bridge, as STAMBRIDGE, RISBRIDGE (the name of a hundred in Suffolk), STALBRIDGE. See also BOW. BRIDGFORD is doubtless generally 'ford with a footbridge'. Other names tell of stepping stones or other contrivances to facilitate the crossing of a stream, as CLAPPERSGATE, BAMFORD, STAPLEFORD, or for crossing marshy land, as RUNCTON, SOCKBRIDGE, WARPSGROVE.

Numerous names indicate early systems of defence, look-out places, and the like. Examples are WARDLOW, WARTHILL 'watch place', TOTTERNHOE 'spur of land with a look-out house'. Many other names contain the stem *tōt-* 'to look out', as TOTHILL, TOTHAM, &c. To this group belong other names, as HALTON in Northumberland, very likely GLANTLEES and the like. *Beacon* is found in BEACONSFIELD and BECKNEY.

Prehistoric stone circles may be referred to by names such as QUARLES, WHARLES, WHEELTON. STANION may well refer to a cromlech, as do certainly FEATHERSTONE, SHILSTONE. THURLESTONE really denoted a stone with a hole in it.

5 Place-names give information on early institutions, social conditions, and the like. Important information is obtained on early meeting-places. Here belong such names as MUTLOW, SPELLOW, SPETCHLEY, STOULTON, THINGWALL. A study of such names, many preserved as names of hundreds or wapentakes, gives clues to Anglo-Saxon and Scandinavian customs. It is obvious that grave-mounds were often used for meeting-places. In other cases a conspicuous hill, a prominent tree, a ford, was chosen for this purpose. The word *hlōse* found in the hundred-names Loes in Suffolk, Clackclose in Norfolk, probably refers to some temporary shelter set up at a meeting-place, and hardly has its usual meaning 'pigsty'. The hundred name Gartree in Leicestershire should very likely be explained in connexion with the Longobardic *gairethinx* 'the common thing', whose first element is *gair* 'spear' (= Old English *gār*).

Names such as KINGSTON, QUINTON, ATHELNEY, tell us that the places once belonged to the king, the queen, some princes. REEPHAM must have been under the supervision of a reeve. DAMERHAM is 'the judges' manor'. ABBOTSTON(E) is 'manor belonging to an abbot or abbess'. KNIGHTON was a village held by knights, DROINTON one held by *drengs*. CHARLTON (CHORLTON) is 'village of free peasants'. The name indicates that other villages had some other status and tells of early manorialism. BUCKLAND was an estate held by charter.

Many place-names tell of early industry and the like. Many names, of course, contain the word *mill*, as MELLIS, MELLS, MELFORD, MILLBROOK. In some cases windmills must be meant. CROFT in Leicestershire (from OE *cræft*), WILD seem to mean 'mechanical contrivance'. A wind- or watermill may be referred to. ORGRAVE, STANDHILL and others testify to mining industry, as do names like QUERNMORE, QUORNDON. KIRKBY OVERBLOW contains an otherwise unknown Old English *ōrblāwere* 'smelter'. SALT and names in SALT-, SALTER- tell of the salt-making industry. Many names contain words for trades or tradesmen, as HUNTINGTON, FULLERTON, FISHERTON, WOODMANCOTE, COLSTERDALE, BICKERTON; SMEATON, SUTTERTON; HOPPERTON, SAPPERTON, POTTERTON; MANGERTON; BEMERTON, HARPERLEY, HORNBLOTTON.

Names like PLAISTOW, PLAYFORD, HESKETH, perhaps FOLLIFOOT tell of ancient sports or horse-racing. Ancient deer-parks are commemorated by names like HARTLIP, HINDLIP, DARTON, DASSETT, ROFFEY.

Traps for catching animals are referred to by such names as BAWDRIP, SNARGATE, STILDON, TRAFFORD in Northants, WOOKEY; KEPIER, YARM.

Something may be gathered from place-names on early agriculture and cattle-farming.

Many names contain words for cereals, as BARLEY, RYTON, WHEATLEY. It is remarkable that *oats* is very rare in place-names: OTELEY is an exception. But pilloats is found early in PILLATON, and very likely *Haver-* in place-names is partly an Old English *hæfera* 'oats' or Old Scandinavian *hafri* the same, as in HAVERHILL, HAVERBRACK. Fruit-trees must have been extensively grown, as indicated by numerous names containing the words for apple, pear, plum. *Cherry* seems to occur several times as a distinctive addition, as in CHERRY WILLINGHAM.

Names of domestic animals are common, as in COWLEY, OXTON, SHEPTON, SHAPWICK. It is of interest to find that the custom of grazing cattle at some distance from the home village or homestead, which is still common in Scandinavia, must have been prevalent in England, not only in Scandinavian districts, but also in purely English areas. In the north, names in *-sett* (ON *sætr*), *-erg* testify to it. In the south, numerous names in *-stoc*, *-wīc* doubtless belong here. SOMERTON must have been a place to which people moved in summer for the sake of better pasture. There is even a case where a SOMERTON and a WINTERTON are found close together. In Kent and Sussex, villages in low-lying districts had outlying pastures in the Weald districts. They were called *denn* and seem to have been mostly used for swine-pastures. Likewise marshland was allotted to various villages. Place-names sometimes give a hint as to the mother-village of a *denn* or piece of marsh. TENTERDEN is 'the *denn* of the Thanet people', BURMARSH, in South Kent, 'the marsh of the Canterbury people'. Cf. also DUNGE MARSH.

6 Place-names are of great value for linguistic study.

i) They frequently contain personal names, and are therefore a source of first-rate importance for our knowledge of the Anglo-Saxon personal nomenclature. A systematic study of personal names found in place-names will give important information on the personal names of the early tribes. It is interesting to find, for instance, that names in *Sax-* and *-mund* are particularly common in East Anglia (SAXLINGHAM, SAXMUNDHAM, MUNDHAM, MENDHAM, MENDLESHAM, &c.). Many personal names are only recorded in place-names. Thus *Godhelm*, the base of GODALMING, has only been found with certainty in this name, though very likely it is also the first element of GOLDSBOROUGH in the West Riding. Old English *god* (*gōd*) and *helm* are common in personal names, and it would be remarkable if they should not sometimes have been combined into *Godhelm*. THIRSTON contains an Old English *Þræsfriþ*. This is the only known example of the element *Thras-* so common in Continental names.

Women's names are quite common. Particularly frequent is *Ēadburg* (ABBERTON, ABRAM, &c.). Perhaps some of the places were named from Eadburg, wife of Beorhtric, king of Wessex. But many other women's names occur, as *Beaduburg* in BABRAHAM, *Cēngifu* in KNAYTON, KNIVETON and others, *Ēadgifu* in EDDINGTON Berks. An interesting group is formed by AUDLEY, BALTERLEY, BETLEY, and BARTHOMLEY, containing the women's names *Aldgȳþ*, *Baldþrȳþ*, *Bettu*, and probably *Beorhtwynn*. The four places are situated close together on the border of Cheshire and Staffordshire. All have for their second element Old English *lēah*.

ii) Place-names contain many old words not otherwise recorded. They show that Old English preserved several words found in other Germanic languages, but not found in Old English literature. Thus the names BEESTON, BESSACAR, &c., have as first element an Old English *bēos* 'bent grass', corresponding to Dutch *Bies*, Low German *bēse*. BLEAN contains a word identical with Old High German *blacha* 'coarse cloth'. DOILEY shows that Old English had an adjective *diger* corresponding to Old Norse *digr* 'thick'. HARDRES contains an old word for 'forest' found in German *Harz*. REDLYNCH, LYSCOMBE in Dorset show that Old English had a word *lisc* identical with Old High German *lisca*, Dutch *lisch* 'reeds'. SOMPTING, SUNT testify to an Old English *sumpt* corresponding to Old High German *sunft* 'marsh'. THE SWIN is identical with HET ZWIN in Holland and shows that Old English had a word *swin* 'creek', identical with Dutch *zwin*.

Other place-names prove the existence of Old English words otherwise unknown in any Germanic language. A very interesting case is offered by the names ENHAM and YEN HALL, which contain an Old English *ēan* 'lamb,' corresponding to Latin *agnus*, but hitherto found only in derivatives (OE *ēanian* 'to lamb', *geēan* 'with lamb'). PEAK and several other names presuppose a word *pēac* 'hill', cognate with Swedish *pjuk* 'a mound'. PRAWLE has as first element an Old English *prāw* 'peering', cognate with *prīwan* 'to wink'. Several names such as WYTHAM in Berks must contain an Old English *wiht* 'bend', which is unknown outside place-names.

Some place-names testify to otherwise unknown side-forms of Old English words, as an *ēstre* by the side of *eowestre* 'sheepfold' (EASTER), or *hagga* by the side of *haga* 'haw' (HAGLEY). Some tell us of unknown derivatives with suffixes, as FRANT, ETCHELLS, NECHELLS.

iii) Place-names often afford far earlier references for words than those found in literature. Only a few examples can be given here. *Dimple* is recorded in OED from *c.* 1400. In the topographical sense 'depression in the ground' it is recorded *c.* 1205 (*Kerlingedimpel* in the Furness Cartulary, apparently 'ducking-pool'). *Dod* 'a round hill' is first exemplified in OED from 1843. As a place-name the word is found in 1230. *Hunter* (first quotation in OED *c.* 1250) occurs in a place-name recorded in Domesday (HUNSTON in Suffolk). *Potter* is found in a place-name in 951 (*Potteresleag* BCS 890), otherwise not until 1284 (OED). *Sprod* 'a salmon in its second year' is recorded in OED from 1617. It is evidently found in the place-name *Sprodpulhey* 1418 (Chetham Soc. 95).

iv) Only a few remarks can be made here on the value of place-names for the history of English sounds. They often help in the dating and localization of sound-changes, the fixing of dialect boundaries and the like. The distribution of place-name forms such as STRATFORD, STRATTON, and STRETFORD, STRETTON gives information on the Old English dialects in which the word *street* appears as *strǣt* and as *strēt*, that is, it helps in drawing the line between Saxon and Anglian territory. The distribution of 'fractured' forms such as Saxon-Kentish *ceald*, *cealf* as against Anglian *cald*, *calf*, which is an important dialect criterion, is illustrated by place-names. One of the chief tests for the distinction between Midland and Northern English is the development of Old English *ā*, which becomes Middle English *ō* in the Midlands, but remains in the North. The *ā*-*ō*-line can be drawn with a good deal of accuracy by the help of place-names.

Many sound-changes can be exemplified in place-names that hardly occur in other words, partly because certain combinations of sounds found in them are rarely met with in other words. Loss of consonants, especially *r* and *l*, owing to dissimilation is common. Examples are WENTWORTH from earlier *Wintreworth* and the like, PUNCKNOWLE, which is pretty certainly Old English *plūm-cnoll* 'plum-tree knoll'. Change of *t*, *k*, to *d*, *g* between vowels is common, rare in other words. Change of *nk* to *ng* or *rt* to *rd* is often found, as in many names containing Old English *hlinc*, *ceart*. See e.g. LYNG, CHARD, CHADACRE. A change of *d* to *th* is well known in words like *father*, *mother* (OE *fæder*, *mōdor*). In place-names a similar change of *b* to *v* or *g* to *gh* is sometimes met with. See e.g. PAVENHAM from *Pabenham*, MOGGERHANGER.

13

I. A. RICHARDS

(1893–)

Richards was born in England and lectured at Cambridge before going to America where he became Professor at Harvard University. He has always been interested in the working of words (*The Meaning of Meaning*, with C. K. Ogden, 1923), and in 1943 he published an account of the simplified form of English that he had been using to help English achieve universal currency, 'Basic English'. In this essay—originally a lecture—he develops his theory of contextual meaning and relates it to advances in other kinds of linguistic description.

'The Interinanimation of Words'

(*The Philosophy of Rhetoric*, 1936)

I turn now to that other sense of 'context'—the literary context—which I distinguished last time from the technical sense of 'context,' as a recurrent group of events, that is convenient for the theorem of meaning. Let us consider some of the effects on words of their combination in sentences, and how their meaning depends upon the other words before and after them in the sentence. What happens when we try with a sentence to decide what single words in it mean?

The sentence, of course, as Aristotle taught, is the unit of discourse. We can hardly give too much importance here to the influence of our modern way of separating words in writing. In conversation we do not ordinarily separate them so—unless we are asking questions about words. With languages which have not been used in writing and thus subjected to a special kind of grammatical analysis—it is worth recalling that grammar takes its name from writing—there is often very great uncertainty as to where one word ends and another begins. The written form gives words far more independence than they possess as units of sound in speech and we derive thence a habit of supposing that they have far more independence as regards their meanings than they usually have in either written or spoken discourse.

The mutual dependence of words varies evidently with the type of discourse. At one end of the scale, in the strict exposition of some highly criticized and settled science through technicalized and rigid speech, a large proportion of them are independent. They mean the same whatever other words they are put with; or if a word fluctuates, it moves only into a small number of stable positions, which can be recorded and are anchored to definitions. That is the ideal limit towards which we aim in exposition. Unfortunately we tend—increasingly since the 17th Century—to take rigid discourse as the norm, and impose its standards upon the rest of speech. This is much as if we thought that water, for all its virtues, in canals, baths and turbines, were really a weak form of ice. The other end of the scale is in poetry—in some forms of poetry rather. We know very much less about the behavior of words in these cases—when their virtue is to have no fixed and settled meaning separable from those of the other words they occur with. There are many more possibilities here than the theory of language has yet tried to think out. Often the whole utterance in which the co-operating meanings of the component words hang on one another is not itself stable in meaning. It utters not one meaning but a *movement* among meanings. Of course, even in the strictest prose we always have one thing that may be described as a movement of meaning. We have change as the sentence develops. In 'The cat is on the mat' we begin with the cat and end with the mat. There is a progression of some sort in every explicit sentence. But in the strictest prose the meanings of the separate words theoretically stay put and thought passes from one to another of them. At the other end of the scale the whole meaning of the sentence shifts, and with it any meanings we may try to ascribe to the individual words. In the extreme case it will go on moving as long as we bring fresh wits to study it. When Octavius Cæsar is gazing down at Cleopatra dead, he says,

> She looks like sleep,
> As she would catch another Antony
> In her strong toil of grace.

'Her strong toil of grace.' Where, in terms of what entries in what possible dictionary, do the meanings here of *toil* and *grace* come to rest?

But my subject is Rhetoric rather than Poetics and I want to keep to prose which is not too far from the strict scientific or 'rigid' end of this scale of dependent variabilities. In the kind of prose I am talking now, you have usually to wait till I have gone on a bit before you can decide how you will understand the opening parts of the sentences. If, instead,

I were reading you the first few theorems of Euclid, that would not be so. You would understand, as soon as I said 'a triangle,' what the word meant, and though what I went on to say might qualify the meaning ('having two sides equal'), it would not destroy or completely change the meaning that you had so far given to the word. But in most prose, and more than we ordinarily suppose, the opening words have to wait for those that follow to settle what they shall mean—if indeed that ever gets settled.

All this holds good not only as to the *sense* of the waiting words but as regards all the other functions of language which we can distinguish and set over against the mere sense. It holds for the *feeling* if any towards what I am talking about, for *the relation towards my audience* I want to establish or maintain with the remark, and for the *confidence* I have in the soundness of the remark—to mention three main sorts of these other language functions. In speech, of course, I have the aid of intonation for these purposes. But, as with the meanings of words, so with the intonation structure. The intonation of the opening words is likely to be ambiguous; it waits till the utterance is completed for its full interpretation.

In writing we have to replace intonation as far as we can. Most of the more recondite virtues of prose style come from the skill with which the rival claims of these various language functions are reconciled and combined. And many of the rather mysterious terms that are usually employed in discussing these matters, *harmony*, *rhythm*, *grace*, *texture*, *smoothness*, *suppleness*, *impressiveness*, and so on are best taken up for analysis from this point of view. Or rather the passages which seem to exemplify these qualities (or fail to) are best examined with the multiplicity of the language functions in mind. For we can obviously do nothing with such words as these by themselves, in the blue. They may mean all sorts of different things in different literary contexts.

I have been leading up—or down, if you like—to an extremely simple and obvious but fundamental remark: that no word can be judged as to whether it is good or bad, correct or incorrect, beautiful or ugly, or anything else that matters to a writer, in isolation. That seems so evident that I am almost ashamed to say it, and yet it flies straight in the face of the only doctrine that for two hundred years has been officially inculcated—when any doctrine is inculcated in these matters. I mean the doctrine of Usage. The doctrine that there is a right or a good use for every word and that literary virtue consists in making that good use of it.

There are several bones that can be picked with that doctrine—as it has been expounded in many epochs and, in particular for us, from the middle of the 18th Century onwards. It is the worst legacy we have from that, in other ways, happy Century. At its best it can be found in George Campbell's *Philosophy of Rhetoric*—otherwise an excellent book in many respects. At its worst, or nearly its worst, the doctrine can be found in most of the Manuals of Rhetoric and Composition which have afflicted the schools—American schools especially. It asserts that 'Good use is the general, present-day practice of the best writers.' One bone we could pick would be with that 'best.' How are they the best writers except by using the words in the best ways? We settle that they *are* the best writers because we find them using their words successfully. We do not settle that theirs is the right, the 'good usage' of the words because *they* use them so. Never was there a crazier case of putting the cart before the horse. It is as though we were to maintain that apples are healthy because[1] wise people eat them, instead of recognizing that it is the other way about—that it is what the food will do for us which makes us eat it, not the fact that we eat it which makes it good food.

But that is not the main bone I have to pick with the doctrine, which is that it blanks out and hides the interinanimation between words. I had better cite you a sentence or two in evidence, or you may think I am inventing a ghost to exorcize. I will take them from a *Manual of Rhetoric* which carries the names of three authors: Messrs. Gardiner, Kittredge and Arnold. And I choose this book because the regard which I have for Mr. Kittredge's name makes a doctrine which has that sanction seem the better worth refuting. The authors write: 'Usage governs language. There is no other standard. By usage, however, is meant the practice of the best writers and speakers.' (I have already asked what standard is supposed to settle which are the best.) They go on to consider 'four great general principles of choice: *correctness*, *precision*, *appropriateness* and *expressiveness*,' which, they say, 'within the limits of good usage and in every case controlled by it...should guide us in the choice of words.' And this is what they say of correctness: 'Correctness is the most elementary of all requirements. The meanings of words are settled by usage. If we use a word incorrectly—that is in a sense which does not customarily belong to it—our readers will miss our thought, or, at best, they must arrive at it by inference and guess-work.'

[1] 'Because' is offering to play one of its most troublesome tricks here, of course in the shift from 'cause' to 'reason.'

Inference and guesswork! What else is interpretation? How, apart from inference and skilled guesswork, can we be supposed ever to understand a writer or speaker's thought? This is, I think, a fine case of poking the fire from the top. But I have still my main bit of evidence to give you. My authors say: 'In studying the four great principles of choice, we observe that only the first (correctness) involves the question of right and wrong. The others deal with questions of discrimination between better and worse—that is with the closer adaptation of words to the thoughts and feelings which we undertake to express. Further, it is only in dealing with the first principle (correctness) that we can keep our attention entirely on the single word.'

There! that is the view I wished to illustrate. Let us not boggle about the oddities of its expression: 'right and wrong,' 'better and worse'; or worry as to how by keeping 'our attention entirely on a single word' we could settle anything at all about it—except perhaps about its spelling! The important point is that words are here supposed just sheerly to possess their sense, as men have their names in the reverse case, and to carry this meaning with them into sentences regardless of the neighbour words. That is the assumption I am attacking, because, if we follow up its practical consequences in writing and reading and trace its effects upon interpretation, we shall find among them no small proportion of the total of our verbal misunderstandings.

I am anxious not to seem to be illustrating this sort of misunderstanding myself here, unwittingly, in my interpretation of this passage. I know well enough that the authors probably had in mind such incorrectness as occurs when people say 'ingenious' when they mean 'ingenuous'; and I know that the Usage Doctrine can be interpreted in several ways which make it true and innocuous.

It can say and truly, for example, that we learn how to use words from responding to them and noting how other people use them. Just how we do so learn is a deep but explorable question. It can say equally truly, that a general conformity between users is a condition of communication. *That* no one would dream of disputing. But if we consider conformity we see that there are two kinds of conformity. Conformity in the general process of interpretation, and conformity in the specific products. We all know how the duller critics of the 18th Century (the century that gave us the current Doctrine of Usage), the people Wordsworth was thinking of when he wrote his Preface, confused the poetic product with the poetic process and thought a poem good because it used poetic diction—the words that former good poets had used—and used them in the same ways. The Usage Doctrine, in the noxious interpretation of it, is just that blunder in a more pervasive and more dangerous incidence. The noxious interpretation is the common one. Its evil is that it takes the senses of an author's words to be things we know before we read him, fixed factors with which he has to build up the meaning of his sentences as a mosaic is put together of discrete independent tesserae. Instead, they are resultants which we arrive at only through the interplay of the interpretative possibilities of the whole utterance. In brief, we have to guess them and we guess much better when we realize we are guessing, and watch out for indications, than when we think we know.[1]

There are as many morals for the writer as for the reader in all this, but I will keep to interpretation. A word or phrase when isolated momentarily from its controlling neighbours is free to develop irrelevant senses which may then beguile half the other words to follow it. And this is at least equally true with the language functions *other than sense*, with *feeling*, say. I will give you one example of an erratic interpretation of feeling, and if I take it from the same *Manual of Rhetoric* that is because it illustrates one of the things to which the mosaic view or habit of interpretation, as opposed to the organic, often leads.

The Authors give the following from Bacon's *Advancement of Learning*. And in re-reading it I will ask you to note how cunningly Bacon, in describing some misuses of learning, takes back with one hand what he seems to be offering with the other, indicating both why men do prefer misuses and why they should not do so.

> But the greatest error of all the rest is the mistaking or misplacing of the last or furthest end of knowledge. For men have entered into a desire of learning and knowledge, sometimes upon a natural curiosity and inquisitive appetite; sometimes to entertain their minds with variety and delight; sometimes for ornament and reputation; and sometimes to enable them to victory of wit and contradiction; and most times for lucre and profession; and seldom sincerely to give a true account of their gift of reason, to the benefit and use of men: as if there were sought in knowledge a couch, whereupon to rest a searching or restless spirit; or a terrace, for a wandering and variable mind to walk up and down with a fair prospect; or a tower of state, for a proud mind to raise itself upon; or a fort or commanding ground, for strife and contention; or a shop, for profit or sale; and not a rich storehouse, for the glory of the Creator and the relief of man's estate.

[1] See the Note at the end of this Lecture.

There is much to take to heart here—especially as to the couch aspect of the Usage Doctrine, and, I must admit, the tower and the fort—but what the authors say about it is this:

> Here the splendor of the imagery is no mere embellishment. Without it, Bacon could not have given adequate expression to his enthusiastic appreciation of learning and his fine scorn for the unworthy uses to which it is sometimes put. At the same time, the figures elevate the passage from the ordinary levels of prose to a noble eloquence. (p. 372)

What splendor is there in the imagery? These images have no splendor as Bacon uses them, but are severely efficient, a compact means for saying what he has to say. His 'enthusiastic appreciation' (a poor phrase, I suggest, to smudge over him!) of the use of knowledge and his 'fine scorn' of unworthy uses are given only if we refuse to be beguiled by the possibilities of splendor in the isolated images. Loose them even a little from their service, let their 'splendor' act independently, and they begin at once to fight against his intention. For the terrace, the tower and the fort, if they were allowed to 'elevate,' would make the misplacings of the last and furthest end of knowledge seem much grander than 'a true account of their gift of reason, to the benefit and use of men'—as a terrace or tower of state or a fort will seem grander than a mere rich storehouse.

Let me go on to some further types of the mutual control and interinanimation between words. So far I have considered only the influence of words actually present in the passage, but we have to include words which are not actually being uttered and are only in the background. Take the case of what are variously called expressive, symbolic, or simulative words—words which 'somehow illustrate the meaning more immediately than do ordinary speech forms,' to quote Leonard Bloomfield. Examples are *flip, flap, flop, flitter, flimmer, flicker, flutter, flash, flush, flare, glare, glitter, glow, gloat, glimmer, bang, bump, lump, thump, thwack, whack, sniff, sniffle, snuff*... Why should these seem so peculiarly appropriate, or fitting, to the meanings we use them for? The popular view is that these words just simply imitate, are copies of, what they mean. But that is a short-cut theory which often does not work, and we can, I think, go further and do better. As Bloomfield, in his excellent book, *Language*, says, 'the explanation is a matter of grammatical structure, to the speaker it seems as if the sounds were especially suited to the meaning.' The speaker usually thinks moreover that the word seems suited because in some way it resembles the meaning, or, if this seems unplausible, that there must be *some* direct connection between them. If it is not the sound of the word which resembles the meaning then perhaps the tongue and lip movements instead imitate something to do with the meaning and so on. Sir Richard Paget's theories of imitative gestures are likely to be appealed to nowadays.

The most that the modern linguist—who compares the very different words which are used in different languages for their meanings—is prepared to allow towards this resemblance of sound and sense is that 'we can distinguish, with various degrees of clearness and with doubtful cases on the border line, a system of initial and final root-forming morphemes of vague signification.' Note how guarded Bloomfield is over such a point.

I must explain what a morpheme is. Two or more words are said to share a morpheme when they have, at the same time, something in common in their meaning and something in common in their sound. The joint semantic-phonetic unit which distinguishes them is what is called a morpheme. It is the togetherness of a peculiar sound and a peculiar meaning for a number of words.

Thus *flash*, *flare*, *flame*, *flicker*, *flimmer* have in common the sound (fl-) and a suggestion of a 'moving light'—and this joint possession is the morpheme. Similarly *blare*, *flare*, *glare*, *stare* have the sound (-ɛə) in common and also the meaning 'big light or noise' shall we say, and this couple—sound and meaning—is the morpheme. So with 'smoothly wet' and (sl-) in *slime*, *slip*, *slush*, *slobber*, *slide*, *slither*. But *pare*, *pear*, *pair*, though they have a sound in common, have no meaning in common, so have no common morpheme.

Of course, the existence of a group of words with a common morpheme has an influence on the formation of other words, and on the pronunciation of other words—assimilating them to the group. Thus, given *skid* and *skate*, that is a strong additional reason, against an English convention, for saying *skee* rather than *shee*.

This pedantic looking term, *morpheme*, is useful because with its help we manage to avoid saying that the sound (sl-) somehow itself means something like 'smoothly wet or slippery' and gain a way of saying no more than that a group of words which share that sound also share a peculiar meaning. And that is all we are entitled to say. To go further and say that the words share the meaning *because* they contain this sound and because this sound has that meaning is to bring in more than we know—an explanation or theory to account for what we do know.

And actually it is a bad explanation. For this sound, by itself, means nothing. It is not the shared sound but each of the words which has the meaning. The sound by itself either means nothing at all—as with (fl) in *flame*, *flare*, *flash*, *flicker*—or as with (-ɛə) in *blare*, *flare*, *glare*, *stare* it has by itself only an irrelevant meaning, namely, that of *air*, 'what we breathe.'

The theoretical position here is worth close study because it is typical of a very large group of positions in which we tend, too boldly and too innocently, to go beyond our evidence and to assume, as the obvious explanation, as almost a datum, what is really the conclusion of a vague and quick and unchecked inductive argument, often a bad and unwarrantable argument. Why should a group of words with a sound in common have similar meanings unless there was a correspondence of some kind between the sound and the meaning? That seems plausible. But state the argument more explicitly, look over the evidence carefully, and it becomes unplausible, for then we have to notice the other words which share the sound but do not share the meaning and the other words which share the meaning without the sound. Then we see that we have been applying to words the sort of argument which would represent a fashion as a spontaneous expression of original taste on the part of all who follow it. We find in fact that we have been looking at the problem upside down. That so far from a perceived correspondence between sound and meaning being the explanation of the sharing, the existence of a group of words with a common sound and meaning is the explanation of our belief in a correspondence.

This situation, I said a moment ago, is typical. We can hardly, I think, exaggerate in an estimate of the number of literary and rhetorical problems which, as usually formulated, are upside down in this fashion. For example, our common assumption that when a word such as *beautiful* or *art* or *religion* or *good*, is used in a great variety of ways, there will be found something in common to all the uses, something which is the fundamental or essential meaning of the word and the explanation of its use. So we spend our wits trying to discover this common essential meaning, without considering that we are looking for it, most often, only as a result of a weak and hasty inductive argument. This assumption that the same word ought to have or must have the same meaning, in an important respect, is one of those bullying assumptions that the context theorem of meanings would defend us from.

But to come back to this parallel assumption that some words, apart from other words, and in their own right in virtue of their sound must mean certain things. It was Aristotle who said that there can be no natural connection between the sound of any language and the things signified, and, if we set the problem right side up and remember the other words before examining it, we shall have to agree with him. Indeed, if we ask the question fairly it becomes—when we get it clear—nearly senseless. What resemblance or natural connection can there be between the semantic and phonetic elements in the morpheme? One is a sound, the other a reference. 'Is (fl–) really like "moving light" in any way in which (sl–) or (gl–) is not?' Is that not like asking whether the taste of turkey is like growing in some way that the taste of mint is not?

I conclude then that these expressive or symbolic words get their feeling of being peculiarly fitting from the other words sharing the morpheme which support them in the background of the mind. If that is so, all sorts of consequences are at once evident. In translation, for example, the expressive word in another language will not necessarily sound at all like the original word. It will be a word that is backed up by other words in a somewhat analogous fashion. Evidently again, a proper appreciation of the expressiveness of a word in a foreign language will be no matter of merely knowing its meaning and relishing its sound. It is a matter of having, in the background of the mind, the other words in the language which share morphemes with it. Thus no one can appreciate these expressive features of foreign words justly without a really wide familiarity with the language. Without that our estimates are merely whimsical.

We can, and I think should, extend this notion of a word as being backed up by other words that are not uttered or thought of. A first extension is to words that sound alike but do not share a morpheme, do not have a common meaning but only some relevant meaning. Thus *blare*, *scare* and *dare* do not share a morpheme, but on occasion the peculiar force of *blare* may well come to it in part from the others. This, of course, is only recognizing on a larger, wider scale the principle that Lewis Carroll was using in Jabberwocky. Its relevance to the theory of rhymes and assonances is obvious.

Another and a wider extension would include not only influences from words which in part sound alike, but from other words which in part overlap in meaning. Words, for example, which we might have used instead, and, together with these, the reasons why we did not use them. Another such extension looks to the other uses, in other contexts, of what we, too simply, call 'the same word.' The meaning of a word on some occasions is quite as much in what it keeps out, or at a distance, as in what it brings in. And, on other occasions, the meaning comes from other partly parallel uses whose relevance we can feel, without necessarily being able to state it explicitly. But with these last leaps I may seem in danger of making the force of a word, the feeling that no other word could possibly do so well or take its place, a matter whose explanation will drag in the whole of the rest of the language. I am not sure, though, that we need be shy of something very like this as a conclusion. A really masterly use of a language—in free or fluid, not technical discourse—Shakespeare's use of English for example, goes a long way towards using the language as a whole.

Cleopatra, taking up the asp, says to it:

> Come, thou mortal wretch,
> With thy sharp teeth this knot intrinsicate
> Of life at once untie; poor venomous fool,
> Be angry, and despatch!

Consider how many senses of *mortal*, besides 'death-dealing' come in; compare: 'I have immortal longings in me.' Consider *knot*: 'This knot intrinsicate of life': 'Something to be undone,' 'Something that troubles us until it is undone,' 'Something by which all holding-together hangs,' 'The nexus of all meaning.' Whether the homophone *not* enters in here may be thought a doubtful matter. I feel it does. But consider *intrinsicate* along with *knot*. Edward Dowden, following the fashion of his time in making Shakespeare as simple as possible, gives 'intricate' as the meaning here of *intrinsicate*. And the Oxford Dictionary, sad to say, does likewise. But Shakespeare is bringing together half a dozen meanings from *intrinsic* and *intrinse*: 'Familiar,' 'intimate,' 'secret,' 'private,' 'innermost,' 'essential,' 'that which constitutes the very nature and being of a thing'—all the medical and philosophic meanings of his time as well as 'intricate' and 'involved.' What the word does is exhausted by no one of these meanings and its force comes from all of them and more. As the movement of my hand uses nearly the whole skeletal system of the muscles and is supported by them, so a phrase may take its powers from an immense system of supporting uses of other words in other contexts.

NOTE

The word *usage* itself well illustrates some of the more troublesome shifts of meaning. An improved Rhetoric has among its aims an improved control over these. Here perhaps a list of some of the senses of *usage* may help us in avoiding misunderstanding.

1 The most inclusive sense is 'the entire range of the powers which the word can exert as an instrument of communication in all situations and in co-operation with any other words.'
(In this sense 'Usage, and usage alone, undoubtedly controls language.')

2 'Some specific power which, in a limited range of situations and with a limited type of verbal context the word normally exerts.'
(This is often called a *use* or *sense* and is what the Dictionary attempts to record in its definitions, by giving other words, phrases and sentences with the same specific power.)

3 An instance of 2, at a certain place in Shakespeare, say, which may be appealed to to show that the word can have that power.

4 A supposed fixed 'proper' meaning that the word must be kept to (has in its own right, etc.). This notion is derived from 1, 2 and 3 by over-simplification and a misconception of the working of language which, typically, takes the meaning of a sentence to be something built up from separate meanings of its words—instead of recognizing that it is the other way about and that the meanings of words are derived from the meanings of sentences in which they occur. This misconception assimilates the process by which words have their meanings determined with that by which they have their spelling determined and is the origin of a large part of misinterpretation.

14

ERIC PARTRIDGE

(1894–)

The subject of slang was of particular interest to the Society for Pure English. The present article, by one of the few authorities on this phenomenon, is an attempt to disentangle the many functions of slang, to isolate some of its defining characteristics, to discuss the relationship between slang and other categories of language, and to provide detailed illustration of the many classes of slang which exist. Eric Partridge is the author of a number of books on the vocabulary of English, including the large *Dictionary of Slang and Unconventional English*, which is an important source-book for further information on this topic.

'Slang'

(Society for Pure English, Tract LV, 1940)

1 *Etymology, definition, synonyms*

The etymology of the word *slang* is as obscure as the definition of Slang is difficult. *The O.E.D.* holds that connexion with Norwegian words in *sleng-* is improbable, whereas Dr. Bradley seems to have thought, Professors H. C. K. Wyld and Ernest Weekley actually think, that *slang* is cognate with *slengjeord*, 'a new slang word', *slengjenamn*, 'a nickname' (a word slung at one), and *slengja kjeften*, literally 'to sling the jaw', hence 'to abuse a person'; *Webster's New International Dictionary* shares their opinion; but they do not actually derive *slang* from Norwegian. Although I cannot prove it, my theory is that *slang* is language *slung*[1] about. This 'sling' etymology was suggested to me by a quotation[2] of *ca.* 1400,

> The bolde wordes that [he] did sling.

Unconventional English affords several parallels: *to sling words* and *sling language* mean 'to talk'; to *sling the bat* is to speak the vernacular,

[1] The fact that *slang* is nowhere recorded as a past participle may appear insuperable to many: but *slang* was originally a cant word; perhaps, therefore, a deliberate perversion of *slung* (recorded long before our noun *slang*).

[2] *O.E.D. sling*, v. 3.

especially to speak the everyday language of the foreign country in which one resides or serves; the soldier of the Regular Army employs it for 'to speak Hindustani', hence 'to speak Arabic', or even 'to speak French'; perhaps relevant is *sling off at*, 'to jeer at or taunt', which approximates to the colloquial *slang*, 'to scold or to address abusively'; more remote is *slanging*, a music-hall term of the 1880's for 'singing', from the practice of interpolating 'gags' between the verses of a song.

And is slang capable of definition? Professor G. H. McKnight holds that no exact definition can be given. *The O.E.D.*, however, succeeds admirably with its 'language of a highly colloquial[1] type, considered as below the level of standard educated speech, and consisting of either new words or of current words employed in some special sense', to which the following definition by H. W. Fowler, inadequate by itself, is complementary: 'the diction that results from the favourite game among the young and lively of playing with words and renaming things and actions'.

Only since *ca.* 1850 has *slang* been the predominant name of 'illegitimate' colloquial speech; in the eighteenth century it usually meant cant (or the language of the underworld). From 1718 until *ca.* 1850 a common synonym was *flash*, properly applied to cant. Before 1850 *slang* tended to be a generic term for all non-Standard English except dialect. And in the nineteenth century, at least three other synonyms of *slang*, in our sense, were used: *lingo* among the lower classes, *jargon* in the middle and upper classes, and *argot* among the cultured and the pretentious: and they are still so used. So late as 1873, John Camden Hotten protested against the restriction of Slang to proletarian slang (and illiteracies) and to cant.

2 *Origin and uses; attitudes to slang*

Slang, the acme and quintessence of spoken and informal language, is to be related, not to phonetic laws, grammatical rules, and philosophical ideals, but to topicality, convenience, human nature at its most natural. As it originates, so it flourishes best, in unconventionality. 'Among the impulses which lead to the invention of slang, the two most important seem to be the desire to secure increased vivacity and the desire to secure increased sense of intimacy in the use of language' (Henry Bradley), and the most favourable conditions are those of 'crowding and excitement,

[1] I.e. sub-Standard. I use 'colloquial' in the narrower sense: that class of non-Standard English which lies between Standard English (above it) and slang (below it). See 'English: Good; Bad; and Worse', a chapter in my *The World of Words* (1938).

and artificial life.... Any sudden excitement or peculiar circumstance is quite sufficient to originate and set going a score of slang words' (John Camden Hotten). Slang is the self-expression of the individual at least as much as of the clique, the profession, the trade, the class; and, as Greenough and Kittredge remarked, 'its coinage and circulation comes rather from the wish of the individual to distinguish himself by oddity or grotesque humour'. Another potent force that makes for slang is 'an honourable discontent with the battered or bleached phrases in far too general use', this fresh slang being 'the plain man's poetry, the plain man's aspiration from penny plain to twopence coloured' (Earle Welby). Slang is personal in its origin; 'it is the user that determines the matter, and particularly the user's habitual way of thinking' (Mencken). Slang is 'devised... by individuals of wit and ingenuity'—by Cockney and cleric, by stockbroker and scholar, by labourer and lawyer, by soldier and sailor, by the man in the street and the man in the car. And, whatever the source of slang, personality and environment (whether social or occupational) are the two coefficients, the two principal factors, the most powerful determinants of the nature of slang: as they are also, one supposes, of language as a whole and of style in general.

But, in answering the question 'Why is slang used at all?', can we not go farther than Bradley and Welby and Whitney (slang is the product of an 'exuberance of mental activity, and the natural delight of language-making')? Slang is employed for one or more of sixteen reasons. That there may be others is probable; nevertheless, the following reasons are, or have been, operative and valid:

1 In high spirits, by the young in heart and mind, whether youthful, mature, or elderly; for the fun of the thing, or, as slang would have it, 'just for the hell of it'; in playfulness or waggishness.
2 As an exercise of wit and ingenuity, or as an outlet for humour. The motive is usually snobbishness or self-display or emulation on the one hand; or, on the other, a lively responsiveness to one's interlocutors or a delight in virtuosity.
3 To be novel or 'different'.
4 To be picturesque, either positively (graphic self-expression) or negatively (from a desire to avoid insipidity or dullness).
5 Or to be arresting or startling, with no intention of leaving one's wish unperceived.
6 To escape from the bondage of clichés.
7 Or—likewise from impatience with existing words and phrases—to be concise and brief.

8 To enrich the language. (Literary and deliberate rather than spontaneous—except among Cockneys, who have a highly developed inventive faculty.)

9 To invest the abstract with solidity and concreteness, and the remote with immediacy and appositeness; to terrestrialize the ethereal; and to reduce the idealistic to the materialistic. (Among the cultured the desire and the process are usually premeditated, whereas among the uncultured they are instinctive and democratic.)

10 *a*) To disperse or, at the least, to lessen the solemnity or excessive gravity of a conversation, or the pomposity of a piece of writing.

b) To deaden the sting of a refusal, a rejection, a recantation; or, on the other hand, to give additional point to one.

c) To mitigate the tragedy, to lighten the inevitability of death or the seeming inevitability of madness; to 'prettify' folly or drunkenness; to mask the ugliness or the starkness of profound turpitude (e.g. cruel treachery, utter and flagrant ingratitude). And thus to enable the speaker or his auditor to 'carry on'; for such things have to be faced and overcome.

11 To speak or write down to an inferior, or to amuse a superior, public: to phrase it more broadly and basically, to put oneself on an emotional and mental level with one's audience, or on a friendly level with one's subject-matter.

12 For ease of intercourse, on social rather than psychological grounds. (Not to be confused, even though it occasionally merges, with the preceding.)

13 To induce friendliness or intimacy of a deeper, more durable kind.

14 To let it be known, rather than to assert, that one belongs or has belonged to a certain school or university, a certain trade or profession, an artistic or intellectual set, or social class; in brief, to be 'in the swim' and establish contact.

15 To prove, to show, or especially to imply that some one is *not* 'in the swim' or is an 'outsider'.

16 To be mysterious or even secret, not understood by those around one. (Schoolchildren and students, very close friends and lovers, members of political secret societies, persons in prison or in danger of being there, these are the principal exponents.)

From the preceding paragraph, it is evident that the general attitude towards slang has considerably changed. In 1825, J. P. Thomas (not a notability) expressed himself thus vigorously in *My Thought Book*: 'The language of slang is the conversation of fools.... The friends of literature will never adopt it, as it is actively opposed to pure and grammatical diction.' Actually it may be used with the nicest grammatical discrimination. Hotten, in 1859, frankly declared that 'the squeamishness which tries to ignore the existence of slang fails signally, for not only in the streets, and in the prisons, but at the bar, on the bench, in the pulpit, and in the Houses of Parliament, does slang make itself heard and...understood too'. By 1893, as appears from a well-known essay by J. Brander Matthews, a kindly feeling towards slang had become noticeable even in academic circles, although Greenough and Kittredge in 1901 were slightly, and the brothers Fowler in *The King's English*, a few years later, were very reactionary. 'As style is the great antiseptic, so slang is the great corrupting matter', said the Fowlers; but Professor H. C. K. Wyld redressed the balance with the temperate verdict, 'While slang is essentially part of familiar and colloquial speech, it is not necessarily incorrect or vulgar in its proper place.'

Not even Americans, very generally regarded as ardent supporters and picturesque partisans of slang, have always been well disposed towards it. 'The use of slang is at once a sign and a cause of mental atrophy' (Oliver Wendell Holmes, *ca.* 1857); 'Slang is the speech of him who robs the literary garbage cans on their way to the dumps' (Ambrose Bierce, *ca.* 1900). Nevertheless, the prevailing American attitude of twentieth-century Americans is that of Carl Sandburg: 'Slang is language which takes off its coat, spits on its hands, and goes to work.'

3 *Characteristics of slang, in relation to language in general*

Slang is on many levels and of many grades: innocent, cultured; cheaply vulgar or vigorously racy, healthily or disgustingly low; linguistically debased; picturesque and imaginative, or nauseatingly repetitive. And at all levels and for all grades, one of the most serviceable bases of judgement is the degree of dignity, or perhaps rather the degree of impudence, casualness, familiarity. Viewed as a whole, slang is an accumulation of terms that, coming from every quarter and every class, are understood by the majority. Viewed analytically, slang has a hierarchy, exemplified, in ascending order of respectability, by the following phrases: *be knocked out in an exam.—come a cropper—mortgage one's reputation—be at fault* (long a dignified idiom).

At fault (from a dog's losing the scent) exemplifies a frequent and important characteristic of slang: the tendency of slang expressions to rise in the verbal world and thus to be ennobled. 'Many of these [slang] words and phrases are but serving their apprenticeship and will eventually become the active strength of our language' (H. T. Buckle); 'The slang of one generation has often become the literary language of the next, and the manners which distinguish contemporary life suggest that this will be still more frequently the case in the future' (Ernest Weekley, *ca.* 1920); 'Most idiom is well-proven slang....Idiom is the most distinctively English (or American) constituent of the language, and... idiom is fed by the tested inventions of slang' (John Brophy, 1932). Among the slang phrases that have improved their status are *to start in, on the stocks, to peter out, to be in at the death, to come (up) to (the) scratch, below the belt, cock of the walk.*

But while linguistic parvenus are mounting to respectability, certain aristocrats pass them in a gloomy declension to the literary depths: *blooming* and *bloody, by the skin of the teeth,* and *tell the world.*

More important is another kind of descent. Of slang in general, Niceforo has said that 'tout ce qui est abstrait doit se matérialiser; tout ce qui est matériel doit...se dégrader et se déprécier'.[1] We see this tendency at work in pejorative formations, in depreciative irony, and, at the extreme, in violent reprobation. Of these, the most interesting psychologically is irony; especially in military slang. 'Some of the terror disappeared, together with the pomp, from war and military glory,' wrote John Brophy in 1930, 'when the soldier decided to call his steel helmet a *tin hat,* his bayonet a *toothpick,* his entrenching-tool handle a *piggy-stick,* and a murderous bombardment a *strafe* or *hate.*' The profoundest account of pejoratizing, however, is that by Professor A. Carnoy in *La Science du Mot,* 1927. 'Dysphemism', he says, 'is a reaction against pedantry, stiffness, and pretentiousness, but also against nobility and dignity in language. It seeks to keep language, especially spoken language, at a low level....On the other hand, it displays good humour in poverty and in adversity....Dysphemism consists, above all, in the substitution for dignified or merely normal terms, of expressions borrowed from more vulgar, familiar, joyous spheres....It is a way of regarding serious and important things as realities that, for all their triviality, are reassuring.' A minor species of dysphemism is the pejorative suffix, as in 'robust*ious*' (now almost respectable) and 'golupt*ious*'.

[1] [*tout ce...déprécier* All that is abstract must be made concrete; all that is concrete must become debased and depreciated.]

To dysphemism is opposed euphemism, which is indulgent where the other is pitiless; kindly where the other is mocking; discreet where the other is brutally frank. Dysphemism aims to stimulate, irritate, shock; euphemism seeks to evade unpleasantness and to calm the person addressed. Euphemism does not pass over or ignore the painful, ugly, filthy, tragic, for silence is best when that is the aim; it tries only to minimize or to prettify. Euphemism is both a sedative and a means to gradual, non-violent assimilation and acceptance. In slang, euphemism may be vague or particular, closely connected or remotely associated, enigmatically affirmative or obviously litotic, solemn or ludicrous, unconventionally droll or conventionally serious, verbally analogous or verbally perverted, as in the following short list: *Good gracious*, *geewhiz* (originally *Je-whizz*); *all-fired* (hell-fired); *make easy* (to kill) and *step into one's last bus* (to die); *hop the bags* (to attack the enemy across no man's land); *barmy*, *bats*, *bug-house*, *cracked*, *crackers*, *dippy*, *goofy*, *loopy*, *not all there*, *nuts* (mad); *in Adam and Eve's togs* (naked); *angel-makers* (baby-farmers); *excuse my French!* (forgive me my strong language) and *to loose French* (to swear and curse in English).

In several of those examples there is humour. 'An element of humour is almost always present in slang.... Thus to call a hat a *lid* is amusing because it puts a hat and a pot-lid in the same class.... [Slang] sets things in their proper places with a smile' (Bradley). The humour of some slang words, however, consists less in association than in sound, as in *biff*, a blow or to strike; *flummox* 'to disconcert'; *spiflicate* 'to punish'; *catawampus* 'vermin'. At a lower level, *picture-askew* 'picturesque', and *gust* 'guest'; *finance* 'fiancé' is wittier.

Of such mutilations, some are caused by an instinctive desire to speak badly. Much of the spirit of slang is openly hostile to linguistic respectability; hence the tendency of slang to adopt words from the underworld: *booze*; *cove*, *cully*, *pal*; *bilk*, *ramp*, to select six from perhaps sixty.

In unconventional language, certain upstart qualities and part of the aesthetic as distinct from the moral impropriety spring from four characteristics of the slang of all periods and countries: volatility and light-headedness, so much less amiable, so much less enduring than light-heartedness; ephemerality; the search for novelty; and the sway of fashion. One of the motives behind metaphors and neologisms is the desire to avoid the accepted phrase. This desire for novelty operates more freely, audaciously, rapidly in slang than in standard speech. The volatility of the slang of the upper classes is well known: and need not be laboured here. The ephemerality of slang is more important. Most slang words and phrases die within a generation or, at most, a generation and a half; when they die, novelties no less transitory take their place; the slang expression is dead, long live the new slang expression! Slang, short-lived, is unsuitable as a means of general intercommunication. And if a slang expression becomes a fashion, and is publicized as a fashion, it is doomed to rapid extinction; but if it is found to be useful, that expression will soon take its place in general speech. Yet even the merely fashionable part of slang, including parroted catch-phrases, has a sociological value, for it annalizes the fashion or the craze and, occasionally, helps the historian. 'Were we able to explain just why a fashion, a catchword, or a phrase of slang becomes popular, we should likewise be able to account for the initial acceptance of a myth. All we can say concerning such things is that they supply a need, or answer a craving, or arouse the interest of the majority of a social group' (William Sherwood Fox, *Greek and Roman Mythology*, 1930).

But most slang, whether ephemerally fashionable among a clique or durably general in a class or even a people, falls into the dichotomy of good and bad. Good slang says, vigorously, concisely, pellucidly, what too much literary language says feebly, diffusely, obscurely. 'The distinctive test of good slang...is that it has a real meaning. Bad slang has no meaning; it is simply a succession of sounds which, because they come trippingly from the tongue, impose upon the ignorant imagination of the reader...Good slang is idiomatically expressive, and has a narrow escape sometimes from being poetical.'[1] It does not always escape: *wife in water-colours*, a temporary mistress; *whispering syl-slinger*, a prompter (theatrical); *push up daisies*, to be dead (military); *go West*, to die: these are of the essence of poetry; poetry not epic, not metaphysical, not mystical, but at least popular. 'Plusieurs termes populaires conviennent si bien à l'expression de certaines idées que les Français cultivés les emploient à tout instant';[2] this remark would have been equally true if the author had substituted 'les Anglais'; consider such slang words as *the movies*, *wangle*, *Tommy* (the soldier in the ranks). 'Good slang is that which gives new life to old or abstract ideas. Bad slang lacks the precision of statement of good slang. It arises from mental sloth instead of from mental acuteness...It puts the imagination to sleep instead of awakening it. It is usually cumbersome, where good

[1] The *Atlantic Monthly* (March 1893): (?) J. Brander Matthews.

[2] [*Plusieurs termes...instant* Several popular terms fit in so well with the expression of certain ideas that the cultivated French use them immediately.] Henri Bauche, *Le Langage populaire* (2nd ed. 1928).

slang is compact' (John Brophy). It may also be colourless instead of bright, silly instead of sensible, unconvincing instead of inevitable, strained instead of natural. Examples of bad slang are these: *As I used to was*, *ace of spades* (a widow), *altogethery* (drunk), *booth-burster* (a ranting 'barn-stormer'), *everlasting shoes* (feet), *furniture picture* (one of no artistic merit), *headguard* (a hat), *machiner* (a coach horse), *olive oil!* and, more ephemeral still, *au reservoir!* for 'au revoir!'; *scripturience*, an itch to write (*cacoëthes scribendi*); *tannergram* (a sixpenny telegram), *yawney* (a dolt, or *sawney*).

But how much slang is creative in the absolute sense? The old saying holds good: *ex nihilo nihil fit*.[1] Most slang consists of old words changed in form or, far more often, changed in sense; such common, basic words as *do* (to kill, rob, swindle), *make* (to steal), *go* (an event or occurrence or incident), *out* (to render senseless), *off* (to depart), are, in their slang senses, as truly creations as are derivative and compound formations from a root. Consider what Carnoy has called the 'slipping of the dominant note' in *That's funny!* (odd or strange), *None of your funny* (dishonest) *tricks!*, *He looks funny* (ill, or drunk), *I'll funny you* (teach you not to play practical jokes), *the funny man of the show* (the comedian or, in a circus, the clown).

A significant group of sense-changes is that in which established slang, officialized by a general acceptance or relegated to the obsolescent or the obsolete, is renewed by ramifications that are genuinely creative. As McKnight remarked in 1923, '*Stop crowing* becomes *come off the perch*; keep your eyes *open* becomes keep your eyes *peeled* [or *skinned*]; *numskull* becomes *bonehead*; ...*give* a boy *the mitten* becomes *to jipp* [or *gyp*] a boy; ...*Camel* cigarettes become *Humps*; *bluffer* becomes *four-flusher*; *take the cake* becomes *take the Huntley and Palmer* [or *take the biscuit*].... The successive names applied to the "man of fashion" run in chronological sequence somewhat as follows: *trig—blood—macaroni—buck—incroyable—dandy—dude—swell—toff*' (all originally slang).

But the most important factor in the renewal of language is metaphor. With characteristic exaggeration and epigrammatic force, G. K. Chesterton, in his essay on slang in *The Defendant* (1901), delivered himself thus: 'The world of slang is...full of blue moons and white elephants, of men losing their heads, and men whose tongues run away with them.' Compare the following expressions from soldiers' slang (1914–18, and after): *angel-face*, a boyish-looking officer; *bag of rations*, a fussy person (whose words rattle in his head); *bantams* (infantrymen

[1] [*ex nihilo nihil fit* nothing is made out of nothing.]

5 ft. 1 in. to 5 ft. 4 in. in height), soon standardized; *bird-lime*, a recruiting sergeant; *bomb-proofer*, a man with a safe job; *bosom chums*, lice. Figurativeness abounds in slang: *cheek* or *face* for impudence; *bracelets* for handcuffs. Restriction by specialization is less common: *cackle*, to divulge a secret; *nob*, the head.

Restriction may operate also in form: by curtailment or by abbreviation. *Biz* 'business'; *bus* 'omnibus', which it has virtually supplanted by becoming Standard English; *cab* 'cabriolet'; *loony* 'lunatic'; *mental* 'mentally defective' (via *mental case*); *monk* 'monkey'; *rhino* and *hippo*; *varsity*; *vert*, a 'convert' or (a religious) 'pervert'. Note, too, how words have been formed from phrases: *chevy* (or *chivvy*) from *Chevy Chase*; *hoax* from *hocus pocus*; *nincompoop* from *non compos mentis*.

Playing on words may be mechanical, as in Foote's *anti-queer-uns*, antiquarians, and in *drinketite*, thirst, and *bite-etite*, appetite; or witty, as in the *canned music* of the phonograph and gramophone, and *dead above the ears*, brainless.

Less amusing and witty, but, for a time, much more widespread, are catch-phrases. *That's the barber*; *have a banana!*; *so is your old man*; *how's your poor feet?*; *I hope it keeps fine for you*; *chase me, Charlie*; *Ginger, your're barmy*; *get your hair cut!*; *have a heart!*; *what do you know about that?*; *this is the life!*; *the answer is a lemon*; *oh yeah?*; *sez you!* These 'blank checks of intellectual bankruptcy' (Oliver Wendell Holmes) capture the public fancy and, like too popular tunes, are repeated until they become exasperating and exacerbating. 'Here is a kind of shorthand language which enables the group to express and to realize its experiences without elaborate analysis.'

In such repetition there is exaggeration. But the commonest form of exaggeration is that which is technically known as hyperbole. Slangy violence requires less imagination, perceptiveness, taste, and delicacy than does literary style. Violence is often abused, especially in adjectives and adverbs: *awful* and *awfully*, *horrible* and *horribly*, *dreadful* and *dreadfully*, *terrible* and *terribly* ('awfully nice', 'terribly jolly', and other absurdly contradictory collocations).

But slang is also notable for the abundance of its synonyms and its artistic potentialities. These potentialities have been fully exploited in England perhaps only by *The Pink 'Un* and P. G. Wodehouse; in the United States, however, there have been many masters, of whom we may mention Artemus Ward, George Ade, O. Henry, Harry Witwer, Ring Lardner and Walter Winchell.

In slang and colloquialism, as also, though rather less prolifically, in cant, astonishingly rich synonymies express, with subtle variations, the primary necessities of life, the commonest functions, the most frequent actions, the most useful parts of the body, the most frequently recurring qualities (as connoted by their adjectives). The force of the Standard word, representative of a basic idea, determines the number and success of the slang synonyms; and the less 'reputable' the action, process, or object, the larger the number of synonyms. *To drink*, *a drink*, and *drunk* have occasioned far more synonyms than *to eat*, *food*, and *replete*; *to run away* than *to run*; *to go stealthily* than *to go*; *stomach* than *chin*; *fear* and *cowardice* than *courage*; *to kill* than *to be kind to*; *bad* than *good*. Squeamishness accounts for many, unconscious or deliberate virtuosity for yet more, of these.

In English, the ideas and facts most fertile in synonyms are money; drinking; drunkenness; the sexual organs and the sexual act. In *The Slang Dictionary*, Hotten lists 130 synonyms for money and particular coins, remarks that next comes drink 'from small beer to champagne', and sets 'intoxication and fuddlement generally' in the third place. But the tabooed words of Standard English are hardly less productive of slang synonyms: because of the need for euphemism or of a desire to give them a different appearance and complexion, these taboos result in synonyms more ingenious and, many of them, more picturesque than those for money and drink.

This synonymous abundance constitutes one of the factors in a subsidiary characteristic of slang: the difficulty of discovering the correct etymology of so many of its units. The origins are often topical, the mutilations irresponsible and violent, the imagery far-fetched. If the origin is not seized and nailed down while the word or the phrase is new and unstaled, it is often irrecoverable, for slang rarely gains admittance to a good dictionary until it has been in circulation for some years. Etymological puzzles are presented by the following words: *bamboozle*, *banter*, *Cockney*, *doggerel*, *pozzy* 'jam', *sham*, *tizzy*, and *Yankee*, all of which began as slang. Folk-etymology has rendered the etymologist's task more difficult: for example, in *upon my sam* (oath), which has nothing to do with a *Samuel* either Scriptural or profane.

4 *Affiliations*[1]

In one's own mind, one can perhaps determine the demarcations of slang and cant and colloquialism and illiteracy and vulgarity and dialect. To definitely establish them is almost impossible.

[1] See pp. 129–42 of my *Slang To-Day and Yesterday* for a much fuller treatment of this aspect.

But need we? The difference between slang and colloquialism has already been implied; dialect is not likely to be misapprehended; illiteracy is merely incorrectness of accidence, syntax, pronunciation; vulgarity is the use of words likely to give offence in polite circles and among sensitive persons. Slang enlists occasional help from dialect and from cant; slang, becoming general, useful, and widely recognized, mounts to the sphere of colloquialisms. Such, roughly, is the relationship: for cant promoted is slang, slang promoted is colloquialism, colloquialism promoted is Standard; dialect stands at one side, technicalities at another; illiteracy and vulgarity are social solecisms. But it must be realized that cant is not properly a low slang; it is not a slang at all. It is the secret vocabulary of the underworld (criminals; beggars and tramps): a glossary of words significant to the underworld: not properly a language.

5 *The Norm*

As there is a hierarchy of language, with Standard Speech at the top, so there is, if not a hierarchy, at least a group of slangs, with a Standard Slang at the top. Obviously it would be foolish to speak of military slang, nautical slang, commercial slang, school slang, university slang, if there were not such a standard; obviously, too, we could not pretend to chart those regions of slang unless we had a measure with which to separate and delimit the regions. We are obliged to begin with that nucleus and proceed from that norm which consists of the slang, and is in fact the slang, employed by those users of the Standard who do not speak, or are in fact not speaking, a vocational or social slang. There is a central body of slang: normal slang: Standard Slang. To it there come, ultimately and inevitably, accretions from the trades and professions, the classes, and the educational establishments.

6 *Classes of slang*

Of Standard Slang there is no need to speak at greater length; and it would be fatally easy to dogmatize. But it is necessary to preface the particular slangs (of which I give only a few, from among the more important) with Bradley and Krapp's dictum[1] that 'slang develops most freely in groups with a strong realization of group activity and interest, and groups without this sense of unity, e.g. farmers, rarely invent slang terms'.

[1] 'Slang', in *The Encyclopaedia Britannica.*

The most important classes of slang are Cockney and Public-House; Workmen's; Tradesmen's; Commercial; those of Publicity, Journalism, Literary Criticism, Publishing and Printing; Legal; Medical; Ecclesiastical and Theological; Parliamentary and Political; Public Schools' (the richest being that of Winchester); University; Social; Artistic; Theatrical; that of Games and that of Sport, including the Turf; Circus; Nautical, including Naval; Military; Yiddish; Family and Domestic; Rhyming Slang. From these I select six for brief comment:

I COCKNEY; PUBLIC-HOUSE; RHYMING SLANG

Rhyming slang, which consists of two or more words for one and which has always been popular in public-houses and among Cockneys, was originated in the underworld slums; public-house slang is mostly Cockney in origin and is much more widely used by Cockneys than by provincials. By Cockney slang[1] I mean *slang*, not that regional modification of Standard English which is indicated by differences in pronunciation only; and I further mean, not the Standard Slang spoken by educated Londoners, but the non-Standard slang spoken by the semi-literate and the illiterate—by costermongers, porters, carriers, publicans, and by others engaged at such centres of Cockney as Covent Garden, Smithfield, Billingsgate, Whitechapel. Here are four unmistakably Cockney expressions:

barrikin, chatter, especially if unintelligible; shouting; whence the Australian cricket-slang, *barracking*, now accepted by Standard English.

dinah, a corruption of the equally Cockney *donah*: one's best girl.

monaker, *monni(c)ker*: a person's name or signature.

weak in the arm: (a drink that is, a barmaid that serves) short measure.

The first three are none the less Cockney for being adoptions, respectively, from (Breton) French, Italian, and cant. Nor is rhyming slang any the less Cockney for having, *ca.* 1835–65, been predominantly an underworld mode of speech; even now, certain rhyming expressions are used only in cant. The rhyme is often imperfect; more often than not, there is no sense in the phrase (*Chatham and Dover*, over; *hot potater*, a waiter; *Scotch peg*, a leg). The following, however, convey shrewd comments on life: *Gawd forbids*, children (or *kids*); *trouble and strife*, a wife; *typewriter*, a pugilist (or *fighter*); *tumble down the sink* (n. and v.),

[1] On Cockney in general and on Cockney slang, there is only one comprehensive, reliable book: Wm. Matthews, *Cockney Past and Present* (1938).

drink. Often the second element is omitted: as in *elephant's*, drunk; *china*, companion or friend; *plates*, feet: where the missing words are *trunk*, *plate* (or *mate*), and *of meat*. The most brilliant and scholarly etymologist, unless he is familiar with rhyming slang, may rack his poor head—and guess with a pitiable degree of error. Two further examples will help to prove my point: (*get down to*) *brass tacks* rhymes *hard facts*; *carpet*,[1] a certain prison sentence, is short for *carpet bag*, which is rhyming slang for *drag*, which is a cant term for a three-months' sentence.

II PUBLISHING, LITERARY CRITICISM, JOURNALISM

In Cockney slang, there is natural wit, sharpened by the struggle for life; in the newspaper and publishing world, there is natural wit, refined by education and sharpened by cut-throat competition. The slang of journalism and publishing, authors and critics, is often indistinguishable from jargon; much of it very rapidly becomes, first colloquial, then part of the Standard language. Even *Jeames* for *The Morning Post* and *The Thunderer* for *The Times* had, by 1900, ceased to be journalistic and become Standard Slang; the latter is now Standard English. Here are a few other journalistic expressions (originally slang) that have gained a wider public: *eventuate*, a *flimsy*, *gin crawl*, *leaderette*, *screed*, *scribe*, *tripe*. Certain words are so much overdone by literary critics that they verge on slang: *Bohemian*, *frank*, *petticoat interest*, *problem novel*, *sensational writing*, *significant* (also in Art). To publishing and authorship belong *mag* (a magazine), *puff* (noun and verb), *blurb*, *hooey* (American), to *ghost*, to *vet*, a *re-write*, *penny dreadfuls*, *shilling shockers*, *yellowbacks* and *thrillers*.

To this group, printers have contributed certain terms from their extensive and often very technical slang: a *comp*, an *ad*, *pie* (type all mixed up), a *rag* (newspaper).

III UNIVERSITIES

The specific slangs of the three genteel professions, the Church, the Law, Medicine, are too technical to be of general interest; and the non-professional slang of clergymen, lawyers, doctors is either Standard Slang or a survival of the slang of their university. A small amount of Public School slang has been adopted by Oxford and Cambridge, but

[1] It is this sort of problem which makes cant etymologies a matter of more than philology and phonetics, as I am constantly finding in my slowly progressing *Dictionary of the English and American Underworld*.

usually the freshman doffs his old slang and hastens to don the slang of the university to which he goes. London and 'the provincial universities' have far less slang than either Cambridge or especially Oxford; 'the Universities of Oxford and Cambridge[1]...are the hotbeds of fashionable slang' (Hotten, 1859).

It is not generally realized that Oxford has produced a large number of slang expressions other than those in *-er* (these latter are on the wane): e.g. *Smalls*, *Mods*, and *Greats* (with which compare the Cambridge *Little-go* and *Trip*); *dim*. Several of the *-er* words have become Standard Slang: *rugger* and *soccer*; *bed-sitter* and *brekker*.

IV CRICKET

In sport, boxing and horse-racing have the richest jargons and slangs; among games, cricket[2] ranks an easy first, as might be expected from its having been played so much longer than the four kinds of football (Rugby, Association, Australian, American), hockey, golf, lacrosse, lawn tennis. Among the well-established slang expressions are *duck*, for *duck's egg* (0); *spectacles*, two scores of 0 in a match; 'a *rot* set in'; *sitter*,[3] an easy catch, called also a *dolly*; *tosh*, (loose and) easily hit bowling, as in *to send up* (cricket reporters' *wheel up*) *tosh*; *to tie up* (of the bowler), to have the batsman in difficulties; *the sticks* (stumps) and *behind the sticks*; the *country* or outfield; *to get work on a ball* (in the 1880's and 90's, *put stuff on the ball*); *to bowl for timber*, or at a batsman's legs, is obsolete—but interesting in relation to *body-line bowling*; a *bowler's double*,[4] 100 wickets and 100 runs in a season.

V MILITARY

The Regular Army has had a slang from at least as early as the seventeenth century; Grose lists many eighteenth-century terms; little survives from the Napoleonic and Crimean Wars, rather more from the Boer War; much from the War of 1914–18. Whereas the Regular Army's pre-1914 slang (see especially Kipling's poems and stories of soldiers) consisted mainly of words from Hindustani and Arabic (e.g.

[1] For early Cambridge slang, see the anonymous *Gradus ad Cantabrigiam* and Hotten; for early Oxford slang, see Pierce Egan's recension (1823), of Grose's *The Vulgar Tongue*; Cuthbert Bede's (i.e. Edward Bradley's) *Verdant Green* (1853–6), and again Hotten.

[2] See that admirable glossary, W. J. Lewis's *The Language of Cricket* (Oxford University Press, 1934).

[3] A catch that one could make even if one were sitting on the ground; probably but not certainly adopted from shooting at birds.

[4] Only since *ca.* 1935.

rooty 'bread', *pawny* 'water', *wallah* 'fellow', *Blighty* 'England', *buckshee* 'free'; *maalish* 'never mind!', *bint* 'girl') and abbreviations (*F.A.* 'nothing', *rooky* 'recruit', *how* 'howitzer', *ammo* 'ammunition', *sarge* 'sergeant'), the civilian soldiers' slang comes from all quarters of the world: *Fritz, kamerad!, strafe* 'to bombard', *minnie* 'minenwerfer', from German; *bocoo* 'much', *finee* 'finished', *apree la gare, napoo* 'there is no more', *Boche, san fairy ann* 'it doesn't matter', from French; many words from Cockney (*cop a packet* 'to get wounded', *dead-meat ticket* 'identity disc'); a few from the Dominions (*bonza* 'excellent', *cobber* 'friend', *dinkum* 'genuine', and probably *to go West*); some from the underworld (*wonky* 'defective', *to make* and *win* 'steal', *kip* 'bed'); a few from dialect (*to scrounge* 'forage'). There are also neologisms (*Asquiths* 'French matches', *to hop the bags* 'to attack', *to get the wind up, to become a landowner* 'to die'). Courage and cheerfulness, realism and humour, irony and ingenuity: such are the dominant qualities of military slang, especially in the twentieth century.[1]

VI AIR FORCE: 1914–18

The technical vocabulary of airmen was smaller in 1914–18 than it is now; the composition of the Air Force was less intricate; the men engaged, in the air and on the ground, were fewer. But that vocabulary had its merits. Some of the terms have passed into Standard English. They have been decorated and promoted. Others have changed their meanings.

As the sailor is *Jack* and the soldier is *Tommy*, so the airman is[2] *George*. A squadron is an *outfit* (adopted from the Canadians). Non-flying airmen are *ground wallahs*; air mechanics are *irks, irk* concertina-ing 'air-mechanic'; *Raffish* is applied to persons or things in the Royal Aircraft Factory; a probationary flight officer is nicknamed *Angel Face*, much as a young subaltern is a *flapper's delight*; an apprentice officer was a *quirk*, as also was a slow-but-sure plane, such officers and planes being, to experienced airmen, 'freaks' and sorry jests; an observer is a *shock-absorber*, the pilot a *taxi-driver*. Daring, experience, and success made an airman an *ace* (a word now accepted in the best word-circles), obviously from card-playing.

[1] See especially John Brophy and Eric Partridge, *Songs and Slang of the British Soldier: 1914–18* (3rd ed. Oxford University Press, 1931).

[2] The use of the present tense is not to be taken as necessarily holding good for the war of 1939– ?: throughout this section, the present tense refers only to, and is valid only for, the war of 1914–18, although many of the slang terms have, in fact, survived.

An aeroplane is a *bus*, which, if armed with a machine-gun, is a *gun bus*; a plane is also a *crate*, never applied to enemy planes; less commonly, a *flying kite*. Of the various kinds of plane, here are some: *baby*, the small Sopwith plane of the R.N.A.S. in the first year of the war of 1914–18; *bullet*, a small plane used in 1915; *camel*, a Sopwith scouting plane; *fly-catchers*, officially known as Fleet Fighters (fast protective planes); *Harry Tate*, rhyming slang for the R.E. 8, a slow plane used for observation only; *joy-waggon*, a practice plane. A *long-horn* is a Farman two-seater bi-plane, and a *short-horn* a Farman bi-plane with short skids, the names coming from breeds of cattle; compare *mechanical cow*, a Farman bi-plane with long skids; *pup* (short for *Sopwith pup*) is a small, fast, single-seater 80 h.p. plane; a *pusher* is a plane that has its propeller in the rear, whereas a *tractor* has its propeller in front; *salamander*, the first type of Sopwith with armoured fuselage; *spad*, a type of single-seater bi-plane, from the initials of the official name; *tabloid*, a small, fast Sopwith.

Of the parts and requisites of a plane, *prop* (propeller) was taken over from marine engineering; any gadget, instrument, or tool is a *doohickey* (compare the infantryman's *oojah* and *doings*); *joystick* (the pilot's control-lever), now very widely known, derives its name from the thrills its operation could give; this lever is also a *wind stick*; *juice* (petrol) was adopted from motorists' slang; *office* is the cockpit.

Other kinds of aircraft are *blimp*, a small, dirigible airship used mostly for anti-submarine surveys over the Channel, whence Low's 'Colonel Blimp'; an observation balloon is an *obbo* or a *sausage*. The men operating these balloons were *balloonatics*, a blend of *balloon* and *lunatics*.

Operations in the air yield the following terms: *to take the air* is to fly, whereas flying is *comic business*; *flip* is a flight, or to fly; to *go like a bat out of hell* is to fly at great speed; *beetle off* is to depart; *blip* is to switch an engine on and off; *hectic show* is any dangerous flying, *hedge-hopping* (still current) is deliberate low flying; *contour-chasing* is low flying for observation purposes; *hickaboo* is an air raid, *Hun-hunting* is seeking or chasing the enemy, whether in *Hunland* or in Allied country; *hoick* is to jerk a plane rapidly up and cause it to climb rapidly, whereas to *yank* is simply to jerk; a *pancake* is a very flat landing; *revving*, 'rapidly circling in the air', is used either of the plane or its pilot, and *porpoising* is a plane's motion resulting from a poor take-off; *roof* is the zenith of a plane's ascent; *solo-flight* (or *flying*) has become official and Standard English; to *snaffle* is to cut off an enemy plane, this word ('to steal or rob') coming from the eighteenth-century underworld; to *stunt* is to fly cleverly, or to show off in the air, and is derived from the noun, which immigrated from the sphere of American athletics; to *unstick* is to start on a flight, but to *unload* is to drop bombs; to *get on the tail of* (*a Hun*) is to attack an enemy plane in the rear; to *yaw* is to produce a laterally see-saw movement in one's plane—adopted from nautical language; to *stall* is to lose steadiness through diminishing one's speed; and to *zoom* (now Standard English) is to cause a plane, going at speed and flying level, to dive and then to ascend sharply, the latter movement being made on impetus alone.

Anti-aircraft fire comes from the *Archies*, a term applied to the batteries, the guns, and the shell-bursts; to *Archie* is to shell aircraft. To *drop eggs* is to release bombs from the air. *Flying darts* were aeroplane darts (used in 1914–15), whereas *grass-cutters* (1917–18) were small bombs dropped from the air and bursting, on impact, with a lateral scatter. A machine-gun is a *mangle*. The cry, *Jerry up!*, announces the approach of German planes. *The Circus* is Count von Richthofen's combination of fighting planes, at one time (1917) invincible: so called from the fact that Richthofen's squadrons moved from sector to sector, as a circus does from district to district.

Disaster, whether caused by Richthofen or by other German aviators, has a small vocabulary of its own. A neutral term is *to be earthed*, applied to a plane brought down; compare the Tank Corps's *to be ditched*, used of a tank that has been disabled. One's engine may *conk* (or *conk out*: since adopted by motorists) and take a *noser* or nose-dive, with the result that the aviators *come a regimental* or suffer an *abdominal crash*; later in the war, they *come a gutser* or they simply, as nowadays, *crash* (also a noun). The irreparable smashing of a plane, or the plane thus smashed, is a *write-off*, because it is to be written off as a bad debt.

Finally, three miscellaneous terms. To *be on the tarmac* is to have been warned for flying duty, from the asphalt or the tarmac (a particular kind of *tar mac*adam) in front of a hangar. A *maternity jacket* is the old R.F.C. double-breasted tunic fastening along the right side of the body. And *Tit-Bits* is the facetious name bestowed on the R.A.F.'s weekly communiqué: with which name, compare *Comic Cuts*, as the Intelligence summary issued to the Army was called.

The 1914–18 airman's vocabulary was, in the main, terse and apposite; cheerful and courageous; realistic but not pessimistic; unhysterical, unromantic, yet youthful and picturesque—a heritage of which the present R.A.F. need not be ashamed.

7 *A note on American slang*

In essentials, American is at one with English slang. The remarks made in sections 1–6 hold good for the one as for the other: and indeed, those remarks were based as much on American as on English slang. Apart from the variations of vocabulary (although there is, in this respect, considerable interaction between the two countries), the differences are less intrinsic than extrinsic, less in the slang itself than in the circumstances. 'American idiom is in a constant state of flux, slang being more copiously produced, more quickly taken up into established usage, but also more quickly discarded.'[1] At any given moment, there are far more slang terms in use in the United States than in England, because of the much larger population and the much greater area, but comparatively few more in New York than in London. Five years later, the slang vocabulary of 'the States' will have strikingly changed, whereas that of England will, unless a cataclysm supervenes, have remained very much the same as before: in the States, a larger proportion of slang expressions will have been ennobled, and a much larger proportion discarded (and even forgotten), than in England. American slang, more volatile than English, has richer synonymies, but many of the synonyms are ephemeral; English synonyms are employed rather for variety than, like the American ones, from weariness or a desire to startle. American slang is, on the whole, more callous and brutal than English, as American cant is even more brutal than English cant. English slang, although slower to obtain general acceptance, is concerned with enduring things more than American is, and therefore it less quickly becomes superannuated. American is the more witty and facetious, English the more genuinely humorous; humour lasts better than wit, much longer than facetiousness. And finally, the affiliations of slang with colloquialism and low speech on the one side and with cant[2] on the other are far harder to determine in the United States than they are in England.

The best American slang (surviving from myriads of inferior expressions, as we in England are prone to forget) possesses a terse expressiveness and a brilliant appositeness that ensure its almost prompt acceptance by Standard American and a faintly reluctant welcome in England. Here is a short list of American slang words and phrases that have justified themselves—many of them in England as well as in the United

[1] John Brophy, *English Prose*, chapter 'Idiom and Slang'.

[2] See *passim* [in various places] Godfrey Irwin, *American Tramp and Underworld Slang* (Oxford University Press, 1931; Sears, New York, 1932).

States, some to the extent of being standardized in both countries: A *crook*, a *crank*, a *fan*(atic), a *vamp*(ire), a *dope-fiend*; *high-brow* and *low-brow* (noun and adjective); *stunt*; *sob-stuff*. *Movies* and *talkies*, a *close-up* and a *fade-out*, to *register* an emotion, to *feature* and to *star*, come from American cinematography, which has popularized in England many other terms, e.g. *mush* and *mushy*; *guy*, *boob*, *mutt*; *to get wise* and *to put wise*, *beat it* and *make a getaway*, *bump off* and *put on the spot* and *take for a ride*. And, in alphabetical order, *baby* (vocative to a girl) and *old-timer* (vocative to a male friend); *bark up the wrong tree* (over a century old); *boiled shirt*; *boloney*; *boom* and *boost*; *brain-storm*; *bum* (a loafer); *bunkum*; *chicken-feed* (small change); it's a *cinch*; *cute*; *dame*; *deck* (of cards); *doughboy*; *fizzle* (a failure); *gangster*; *go over big*; *ham*, a third-rate actor; a *hard-boiled* person; *hobo*; *ivory-domed*; *jay walker*, the victim of *joy rider* and *road-hog*; *let it slide!*; *medicine man* (a doctor); *the nineteenth hole*; *nuts*; (give a person the) *once over*; *paint the town red*; *poppycock*; *pussyfoot*; *quitter*; *racket*; *to reel off*; *rough house* and *roughneck*; to *scram*; *sheikh* and *sheba*; *shoot!* (go ahead!); *sleuth*; *slush* (counterfeit paper money); *smart Alec*; *sob-sister*; *soused*; *take a back seat*; *tickle the ivories*; *wade in*; *where the flies won't get it*; *the willies*; *wise crack*; *Wop*; (*give* a person) *the works*; *yellow streak*; *you make me tired*.

15

C. C. FRIES

(1887–1967)

This is the introductory chapter of a report sponsored by the National Council of Teachers of English in America. The aim of the project was to collect materials on which to base a preliminary sketch of the syntax and morphology of American English with special reference to social class differences, so that the teaching of the English language in schools should be based on sound views of language and a knowledge of the facts. In the introduction, Fries, Professor of English at the University of Michigan, and author of a number of works on the structure of English and applied Linguistics, makes a succinct presentation of the arguments in favour of a linguistic approach to the study of English grammar.

'The Social Significance of Differences in Language Practice and the Obligation of the Schools'

(*American English Grammar*, 1940)

'English' maintains its place as the most frequently *required subject* of our school and college curriculums because of the unanimous support given it both by the general public and by education authorities. This support rests upon the general belief that the mastery of *good English* is not only the most important asset of the ambitious, but also an obligation of every good citizen. There is, however, in many quarters, a very hazy idea of the specific elements which make *good English*. A great deal of vigorous controversy ignores all the larger problems of effective communication and centers attention upon the criteria to be applied in judging the acceptability of particular words and language forms. All of this controversy is direct evidence that there do exist many differences in the language practice of English speaking people; for no controversy could arise and no choice be offered unless differing language forms presented themselves in the actual practice of English speech. It is the purpose of this chapter to set forth the general character of these differences and to analyze their significance in relation to the obligations resting upon our schools. The chapter as a whole will therefore present the principles underlying this whole investigation and the point of view which has determined its material and method.

I

Underlying many of the controversies concerning words and language forms is a very common attitude which I shall call here the 'conventional point of view.' Frequently stated explicitly, sometimes only implied, it appears in most handbooks and manuals of correct English, in grammars and rhetorics, in educational tests and measures, and in many editorials of the press. This conventional point of view assumes not only that there is a correctness in English language as absolute as that in elementary mathematics but also that the measures of this correctness are very definite rules. The following quotations are typical:

'A college professor rises to defend "ain't" and "it is me" as good English. The reed upon which he leans is majority usage..."Ain't," as a legitimate contraction of "am not," would not require defense or apology if it were not for widespread misuse. Unfortunately the same cannot be said of "it is me." This solecism could not be given the odor of good English by a plurality as great as Warren G. Harding rolled up in 1920...A vast amount of wretched English is heard in this country. The remedy does not lie in the repeal of the rules of grammar; but rather in a stricter and more intelligent enforcement of those rules in our schools...This protest against traditional usage and the rules of grammar is merely another manifestation of the unfortunate trend of the times to lawlessness in every direction...Quite as important as keeping undesirables out of the vocabulary is the maintaining of respect for the rules of grammar, which govern the formation of words into phrases and sentences...Students should be taught that correct speaking is evidence of culture; and that in order to speak correctly they must master the rules that govern the use of the language.'[1]

'Grammar consists of a series of rules and definitions...Since...ninety-five per cent of all children and teachers come from homes or communities where incorrect English is used, nearly everyone has before him the long, hard task of overcoming habits set up early in life before he studied language and grammar in school...Such people are exposed to the ridicule of those who notice the error, and the only way in which they can cure themselves is by eternal vigilance and the study of grammar.'[2]

'This is a test to see how well you know correct English usage and how well

[1] From an editorial in *The Detroit Free Press* (9 December 1928).

[2] W. W. Charters, *Teaching the Common Branches* (rev. ed. Macmillan, New York, 1924), pp. 96, 98, 115.

you can select the *rule or principle in accordance with which a usage is correct.* In the left hand column a list of sentences is given. In each sentence there are two forms in parentheses, one correct, and the other incorrect. In the right hand column a list of rules or principles is given, some one of which applies to each sentence...

Sentences	*Principles*
[] 1 (Whom) (Who) did you meet?	*a* The indirect object is in the objective case.
[] 2 He told John and (I) (me) an interesting story.	*b* The subject of the verb is in the nominative case.
	c The object of a verb is in the objective case.

Read the first sentence in Section I; then mark out the incorrect form. Read the rules in Section I, until you find one that applies to this first sentence. Place the letter of this rule in the square preceding the first sentence...'[1]

'One purpose of this report is to describe and illustrate a method of constructing a grammar curriculum upon the basis of the errors of school children...it is apparent that the first step is *to ascertain* the rules which are broken and to determine their relative importance.'[2]

The point of view expressed in these quotations, assuming as it does that certain definite rules[3] are the necessary standards by which to measure language correctness, also repudiates *general usage* as a valid guide to acceptability, even the usage of the so-called 'educated.' The following quotation represents dozens of similar statements:

'The truth is, however, that authority of general usage, or even of the usage of great writers, is not absolute in language. There is a misuse of words which can be justified by no authority, however great, and *by no usage however general.*'[4]

From this, the 'conventional point of view,' the problem of the differences in our language practice is a very simple one. Only two kinds of forms or usages exist—correct forms and mistakes. In general, the mistakes are thought to be corrupt forms or illegitimate meanings derived by carelessness from the correct ones. In some cases a grudging acquiescence accepts some forms which are contrary to the rules when

[1] T. J. Kirby, *Grammar Test*, University of Iowa Standard Tests and Scales.

[2] 'Minimal Essentials in Language and Grammar', in *Sixteenth Yearbook* of the National Society for the Study of Education (Bloomington, Ind., Public School Publishing Co., 1917), pp. 86, 87.

[3] For a statement of the development of this point of view see C. C. Fries, *Teaching of the English Language* (Thomas Nelson, New York, 1927), chapter 1, 'The Rules of Grammar as the Measure of Language Errors'.

[4] R. G. White, *Words and Their Uses* (rev. ed. Houghton Mifflin, Boston, 1899), p. 14.

these forms are sanctioned by an overwhelming usage, but here the view remains that these forms, although established by usage, are still *incorrect* and must always be incorrect. To this point of view these incorrect forms sanctioned by usage are the 'idioms' of the language. In all the matters of differing language practices, therefore, those who hold this point of view regard the obligation of the schools as perfectly clear and comparatively simple—the schools must root out the *mistakes* or *errors* and cultivate the language uses that are *correct according to the rules*.[1]

Opposed to this 'conventional point of view' is that held by the outstanding scholars in English language during the last hundred years. I shall call it here 'the scientific point of view.' Typical expressions of it abound.

'In considering the use of grammar as a corrective of what are called "ungrammatical" expressions, it must be borne in mind that the rules of grammar have no value except as statements of facts: whatever is in general use in a language is for that very reason grammatically correct.'[2]

'The grammar of a language is not a list of rules imposed upon its speakers by scholastic authorities, but is a scientific record of the actual phenomena of that language, written and spoken. If any community habitually uses certain forms of speech, these forms are part of the grammar of the speech of that community.'[3]

'It has been my endeavor in this work to represent English Grammar not as a set of stiff dogmatic precepts, according to which some things are correct and others absolutely wrong, but as something living and developing under continual fluctuations and undulations, something that is founded on the past and prepares the way for the future, something that is not always consistent or perfect, but progressing and perfectible—in one word, human.'[4]

'A Grammar book does not attempt to teach people how they ought to speak, but on the contrary, unless it is a very bad or a very old work, it merely states how, as a matter of fact, certain people do speak at the time at which it is written.'[5]

In these typical expressions of 'the scientific point of view' there is, first of all, a definitely stated opposition to the fundamental principle of

[1] 'Some better reason than a custom arising from ignorance...is needed for changing the English language. It would seem to be still the part of the schools to teach the language *strictly according to rule*, and to place emphasis on such teaching, rather than to encourage questionable liberties of usage.' From an editorial in *The Christian Science Monitor* (Boston, 23 February 1923).

[2] Henry Sweet, *New English Grammar*, vol. 1 (Clarendon Press, Oxford, 1891), p. 5.

[3] Grattan and Gurrey, *Our Living Language* (Thomas Nelson, London, 1925), p. 25.

[4] Otto Jespersen, *A Modern English Grammar* (Heidelberg, 1909), vol. 1, Preface.

[5] H. C. Wyld, *Elementary Lessons in English Grammar* (Clarendon Press, Oxford, 1925), p. 12.

the 'conventional attitude.' All of them insist that it is unsound to take the rules of grammar as the necessary norms of correct English and to set out to make all usage conform to those rules. In these expressions of the scientific view there is, also, a clear affirmation of the fundamental principle of the attitude that usage or practice is the basis of all the *correctness* there can be in language.[1] From this, the scientific point of view, the problem presented by the differences in our language is by no means a simple one. Instead of having to deal with a mass of diverse forms which can be easily separated into the two groups of *mistakes* and *correct language* according to perfectly definite measures, the language scholar finds himself confronted by a complex range of differing practices which must be sorted into an indefinite number of groups according to a set of somewhat indistinct criteria called 'general usage.'[2] Those who hold this scientific point of view insist, therefore, that the first step in fulfilling the obligation of the schools in the matter of dealing with the English language is to record, realistically and as completely as possible, the facts of this usage.

This investigation and report assumes as its first principle this scientific point of view with its repudiation of the conventional attitude toward language errors. We shall, therefore, ignore the conventional classification of *mistakes* and *correct forms*, and attempt to outline the types of differences that appear in our American language practices.

II

All of us upon occasion note and use for the purpose of identification the many differences in the speech of those about us. By differences in pitch of voice, for instance, we can usually tell whether the person talking to us over the telephone is a man, or a woman, or a child. By certain characteristic differences of pronunciation and of grammar, the speech of 'Amos and Andy' as it comes over the radio makes us visualize

[1] This statement must not be taken to imply that *mere correctness* is to be considered the ultimate ideal of language. The scientific point of view does not in any way conflict with the artistic view of *good English*. See the discussion of 'The Scientific and the Artistic Points of View in Language,' in C. C. Fries, *The Teaching of the English Language*, pp. 102–21.

[2] One should, perhaps, call attention at this point to the fact that the great *Oxford English Dictionary* is the outstanding document in this 'scientific view of language.' The principle underlying the production of the *Oxford Dictionary*, the very foundation of its method, was the insistence upon use or practice as the sole criterion of the legitimate meaning of words. Compare, for example, the treatment of the word *nice* (especially sense 15) in this dictionary with the usual statements concerning it as given in the conventional handbooks.

two uneducated negroes. Through the speech of 'Clara, Lou, and Em,' we see three women of little education who have had a very limited range of social contacts. In similar fashion we should with little difficulty recognize the speech of a Scot like Harry Lauder as differing from that of a native of Georgia or Alabama. If one could conjure up Shakspere or Spenser or Milton, he would find their English strange to his ears not only in pronunciation but in vocabulary and in grammar as well. The speech of Chaucer and of Wycliffe would sound even less like English. In other words, even if one ignores such details as separate the speech of every single person from that of any other, there are at least four large types of differences to be noted in our discussion here.

First, there are historical differences. Chaucer used, as we do, *they* as the nominative plural of the pronoun of the third person, but he did not use *their* as the genitive and *them* as the dative-accusative form. Instead, he used the forms *her* or *hir*, for the genitive plural, and *hem* for the dative-accusative or objective forms. In Chaucer's language it was still the practice to distinguish carefully between the singular and plural forms of the past tense of many verbs. He would say *I rood* (rode) but we *ride*(*n*), *he sang* but they *sunge*(*n*). In the late sixteenth century it was no longer the practice to distinguish between the singular and plural in the past tense, and Shakspere therefore used *we rode* as well as *I rode*. For him, however, *learn* was often used with the meaning we give to *teach*, and *thou* was frequently used to address those of inferior rank or intimate friends. Thus the language forms of each age have differed in some respect from those of any other time. Constant change is the outstanding characteristic of a live language used by an intellectually active people. The historical changes do not come suddenly, nor do they affect all the users of a language equally. Thus at any time there will be found those who cling to the older methods and those who use the newer fashion. Many of the differences we note in the language of today find their explanation in this process of historical change. These older forms constitute a fairly large proportion of the materials usually called errors by those who maintain the conventional point of view. The so-called double negative, as in 'They didn't take no oil with them,' is thus a perpetuation of an old practice exceedingly common in the English language for centuries. It was formerly the normal way of stressing a negative. The form *foot*, in such expressions as 'He is six foot tall,' 'The height of the bar is now six foot and two inches,' is again the perpetuation of an old practice in the English language which the modern fashion has abandoned. It is an old genitive plural following the numeral. A few other examples out of dozens of such historical differences are *clomb*, usually spelled *clum*, as the past tense of the verb *climb*, instead of *climbed*; *wrought*[1] as the past tense of the verb *work*, instead of *worked*; *stang* as the past tense of the verb *sting*, instead of *stung*. Such differences belong not only in this group called 'historical differences' but often also to some of the other three groups to be explained below. In fact, the four types of differences are not by any means mutually exclusive classifications but merely loose divisions with convenient labels.

Second, there are regional differences. In the south of England, in early Modern English, the inflectional ending of the verb in the third person singular present indicative was *-eth*, as in 'God *loveth* a cheerful giver.' In the north of England this inflectional ending was *-es*, as 'God *loves* a cheerful giver.' Late Modern English has adopted the form that was used only in the northern region. In the language practice of the United States, *gotten* as a past participle form of *get* is fairly general; in England it seldom appears. *You all* as a plural of *you* is especially characteristic of southern United States. In some colleges one takes a course *under* a professor; in others it is *from* one or *with* one; in still others it is *to* one. Some of the differences we note in the language practices of those about us find their explanation in the fact that the fashions in one community or section of the country do not necessarily develop in others. Regional or geographical differences show themselves more clearly in matters of vocabulary. That part of an automobile that is called a *hood* in the United States is called a *bonnet* in England. That which they call the *hood* in England we call the *top*. *Lumber*, to most of us in the United States means *timber*; in England it still means *rubbish*. In some sections of the United States, a *paper bag* is usually called a *sack*, in others a *poke*. Such regional differences become especially noticeable when a person from one section of the country moves into another bringing with him the peculiar fashions of the district from which he comes. In the new community these language differences challenge attention and give rise to questions of correctness and preference.

Third, there are literary and colloquial differences. The language practices of conversation differ in many subtle ways from those used in formal writing. Most apparent is the abundance of contractions in the language of conversation. Thoroughly unnatural would sound the

[1] One should note that in the case of *wrought* the old form has not the flavor of 'vulgar' English as have the other examples here given but suggests super-refinement.

speech of those who in conversation did not constantly use *I'm, you'll, isn't, don't, aren't, they'd better, we've,* instead of the fully expanded *I am, you will, is not, do not, are not, they had better, we have.* And in similar fashion the formal writing that habitually employed such contractions would seem equally unnatural because of the impression of very informal familiarity which they would create. Apparent, too, although less obvious are the differences between conversation and formal writing in the matter of sentence completeness. Conversation abounds in groups of words that do not form conventionally complete and logical sentences. Many verbs are omitted; clauses are uttered which are to be attached to the whole context of the conversation rather than to any particular word in a parsable sentence; single words stand for complete ideas. In formal writing the situation demands much more logical completeness of expression, and most of the sentences appear to satisfy the demands of a conventional grammatical analysis. Less apparent but not less real are the differences which arise out of the fact that many perfectly familiar expressions occur practically only in conversational situations and are found very seldom in literary English unless they appear in attempts to report conversation in writing. Occasions seldom arise in anything except conversational situations to use *Who* (or *whom*) *did you call?* or *It is me* (or *I*).

Many assume that the language practices of formal writing are the best or at least that they are of a higher level than those of colloquial or conversational English. When, therefore, they find an expression marked 'colloquial' in a dictionary, as is the phrase '*to get on one's nerves*' in Webster's *New International Dictionary*, they frown upon its use. As a matter of fact, thus to label an expression 'colloquial' is simply to say that it occurs in good conversation but not in formal writing.[1] Unless one can assume that formal writing is in itself more desirable than good conversation, the language practices peculiar to conversation cannot be

[1] The word *colloquial* as applied to English words and structures is frequently misunderstood, even by teachers of English. Some confuse it with *localism*, and think of the words and constructions marked 'colloquial' as peculiarities of speaking which are characteristic of a particular locality. Others feel that some stigma attaches to the label 'colloquial' and would strive to avoid as *incorrect* (or as of a *low level*) all words and phrases so marked. The word *colloquial*, however, as used to label words and phrases in a dictionary like Webster's *New International Dictionary* has no such meaning. It is used to mark those words and constructions whose range of use is primarily that of the polite conversation of cultivated people, of their familiar letters and informal speeches, as distinct from those words and constructions which are common also in formal writing. As a matter of fact, even the language of our better magazines and of public addresses has, during the last generation, moved away from the formal toward the informal.

rated in comparison with those of formal writing. Each set of language practices is best in its own special sphere of use; one will necessarily differ from the other.

Fourth, there are social or class differences. Despite the fact that America in its national life has struggled to express its belief in the essential equality of human beings and to free the paths of opportunity from arbitrary and artificial restraints, there still do exist some clear differences between the habits and practices of various social groups. It is, of course, practically impossible to mark the limits of any social class in this country. It is even extremely difficult to describe the special characteristics of any such class because of the comparative ease with which one passes from one social group to another, especially in youth, and the consequent mixture of group habits among those so moving. Our public schools, our churches, our community welfare work, our political life, all furnish rather frequent occasions for social class mixture. All that can be done in respect to such a description is to indicate certain facts which seem generally true for the *core* of any social group, realizing that these same facts may also be true separately of many who have connections with other groups. There are, for example, those who habitually wear formal dress clothes in the evening and those who never wear them. Many of the former frequent the opera and concerts of the best music; many of the latter find their entertainment solely in the movies. The families of the wealthy, especially those whose wealth has continued for several generations, ordinarily mix but little with the families of unskilled laborers; and the families of college professors even in a small city have usually very little social life in common with the families of policemen and firemen.

Just as the general social habits of such separated social groups naturally show marked differences, so their language practices inevitably vary. Pronunciations such as '*ketch*' for *catch* and '*git*' for *get*; and grammatical forms such as 'he *seen* his mistake as soon as he *done* it' or '*You was*' are not the characteristic modes of speech of university professors, or of the clergymen who preach from the pulpits in our large city churches, or of the judges of the supreme court, or of the presidents of our most important banks, or even of those who habitually patronize the opera. Such language practices, therefore, if used in these particular social groups attract as much attention as a pair of overalls might at an evening gathering where custom demands formal dress clothes. In fact, part of the significance of the social differences in language habits can well be illustrated by a comparison with clothes.

Fundamentally the clothes one wears fulfill the elementary practical functions of comfort by keeping one warm and of modesty by avoiding indecent exposure of one's person. These two practical purposes could just as well be accomplished by rather shapeless simple garments produced over a standard pattern for every one and worn upon all occasions. Such clothes could be made to fulfill their primary functions very efficiently with a minimum of cost. In such a situation, however, aside from the significance of differing degrees of cleanliness, the clothes would show us very little concerning the individuals who wore them. With our present habits of dress the clothes connote or suggest, in a broad general way, certain information concerning the wearers. Among other things they suggest the *circumstances in which we usually see them worn*. A dress suit suggests an evening party (or in some places a hotel waiter); overalls suggest a piece of dirty work or possibly a summer camp. In like manner language forms and constructions not only fulfill a primary function of communicating meaning; they also suggest the circumstances in which those particular forms and constructions are usually employed. If, then, one uses the pronunciations and grammatical forms given earlier in this paragraph, they may serve to communicate his meaning unmistakably, but they will also suggest that he habitually associates with those social groups for whom these language forms are the customary usage and not with those for whom they are not characteristic. We must, therefore, recognize the fact that there are separate social or class groups even in American communities and that these groups differ from one another in many social practices including their language habits.

As indicated earlier the four kinds of differences in language practice here outlined are by no means mutually exclusive. Many historical differences and some sectional differences have become also social differences. For our purpose here the social or class differences are of most concern; other types of differences will be treated only as they bear upon these social or class dialects.

III

In order to grasp the significance of these social differences in language practice for the obligation of the schools one must understand clearly what is meant by 'standard' English, and that can perhaps best be accomplished by tracing the course by which a particular kind of English became 'standard.' As one examines the material written in England during the twelfth and thirteenth centuries—a period from one hundred to two hundred years after the Norman Conquest—he finds a situation in which three things are of especial note:

1 Most of the legal documents, the instruments which controlled the carrying on of the political and the business affairs of the English people, were not written in the English language but in French or in Latin. This fact was also true of much of the literature and books of learning familiar to the upper classes.

2 Although some books, especially historical records and religious and moral stories and tracts, were written in English, there was no single type of the English language common to all English writings. The greatest number used what is called the Southern dialect. This particular kind of English had been centered in Winchester, which was the chief city of King Alfred and his successors until the time of the Norman Conquest.

3 There was, therefore, no 'standard' English in twelfth and thirteenth century England, for no single type of the English language furnished the medium by which the major affairs of English people were carried on. Instead, English people used for these purposes French, Latin, and at least four distinct varieties of English. The particular kind of English spoken in southern England came nearest to fulfilling the function of a 'standard' English because more writings and more significant writings were produced in this type of English than in any other.

In the fourteenth and early fifteenth centuries, however, this situation changed. London had become the political and in some respects the social head of English life in a much more unified England. Many of the major affairs of the realm had to be handled in London. More and more the English language, the English of London, was used in the legal documents of politics and business. Solely because of the fact that more of the important affairs of English life were conducted in this London English rather than in Winchester English, London English became 'standard' English. Naturally, then, the growing use of this particular type of English for the important affairs of English life gathered such momentum that even writers to whom other types of English were more natural felt constrained to learn and to use the fashionable London English. Gower, for example, a Kentishman, did not write his native kind of English but practically the same forms, constructions, and spellings as Chaucer, a Londoner born. Naturally, too, this London English gained a social prestige because of the fact that its use connoted or suggested relations with the center of affairs in English life, whereas the inability to use London English suggested that one did not have such social contacts. 'Standard' English, therefore, is, historically, a local dialect, which was used to carry on the major affairs of English life and which gained thereby a social prestige.[1]

Many changes occurred in this dialect of English and these changes especially affected the usage of the younger rather than of the older generations in the centers of fashionable social life. Thus the continued use of the older forms rather than the newer changes always suggested a lack of direct contacts with those who were active in the conduct of important matters. In this connotation lay the power of 'standard' English to compel the ambitious to conform to its practices.

In America, however, we have had no one recognized center for our political, business, social, and intellectual affairs. More than that, the great distances between various parts of the United States made very difficult frequent actual social contacts in the earlier days. Our coast cities, Boston and New York, maintained direct relations with London long after the earlier settlers had moved west, but the middle western settlements had practically no relations with Boston and New York. This fact can probably explain the differences between our middle-western speech and that of nineteenth century Boston and New York. Because of the fact that New England so long dominated our intellectual life there has been a good deal of feeling in many parts of the United States that the language usages of New England connoted a connection with a higher culture than did the language of the Middle West. Hence the rather widespread attempt to imitate certain New England speech characteristics. On the whole, however, if we ignore the special differences that separate the speech of New England, the South, and the Middle West, we do have in the United States a set of language habits, broadly conceived, in which the major matters of the political, social, economic, educational, religious life of this country are carried on. To these language habits is attached a certain social prestige, for the use of them suggests that one has constant relations with those who are responsible for the important affairs of our communities. It is this set of language habits, derived originally from an older London English, but differentiated from it somewhat by its independent development in this country, which is the 'standard' English of the United States. Enough has been said to enforce the point that it is 'standard' not because it is any more correct or more beautiful or more capable than

[1] 'Standard' French, 'Standard' Italian, 'Standard' Dutch, etc., have similar histories.

other varieties of English; it is 'standard' solely because it is the particular type of English which is used in the conduct of the important affairs of our people. It is also the type of English used by the *socially acceptable* of most of our communities and insofar as that is true it has become a social or class dialect in the United States.

IV

With this analysis it is not difficult to understand the nature of the obligation assumed by our schools in respect to the teaching of the English language. Long have we in our national life adhered to the principle that no individual in his attempts to rise to the highest positions should be disqualified by artificial restraints. Our people have been devoted to education because education has furnished the most important tool of social advancement. Our public schools have therefore held to the ideal that every boy and girl should be so equipped that he shall not be handicapped in his struggle for social progress and recognition, and that he may rise to the highest positions. In the matter of the English language it is clear that any one who cannot use the language habits in which the major affairs of the country are conducted, the language habits of the socially acceptable of most of our communities, would have a serious handicap. The schools, therefore, have assumed the burden of training every boy and girl, no matter what his original social background and native speech, to use this 'standard' English, this particular social or class dialect. To some pupils it is almost a foreign language; to others it is their accustomed speech. Many believe that the schools have thus assumed an impossible task. Certainly the widespread and almost unanimous condemnation of the results of their efforts convinces us that either the schools have not conceived their task adequately or they have chosen the wrong materials and methods to accomplish it. We shall find, I think, that seldom have school authorities understood the precise nature of the language task they have assumed and very frequently have directed their energies to teaching not 'standard' English realistically described, but a 'make-believe' correctness which contained some true forms of real 'standard' English and many forms that had and have practically no currency outside the classroom.[1]

[1] See, for example, H. B. Allen's article 'The Standard of Usage in Freshman Textbooks,' in *English Journal*, vol. 24 (college ed. 1935), pp. 564–71; and R. C. Pooley, *Grammar and Usage in Textbooks on English*, Bulletin 14, Bureau of Educational Research (University of Wisconsin, 1933).

A few brief statements will serve both to summarize the preceding discussion and to bring into a single view the principles which underlie this investigation and report.

1 All considerations of an *absolute* 'correctness' in accord with the conventional rules of grammar or the dicta of handbooks must be set aside, because these rules or these dicta very frequently do not represent the actual practice of 'standard' English but prescribe forms which have little currency outside the English classroom. We assume, therefore, that there can be no 'correctness' apart from usage and that the *true* forms of 'standard' English are those that are actually used in that particular dialect. Deviations from these usages are 'incorrect' only when used in the dialect to which they do not belong. These deviations suggest not only the particular social dialect or set of language habits in which they usually occur, but also the general social and cultural characteristics most often accompanying the use of these forms.

2 It is the assumed obligation of the schools to attempt to develop in each child the knowledge of and the ability to use the 'standard' English of the United States—that set of language habits in which the most important affairs of our country are carried on, the dialect of the socially acceptable in most of our communities.

3 The first step in fulfilling that obligation is the making of an accurate and realistic survey and description of the actual language practices in the various social or class dialects. Only after we have such information in hand can we know what social connotations are likely to attach to particular usages.

16

GEORGE ORWELL

(1903–1950)

George Orwell (the *nom de plume* of Eric Blair) was born in India, received an English education, and returned to the East for a time before beginning a nomadic life in Europe. His books and articles, fiction and non-fiction, are those of a democratic socialist untrammelled by party loyalties, and their subjects, whether literary, geographical, or social, all have immediate political application. This essay, written late in his life, was contributed to a London literary magazine edited by the critic Cyril Connolly.

'Politics and the English Language'

(*Horizon*, vol. 13, 1946)

Most people who bother with the matter at all would admit that the English language is in a bad way, but it is generally assumed that we cannot by conscious action do anything about it. Our civilization is decadent, and our language—so the argument runs—must inevitably share in the general collapse. It follows that any struggle against the abuse of language is a sentimental archaism, like preferring candles to electric light or hansom cabs to aeroplanes. Underneath this lies the half-conscious belief that language is a natural growth and not an instrument which we shape for our own purposes.

Now, it is clear that the decline of a language must ultimately have political and economic causes: it is not due simply to the bad influence of this or that individual writer. But an effect can become a cause, reinforcing the original cause and producing the same effect in an intensified form, and so on indefinitely. A man may take to drink because he feels himself to be a failure, and then fail all the more completely because he drinks. It is rather the same thing that is happening to the English language. It becomes ugly and inaccurate because our thoughts are foolish, but the slovenliness of our language makes it easier for us to have foolish thoughts. The point is that the process is reversible. Modern English, especially written English, is full of bad habits which spread by imitation and which can be avoided if one is willing to take the necessary trouble. If one gets rid of these habits one can think more clearly, and to think clearly is a necessary first step towards political regeneration: so that the fight against bad English is not frivolous and is not the exclusive concern of professional writers. I will come back to this presently, and I hope that by that time the meaning of what I have said here will have become clearer. Meanwhile, here are five specimens of the English language as it is now habitually written.

These five passages have not been picked out because they are especially bad—I could have quoted far worse if I had chosen—but because they illustrate various of the mental vices from which we now suffer. They are a little below the average, but are fairly representative samples. I number them so that I can refer back to them when necessary:

1 'I am not, indeed, sure whether it is not true to say that the Milton who once seemed not unlike a seventeenth-century Shelley had not become, out of an experience ever more bitter in each year, more alien [*sic*] to the founder of that Jesuit sect which nothing could induce him to tolerate.'

Professor Harold Laski (Essay in *Freedom of Expression*).

2 'Above all, we cannot play ducks and drakes with a native battery of idioms which prescribes such egregious collocations of vocables as the Basic *put up with* for *tolerate* or *put at a loss* for *bewilder*.'

Professor Lancelot Hogben (*Interglossa*).

3 'On the one side we have the free personality: by definition it is not neurotic, for it has neither conflict nor dream. Its desires, such as they are, are transparent, for they are just what institutional approval keeps in the forefront of consciousness; another institutional pattern would alter their number and intensity; there is little in them that is natural, irreducible, or culturally dangerous. But *on the other side*, the social bond itself is nothing but the mutual reflection of these self-secure integrities. Recall the definition of love. Is not this the very picture of a small academic? Where is there a place in this hall of mirrors for either personality or fraternity?'

Essay on psychology in *Politics* (New York).

4 'All the "best people" from the gentlemen's clubs, and all the frantic fascist captains, united in common hatred of Socialism and bestial horror of the rising tide of the mass revolutionary movement, have turned to acts of provocation, to foul incendiarism, to medieval legends of poisoned wells, to legalize their own destruction of proletarian organizations, and rouse the agitated petty-bourgeoisie to chauvinistic fervour on behalf of the fight against the revolutionary way out of the crisis.'

Communist pamphlet.

5 'If a new spirit *is* to be infused into this old country, there is one thorny and contentious reform which must be tackled, and that is the humanization and galvanization of the B.B.C. Timidity here will bespeak canker and atrophy of the soul. The heart of Britain may be sound and of strong beat, for instance, but the British lion's roar at present is like that of Bottom in Shakespeare's *Midsummer Night's Dream*—as gentle as any sucking dove. A virile new Britain cannot continue indefinitely to be traduced in the eyes, or rather ears, of the world by the effete languors of Langham Place, brazenly masquerading as "standard English". When the Voice of Britain is heard at nine o'clock, better far and infinitely less ludicrous to hear aitches honestly dropped than the present priggish, inflated, inhibited, school-ma'amish arch braying of blameless bashful mewing maidens!' Letter in *Tribune*.

Each of these passages has faults of its own, but, quite apart from avoidable ugliness, two qualities are common to all of them. The first is staleness of imagery: the other is lack of precision. The writer either has a meaning and cannot express it, or he inadvertently says something else, or he is almost indifferent as to whether his words mean anything or not. This mixture of vagueness and sheer incompetence is the most marked characteristic of modern English prose, and especially of any kind of political writing. As soon as certain topics are raised, the concrete melts into the abstract and no one seems able to think of turns of speech that are not hackneyed: prose consists less and less of *words* chosen for the sake of their meaning, and more and more of *phrases* tacked together like the sections of a prefabricated hen-house. I list below, with notes and examples, various of the tricks by means of which the work of prose-construction is habitually dodged:

DYING METAPHORS. A newly invented metaphor assists thought by evoking a visual image, while on the other hand a metaphor which is technically 'dead' (e.g. *iron resolution*) has in effect reverted to being an ordinary word and can generally be used without loss of vividness. But in between these two classes there is a huge dump of worn-out metaphors which have lost all evocative power and are merely used because they save people the trouble of inventing phrases for themselves. Examples are: *Ring the changes on, take up the cudgels for, toe the line, ride roughshod over, stand shoulder to shoulder with, play into the hands of, no axe to grind, grist to the mill, fishing in troubled waters, on the order of the day, Achilles' heel, swan song, hotbed.* Many of these are used without knowledge of their meaning (what is a 'rift', for instance?), and incompatible metaphors are frequently mixed, a sure sign that the writer is not interested in what he is saying. Some metaphors now current have been twisted out of their original meaning without those who use them even being aware of the fact. For example, *toe the line* is sometimes written *tow the line*. Another example is *the hammer and the anvil*, now always used with the implication that the anvil gets the worst of it. In real life it is always the anvil that breaks the hammer, never the other way about: a writer who stopped to think what he was saying would be aware of this, and would avoid perverting the original phrase.

OPERATORS, *or* VERBAL FALSE LIMBS. These save the trouble of picking out appropriate verbs and nouns, and at the same time pad each sentence with extra syllables which give it an appearance of symmetry. Characteristic phrases are: *render inoperative, militate against, prove unacceptable, make contact with, be subjected to, give rise to, give grounds for, have the effect of, play a leading part (role) in, make itself felt, take effect, exhibit a tendency to, serve the purpose of, etc., etc.* The keynote is the elimination of simple verbs. Instead of being a single word, such as *break, stop, spoil, mend, kill,* a verb becomes a *phrase*, made up of a noun or adjective tacked on to some general-purposes verb such as *prove, serve, form, play, render*. In addition, the passive voice is wherever possible used in preference to the active, and noun constructions are used instead of gerunds (*by examination of* instead of *by examining*). The range of verbs is further cut down by means of the *-ize* and *de-* formations, and banal statements are given an appearance of profundity by means of the *not un-* formation. Simple conjunctions and prepositions are replaced by such phrases as *with respect to, having regard to, the fact that, by dint of, in view of, in the interests of, on the hypothesis that*; and the ends of sentences are saved from anti-climax by such resounding commonplaces as *greatly to be desired, cannot be left out of account, a development to be expected in the near future, deserving of serious consideration, brought to a satisfactory conclusion*, and so on and so forth.

PRETENTIOUS DICTION. Words like *phenomenon, element, individual* (as noun), *objective, categorical, effective, virtual, basic, primary, promote, constitute, exhibit, exploit, utilize, eliminate, liquidate*, are used to dress up simple statement and give an air of scientific impartiality to biased judgements. Adjectives like *epoch-making, epic, historic, unforgettable, triumphant, age-old, inevitable, inexorable, veritable*, are used to dignify the sordid processes of international politics, while writing that aims at glorifying war usually takes on an archaic colour, its characteristic words being: *realm, throne, chariot, mailed fist, trident, sword, shield, buckler, banner, jackboot, clarion*. Foreign words and expressions such as *cul de sac, ancien régime, deus ex machina, mutatis mutandis, status quo, gleichschaltung, weltanschauung*, are used to give an air of culture and elegance. Except for the useful abbreviations *i.e.*, *e.g.*, and *etc.*, there is no real need for any of the hundreds of foreign phrases now current in English. Bad writers, and especially scientific, political and sociological writers, are nearly always haunted by the notion that Latin or Greek words are grander than Saxon ones, and unnecessary words like *expedite, ameliorate, predict, extraneous, deracinated, clandestine, subaqueous* and hundreds of others constantly gain ground from their Anglo-Saxon opposite numbers.[1] The jargon peculiar to Marxist writing (*hyena, hangman, cannibal, petty bourgeois, these gentry, lacquey, flunkey, mad dog, White Guard*, etc.) consists largely of words and phrases translated from Russian, German or French; but the normal way of coining a new word is to use a Latin or Greek root with the appropriate affix and, where necessary, the -ize formation. It is often easier to make up words of this kind (*de-regionalize, impermissible, extramarital, non-fragmentatory* and so forth) than to think up the English words that will cover one's meaning. The result, in general, is an increase in slovenliness and vagueness.

MEANINGLESS WORDS. In certain kinds of writing, particularly in art criticism and literary criticism, it is normal to come across long passages which are almost completely lacking in meaning.[2] Words like *romantic, plastic, values, human, dead, sentimental, natural, vitality*, as used in art criticism, are strictly meaningless, in the sense that they not only do not point to any discoverable object, but are hardly even expected to do so by the reader. When one critic writes, 'The outstanding feature of Mr. X's work is its living quality', while another writes, 'The immediately striking thing about Mr. X's work is its peculiar deadness', the reader accepts this as a simple difference of opinion. If words like *black*

[1] An interesting illustration of this is the way in which the English flower names which were in use till very recently are being ousted by Greek ones, *snapdragon* becoming *antirrhinum, forget-me-not* becoming *myosotis*, etc. It is hard to see any practical reason for this change of fashion: it is probably due to an instinctive turning-away from the more homely word and a vague feeling that the Greek word is scientific.

[2] Example: 'Comfort's catholicity of perception and image, strangely Whitmanesque in range, almost the exact opposite in aesthetic compulsion, continues to evoke that trembling atmospheric accumulative hinting at a cruel, an inexorably serene timelessness... Wrey Gardiner scores by aiming at simple bullseyes with precision. Only they are not so simple, and through this contented sadness runs more than the surface bittersweet of resignation.' *Poetry Quarterly*.

and *white* were involved, instead of the jargon words *dead* and *living*, he would see at once that language was being used in an improper way. Many political words are similarly abused. The word *Fascism* has now no meaning except in so far as it signifies 'something not desirable'. The words *democracy*, *socialism*, *freedom*, *patriotic*, *realistic*, *justice*, have each of them several different meanings which cannot be reconciled with one another. In the case of a word like *democracy*, not only is there no agreed definition, but the attempt to make one is resisted from all sides. It is almost universally felt that when we call a country democratic we are praising it: consequently the defenders of every kind of régime claim that it is a democracy, and fear that they might have to stop using the word if it were tied down to any one meaning. Words of this kind are often used in a consciously dishonest way. That is, the person who uses them has his own private definition, but allows his hearer to think he means something quite different. Statements like *Marshal Pétain was a true patriot*, *The Soviet Press is the freest in the world*, *The Catholic Church is opposed to persecution*, are almost always made with intent to deceive. Other words used in variable meanings, in most cases more or less dishonestly, are: *class*, *totalitarian*, *science*, *progressive*, *reactionary*, *bourgeois*, *equality*.

Now that I have made this catalogue of swindles and perversions, let me give another example of the kind of writing that they lead to. This time it must of its nature be an imaginary one. I am going to translate a passage of good English into modern English of the worst sort. Here is a well-known verse from *Ecclesiastes*:

I returned, and saw under the sun, that the race is not to the swift, nor the battle to the strong, neither yet bread to the wise, nor yet riches to men of understanding, nor yet favour to men of skill; but time and chance happeneth to them all.

Here it is in modern English:

Objective consideration of contemporary phenomena compels the conclusion that success or failure in competitive activities exhibits no tendency to be commensurate with innate capacity, but that a considerable element of the unpredictable must invariably be taken into account.

This is a parody, but not a very gross one. Exhibit 3), above, for instance, contains several patches of the same kind of English. It will be seen that I have not made a full translation. The beginning and ending of the sentence follow the original meaning fairly closely, but in the middle the concrete illustrations—race, battle, bread—dissolve into the vague phrase 'success or failure in competitive activities'. This had to be so, because no modern writer of the kind I am discussing—no one capable of using phrases like 'objective consideration of contemporary phenomena'—would ever tabulate his thoughts in that precise and detailed way. The whole tendency of modern prose is away from concreteness. Now analyse these two sentences a little more closely. The first contains 49 words but only 60 syllables, and all its words are those of everyday life. The second contains 38 words of 90 syllables: 18 of its words are from Latin roots, and one from Greek. The first sentence contains six vivid images, and only one phrase ('time and chance') that could be called vague. The second contains not a single fresh, arresting phrase, and in spite of its 90 syllables it gives only a shortened version of the meaning contained in the first. Yet without a doubt it is the second kind of sentence that is gaining ground in modern English. I do not want to exaggerate. This kind of writing is not yet universal, and outcrops of simplicity will occur here and there in the worst-written page. Still, if you or I were told to write a few lines on the uncertainty of human fortunes, we should probably come much nearer to my imaginary sentence than to the one from *Ecclesiastes*.

As I have tried to show, modern writing at its worst does not consist in picking out words for the sake of their meaning and inventing images in order to make the meaning clearer. It consists in gumming together long strips of words which have already been set in order by someone else, and making the results presentable by sheer humbug. The attraction of this way of writing is that it is easy. It is easier—even quicker, once you have the habit—to say *In my opinion it is a not unjustifiable assumption that* than to say *I think*. If you use ready-made phrases, you not only don't have to hunt about for words; you also don't have to bother with the rhythms of your sentences, since these phrases are generally so arranged as to be more or less euphonious. When you are composing in a hurry—when you are dictating to a stenographer, for instance, or making a public speech—it is natural to fall into a pretentious, Latinized style. Tags like *a consideration which we should do well to bear in mind* or *a conclusion to which all of us would readily assent* will save many a sentence from coming down with a bump. By using stale metaphors, similes and idioms, you save much mental effort, at the cost of leaving your meaning vague, not only for your reader but for yourself. This is the significance of mixed metaphors. The sole aim of a metaphor is to call up a visual image. When these images clash—as in *The Fascist octopus has sung its swan song, the jackboot is thrown into the melting pot*—it can be taken as certain that the writer is not seeing a mental image of the objects he is naming; in other words he is not really thinking. Look again at the examples I gave at the beginning of this essay. Professor Laski 1) uses five negatives in 53 words. One of these is superfluous, making nonsense of the whole passage, and in addition there is the slip *alien* for akin, making further nonsense, and several avoidable pieces of clumsiness which increase the general vagueness. Professor Hogben 2) plays ducks and drakes with a battery which is able to write prescriptions, and, while disapproving of the everyday phrase *put up with*, is unwilling to look *egregious* up in the dictionary and see what it means. 3), if one takes an uncharitable attitude towards it, is simply meaningless: probably one could work out its intended meaning by reading the whole of the article in which it occurs. In 4), the writer knows more or less what he wants to say, but an accumulation of stale phrases chokes him like tea leaves blocking a sink. In 5), words and meaning have almost parted company. People who write in this manner usually have a general emotional meaning—they dislike one thing and want to express solidarity with another—but they are not interested in the detail of what they are saying. A scrupulous writer, in every sentence that he writes, will ask himself at least four questions, thus: What am I trying to say? What words will express it? What image or idiom will make it clearer? Is this image fresh enough to have an effect? And he will probably ask himself two more: Could I put it more shortly? Have I said anything that is avoidably ugly? But you are not obliged to go to all this trouble. You can shirk it by simply throwing your mind open and letting the ready-made phrases come crowding in. They will construct your sentences for you—even think your thoughts for you, to a certain extent—and at need they will perform the important service of partially concealing your meaning even from yourself. It is at this point that the special connection between politics and the debasement of language becomes clear.

In our time it is broadly true that political writing is bad writing. Where it is not true, it will generally be found that the writer is some kind of rebel, expressing his private opinions and not a 'party line'. Orthodoxy, of whatever colour, seems to demand a lifeless, imitative style. The political dialects to be found in pamphlets, leading articles, manifestos, White Papers and the speeches of under-secretaries do, of course, vary from party to party, but they are all alike in that one almost never finds in them a fresh, vivid, home-made turn of speech. When one watches some tired hack on the platform mechanically repeating the familiar phrases—*bestial atrocities*, *iron heel*, *bloodstained tyranny*, *free peoples of the world*, *stand shoulder to shoulder*—one often has a curious feeling that one is not watching a live human being but some kind of dummy: a feeling which suddenly becomes stronger at moments when the light catches the speaker's spectacles and turns them into blank discs which seem to have no eyes behind them. And this is not altogether fanciful. A speaker who uses that kind of phraseology has gone some distance towards turning himself into a machine. The appropriate noises are coming out of his larynx, but his brain is not involved as it would be if he were choosing his words for himself. If the speech he is making is one that he is accustomed to make over and over again, he may be almost unconscious of what he is saying, as one is when one utters the responses in church. And this reduced state of consciousness, if not indispensable, is at any rate favourable to political conformity.

In our time, political speech and writing are largely the defence of the indefensible. Things like the continuance of British rule in India, the Russian purges and deportations, the dropping of the atom bombs on Japan, can indeed be defended, but only by arguments which are too brutal for most people to face, and which do not square with the professed aims of political parties. Thus political language has to consist largely of euphemism, question-begging and sheer cloudy vagueness. Defenceless villages are bombarded from the air, the inhabitants driven out into the countryside, the cattle machine-gunned, the huts set on fire with incendiary bullets: this is called *pacification*. Millions of peasants are robbed of their farms and sent trudging along the roads with no more than they can carry: this is called *transfer of population* or *rectification of frontiers*. People are imprisoned for years without trial, or shot in the back of the neck or sent to die of scurvy in Arctic lumber camps: this is called *elimination of unreliable elements*. Such phraseology is needed if one wants to name things without calling up mental pictures of them. Consider for instance some comfortable English professor defending Russian totalitarianism. He cannot say outright, 'I believe in killing off your opponents when you can get good results by doing so'. Probably, therefore, he will say something like this:

> While freely conceding that the Soviet régime exhibits certain features which the humanitarian may be inclined to deplore, we must, I think, agree that a certain curtailment of the right to political opposition is an unavoidable concomitant of transitional periods, and that the rigours which the Russian people have been called upon to undergo have been amply justified in the sphere of concrete achievement.

The inflated style is itself a kind of euphemism. A mass of Latin words falls upon the facts like soft snow, blurring the outlines and covering up all the details. The great enemy of clear language is insincerity. When there is a gap between one's real and one's declared aims, one turns as it were instinctively to long words and exhausted idioms, like a cuttlefish squirting out ink. In our age there is no such thing as 'keeping out of politics'. All issues are political issues, and politics itself is a mass of lies, evasions, folly, hatred and schizophrenia. When the general atmosphere is bad, language must suffer. I should expect to find—this is a guess which I have not sufficient knowledge to verify—that the German, Russian and Italian languages have all deteriorated in the last ten or fifteen years, as a result of dictatorship.

But if thought corrupts language, language can also corrupt thought. A bad usage can spread by tradition and imitation, even among people who should and do know better. The debased language that I have been discussing is in some ways very convenient. Phrases like *a not unjustifiable assumption*, *leaves much to be desired*, *would serve no good purpose*, *a consideration which we should do well to bear in mind*, are a continuous temptation, a packet of aspirins always at one's elbow. Look back through this essay, and for certain you will find that I have again and again committed the very faults I am protesting against. By this morning's post I have received a pamphlet dealing with conditions in Germany. The author tells me that he 'felt impelled' to write it. I open it at random, and here is almost the first sentence that I see: '(The Allies) have an opportunity not only of achieving a radical transformation of Germany's social and political structure in such a way as to avoid a nationalistic reaction in Germany itself, but at the same time of laying the foundations of a co-operative and unified Europe.' You see, he 'feels impelled' to write—feels, presumably, that he has something new to say—and yet his words, like cavalry horses answering the bugle, group themselves automatically into the familiar dreary pattern. This invasion of one's mind by ready-made phrases (*lay the foundations*, *achieve a radical transformation*) can only be prevented if one is constantly on guard against them, and every such phrase anaesthetizes a portion of one's brain.

I said earlier that the decadence of our language is probably curable. Those who deny this would argue, if they produced an argument at all, that language merely reflects existing social conditions, and that we cannot influence its development by any direct tinkering with words and constructions. So far as the general tone or spirit of a language goes, this may be true, but it is not true in detail. Silly words and expressions have often disappeared, not through any evolutionary process but owing to the conscious action of a minority. Two recent examples were *explore every avenue* and *leave no stone unturned*, which were killed by the jeers of a few journalists. There is a long list of flyblown metaphors which could similarly be got rid of if enough people would interest themselves in the job; and it should also be possible to laugh the *not un-* formation out of existence,[1] to reduce the amount of Latin and Greek in the average sentence, to drive out foreign phrases and strayed scientific words, and, in general, to make pretentiousness unfashionable. But all these are minor points. The defence of the English language implies more than this, and perhaps it is best to start by saying what it does *not* imply.

To begin with, it has nothing to do with archaism, with the salvaging of obsolete words and turns of speech, or with the setting-up of a 'standard English' which must never be departed from. On the contrary, it is especially concerned with the scrapping of every word or idiom which has outworn its usefulness. It has nothing to do with correct grammar and syntax, which are of no importance so long as one makes one's meaning clear, or with the avoidance of Americanisms, or with having what is called a 'good prose style'. On the other hand it is not concerned with fake simplicity and the attempt to make written English colloquial. Nor does it even imply in every case preferring the Saxon word to the Latin one, though it does imply using the fewest and shortest words that will cover one's meaning. What is above all needed is to let the meaning choose the word, and not the other way about. In prose, the worst thing one can do with words is to surrender to them. When you think of a concrete object, you think wordlessly, and then, if you want to describe the thing you have been visualizing, you probably hunt about till you find the exact words that seem to fit it. When you think of something abstract you are more inclined to use words from the start, and unless you make a conscious effort to prevent it, the existing dialect will come rushing in and do the job for you, at the expense of blurring or even changing your meaning. Probably it is better to put off using words as long as possible and get one's meaning as clear as one can through pictures or sensations. Afterwards one can choose—not simply *accept*—the phrases that will best cover the meaning, and then switch round and decide what impression one's words are likely to make on another person. This last effort of the mind cuts out

[1] One can cure oneself of the *not un-* formation by memorizing this sentence: *A not unblack dog was chasing a not unsmall rabbit across a not ungreen field.*

all stale or mixed images, all prefabricated phrases, needless repetitions, and humbug and vagueness generally. But one can often be in doubt about the effect of a word or a phrase, and one needs rules that one can rely on when instinct fails. I think the following rules will cover most cases:

1 Never use a metaphor, simile or other figure of speech which you are used to seeing in print.

2 Never use a long word where a short one will do.

3 If it is possible to cut a word out, always cut it out.

4 Never use the passive where you can use the active.

5 Never use a foreign phrase, a scientific word or a jargon word if you can think of an everyday English equivalent.

6 Break any of these rules sooner than say anything outright barbarous.

These rules sound elementary, and so they are, but they demand a deep change of attitude in anyone who has grown used to writing in the style now fashionable. One could keep all of them and still write bad English, but one could not write the kind of stuff that I quoted in those five specimens at the beginning of this article.

I have not here been considering the literary use of language, but merely language as an instrument for expressing and not for concealing or preventing thought. Stuart Chase and others have come near to claiming that all abstract words are meaningless, and have used this as a pretext for advocating a kind of political quietism. Since you don't know what Fascism is, how can you struggle against Fascism? One need not swallow such absurdities as this, but one ought to recognize that the present political chaos is connected with the decay of language, and that one can probably bring about some improvement by starting at the verbal end. If you simplify your English, you are freed from the worst follies of orthodoxy. You cannot speak any of the necessary dialects, and when you make a stupid remark its stupidity will be obvious, even to yourself. Political language—and with variations this is true of all political parties, from Conservatives to Anarchists—is designed to make lies sound truthful and murder respectable, and to give an appearance of solidity to pure wind. One cannot change this all in a moment, but one can at least change one's own habits, and from time to time one can even, if one jeers loudly enough, send some worn-out and useless phrase—some *jackboot*, *Achilles' heel*, *hotbed*, *melting pot*, *acid test*, *veritable inferno* or other lump of verbal refuse—into the dustbin where it belongs.

17

BERNARD BLOCH

(1907–1966)

Bloch was Professor of Linguistics at Yale University from 1950 until his death. This article is a detailed and fairly technical example of the methods of linguistic analysis practised by many scholars during the late 1940s, who took as fundamental the essentially bloomfieldian notion of the morpheme—the smallest contrastive grammatical unit in a language—and applied this, through a defined set of methodological principles, to the clarification of a specific linguistic problem. Much of the theory has now been superseded, and some of the technicalities may seem unduly cumbersome, particularly if one is not used to an approach of this kind; but the paper stands as an instance of a clear and consistent analytical method displaying the underlying pattern in a mass of complex material. (The second half of the essay is here omitted.)

'English Verb Inflection'

(*Language*, vol. 23, 1947)

1 *Introductory*

1.1. The inflection of verbs in present-day colloquial English[1] has been described in many works—most clearly and exhaustively, perhaps, by Sweet, Palmer, Curme, Fries, Jespersen, and Hockett.[2] In view of the

[1] The dialect here studied is a somewhat generalized northeastern variety of standard American English. For the methodological groundwork of this paper, see Zellig S. Harris, 'Morpheme Alternants in Linguistic Analysis', *Language*, vol. 18 (1942), pp. 169–80; Rulon S. Wells, 'Immediate Constituents', *Language*, vol. 23 (1947), pp. 81–117; and C. F. Voegelin, 'A Problem in Morpheme Alternants and their Distribution', *Language*, vol. 23, pp. 245–54. Compare now also Charles F. Hockett, 'Problems of Morphemic Analysis', *Language*, vol. 23, pp. 321–43. Though my views in general agree with Hockett's, it will be observed that his treatment of certain problems of English inflection (especially in §24 of his paper) differs markedly from the one here proposed.
I have profited from discussions with R. S. Wells, W. F. Twaddell, and Martin Joos.

[2] Henry Sweet, *A New English Grammar Logical and Historical*, vol. I (Oxford, 1892), pp. 391–428 = §§1283–493; Harold E. Palmer, *A Grammar of Spoken English on a Strictly Phonetic Basis* (Cambridge, 1930), pp. 88–122 = §§199–270; George O. Curme, *A Grammar of the English Language*, II (Boston, etc., 1935), Parts of Speech and Accidence, pp. 241 ff., esp. pp. 269–96 = §60, pp. 304–19 = §63; Charles Carpenter Fries, *American English Grammar* (New York and London, 1940), pp. 59–71; Otto Jespersen, *A Modern*

number and fullness of these descriptions, no new treatment can hope to add any facts hitherto overlooked: at most, a new treatment may be able to arrange the known facts more systematically than has been done before, or in a way that will be more useful to other linguists.

In all previous works, the inflection of English verbs is described in terms of the PROCESSES by which various inflected forms are derived from underlying bases. Thus, the preterit *waited* is said to be derived from *wait* by the addition of a suffix, *took* from *take* by vowel change, *built* from *build* by consonant change, *sold* from *sell* by vowel change and suffixation together, *went* from *go* by suppletion, *put* from *put* by zero change, and so on. Statements of this kind, referring to processes of derivation, are useful for showing the relation of any inflected form to its base; but they have at least one serious shortcoming: they cannot be readily used for the description of specific forms, viewed as words in their own right.

1.2. To describe the structure of a language as a whole, the linguist must be able to describe also the structure of any single sentence or part of a sentence that occurs in the language. He does this in terms of constructions—essentially, in terms of MORPHEMES and their ORDER.[1] Any sentence, phrase, or complex word can be described as consisting of such-and-such morphemes in such-and-such an order; each morpheme has a meaning, and so also has the order in which they occur (the 'constructional meaning').

For the purposes of this paper we adopt Bloomfield's definition of a morpheme, which has been accepted by nearly all descriptive linguists. A morpheme, according to Bloomfield, is 'a linguistic form which bears no partial phonetic-semantic resemblance to any other form'; a linguistic form is 'any combination of phonemes...which has a meaning'.[2]

To illustrate: the preterit form *waited*—considered simply as a word, without the morphemes of stress and pitch that would accompany it in a real utterance—can be described as follows. It consists of two morphemes, /weyt/ and /ed/,[3] occurring in that order. The meaning of the

English Grammar on Historical Principles, VI (Copenhagen, 1942), Morphology, pp. 28–83 = chapters 4–5; Charles F. Hockett, 'English Verb Inflection', *SIL*, vol. 1, no. 2 (1942). For an entertaining travesty of American English verb inflection, see H. L. Mencken, *The American Language* (New York, 1936), pp. 427–47.

[1] Wells, *Language*, vol. 23, pp. 93–8.

[2] Leonard Bloomfield, *Language* (New York, 1933), pp. 161, 138.

[3] The phonemic transcriptions in this paper necessarily reflect my own speech, except that a few distinctions not commonly made in other dialects of English have been disregarded. On the transcription of vowels and diphthongs see George L. Trager and Bernard Bloch, 'The Syllabic Phonemes of English', *Language*, vol. 17 (1941), pp. 223–46, and cf.

first morpheme is a particular action that we need not specifically define here; that of the second is 'past time' or the like. The constructional meaning of the order in which the two morphemes occur is approximately 'perform a certain action at a certain time'.

How shall we describe, now, the preterit form *took*? Its relation to the uninflected form *take* is irrelevant, because we are concerned here simply with the structure of this one word, not with its derivation. Either *took* is one morpheme, or it is two morphemes; the possibility of its being more than two may be neglected as improbable. If it is one morpheme, it is either the same morpheme as *take*, or a different morpheme: as a morpheme, it cannot be partly the same and partly different. If it is the same morpheme as *take*, its meaning must be the same also; but of course we know that *took* and *take* are not synonymous. If *took* is a single morpheme different from *take*, then there can be no morphological connection between them—just as there is none between *took* and *talk*; but since the semantic and syntactic relation of *took* to *take* is exactly the same as that of *waited* to *wait*, we do not like to give up the possibility of connecting them in a morphological system. Finally, if *took* consists of two morphemes, what are they? Perhaps they are 1) /teyk/ and 2) vowel change; but if a morpheme is ultimately a combination of phonemes, then it is clear that vowel change, a process, is not a morpheme. Perhaps, instead, the two morphemes in *took* are 1) /t...k/ and 2) /u/; but then what about *take*? Does *take* then consist of the two morphemes /t...k/ and /ey/? If so, it differs in a fundamental respect from a verb like *wait*, which consists of only a single morpheme; and we must classify English verbal bases into two morphological groups according to the number of their morphemes. Or perhaps *take* is only one morpheme, and the two morphemes in *took* are 1) /teyk/ and 2) /−ey+u/;[1] but again the second of these entities fits no definition of a morpheme that linguists are commonly agreed upon.

Language, vol. 19 (1943), p. 189, fn. 15. The following stressed syllabics occur in the dialect here transcribed: /i/ in *pit*, /e/ in *pet*, /æ/ in *pat*, /a/ in *pot*, /ʌ/ in *cut*, /o/ in *coffin*, /u/ in *put*, /ə/ in *just* (adverb); /iy/ in *beat*, /ey/ in *bait*, /ay/ in *bite*, /oy/ in *boil*, /uy/ in *ruin* (monosyllabic); /aw/ in *bout*, /ow/ in *boat*, /uw/ in *boot*; /ih/ in *theater*, /eh/ in *yeah*, /æh/ in *mad*, /ah/ in *calm*, /oh/ in *law*, /əh/ in *er* (hesitation form); /ir/ in *here*, /er/ in *there*, /ar/ in *part*, /or/ in *port*, /ur/ in *sure*, /ər/ in *curt*; /ihr/ in *beer*, /ehr/ in *bare*, /ahr/ in *bar*, /ohr/ in *bore*, /uhr/ in *boor*, /əhr/ in *burr*. Pitch will not be marked in this paper: stress will be marked only in transcriptions of whole utterances. A space between words has no phonetic or phonemic significance.

Needless to say, the treatment of verb inflection offered here does not depend on the system of transcription. The cited forms could be written just as well according to any other system, so long as it recognized the existing phonemic distinctions in American English.

[1] Read: minus /ey/ plus /u/. Cf. Zellig S. Harris, *Language*, vol. 21 (1945), p. 121 and fn. 3.

The difficulty is even greater with an 'unchanged' preterit like *put* (*He put it there yesterday*). How can we phrase a description of this word that will be different from a description of *put*, the corresponding base form?

1.3. The treatment of inflection to be given here is intended to make possible a clear and unambiguous description of all verb forms. By analyzing every inflected form as a combination of morphemes in a particular order, and by avoiding all reference to the process by which the form is derived, we shall be able to systematize the facts of English verb inflection in a way that will be not only more useful to the descriptive linguist than the treatments hitherto published, but also more uniform and in the long run simpler.

2 *Categories and assumptions*

2.1. A verbal base, in English, is used without any suffix in several different functions: as an INFINITIVE (*I can't wait*; *I don't want to wait*), as an IMPERATIVE (*Wait a minute*), as a FINITE PRESENT with a subject in the 1st or 2d person singular or in the plural (*I wait here every day*; *If you wait for him*; *They wait in line for it*), and in some other ways. In other functions, the verbal base appears with a following INFLECTIONAL SUFFIX:[1] as a FINITE PRESENT with a subject in the 3d SINGULAR (*He waits here every day*), as a FINITE PRETERIT (*I waited for him*), as a PARTICIPLE (*I've waited long enough*), and as a GERUND (*I'm still waiting*; perhaps also *Waiting is tiresome*).

We shall speak of 3d singular, preterit, participle, and gerund as the four INFLECTIONAL CATEGORIES of English verbs; and we shall speak of every verb form that is used in one of these four functions as an INFLECTED FORM.[2]

2.2. To prepare the ground for further discussion, we shall briefly examine a number of typical verb forms. Comparing the 3d-singular forms *passes*, *waits*, and *lives* /pæhs-ez, weyt-s, liv-z/,[3] we note that the

[1] We shall pay no attention in this paper to derivational suffixes (like the *-er* in *waiter*, the *-ful* in *wakeful*, or the *-th* in *growth*), except for a brief mention in §4.5. On the difference between inflection and derivation see Bloch and Trager, *Outline of Linguistic Analysis* (Baltimore, 1942), pp. 54–5 = §4.3.

[2] The verb *be* has inflected forms not included among these four categories. Since this verb presents a special and vexing problem, we shall postpone all reference to it until §5. Inflected verb forms used only with a subject in the 2d person singular (archaic forms like *waitest*, preterit *waitedst*, and Quaker forms like [*thee*] *waits*) are not regarded in this paper as part of present-day standard American English.

[3] Hyphens in the phonemic transcription throughout this paper indicate morphological boundaries, not phonemic junctures.

inflectional suffix appears in three different phonemic shapes /ez, s, z/, whose choice depends on the last phoneme in the base. If we now add the 3d-singular form *need* (*He need not go*) and interpret this like the others as consisting of a base plus an inflectional suffix, we find that the suffix has yet another phonemic shape, namely zero, and that the occurrence of this shape cannot be predicted from the last phoneme in the base but only from the base itself; i.e. the choice of zero instead of /z/ depends on the fact that the base here is *need* and not some other base, such as *lead*.

Again, the preterit forms *waited*, *passed*, and *lived* /weyt-ed, pæhs-t, liv-d/ reveal three phonemic shapes of the preterit suffix. In general, the choice among them depends on the last phoneme in the base; but a form like *dwelt* /dwel-t/ instead of the expected /dwel-d/ shows that the alternation among the three shapes is not wholly determined by this criterion. The preterit form *put* (*He put it there yesterday*) contains an additional shape of the same suffix, namely zero again.

Not only the inflectional suffixes but bases also may have more than one phonemic shape. If we compare the preterit forms *cried* and *fled* /kray-d, fle-d/ with the corresponding uninflected forms, we find that the base *cry* /kray/ remains unchanged before the suffix /d/, whereas the base *flee* /fliy/ appears before this suffix in the special shape /fle/. In just the same way, the base *take* /teyk/ appears before the same suffix in the special shape /tuk/—the only difference being that after this particular base the preterit suffix has the phonemic shape zero, as it has also after the base *put*.

2.3. We are now ready to state the special assumptions that underlie our treatment of English verb inflection. 1) Every verb form functioning as a 3d-singular finite present, as a finite preterit, as a participle, or as a gerund consists of a base and an inflectional suffix. 2) Different phonemic shapes of a given base appearing before different suffixes, and different phonemic shapes of a given suffix appearing after different bases, are morpheme alternants of the same morpheme.[1] 3) One of the alternants of a given morpheme may be zero but no morpheme has zero as its only alternant. 4) Different morphemes may have one or more alternants (including zero) in common. 5) Phonemically different forms that occur in the same environment, and are not in completely free variation with each other, are morphemically different.

[1] On morpheme alternants and morpheme units see Harris, *Language*, vol. 18, pp. 170–3; and cf. Hockett, *Language*, vol. 23, pp. 341–2.

3 Inflectional suffixes

3.1. We list here the four morphemes that appear as inflectional suffixes after verbal bases, together with their morpheme alternants. Alternants whose choice depends on the last preceding phoneme (automatic alternants) are connected by a curve (~); alternants whose choice depends not on a phonemic feature but on the base itself (non-automatic alternants) are separated by a semicolon. The four suffix morphemes are designated by italic numerals.

SUFFIX *1* (3d singular): /ez/ after sibilant ~ /s/ after voiceless non-sibilant ~ /z/ elsewhere; /o/ (zero).

SUFFIX *2* (preterit): /ed/ after apical stop ~ /d/ after voiced sound other than apical stop; /t/; /o/.

SUFFIX *3* (participle): /ed/ after apical stop ~ /d/ after voiced sound other than apical stop; /t/; /n/ after syllabic[1] ~ /ən/ elsewhere; /o/.

SUFFIX *4* (gerund): /iŋ/.

3.2. Certain alternants of different suffix morphemes are associated, in the sense that if a given base is followed by one of them, it will be followed also by the other; thus the /t/ alternant of suffix *2* occurs only after bases that are followed also by the /t/ alternant of suffix *3*, and conversely. On the other hand, certain alternants of different suffix morphemes are mutually exclusive, in the sense that they never appear after the same base; thus no base that is followed by the zero alternant of suffix *1* is followed also by the zero alternant of suffix *2* or *3*.

Among verbs inflected for all four of the categories we have listed, we find that the alternants of the four suffix morphemes appear in seven different combinations. (Automatic alternants are not differentiated in this count.) These combinations provide a basis for grouping such verbs into seven INFLECTIONAL CLASSES (A to G). To these we must add two more (H and I) to accommodate verbs that are not inflected for all four of the categories. Some verbs have no participle or gerund; other verbs lack not only these forms but a preterit also.

The following list shows the nine inflectional classes of English verbs, based on the combinations of suffix alternants that accompany their bases. To simplify the listing, the automatic alternants /ez ~ s ~ z/ are represented by /z/, the alternants /ed ~ d/ by /d/, and the alternants /n ~ ən/ by /n/. One example is given for each class.

[1] A syllabic is a vowel alone or a vowel plus /y, w, h, r, hr/; cf. fn. 3, p. 230.

Class	Suffix 1	Suffix 2	Suffix 3	Suffix 4	Example
A	z	d	d	iŋ	*live*
B	z	t	t	iŋ	*pass*
C	z	o	n	iŋ	*fall*
D	z	o	o	iŋ	*put*
E	z	d	n	iŋ	*show*
F	z	o	d	iŋ	*dive*
G	o	d	d	iŋ	*need*
H	o	d			*can*
I	o				*must*

3.3. In traditional terminology, verbs in classes A and B are weak verbs; those in classes C and D are strong verbs; those in classes E, F, and G are mixed or anomalous verbs; and those in classes H and I are auxiliaries.

Auxiliaries are not only defective in their morphology, but syntactically peculiar as well. The uninflected form (*can*, *shall*, *must*, *may*, etc.) is used as a finite present with a subject in the 1st or 2d person singular or in the plural (cf. §2.1), but not as an infinitive or as an imperative.

4 *Verbal bases*

4.1. Turning now from the suffix morphemes to the base morphemes, we observe that some verbs (*wait*, *live*, *beat*, *show*, etc.) have a base with only one phonemic shape—in other words, with only one morpheme alternant.[1] Other verbs (*flee*, *take*, *fall*, *bite*, etc.) have a base with two different morpheme alternants: one that appears when the base is used alone and before certain of the inflectional suffixes, another that appears before certain other suffixes. And some verbs (*sing*, *fly*, *drive*, *do*, etc.) have a base with three different morpheme alternants.

[1] Strictly considered, every verbal base has at least two alternants differing in stress; see Wells, *Language*, vol. 23, pp. 108–14 = §§66–78. Thus, *wait* has the following alternants: 1) /weyt/, without inherent stress, when the base is accompanied in an utterance by the emphatic stress morpheme /ʹ/, e.g. WAIT *a minute* /wéyt ə mînit/; 2) /wêyt/, with 'reduced-loud' stress, when the base is not accompanied by the emphatic stress morpheme, e.g. *Let's wait* HERE /lèt s wêyt hír/; 3) /wèyt/, with 'medial' stress, again when the base is not accompanied by the emphatic stress morpheme, e.g. *Let's not wait* HERE /lèt s nât wèyt hír/. (The first of these alternants would appear also if the base were pronounced without any phonemic stress; but this would scarcely happen with a word like *wait*.) In our discussion we shall disregard all stress differences among morpheme alternants.

This divergence among the base morphemes allows us to divide them into seven BASE GROUPS according to the number of their morpheme alternants and the particular suffix morphemes before which the alternants occur. When a given base has two alternants or more, they are designated as 'first alternant', 'second alternant', and so on: the first alternant being the one that appears when the base is used alone, and the others being numbered arbitrarily.

BASE GROUP 1 Single alternant. (Example: *wait.*)

BASE GROUP 2 Second alternant before suffix *2*. (Example: *take.*)

BASE GROUP 3 Second alternant before suffixes *2* and *3*. (Example: *break.*)

BASE GROUP 4 Second alternant before suffixes *1*, *2*, and *3*. (Example: *say.*)

BASE GROUP 5 Second alternant before suffix *2*; third alternant before suffix *3*. (Example: *sing.*)

BASE GROUP 6 Second alternant before suffix *2*; third alternant before suffixes *1* and *3*. (Only example: *do.*)

BASE GROUP 7 Second alternant before suffixes *2* and *3*; third alternant before suffix *1*; fourth alternant before suffix *4*. (For the only example see §6.1 s.v. *have.*)

4.2. In citing a verbal base (in the lexicon or elsewhere) we must give all its morpheme alternants, listed in the order determined by the tabulation in §4.1. If we do this, it is obvious that the complete inflection of the verb can then be defined simply by noting the inflectional class and the base group to which it belongs. The following illustrations will make this clear:

wait (A 1) /weyt/	*take* (C2) /teyk; tuk/
build (B 3) /bild; bil/	*put* (D 1) /put/
beat (C 1) /biyt/	*sing* (D5) /siŋ; sæŋ; sʌŋ/

The indication A 1 after *wait* means that the suffix morphemes appear after this base in the alternants /s, ed, ed, iŋ/, and that the base appears before all these suffixes in the single form /weyt/; the complete inflection of this verb is accordingly /weyt-s, weyt-ed, weyt-ed, weyt-iŋ/. The indication B3 after *build* means that the suffix morphemes appear in the alternants /z, t, t, iŋ/, and that the base has two alternants of its own: one, /bild/, appearing before the suffixes /z/ and /iŋ/, the other, /bil/, appearing before /t/ and /t/. The indication C1 after *beat* means that the suffix morphemes appear as /s, o, ən, iŋ/, and that the base is uniformly /biyt/ before all the suffixes. In the same way, the indications C2, D1, and D5 after *take*, *put*, and *sing* respectively, mean that the complete inflection of these verbs is /teyk-s, tuk-o, teyk-ən, teyk-iŋ; put-s, put-o, put-o, put-iŋ; siŋ-z, sæŋ-o, sʌŋ-o, siŋ-iŋ/.

The twofold classification of a verb according to its inflection class and its base group (indicated by a double symbol such as A1, B3, C2) we shall call its CONJUGATION TYPE.

4.3. The overwhelming majority of English verbs belong to one of two conjugation types: to B1 if the base ends in a voiceless consonant except /t/, otherwise to A1. Such verbs are REGULAR; all others are IRREGULAR.

A considerable number of verbs belong to both a regular and an irregular conjugation type. Thus, *burn* belongs to both A1 and B1 (with inflected forms /bəhrn-z, -d, -d, -iŋ/ and /bəhrn-z, -t, -t, -iŋ/ respectively); *fit* belongs to both A1 and D1 (with inflected forms /fit-s, -ed, -ed, -iŋ/ and /fit-s, -o, -o, -iŋ/ respectively); *heave* belongs to both A1 and D3 (with inflected forms /hiyv-z, -d, -d, -iŋ/ and /hiyv-z, howv-o, howv-o, hiyv-iŋ/ respectively). There are also verbs that belong to two or more different irregular conjugation types. Thus, *spit* belongs to D1 and D3 (with inflected forms /spit-s, -o, -o, -iŋ/ and /spit-s, spæt-o, spæt-o, spit-iŋ/ respectively); *tread* belongs to C3 and D3 (with inflected forms /tred-z, trad-o, trad-ən, tred-iŋ/ and /tred-z, trad-o, trad-o, tred-iŋ/ respectively); and *shrink* belongs to four different types —C3, C5, D3, and D5 (with inflected forms /šriŋk-s, šrʌŋk-o, šrʌŋk-ən, šriŋk-iŋ/, /šriŋk-s, šræŋk-o, šrʌŋk-ən, šriŋk-iŋ/, /šriŋk-s, šrʌŋk-o, šrʌŋk-o, šriŋk-iŋ/, and /šriŋk-s, šræŋk-o, šrʌŋk-o, šriŋk-iŋ/ respectively).

Some verbs exhibit a difference in meaning according to their conjugation type; thus, *shine* is transitive in A1 (*I shined my shoes*) but intransitive in D3 (*The sun shone*). Other verbs have the same or approximately the same denotation, but slightly different stylistic and social connotations: the participle *shown* (E1) is for many speakers more elegant than the participle *showed* (A1). Still other verbs are apparently identical in both meaning and connotation regardless of their conjugation type, so that the different inflected forms (e.g. *burned* and *burnt*) occur interchangeably in all situations—i.e. in completely free variation. According to our assumptions (§2.3), if a verb that belongs to a given conjugation type differs in meaning or connotation, however slightly, from a verb with a phonemically identical base that belongs to another type, the verbs are different morphemes: the *shine* whose preterit is *shined* is a different verb from the *shine* whose preterit is *shone*; and by the same argument the *show* whose participle is *shown* is a different verb from the *show* whose participle is *showed*.[1]

Since in practice it is often difficult to decide whether a given phonemic shape that belongs to two or more conjugation types is one verbal base or more than one, we shall not attempt the distinction. Hereafter, we shall use an asterisk to identify all bases that either 1) belong to both a regular and an irregular type, or 2) belong to an irregular type and are homonymous (in at least their first morpheme alternant) with a base belonging to a regular type.

4.4. A number of bases have morpheme alternants whose appearance is controlled not by an inflectional suffix but by some other following element. Chief among such elements is the unstressed morpheme *n't*—/nt/ after a syllabic, /ənt/ elsewhere—that occurs after eleven of the uninflected bases and after some of the corresponding inflected forms.[2] The following verb forms appear before this morpheme unchanged:[3]

can, pret. /kud/:/kud-ənt/.
dare, /dehr/:/dehr-nt/.
do, 3d sg. /dʌz/, pret. /did/:/dʌz-ənt, did-ənt/.
have, uninflected /hæv/, 3d sg. /hæz/, pret. /hæd/:/hæv-ənt, hæz-ənt, hæd-ənt/.
may, /mey/:/mey-nt/.
might, /mayt/:/mayt-ənt/.
ought, /oht/:/oht-ənt/.
need, /niyd/:/niyd-ənt/.
shall, pret. /šud/:/šud-ənt/.
will, pret. /wud/:/wud-ənt/.

Certain other bases (and homonymous 3d-singular forms including the zero alternant of suffix *1*) appear before the morpheme *n't* in an alternant that occurs nowhere else:

[1] The argument: Phonemically different forms that occur in the same environment and are not in completely free variation with each other, are morphemically different (§2.3). In the two participles *shown* / šow-n/ and *showed* / šow-d/, the phonemically different elements /n/ and /d/ both follow the base / šow/. They are not in free variation, since the two forms have different connotations of elegance and hence are not interchangeable. Therefore, either /n/ and /d/ are different morphemes, or the environment in which they occur is after all not the same for both. Since we wish to identify /n/ and /d/ as alternants of the same morpheme (suffix *3*), we assume that the / šow/ that precedes /n/ is morphemically different from the / šow/ that precedes /d/. In other words, we choose to set up two different but homonymous morphemes / šow/, and to refer to them—rather than to the suffix alternants—the stylistic or connotative difference between the inflected forms *shown* and *showed*.

[2] The form *n't* is best regarded as a separate morpheme, not as an alternant of the full form *not*. The two forms contrast, at least stylistically and in their connotations, in such phrases as *I cannot go*: *I can't go*.

[3] Any form in this list not otherwise identified is both the uninflected form of the verb and the homonymous 3d-singular form with zero suffix.

can, /kæn/ : /kæh-nt/.
do, uninflected /duw/ : /dow-nt/.
must, /mʌst/ : /mʌs-ənt/.
shall, /šæl/ : /šæh-nt/.
will, /wil/ : /wow-nt/.

4.5. There are also bases that appear in a special alternant shape before certain derivational suffixes. Thus, the base of the verb *see* has the alternants /siy/ and /soh/ before the inflectional morphemes, but the alternant /say/ before /t/ in the derivative noun *sight* /say-t/; the base of the verb *sing* has the alternants /siŋ/, /sæŋ/, and /sʌŋ/ before the inflectional morphemes, but the alternant /sohŋ/ before a zero derivational suffix in the noun *song*.[1]

Finally, some bases have special sandhi alternants when followed in the same phrase by a word with an initial consonant, especially one that is homorganic or identical with the last consonant of the base in its fuller form. This is especially true of bases ending with /t/ or /d/ after another consonant. Thus, the verb form *last*, normally /læhst/, may appear as /læhs/ in the phrase *How long will it last today?* or the like; the verb forms *find* and *found*, normally /faynd/ and /fawnd/, may lack the final /d/ in the phrases *Did you find time to do it?* and *I found two dollars.* The use of such sandhi alternants is optional: the same person will speak sometimes the shorter form, sometimes the longer in the same context. In the remainder of this paper we shall ignore them entirely.

5 *The Verb* be

5.1. The base of the verb *be* has a greater number of morpheme alternants than any other. As the first alternant—the one that appears when the base is used without any inflectional suffix—we may set up the shape /biy/; but this has a more limited use than the first alternant of other verbs except the auxiliaries (§2.1, §3.3). It occurs freely as an infinitive (*I can't be there*; *I don't want to be there*) and as an imperative (*Be quiet*); but as a finite present it occurs only after *if*, and only in rather formal style (*If I be not mistaken*; *If you be he*; *If they be still there*). In the latter use, /biy/ occurs also with a 3d-singular subject (*If it be not presumptuous*), thus differing again from other verbal bases. Moreover,

[1] It goes without saying that historical considerations play no part in a structural description. The actual historical relation between *sing* and *song* is irrelevant here; all that is relevant is their morphological relation in the structure of present-day English.

/biy/ is unique in its optative and concessive uses (*God be praised*; *The public be damned*; *Be it never so humble*; *Be that as it may*).[1]

5.2. The inflected forms of the verb *be* in the four usual inflectional categories are as follows: 3d singular *is* (base alternant /i/, suffix alternant /z/); preterit *was* and *were* (base alternants /wʌz/ and /wəhr/ in complementary distribution,[2] suffix alternant zero); participle *been* (base alternant /bi/,[3] suffix alternant /n/); gerund *being* (base alternant /biy/, suffix alternant /iŋ/).

But there are still other inflected forms of *be* that belong to none of these four categories. This constitutes the most striking idiosyncrasy of the verb: that its inflection distinguishes categories not recognized by the morphology of any other verb. We find, first, the forms *am* and *are* /æm, ahr/. These might be regarded as uninflected forms, in complementary distribution with the alternant /biy/; for the three words together have the same distribution as the uninflected form of such a verb as *wait*. The objection to this view is that the alternant /biy/ occurs, as already mentioned, in clauses with *if* (§ 5.1), contrasting in this position with /æm/ and /ahr/ (*If I be not mistaken*: *If I am not mistaken*; *If you be he*: *If you are he*). If the contrast is valid, we must set up a new inflectional category for *am* and *are*, perhaps to be called GENERAL PRESENT (i.e. non-3d-singular present). But in that case *am* and *are* include an inflectional suffix; and this cannot be zero, since we have assumed (§2.3) that no morpheme has zero as its only alternant. Any solution of the problem is inescapably ad hoc; we propose to regard the alternants of the base here as /æ/ and /ah/ in complementary distribution, and to posit a suffix morpheme with two alternants /m/ and /r/, the choice between them being regulated by the shape of the base alternant: /m/ after /æ/, /r/ after /ah/.

Complementary distribution and identity of meaning have allowed us to treat the two preterit forms *was* and *were* as both containing the zero alternant of suffix 2. But there is another form *were* which is not preterit and which contrasts with *was*: the form that appears in conditional clauses after *if* with a subject in the 1st or 3d person singular (*If I were rude, I'd apologize*; *If he were here, he'd see it*; contrast *If I was*

[1] The optative use of *be* is paralleled by other verbs in a few formulas: *God have mercy*; *God forbid*; *Perish the thought*. The concessive use of other verbs than *be* is limited to such archaic locutions as *Try they never so hard*.

[2] The alternant /wʌz/ occurs only with a subject in the 1st or 3d person singular; the alternant /wəhr/ occurs with all other subjects.

[3] Or /biy/ in British English, identical with the alternant that appears in the uninflected form.

rude, I apologize; *If he was here, he saw it*). This *were* must be an inflected form different from the preterit *were*; its category we may call (with Hockett) the UNREAL. Again we analyze the form ad hoc: base alternant /wəh/, suffix morpheme /r/.[1]

5.3. Our analysis results in the following array of forms for the verb *be*: uninflected /biy/; 3d singular /i-z/; preterit /wʌz-o/ and /wəhr-o/ in complementary distribution; participle /bi-n/; gerund /biy-iŋ/; general present /æ-m/ and /ah-r/ in complementary distribution; unreal /wəh-r/. The base morpheme has eight alternants: /biy, i, wʌz, wəhr, bi, æ, ah, wəh/; and the six inflectional morphemes appear in the following alternants: *1* /z/, *2* /o/, *3* /n/, *4* /iŋ/, *5* /m/ and /r/ in complementary distribution, *6* /r/. This multiplicity of forms calls for an addition both to our list of inflectional classes (§3.2) and to our list of base groups (§4.1). Accordingly, we set up (again ad hoc) class J and base group 8 to accommodate the verb *be*. The former has been defined already in the list of suffix alternants just given; the latter is defined as follows:

BASE GROUP 8 Second alternant before suffix *1*; third and fourth alternants before suffix *2*; fifth alternant before suffix *3*; sixth and seventh alternants before suffix *5*; eighth alternant before suffix *6*.

5.4. Three of the inflected forms of *be* (but not the uninflected form) appear unchanged before the morpheme *n't* (§4.4). These are 3d singular /iz/, preterit /wʌz/ and /wəhr/, general present /ahr/ but not /æm/: /iz-ənt, wʌz-ənt, wəhr-nt, ahr-nt/. In the substandard form *ain't* /ey-nt/, the /ey/ is a ninth alternant of the base, here followed by the zero alternants of suffixes *1* and *5*...

[1] Since *be* has more inflected forms than any other verb, we might have begun our discussion with it instead of saving it for the end. In that case we should have said that all other verbs (except the auxiliaries) have the same inflectional categories as *be*, but that only *be* formally distinguishes the general present from the uninflected form or the unreal from the preterit. This is essentially what Hockett did in his rigorously systematic treatment of English verbs ('English Verb Inflection', *SIL*, vol. 1, no. 2). The treatment here adopted seems preferable because it results in a simpler statement.

18

H. L. MENCKEN

(1880–1950)

Mencken, the American reporter and editor, produced also verse, plays, a series of satirical *Prejudices*, books about George Bernard Shaw and Nietzsche, and other works. *The American Language* went through four editions in his lifetime, to which he added two supplements (1945, 1948). Although he thought of it as mere journalism, most scholars of the language received it with high approval. Among school teachers of English his views did not fare so well.

'English or American?'

(*The American Language*, 1919; the text is from the fourth edition, 1947)

But as English spreads over the world, will it be able to maintain its present form? Probably not. But why should it? The notion that anything is gained by fixing a language in a groove is cherished only by pedants. Every successful effort at standardization, as Dr. Ernest Weekley has well said, results in nothing better than emasculation.[1] 'Stability in language is synonymous with *rigor mortis*.' It is the very anarchy of English, adds Claude de Crespigny, that has made it the dominant language of the world today.[2] In its early forms it was a highly inflected tongue—indeed, it was more inflected than modern German, and almost as much so as Russian. The West Saxon dialect, for example, in the days before the Norman Conquest, had grammatical gender, and in addition the noun was inflected for number and for case, and there were five cases in all. Moreover, there were two quite different declensions, the strong and the weak, so that the total number of inflections was immense. The same ending, of course, was commonly used more than once, but that fact only added to the difficulties of the language. The impact of the Conquest knocked this elaborate gram-

[1] 'English as She Will be Spoke', *Atlantic Monthly* (May 1932). The quotation following is from *The English Language*, by the same author (New York, 1929), p. 9.

[2] 'Esperanto', *American Speech* (September 1926).

matical structure into a cocked hat. The upper classes spoke French, and so the populace had English at its mercy. It quickly wore down the vowels of the endings to a neutral *e*, reduced the importance of their consonants by moving the stress forward to the root, and finally lopped off many inflections *in toto*. By the time of Chaucer (1340?–1400) English was moving rapidly toward its present form. It had already become a virtually analytical language, depending upon word position rather than upon inflection for expressing meanings, and meanwhile the influence of French, which had been official from 1066 to 1362, had left it full of new words, and made it a sort of hybrid of the Teutonic and Romance stocks. It has remained such a hybrid to this day, and in some ways, indeed, its likeness to French, Italian and Spanish is more marked than its likeness to German. Once its East Midland dialect had been given preëminence over all other dialects by Chaucer and his followers, it began to develop rapidly, and in the time of Shakespeare it enjoyed an extraordinarily lush and vigorous growth. New words were taken in from all the other languages of Europe and from many of those of Africa and Asia, other new words in large number were made of its own materials, and almost everything that remained of the old inflections was sloughed off.[1] Thus it gradually took on a singularly simple and flexible form, and passed ahead of the languages that were more rigidly bound by rule.

I think I have offered sufficient evidence in the chapters preceding that the American of today is much more honestly English, in any sense that Shakespeare would have understood, than the so-called Standard English of England. It still shows all the characters that marked the common tongue in the days of Elizabeth, and it continues to resist stoutly the policing that ironed out Standard English in the Seventeenth and Eighteenth Centuries. Standard English must always strike an American as a bit stilted and precious. Its vocabulary is patently less abundant than his own, it has lost to an appreciable extent its old capacity for bold metaphor, and in pronunciation and spelling it seems to him to be extremely uncomfortable and not a little ridiculous. When

[1] The process is described at length in George H. McKnight, *Modern English in the Making* (New York, 1928). See also George Philip Krapp, *Modern English* (New York, 1910), especially chapter IV; and T. R. Lounsbury, *A History of the English Language* (rev. ed. New York, 1894). 'English,' says Harold Cox in 'English as a World Language', London *Spectator* (10 May 1930), 'has the great advantage that it more or less represents an amalgam of languages. It is largely Scandinavian in origin, but it also embodies a vast number of words directly derived from Latin, and many others coming to us from French and Italian, besides not a few coming from German.'

he hears a speech in its Oxford (or Public-School) form he must be a Bostonian to avoid open mirth. He believes, and on very plausible grounds, that American is better on all counts—clearer, more rational, and above all, more charming. And he holds not illogically that there is no reason under the sun why a dialect spoken almost uniformly by nearly 125,000,000 people should yield anything to the dialect of a small minority in a nation of 45,000,000. He sees that wherever American and this dialect come into fair competition—as in Canada, for example, or in the Far East—American tends to prevail,[1] and that even in England many of its reforms and innovations are making steady headway, so he concludes that it will probably prevail everywhere hereafter. 'When two-thirds of the people who use a certain language,' says one of his spokesmen,[2] 'decide to call it a *freight-train* instead of a *goods-train* they are "right"; and the first is correct English and the second a dialect.'

Nor is the American, in entertaining such notions, without English support. The absurdities of Standard English are denounced by every English philologian, and by a great many other Englishmen. Those who accept it without cavil are simply persons who are unfamiliar with any other form of the language; the Irishman, the Scotsman, the Canadian, and the Australian laugh at it along with the American—and with the Englishman who has lived in the United States. As an example of the last-named class I point to Mr. H. W. Seaman, a Norwich man who had spent ten years on American and Canadian newspapers and was in practice, when he wrote, as a journalist in London. He says:

I speak for millions of Englishmen when I say that we are as sick and tired of this so-called English as you Americans are. It has far less right to be called Standard English speech than Yorkshire or any other country dialect has—or than any American dialect. It is as alien to us as it is to you. True, some of my neighbors have acquired it—for social or other reasons—

[1] Its influence upon the English of Australia and of South Africa is already marked. In a glossary of Australianisms appended by the Australian author, C. J. Dennis, to his *Doreen and the Sentimental Bloke* (New York, 1916), I find the familiar verbs and verb-phrases, *to beef, to biff, to bluff, to boss, to break away, to chase one's self, to chew the rag, to chip in, to fade away, to get it in the neck, to back and fill, to plug along, to get sore, to turn down* and *to get wise*; the substantives, *dope, boss, fake, creek, knockout-drops* and *push* (in the sense of *crowd*); the adjectives, *hitched* (in the sense of *married*) and *tough* (as before *luck*), and the adverbial phrases, *for keeps* and *going strong*. In South Africa many Americanisms have ousted corresponding English forms, even in the standard speech.

[2] William McAlpine, *New Republic* (26 June 1929).

but then some of the Saxon peasants took pains to acquire Norman French, which also was imposed upon them from above.[1]

Mr. Seaman describes with humour his attempts as a schoolboy to shed his native Norwich English and to acquire the prissy fashionable dialect that passes as Standard. He managed to do so, and is thus able today to palaver on equal terms with 'an English public-school boy, an Oxford man, a clergyman of the Establishment, an announcer of the British Broadcasting Company, or a West End actor,' but he confesses that it still strikes him, as it strikes an American, as having 'a mauve, Episcopalian and ephebian ring.' And he quotes George Bernard Shaw as follows:

The English have no respect for their language...It is impossible for an Englishman to open his mouth without making some other Englishman hate or despise him...An honest and natural slum dialect is more tolerable than the attempt of a phonetically untaught person to imitate the vulgar dialect of the golf club.

The views of Basil de Sélincourt, author of 'Pomona, or The Future of English,' and of J. Y. T. Greig, author of 'Breaking Priscian's Head,' I have quoted in previous chapters. Both cling to the hope that some form of English denizened in England may eventually become the universal form of the language, but both are plainly upset by fears that American will prevail. 'Right and wrong in such a matter,' says Mr. de Sélincourt, 'can be decided only by the event. However it be, the United States, obviously, is now the scene of the severest ordeals, the vividest excitements of our language...The contrasting and competitive use of their one language by the English and the Americans gives it a new occasion for the exercise of its old and noble faculty of compromise. In a period of promise and renewal, it was beginning to grow old; the Americans are young...Its strong constitution will assimilate tonics as fast as friends can supply them, and take no serious harm. Changes are certainly in store for it.' Mr. Greig is rather less sanguine about the prospects of compromise between English and American. 'It is possible,' he says gloomily, 'that in fifty or a hundred years...American and not English will be the chief foreign language taught in the schools of Asia and the European Continent. Some Americans look forward to this without misgiving, nay, with exultation; and I for one would rather have it fall out than see perpetuated and extended that silliest and dwabliest of all the English dialects, Public-

[1] 'The Awful English of England', *American Mercury* (September 1933), p. 73.

School Standard.' To which I add an extract from an English review of Logan Pearsall Smith's 'Words and Idioms' (1925), quoted by the late Brander Matthews:[1]

It is chiefly in America—let us frankly recognize the fact—that the evolution of our language will now proceed. Our business here is to follow sympathetically what happens there, admitting once for all that our title to decide what English is is purely honorary. The more unmistakably we make the admission, the more influence we shall have; for in language it is the *fait accompli* that counts, and in the capacity for putting new words over, the Americans, if only because they have twice the population, are bound to win every time.[2]

The defects of English, whether in its American or its British form, are almost too obvious to need rehearsal. One of the worst of them lies in the very fact that the two great branches of the language differ, not only in vocabulary but also in pronunciation. Thus the foreigner must make his choice, and though in most cases he is probably unconscious of it, he nevertheless makes it. The East Indian, when he learns English at all, almost always learns something approximating Oxford English, but the Latin-American is very apt to learn American, and American is what the immigrant returning to Sweden or Jugoslavia, Poland or Syria, Italy or Finland certainly takes home with him. In Russia, American has begun to challenge English, and in Japan and elsewhere in the Far East the two dialects are in bitter competition, with American apparently prevailing. That competition, which has been going on in Europe since the World War, presents a serious problem to foreign teachers of the language. Says Dr. R. W. Zandvoort of The Hague:

A generation ago, this problem had scarcely arisen. Most Continental language teachers, if interrogated on the subject, would probably have stated that they recognized one standard only, that set by educated usage in the South of England, and that, except perhaps for scientific purposes, local variants did not come within their purview. Nor was this surprising, considering the proximity of the Continent to England, the prestige enjoyed by Southern English within the British Isles, and the distance from that other center of Anglo-Saxon culture, the United States of America. Since the Great War, however, it has become increasingly difficult for European teachers and scholars to ignore the fact that different norms of English usage are being evolved in another hemisphere, and that these norms are beginning to encroach on territory where hitherto Standard

[1] 'American Leadership in the English Idiom', *Literary Digest International Book Review* (March 1926). See also, Frank D. Long, 'Shall We All Speak American?', *Passing Show* (London, 13 July 1935).

[2] 'It is amusing to note', added Matthews, 'that in this last sentence the British reviewer used two Americanisms—*putting new words over* and *every time*; and apparently he used them quite unconscious of their transatlantic origin.'

Southern English has held undisputed sway. Not that they are greatly concerned about the sort of English spoken in Australia, New Zealand, or Canada; these areas as yet exert no appreciable cultural influence upon the rest of the civilized world, and as members of the British Commonwealth of Nations are more or less amenable to the linguistic authority of the mother country. So long, too, as the attitude of educated Americans towards their own form of speech was expressed in the words of Richard Grant White that 'just in so far as it deviates from the language of the most cultivated society of England, it fails to be English,' there was no need for Continental language teachers to take even American English seriously. But with its world-wide dissemination through business, literature, the talking film, the gramophone record, on one hand, and the growing determination of Americans to assert their independence in matters of language on the other, the situation is taking on a different aspect.[1]

Unluckily, neither of the great dialects of English may be described as anything approaching a perfect language. Within the limits of both there are still innumerable obscurities, contradictions and irrationalities. Those in spelling are especially exasperating. 'Eight long vowels,' says Dr. Arthur G. Kennedy,[2] 'are spelled in at least sixty-six different ways; hardly a letter in the alphabet could be named which does not represent from two to eight different sounds; at least six new vowel characters and five new consonant characters are needed; nearly a fifth of the words on a printed page contain silent letters; and the spelling of many words such as *colonel*, *one* and *choir* is utterly absurd.' 'But spelling,' says Dr. George Philip Krapp,[3]

would be only a beginning of the general house-cleaning for which our precious heritage of English speech as we know it today provides a profitable opportunity. The language is burdened with quantities of useless lumber, which from the point of view of common sense and reason might just as well be burned on the rubbish heap... Why should we permit an exceptional plural *feet* or *teeth* when we possess a perfectly good regular way of making plurals by adding *s*? And why should verbs like *write* have two past forms, *wrote* and *written*, when most verbs of the language get along quite satisfactorily with only one?

There is yet another difficulty, and a very serious one. Of it Dr. Janet Rankin Aiken says:

This difficulty is idiom—idiom observable in a large part of what we say and write, but centering particularly in verb and preposition. It has been calculated[4]

[1] 'Standards of English in Europe', *American Speech* (February 1934).

[2] 'The Future of the English Language', *American Speech* (December 1933).

[3] 'The Future of English', in *The Knowledge of English* (New York, 1927), p. 537.

[4] By Dr. Aiken herself in *A New Plan of English Grammar* (New York, 1933), chapter XIX.

that including all phrase constructions there are well over a hundred different forms for even a simple, regular verb like *call*, besides extra or lacking forms for irregular verbs like *speak*, *be* and *set*. Each of these verb forms has several uses, some as high as a dozen or more, to express not only time but such other notions as possibility, doubt, habit, emphasis, permission, ability, interrogation, negation, generalization, expectation, duration, inception, and a bewildering number of other ideas. Native speakers of English have difficulty with verb constructions; how much more so the foreign student of the language![1]

Finally, there are the snarls of sentence order—naturally numerous in an analytical language. Says Dr. Aiken:

Each of the sentence types—declarative, interrogative, imperative, and exclamatory—has its own normal order, but there are many exceptional orders as well. In certain constructions the verb may or must come before the subject, and frequently the complement comes before the subject, or the subject is embedded within the verb phrase. All these orders, both normal and exceptional, must somehow be mastered before the student can be said to use English properly.

I introduce a foreign-born witness of high intelligence to sum up. He is Dr. Enrique Blanco, of the department of Romance languages at the University of Wisconsin, a native of Spain who has acquired a perfect command of English and writes it with vigor and good taste. He says:

English is not easy to learn. It is a puzzling, bewildering language; and the ambitious foreigner who sets himself to the task of learning it soon discovers that it can not be acquired in a short time. As Mr. Mencken quotes in his book: 'The vowel sounds in English are comparatively independent of their surroundings.'[2] We would suggest that the word 'comparatively' be changed to 'absolutely.' That's one of the greatest troubles in the English language; one never knows how to pronounce a vowel. The *a*, for instance, that apparently inoffensive first letter of the alphabet, soon assumes, for the student of English, most terrifying proportions; it has a different sound in nearly every word. Beginning with *meat* and going on through *awful*, *alas*, *mat*, *ate*, *tall*, *fail*, *cap*, *said*, and so forth, one can run across nearly every conceivable sound in human speech. As soon as the enterprising would-be American has learned to pronounce *door* nicely, he is politely informed that *boor* must be pronounced differently. *Arch* and *march* sound very logical, but one gets a frown if he pronounces *patriarch* in the same manner. If a man goes to church he may sit on a humble *chair*, but the word *choir* must be pronounced with a greater degree of respectfulness; coming out of the sacred precinct, a man may be *robbed*, or just simply *robed*. An egg can

[1] 'English as the International Language', *American Speech* (April 1934), p. 104.

[2] The reference is to the third edition of the present work (New York, 1923). The quotation, and the one following, are from Otto Jespersen's *Growth and Structure of the English Language* (3rd ed. Leipzig, 1919).

take a mate unto itself and be *eggs*, but if a child has a friend they are not *childs* but *children*; a pastor may refer to *brother* Jones, but he is careful to speak to his *brethren*. Quotes Mr. Mencken: 'Each English consonant belongs distinctly to its own type, a *t* is a *t*,...and there is an end.' Unfortunately, the end is far from being there, for the *t* in English is often not a *t* at all, but an *sh*, as in *intuition*, *constitution*, where the *t* has two different sounds in the same word, and *nation*, *obligation*, where the *t* is not a *t* but something else. Need I go on? Yet, this language is supposed to be 'vastly easier' than any other.[1]

Efforts to remedy the irrationalities of English spelling have been under way for many years, but so far without much success. The improvement of English in other respects must await a revolutionist who will do for it what Mark Twain tried to do for German in 'The Awful German Language'—but with much less dependence upon logic. 'If English is to be a continuously progressive creation,' said Dr. Krapp,[2] 'then it must escape from the tyranny of the reason and must regain some of the freedom of impulse and emotion which must have been present in the primitive creative origins of language...Suppose the children of this generation and of the next were permitted to cultivate expressiveness instead of fineness of speech, were praised and promoted for doing something interesting, not for doing something correct and proper. If this should happen, as indeed it is already beginning to happen, the English language and literature would undergo such a renascence as they have never known.' Meanwhile, despite its multitudinous defects, English goes on conquering the world. I close with the florid vision of Samuel Daniel:

> And who in time knows whither we may vent
> The treasure of our tongue? To what strange shores
> This gain of our best glory shall be sent,
> T' enrich unknowing nations with our stores?
> What worlds in th' yet unformed Occident
> May come refin'd with th' accents that are ours?[3]

[1] 'American as a World-Language', *Literary Digest International Book Review* (April 1924), p. 342.

[2] *The Future of English*, above cited, p. 543.

[3] *Musophilus* (1599). *Musophilus* is a dialogue between a courtier and a poet, in which the latter defends the worldly value of literary learning.

19

R. B. LEES

(1922–)

A sharp reaction from the methods of linguistic analysis propounded by Bloomfield, Bloch, Fries, and others came with the work of Noam Chomsky (see in particular his *Syntactic Structures*, 1957). This new approach, usually referred to as transformational-generative grammar (or, simply, 'generative' grammar) is now the most influential method of linguistic analysis, though little descriptive material has as yet been produced. Lees wrote his article at a time when the effect of generative grammar was beginning to be felt on a large scale: he therefore prefaces his descriptive analysis illustrating generative principles and procedures with a summary of what he feels to be the major weaknesses in traditional (i.e. pre-1957) linguistic grammar.

'A Multiply Ambiguous Adjectival Construction in English'

(*Language*, vol. 36, 1960)

1 *Syntactic analysis*

I INTRODUCTION

It has often been regretted that, while the methods of modern linguistics have achieved notable progress in the field of phonology, corresponding results for syntax have been considerably less impressive. At least one reason for the truth underlying this regret is undoubtedly the inability of the linguist to satisfy the very requirements which he himself has thought it necessary to impose on an adequate syntactic description. His persistent failure has resulted not so much, I think, from the lack of knowledge or insight into the nature of linguistic systems but rather in large measure from the unrealistic nature of these requirements.

The earlier attitude dominant during the 19th century and persisting into our time was that a syntactic analysis must account for all the various meanings which one could think of, all shades and nuances which could possibly be expressed by utterances—in short, a syntactic analysis must be a grammatically oriented semantic theory.

Reacting vigorously against this notional approach and all the vagueness or, as it was termed, mentalism, to which it must inevitably be heir, the modern linguist has swung to the opposite extreme. In order to render grammatical analysis scientific he advocates a description based on directly observable physical properties of utterances. The idea that the overt shape of sentences might yield taxonomic criteria goes back at least as far as Pāṇini and the Hindu grammarians, but the notion that a linguistic description be based exclusively upon the phonemic shape of expressions is a modern development, arising in part perhaps from a mistaken idea that success in the physical sciences arises from strict empirical induction out of observables.

Along with this latter physicalist view there has also developed, not only in linguistics but also in other social sciences, the notion that description is rendered scientific to the extent that a strict account can be given of how the description, or the analysis, might have been deduced from observations. This rather quaint idea takes its form in linguistic science in the requirement that an adequate linguistic description consist of a series of automatically applicable procedural steps by means of which any trained expert might pass from tape recordings of a corpus of utterances, smoothly through various stages of transcription, to more and more general grammatical analyses of those utterances.

I do not wish to dwell at length here on the reasons why such a view must be deemed quixotic, but the position which I take vis-à-vis the generally accepted doctrine may be summarized briefly in the following way. Most linguists would agree, and I think correctly, that the two central aims of linguistic science are 1) to provide grammatical analyses for as many different sentence-types as possible, and 2) to provide criteria for these analyses. However, the key concepts in this statement are ordinarily INTERPRETED in a very naive and primitive way. The accepted view of 'linguistic analysis' is as a kind of dissection of sentences into segments with a subsequent classification of these fragments into species, genera, families, etc.; and the corresponding accepted view of 'criteria of analysis' is as recipes for this segmentation and taxonomy.[1] This naive physicalist interpretation is in keeping with an

[1] This view is so widely accepted that there is little point in documenting it with citations. Furthermore, although my article is clearly in part polemic, it is not with any particular authors that I wish to take issue. However, lest it be thought that my interpretation of the dominant view in American linguistics is overly severe, I call attention to one single

insistence that the relationship between a grammatical analysis and a material record of the utterances analyzed be a simple, one-one, temporal-order-preserving map of sequences of elements onto sequences of sound segments.

The interpretation which I shall give to these two immediate, or limited, goals of linguistic science is much more like that customary in other fields of research. By ANALYSIS I understand the assignment of grammatical structures to sentences, where these structures may be of a very abstract nature, not necessarily ordered as are the sounds themselves, and not necessarily segmented by nonintersecting hierarchical bracketings, as on a Stammbaum. By CRITERIA of analysis I understand the various constraints which it may become possible to impose on an adequate explanatory linguistic theory of any language, i.e. the general formal features which we may expect the grammar of a language to exhibit.[1]

In the following I shall show how the several generally accepted conceptions of syntactic analysis all fail to provide correct grammatical structures for a certain set of common adjectival constructions in English as a result both of restriction to irrelevant taxonomic criteria and of their inability to reach down to sufficiently deep-lying levels of linguistic structure. In short, I hope to demonstrate that many accepted methods of syntactic analysis are both wrong and superficial.

II TRADITIONAL DOCTRINES

A SEMANTIC ANALYSIS. It is difficult to distinguish clearly demarcated traditions or schools of syntactic analysis, but there are certain widely accepted methodological doctrines which we can adduce as examples.

The old concern with meaning which arose in the conception of grammatical research as a kind of semantic theory centered on natural-language sentences (rather than, say, psychological or philosophical notions) lingers on in modern linguistic literature at least in the form of an irrelevant definition of the term 'morpheme', always called for as a prerequisite to analysis but then usually ignored in the subsequent details

article, chosen simply because it so clearly and overtly states the dogma in question: Wallace L. Chafe, 'The Classification of Morphs in Seneca', *Anthropological linguistics*, vol. I (1959), pp. 1–6. Chafe writes (page 1): 'Let us assume that the utterances of a language have been successfully segmented into morphs...We now wish to classify these morphs into morphemes...I shall use the term morph, incidentally, to mean not a single occurrence, but a class of occurrences with the same meaning and shape.'

[1] This view is clearly taken from the work of N. Chomsky and is advocated in greater detail in his own *Syntactic Structures* ('s-Gravenhage, 1957), especially chapters 1, 2, 6, and 9.

of description. This demand for pre-analytic definitions of terms is again a manifestation of naive physicalism, which can on occasion be extended to the most ludicrous limits; thus, there are studies in which the grammarian has felt the necessity of 'defining' such basic notions as 'sentence', or even 'language', before proceeding to the business of grammar, much as if a geologist were constrained to provide a formal definition of the term 'earth' before analyzing rocks.

B PHONEMIC APPROACH. Out of an increasingly detailed study of sound systems, together with the mistaken conviction that linguistics must provide an automatic procedure for deducing the grammatical analysis of sentences from phonetic transcriptions of them, has grown the recent proposal for a 'phonemic approach' to syntax. This shallow and backward step in linguistic studies would congeal our imperfect understanding of grammatical form at that primitive stage which recognizes only those syntactic features of sentences which are clearly and overtly mirrored in the physical shape of the utterance. An apparently very convincing motivation to accept this view is the argument that since sentences are uttered to be understood, and since all that can be understood must be physically present in the sound waves, the relevant features of our linguistic description also must be found in a physical description, for these are all and only what the speaker perceives. When reminded that the listener in addition to hearing the utterance with his ears also knows the grammar of the language, the proponent of the phonemic approach can retort that while his view may not be absolutely necessary for an explanation of talking and understanding, surely it will be so necessitated if we are to account for the LEARNING of the grammar by the child.

But none of these considerations is quite relevant, for no one would wish to deny that the formal features of sentences which the linguist seeks to describe are, in some sense, 'present' physically in the utterances. The important point is that these features need not be spatially perspicuous, need not be visually obvious, features of arrangement and demarcation; they may be very intricate, abstract characteristics, connected to the immediately perceptible sound features only by means of long chains of involved rules, some of them perhaps not preserving temporal order. Finally, it is not necessary at all to assume that these features are related to phonetic transcriptions bi-uniquely, i.e. in such a manner that to every distinct phonetic sequence there corresponds only one grammatical analysis (as would be required if grammatical analyses are to be deducible from phonetic transcriptions).

C SUBSTITUTION IN DIAGNOSTIC ENVIRONMENTS. Overtly or unconsciously perceiving the severe difficulties in this strict phonemic approach, most linguists have admitted that linguistic analysis must make use also of another, supplementary method, the so-called method of diagnostic environments, or the substitution-in-frames technique. This familiar device is, however, not an analytic technique, as it is usually taken to be, but simply a misleading way to present a proposed grammatical analysis—more accurately, a proposed morpheme-order analysis. This so-called method proceeds to a reasonable result if and only if the correct frames for the putative substitution process have somehow already been chosen, for there is no automatic method for choosing them, nor does anyone ever propose that all possible frames must be investigated (which is, of course, absurd, since there are infinitely many frames). But this is simply to say that the method can be applied only when the answer is in a sense already known, and the method, therefore, already dispensible. Thus it is delusory to pretend that one discovers that English has nouns, or (as Fries called them) Class I words,[1] by noting which words fill a certain blank in a certain frame with preservation of grammaticalness; for knowing which blank in which frame to use is tantamount to knowing beforehand the desired class of words. Furthermore, to say that 'noun in English' means just whatever will substitute in all the frames into which nouns substitute is completely vacuous so long as one has not independently characterized just those particular frames. The same vicious circularity militates equally strongly against the view that 'noun in English' may be 'defined' as whatever appears before some particular ending, say *-s*.[2]

While this difficulty with the prior characterization of the frames has been noted before, there is another fatal defect in the method which has not been so widely recognized. In order to characterize a new taxonomic class it is necessary not only to have the frames but it is also essential to possess an effective procedure for deciding whether or not the expression obtained after substituting a tested item is of the same grammatical form as the prototype expression from which the frame was selected. It is clearly not sufficient that the frame after substitution preserve grammaticalness only, for there is then no way to exclude such absurd results as the classification of *they said he* as a nominal in English because it fits the 'typical' nominal frame: ( ) *was good*. The only general

[1] *The Structure of English* (New York, 1952).

[2] This is apparently the principal analytic device advocated by Smith and Trager as an extension of their otherwise putatively deductive phonological description of English.

principle by means of which we might reject this result is the requirement that the new utterance, namely: *They said he was good*, be 'of the same form' as the model we had in mind, that is such expressions as: *He was good, The man was good.* But this simply forces another vicious circularity, for the principle assumes that we already have that knowledge of grammatical structure which it is the very purpose of the substitution method to reveal.

This analytic doctrine is sometimes expanded to the more indefinite view of 'distributional analysis', according to which all morphemes, words, or other strings are supposed to be classified significantly by the totality of environments or perhaps, more correctly, environment types, in which they occur, or can occur. But unless environments are quite arbitrarily limited to some ad-hoc length, there will always be an infinity of different environments into which any given expression fits, and the class of environments into which one expression substitutes will always differ from that into which any other one does. On the other hand, environment types cannot be surveyed before the types themselves have been distinguished; but making these distinctions is the goal of the very distributional analysis for which they are now required.

D MORPHEME-ORDER CHARTS. We should also take notice of the technique which has become so popular especially in sketches of Amerindian languages, namely, the method of morpheme-order charts. This technique—or, more correctly, method of presentation—of syntactic analysis, like those mentioned above, freezes our conception of sentence structure into that of a sequence of hierarchically subdivided, contiguous, nonoverlapping constituents, and has no natural place for discontinuous components.[1] It also fails to account properly for the notion of sentence-type (such as 'interrogative' in English), which is not characterized by any single morpheme sequence, and for the notion of relationships among certain sentence-types (such as that between an active and its corresponding passive in English).[2]

E 'GRAMEMIC ANALYSIS.' I do not wish to imply that the techniques of syntactic analysis which I have criticized here are the only ideas on the subject which have ever been proposed, but they are surely very widely accepted and might fairly be considered the dominant

[1] Despite Hockett's ingenious attempt to extend morpheme-order chart diagrams to permit the representation of noncontiguous constituents and pro-morphemes. See *A Course in Modern Linguistics* (New York, 1958), especially §17.6 and diagrams on pp. 155, 253, 255. Some of the inadequacies of traditional doctrine are hinted at in chapter 29.

[2] See Chomsky, *Syntactic Structures*, chapter 5.

notions in linguistics today. Other proposals which have been made are in essence elaborations or special variants of the underlying ideas already mentioned. Thus, Kenneth Pike's 'gramemic analysis' is, so far as my rather limited knowledge of its details permits me to judge, an attempt to remedy the confusion in the traditional picture of relations between phonological and syntactic structure by simply severing the relations and substituting for one constituent-structure hierarchy a trinity of three such hierarchies, independent from one another but interwoven in the sentence.[1] But such a view of linguistic structure would seem merely to triple the effects of whatever difficulties may be encountered in attempting to picture grammatical patterns solely as a constituent-structure, to prevent us from ever achieving a coherent description of all levels of linguistic structure in one single theory, and to force recognition of certain fictitious 'units of grammatical form', called 'gramemes', along with a host of other fanciful '-emes'. In view of Pike's long and laudable opposition to the unnecessary strict separation of grammatical and phonemic levels, this theory of separate grammatical, morphological, and phonological hierarchies is, I regret, a backward step for him to take.

III MIRRORED SYNTACTIC RELATIONS

The once rather widely recognized idea that the grammatical relations among constituents in a sentence are duplicated among the internal constituents of derivative expressions is all but lost to present-day linguistics, though in 1933 Bloomfield was still able to make use of this notion in his extended treatment of nominal compounds.[2]

Forty years ago Otto Jespersen used the mirroring of syntactic relations in derivative expressions to explain occasional peculiarities in English, though his treatment was not at all uniform, and his analysis of many constructions, especially nominal compounds, was for the most part notional and inconsistent.[3]

In a very recent article, Benveniste studied certain 'external' syntactic relations shared by definite nominals and relative clauses, arguing that in Ewe, Tunica, Sumerian, and Arabic a kind of relative pronoun plays

[1] K. L. Pike, *Language in Relation to a Unified Theory of the Structure of Human Behavior* (Glendale, Calif., 1954–5).

[2] I have given a critique of his treatment of compounding and conception of syntactic structure in the preface to my book, *The Grammar of English Nominalizations* (Baltimore, 1960).

[3] See especially *A Modern English Grammar on Historical Principles*, VI, Morphology (Copenhagen, 1942).

the role of a determining syntactic article just as the relative phrase, in being connected with an antecedent pronoun or particle, behaves as a 'determined syntactic adjective.'[1] He views this identity, or at least close similarity, of syntactic function and morphological feature thus: 'En somme les unités complexes de la phrase peuvent, en vertu de leur fonction, se distribuer dans les mêmes classes de formes où sont rangées les unités simples, ou mots, en vertu de leurs caractères morphologiques.'[2]

This interesting idea of Benveniste's, while also clearly beyond the range of current doctrine, is not quite the same as that of 'mirrored syntactic relations,' such as concerns us here. The notion to which I refer is that according to which it is correct to describe *our* as the 'subject' of the following verb in *our having written* by virtue of the preservation of the subject-relation during the derivation of *our having written* from an underlying source-sentence: *We wrote*. On the basis of most accepted dogmas there is no cogent relationship at all between *We wrote* and *Our having written*...

2 *A grammatically ambiguous construction*

I PARADIGM EXAMPLES

The construction for which I shall give a detailed analysis in this section consists basically of three constituents: Adjective plus *to* plus Verb. As I shall show, it is really a set of at least eight different constructions and contains in some of its contrasting forms more than these three constituents.[3] As paradigm examples of the eight interpretations I shall cite first the following short sentences, believed to be free from relevant grammatical ambiguities:

1 It's too humid to play.
2 It's tedious to stay.
3 He's free to go.
4 He's too old to send.
5 He's too tired to swim.
6 He's eligible to vote.
7 He's hard to convince.
8 He's splendid to wait.

[1] 'La phrase relative, problème de syntaxe générale', *BSL*, vol. 53 (1958), pp. 39–54.

[2] [*En somme...morphologiques* All things considered, the complex units of the phrase can, by virtue of their function, be distributed in the same classes of forms as are the simple units, or words, by virtue of their morphological characters.]

[3] Lees, *English Nominalizations*, sections in chapter III on Infinitival Nominals and It-Inversions, where a more detailed treatment of the grammatical rules is given for the generation of these constructions.

II AMBIGUOUS EXAMPLES

The first analytic proposal which one might make is the obvious suggestion that these differ, if at all, only in the particular adjective or verb used, and would therefore be distinguished in ANY syntactic treatment. To meet this preliminary objection I cite immediately two more lists of eight sentences each, in corresponding order, the first list containing only sentences with the same adjective, the second with the same verb, so far as contrasting examples are possible to find among bona fide English sentences:

1*a*	It's too nice to loaf.	1*b*	It's too humid to help.
2*a*	It's nice to travel.	2*b*	It's advisable to help.
3*a*	—	3*b*	He's welcome to help.
4*a*	He's too nice to tease.	4*b*	He's too desolate to help.
5*a*	He's too nice to grumble.	5*b*	He's too hostile to help.
6*a*	—	6*b*	He's eligible to help.
7*a*	He's nice to send.	7*b*	He's difficult to help.
8*a*	He's nice to contribute.	8*b*	He's noble to help.

We may also exhibit the manifold grammatical ambiguities in the following similarly numbered table:

1*c*	It's too hot to eat.
4*c*	It's too hot to eat.
5*c*	It's too hot to eat.
2*c*	It's easy to call.
7*c*	It's easy to call.
3*c*	He's ready to call.
6*c*	He's ready to call.
8*c*	He's clever to call.

The correspondingly numbered examples in the three lists are judged to be of the same grammatical form but to differ in grammatical structure from all other examples, and I shall now present evidence in favor of this view and in support of a particular analysis for each type.

III ANALYSIS

A IMPERSONAL SUBJECT. Types 1 and 2 differ from all the others in that these two constructions, and only these, are constrained to the impersonal subject *it* to which there corresponds no interrogative: **What is too humid to play?*, **What is tedious to stay?*. Type 1 furthermore is construed only with *too* plus 'weather' adjectives, such as *sunny*, *hot*, *cool*, *windy*, etc.

It is not absolutely necessary for us to decide here just what origin this 'weather' *it*-subject has in the grammar, though as in the case of sentences like *It's raining* it is likely that this special subject is introduced directly in the kernel-generating constituent-structure grammar as an independently chosen noun. Though it does not undergo the interrogative transformation, it can function like other nominal subjects in nominalization transformations: *For it to be too humid...*, *Its being too humid...*, *That it was too humid...*

On the other hand, the *it*-subject of Type 2 has an entirely different origin and is parallel to a number of other impersonal constructions:[1]

That he came was surprising.	= It was surprising that he came.
What he did was surprising.	= It was surprising what he did.
Going there was fun.	= It was fun going there.
For him to go was good.	= It was good for him to go.
He was crazy to do it.	= It was crazy of him to do it.
To convince him is hard.	= It's hard to convince him.

(We shall return later to the last two examples in this list.) We see from such cases that certain nominalizations when used as subject may be shifted into the predicate of a copulative-type sentence, whose subject is then the impersonal *it*. Leaving aside various minor restrictions on the details, such an optional transformational rule would be roughly of the form:

$$\text{Nom} + \text{VP} \rightarrow \text{it} + \text{VP} + \text{Nom}$$

where Nom represents the appropriate nominalized sentences (such as the *that*-clause, question-word clause, infinitival, gerundive nominals), and VP represents the verb phrase, in this case always copulative (*be*, *seem*, etc., together with their auxiliaries and verbal affixes). Thus, we may analyze Type 2 sentences as *It*-inversion transforms of sentences with Infinitival Nominal subjects and appropriate predicate-adjectival verb phrases:

To stay here is tedious. → It is tedious to stay here.

Notice that the adjective itself may be further modified, say with a *for*-phrase adverbial:

To play tennis is strenuous *for him*.
→ It is strenuous *for him* to play tennis.

[1] Ibid. It-Inversions.

It is also possible that at least some speakers may permit this inversion with a so-called 'factive' type of Infinitival Nominal containing its transformed subject after *for*:

N_a is good.
John does that. } → For John to do that is good. →
It is good for John to do that.

where N_a represents an abstract noun. In such a case we should have another ambiguity, for the latter transform might also have arisen from

To do that is good for John. → It is good for John to do that.

with a different constituent-structure.

It is instructive to note incidentally that while such grammatical ambiguities may often be resolved on particular occasions by the use of contrasting phonological devices, this fact is irrelevant, for there are correspondingly many cases in which they are not, or indeed cannot be so resolved. In this case the two constructions can be (though usually they are not) contrasted phonemically:

^{2}It is ^{3}góod for Jôhn^1/^{1}to ^{1}dó thât^1
^{2}It is ^{3}góod^1/^{1}for Jôhn to ^{1}dó thât^1

while in the case of the by now classical example *Flying planes can be dangerous*, there is no way to contrast the two structures phonologically.

B ADJECTIVAL COMPLEMENT. Types 3 through 8 may all have personal subjects, though with some restrictions; e.g. Type 8 is usually confined to human subjects. On the basis of examples like the following:

He is delighted with it.	
He is delighted with going.	(Gerundive Nominal)
He is delighted that he went.	(Factive Nominal)
He is delighted to go.	(Infinitival Nominal)
He is content with it.	
He is content with going.	(Gerundive Nominal)
He is content to go.	(Infinitival Nominal)

we might suppose that *He is delighted to go* consists of a complex adjectival (*delighted with*, *happy about*, *sure of*, etc.) followed by an Infinitival Nominal *to go* (from *He goes*) with subsequent automatic ellipsis of the preposition before the nominalization (as is required elsewhere in the grammar anyway). However, there are not only other cases in which the Adj+P complex does not occur before the Gerundive Nominal, as in:

He is welcome to it.
He is welcome to go., but not (Infinitival Nominal)
*He is welcome to going. (Gerundive Nominal)

but there are many types in which the complex occurs ONLY in other combinations, as in:

He is unhappy about it.
He is unhappy about going. (Gerundive Nominal)
He is unhappy that he went. (Factive Nominal)

He is sceptical of it.
He is sceptical of going. (Gerundive Nominal)

More important, there is a type in which the adjectival occurs before the infinitive but there is no complex with a preposition, nor does the adjective, at least in many cases, occur alone as predicate:

He is likely to go. (Infinitival Nominal)
He is apt to go. (Infinitival Nominal)
He is prone to go. (Infinitival Nominal)
He is able to go., but not (Infinitival Nominal)
*He is likely.

Furthermore, in most such cases there is also a nominalization of the entire adjectival phrase to produce an abstract which preserves the following infinitival construction intact:

His ability to go...
His freedom to go...
His readiness to go..., etc.

Thus, the latter construction (Type 3) resembles the derived verbalization which has been treated as a 'Complement transform' in which complex verbs are produced from a kernel-sentence string Verb+Complement and a second source-sentence:[1]

He found+C her.
She works.
} → He found-working her. →
He found her working.

He forced+C her.
She works.
} → He forced-to-work her. →
He forced her to work.

[1] See Chomsky, *Syntactic Structures*, pp. 75–84.

in which *found working* and *forced to work* may be considered discontinuous complex verbal constituents, preserved under passive transformation: *She was found working by him* and *She was forced to work by him.* Our adjectival construction can be analyzed similarly as Adj plus a 'complement' which is replaced under transformation by an infinitival construction, as in the latter verb-complement example.[1] Thus:

$$\left.\begin{array}{l}\text{He is free} + \text{Comp.}\\ \text{He goes.}\end{array}\right\} \rightarrow \text{He is free to go.}$$

Now we may also account easily for the failure of certain adjectives to occur without the following infinitival: these adjectives are generated as expansions only of the Adj which occurs before Comp but happen not to be expansions of any other Adj constituent in the grammar. Notice furthermore that among the restrictions which would have to be imposed upon this Adj-Comp rule is that both the subject and the verbal auxiliaries, if present in the second, or constituent-, sentences of the two source-sentences, must be dropped, else we should obtain **He is free for him to go* and **He is free to have been going*.

Thus, the grammatical rule which I propose as source for Type 3 sentences would be roughly of the form:

$$\left.\begin{array}{l}\text{Nom}_1 + \text{be} + \text{A}_y + \text{Comp}\\ \text{Nom}_2 + \text{VP}\end{array}\right\} \rightarrow \text{Nom}_1 + \text{be} + \text{A}_y + \text{to} + \text{VP}$$

where A_y are just the adjectives which may be followed by such complements and $N_1 = N_2$.

C INFINITIVAL INVERSION. Next, I shall distinguish among the three very similar-appearing cases of Types 3, 6, and 7. In the first two:

(3) He's anxious to go.
(6) He's qualified to go.

the subject of the sentences is also the subject of the infinitival after the adjective, as is shown by the exact correlation of selection restrictions in, e.g.

	He admires Cadillacs.	He's apt to admire Cadillacs. and
	Cadillacs please him.	Cadillacs are apt to please him.
but not	*Cadillacs admire him.	*Cadillacs are apt to admire him.
nor	*He pleases Cadillacs.	*He's apt to please Cadillacs.

The point of these examples is simply that the animate subject required before *admire* is also required before *apt to admire*, though not before *apt*

[1] Lees, *English Nominalizations*, section on Adjectivalizations.

by itself (*The machine is apt to stop*). Thus, the subject of *is apt to V* has exactly the same restrictions as does the subject of *V*.

In Type 7 sentences, however, the subject of the sentences is the *object* of the infinitival verb, as is shown by the possibility of including the (deletable) subject of the infinitival, as in:

He is hard *for us* to convince.

This is also shown by the identity of selection restrictions in:

	We astonish him.	He's difficult to astonish. and
	We tune radios.	Radios are difficult to tune.
but not	*We tune him.	*He's difficult to tune.
nor	*We astonish radios.	*Radios are difficult to astonish.

Furthermore, in only the latter case (7) are the adjectives used restricted particularly to those which occur as predicate adjectives after abstract subject nominalizations:

To convince him is hard.
He is hard to convince.
To send him is convenient.
He is convenient to send. but not
*He is blond to send. since no
*To send him is blond.

Another peculiarity of Type 7 sentences is that only in these subject-object cases may the adjective be further shifted to PRE-nominal position:

The man is convenient for Nom to send.
The man is convenient to send.
The man who is convenient to send...
The man convenient to send...
The convenient man to send...

even though these adjectives may NOT occur as predicates to the noun-subjects WITHOUT the accompanying infinitival modifier:

*The man is convenient.
*The convenient man...

Now, the adjectives of Type 7 do occur as predicates to abstract Infinitival Nominals:

To send the man is convenient.
To convince him is hard.

All these correlations suggest that the sentences of Type 7 are best analyzed as transforms of those which have a transitive Infinitival Nominal as subject, simply by permitting the infinitive in these cases to shift around its object to the end of the sentence:

To convince the man is hard (for us). →
The man is hard (for us) to convince.

This transformation will occur in the grammar before the application of the obligatory rule which inserts the object (case) morpheme, else we should enumerate ungrammatical strings of the form **Him is hard to convince.*[1] The required grammatical rule would then be roughly:

$$\text{to}+\text{V}+\text{Nom}+\text{be}+\text{A}_a \rightarrow \text{Nom}+\text{be}+\text{A}_a+\text{to}+\text{V}$$

where the A_a are predicate adjectives occurring with abstract subjects.

D FOR-PHRASE ADVERBIAL. We must now distinguish Type 6 sentences from the case of adjectival complement (Type 3). I have already pointed out that the adjectives of the latter construction are restricted to those which occur as predicates to abstract subjects. The Type 6 adjectives on the other hand, may occur pre-nominally:

He is eligible to vote. An eligible voter..., but not
He is apt to vote. *An apt voter...

Next, we note that some Type 3 sentences are ambiguous, as in the following case:

He is ready to go. = He agrees to go. or
= He has prepared for going.

where the first interpretation correlates with other Type 3 sentences (*He is likely to go*), while the second interpretation is always related to sentences containing a purpose-adverbial in *for*. To each such latter case there also corresponds an interrogative in *what...for*:

He's ready to go. What is he ready for?
He's qualified to vote. What is he qualified for?

Thus, we may analyze Type 6 sentences as derivatives from *for*-sentences by substitution of the (abstract) Infinitival Nominal for an abstract noun in a purpose-adverbial; thus:

He is qualified for N_a.
He votes.
} → He is qualified for for him to vote. →
He is qualified to vote.

[1] Lees, *English Nominalizations*, chapter II, Object.

The latter conversion of *for+for+N+to* into *to* is then automatic, proceeding in steps by several obligatory transformations which are also useful in the generation of other sentence-types.[1] First, the *for*-phrase which contains a nominal identical with the subject of the transform-sentence is deleted, yielding *He is qualified for to vote*, and then the remaining *for* is deleted before the nominalization, as are all prepositions before abstract nominals. (This rule may be absent in certain dialects, or may be restricted to certain nominalizations, for there are speakers who say *I want for to go*.)

Having given to Type 6 sentences this analysis as a *for*-phrase adverbial (with subsequent obligatory deletions of repeated subject and of prepositions), we can now account for similar sentences containing *too* plus descriptive adjective. Except elliptically the particle *too* does not occur without some following 'explanatory' phrase, either *for* plus a nominal or *to* plus a verbal:

She's too weak for housework.
She's too weak to do housework.

Thus, we may consider *too* and the following prepositional phrase to comprise a discontinuous syntactic component attributive to the descriptive adjective. (This does not imply that *too* cannot enter other sentences in some different way, say as do *very*, *quite*, etc., or *either*, *also*, etc.: *His too eager reply*...; *I do too*.)

Since Types 4, 5 and 6 are then all analyzed as transforms of sentences containing *for*-phrase adverbials, we may summarize the required grammatical rules thus:

$$\left.\begin{array}{l}\text{Nom}_1+\text{be}+\text{A(too) for}+\text{N}_a\\ \text{Nom}_2+\text{VP.}\end{array}\right\} \rightarrow \begin{array}{l}\text{Nom}_1+\text{be}+\text{A(too)for}+\text{for}\\ \quad +\text{Nom}_2+\text{to}+\text{VP}\end{array}$$

$$\rightarrow \text{Nom}_1+\text{be}+\text{A(too)for(for}+\text{Nom}_2\text{) to}+\text{VP}$$
$$\text{(where 'for}+\text{Nom}_2+\text{' is deleted if Nom}_1 = \text{Nom}_2)$$

$$\rightarrow \text{Nom}_1+\text{be}+\text{A(too)(for}+\text{Nom}_2\text{) to}+\text{VP}$$

$$\rightarrow \text{Nom}_1+\text{be(too)A(for}+\text{Nom}_2\text{)to}+\text{VP}$$

where *too* is chosen for Types 4 and 5, 'for+Nom_2' is chosen optionally for Type 4, but is automatically deleted for Types 5 and 6 where $\text{Nom}_1 = \text{Nom}_2$.

E ANIMATE ADJECTIVE. It remains now to assign some analysis to the last case, Type 8. This might so far be confused only with Type 3,

[1] Ibid. end of chapter III.

6, or 7 sentences, though there is usually a phonological distinction. Type 8 sentences normally carry the primary stress on the adjective:

²Hè 's ³spléndid to wâit¹.

Furthermore, these sentences have a special *it*-inversion form in *of*:

It's splendid *of* him to wait.

and also a special abstract nominalization in *in*:

He's clever to make so much money.
It's clever *of* him to make so much money.
His cleverness *in* making so much money...

The adjectives in this construction may be confined to those which occur as predicates to animate subjects.

We see then that the adjectival expression in Type 8 sentences functions as a complex adjective, but the Infinitival modifier of the head-adjective is not a reflex of a *for*-phrase adverbial of purpose. Although at the present level of analysis I cannot determine a more detailed relationship between this construction and other adjectival modifiers, we may at least permit it to be generated directly by means of a generalized grammatical transformation parallel to the adjectival complement transformation, thus:

$$\left.\begin{matrix}\text{He is splendid.}\\ \text{He waits.}\end{matrix}\right\} \rightarrow \text{He is spléndid to wait.}$$

This derivation is distinguished from that of the Type 3 complement-sentences in that here the infinitival is inserted after certain adjectives, while in the Type 3 case the infinitival is a replacement of a Comp constituent.

The grammatical rule to generate Type 8 sentences would then look roughly as follows:

$$\left.\begin{matrix}\text{Nom}_1+\text{be}+\text{A}_z\\ \text{Nom}_2+\text{VP}\end{matrix}\right\} \rightarrow \text{Nom}_1+\text{be}+\text{A}_z+\text{to}+\text{VP}$$

where $\text{Nom}_1 = \text{Nom}_2$.

F SUMMARY OF ANALYSES. I have now assigned to each of the eight types of sentence containing the expression *Adj + to + V* eight different grammatical analyses, thus accounting correctly for certain of their syntactic features and relationships and for the ambiguities listed above.

I shall illustrate some of these contrasts by means of the following two sets of ambiguous sentences:

I. (1) It is too hot to eat. = It [the weather] is too hot (for us) to eat (them).

(4) It is too hot to eat. = It [the soup] is too hot (for us) to eat.

$< \begin{cases} \text{It is too hot for } N_a. \\ \text{We eat it.} \end{cases}$

(5) It is too hot to eat. = It [the dog] is too hot to eat (them).

$< \begin{cases} \text{It is too hot for } N_a. \\ \text{It eats them.} \end{cases}$

II. (2) It is easy to call. = It is easy (for us) to call (them).

$<$ To call (them) is easy (for us).

(7) It is easy to call. = It [the fire department] is easy (for us) to call.

$<$ To call it is easy (for us).

(3) It is ready to call. = It [the committee] is ready (and willing) to call (them).

$< \begin{cases} \text{It is ready} + \text{Comp.} \\ \text{It calls them.} \end{cases}$

(6) It is ready to call. = It [the machine] is ready (and waiting) to call (them).

$< \begin{cases} \text{It is ready for } N_a. \\ \text{It calls them.} \end{cases}$

(8) He is noble to suffer. = It is noble of him to suffer.

3 *Summary*

In conclusion, a summary of my argument. Like most other constructions in English, sentences containing the expression

Nom is Adj to Vb

are multiply ambiguous; in fact, I have exhibited three different syntactic structures for *too* + A + to + V and four others for A + to + V. Since in each of its different interpretations the sentence is phonemically the same, no 'phonological approach to syntax' could assign the correct analyses. Since the sentences are also morphemically identical in each interpretation, no substitution-in-frames technique or morpheme-order chart could yield the correct analyses. In fact, since the sentence remains physically unchanged, the grammatical analyses cannot in any way be deduced from a phonetic record.

The analyses given to the eight types exhibited are:

(1) Impersonal subject *it* ('weather'); adjectival predicate with complex modifier, the latter consisting of *too* plus a reduction of a *for*-phrase adverbial in which the abstract noun has been replaced by an Infinitival Nominal.

(2) *It*-inversion of sentences with Infinitival Nominal subject.

(3) Adjectival Complement replaced by Infinitival Nominal.

(4) Like (1) but with personal subject; subject of sentence is object of Infinitival.

(5) Same as (4) but subject of sentence is subject of Infinitival.

(6) Predicate adjective modified by *for*-phrase adverbial in which nominal is replaced by Infinitival Nominal.

(7) Inversion of sentences with abstract Infinitival Nominal subject, leaving object of Infinitival as new subject.

(8) Animate predicate adjective modified by infinitival expression.

20

H. KURATH AND R. I. McDAVID

(1891–) (1911–)

The subject of dialectology has made great strides during the present century, and dialect surveys of most parts of the English-speaking world are now well under way. In America, a major project was undoubtedly the *Linguistic Atlas of the Eastern United States*, chiefly the work of Kurath and McDavid. The present text is the introductory section from a volume describing the segmental phonetics and phonology of the area in some detail. It mainly covers important preliminary matters prerequisite for a proper assessment of the survey's results, such as the character of the source material, the problem of interpreting the phonic record in phonemic terms, the approach the authors used in analysing the vowel system, and an outline of the vowel system they set up from this point of view.

'Introduction'

(*The Pronunciation of English in the United States*, 1961)

1.1 *The character of the source material*

All field recordings of the Linguistic Atlas are *phonic* in intention. Particular utterances of the informants are recorded as heard by trained observers without reference to a general scheme of phonemicization or to the phonemic structure of the separate idiolects. When several variant utterances of the same expression by one and the same speaker are taken down, the observer may classify them as 'fast' or 'slow,' 'natural' or 'guarded,' 'old' or 'modern,' etc., but he does not change the phonic record or attempt to establish the full phonic range of the variant sound. The observer may also comment on the phonemic status of any given phone in a particular idiolect, as often happens, but he does not obliterate the phonic entity. Thus all records of pronunciation are deliberately phonic.

The instrument for phonic recording is a finely graded phonetic alphabet, which is described in full detail in Hans Kurath, Bernard

Bloch, and others, *Handbook of the Linguistic Geography of New England* (1939; second printing 1954, by the American Council of Learned Societies, 345 East 46th Street, New York 17, N.Y.), pp. 122–46. Here only the scheme of vowel symbols is reproduced from the *Handbook*, p. 123. Rounded vowels are enclosed in parentheses.

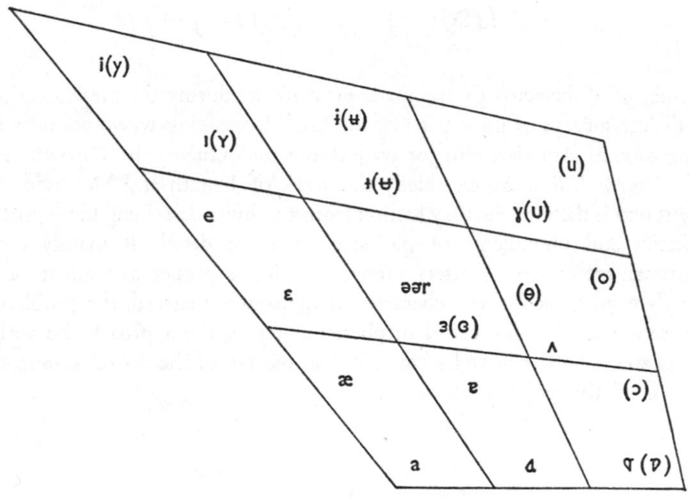

A phonic record of pronunciation is needed for all attempts at establishing the system of phonemes and describing the phonic range of the several phonemes (i.e., their positional and prosodic allophones or their free variations). The preservation of the phonic record is all the more important since all schemes of phonemicization are to some extent arbitrary in view of the present state of our knowledge of the segmentation of utterances. On the other hand, all features of pronunciation must of course be presented from a phonemic point of view. If the basis of the adopted scheme of phonemicization is explicitly stated and each phoneme in that system is described in phonic terms, the phonic data thus preserved can be interpreted in terms of different systems of phonemicization.

For comparative dialectology and historical linguistics in general a phonic record is of the utmost importance. The splitting of phonemes, the merging of one phoneme with another—whether partial or total—are readily comprehensible when the allophones of the phonemes in question are known.

For the study of American English, whose dialects differ rather little in phonemic structure but exhibit rather marked differences in the phonic character of many of the vowel phonemes, a phonic record is of peculiar importance. This observation holds whether one accepts the unitary interpretation of phonically complex syllabics or not.

To emphasize the importance of the phonic data is not to detract from the overriding importance of the system of phonemes, however conceived. Phonic differences between idiolects or between regional and social dialects must be kept strictly apart from differences in the system of phonemes, and these in turn from differences in the incidence of the phonemes in the vocabulary. *Phonemic, phonic,* and *incidental* heteroglosses are of unequal value in determining the degree of difference between dialects and in evaluating the relative importance of the boundaries between speech areas. Of the three types, phonemic heteroglosses obviously outrank the others.

1.2 *The design of the questionnaire*

The work sheets of the Linguistic Atlas of the Eastern States are sufficiently inclusive to provide the phonic data for describing the pronunciation of each of the 1500 speakers interviewed in phonemic and in phonic terms. This expectation was expressed in the *New England Handbook* (1939), p. 148, in these words:

> Care was taken to provide sufficient material for a rather full description, both phonemic and phonic, of the pronunciation of each informant, and hence for determining the regional and social distribution of the phonic variations of all the phonemes of American English, and for establishing differences in phonemic structure.

The work sheets used in New England are printed in the *Handbook*, pp. 150–58. They contain 814 words and phrases. The work sheets for the Middle and the South Atlantic States are somewhat fuller and include all of the key words of the New England set selected for matters of pronunciation.

Extensive experience with the Atlas records over two decades, both in connection with the preparation of the present volume and the direction of doctoral dissertations devoted to particular problems in the pronunciation of English in the Eastern States, leaves no doubt of the essential soundness of the expectation expressed in 1939. There are, however, some minor reservations.

1) Although examples are available for all vowel phonemes in their major positions (e.g., before stops, fricatives, and tautosyllabic /r/ as well as finally), there are some minor omissions, notably the type of *story, glory*.

2) Although the sampling is adequate for describing the pronunciation of speakers living in areas of relatively uniform usage (such as Maine, Metropolitan New York, Philadelphia and vicinity, the Virginia piedmont, the Low Country of South Carolina, and western North Carolina), the speech of informants living in transition belts, and especially in rapidly growing cities located on or near major dialect boundaries (such as Newark, N.J., Baltimore, Md., Roanoke, Va., and Atlanta, Ga.), is at times so mixed and unsettled that some questions have to be left open for lack of sufficient evidence.

1.3 How systematic is speech?

The task of presenting a complicated and fluid linguistic situation in readily intelligible simplified form exposes one to the risk of making the dialects look more regular and systematized than the observed facts warrant. One should, of course, uncover all the regularities; but one should not overlook recalcitrant data or play them down. We have tried to avoid oversystematization and oversimplification in our statements and have taken pains to present the data on which our generalizations rest as fully as we could within our means. Much corroborative material, and some that may require modifications of some of our statements, is available in the collections of the Linguistic Atlas of the Eastern States awaiting publication.

As a means of communication between the members of a community, whether small or large, language is essentially systematic in its sounds and forms. This is as true of the speech ways of the folk as of the dialects of the cultured. It is the first task of the linguist to discover the system and to describe it. Operating on the theory that language is essentially systematic and using a technique for identifying the systematic features, he analyzes the structure of the language or dialect and formulates descriptive statements. Sooner or later he finds features that don't follow the rule, that do not conform to the system; these too he must recognize for what they are. For, though language is essentially systematic, it is never wholly without irregularities and oddities, whatever their origin. This is a simple matter of observation and should surprise no one who is unwilling to forget that all natural languages are historical products developed in the give-and-take between individuals and social groups of a speech community and between speech communities. In this complicated historical process, so different from the creation, once and for all, of an artificial code, features taken from other social and regional dialects are not always adapted to the native system, and innovations in the native system may as yet not be established with consistency, so that elements of an older system survive as relics. To treat such tangible irregularities, current in all natural languages and dialects, as if they were built into the system is to misjudge linguistic realities for the sake of a working theory. The more ingenious the formulations of certain structuralists who are bent upon making oddities look systematic, the more suspect they become.

In our handling of the data we single out the inconsistencies and the vacillations in usage after the regularities have been established. Such deviations from the system are indicative of change in progress, of trends in usage. In fact, changes in systematization, which all living dialects undergo from time to time, are inconceivable without temporary disorganization.

1.4 From phone to phoneme

The analysis, on a purely phonic basis, shows 1) that the preconsonantal segments in such pairs as *grease:crib*, *eight:ten*, *tooth:wood*, *bag:fog*, *nine:down*, etc., are contrastive; 2) that the segments contained in *grease*, *eight*, *tooth*, *fog* occur also at the end of words, as in *three*, *day*, *two*, *law*, whereas those contained in *crib*, *ten*, *wood*, *bag* do not occur in this position; 3) that the 'free' segments—those that occur both before consonants and word-finally—are predominantly upgliding, while the 'checked' segments—those restricted to preconsonantal position—are usually monophthongal or ingliding.

At this point in the analysis of the phonic data the question must be raised whether the contrastive diphthongal segments should be treated as unit phonemes or broken down into a syllabic and a following unsyllabic element. No clear-cut answer can be given to this question in the present state of phonemic theory. Some scholars advocate a 'unitary' interpretation of such segments, others favor a 'binary' analysis, and some hold that the choice is a matter of convenience—not a matter of definitive cognition of a linguistic reality.[1]

[1] This problem has recently been discussed by Hans Kurath and James H. Sledd in *Language*, vol. 33 (1957), pp. 111–22 and vol. 34 (1958), pp. 252–60.

Although admitting that a binary interpretation of diphthongal phones of American English more satisfactory than any advanced so far may in time be devised, a unitary interpretation seems more realistic, and certainly more convenient for comparing the dialects of English spoken in the Atlantic States and establishing degrees of diversity or kinship between them on a stated basis. It has been adopted here and is consistently applied to all features of pronunciation dealt with.

From this point of view the stressed vowels of English fall into two classes: 1) FREE VOWELS, as in *three, two, day, know, law, bur, high, boy, now*, which are usually upgliding diphthongs but have monophthongal allophones and diaphones; they occur also in checked position, as in *grease, tooth, eight, road, frost, worm, five, boil, down*. 2) CHECKED VOWELS, as in *crib, wood, ten, sun, bag, crop*, which are often monophthongal but have ingliding allophones and diaphones.

The phonic characteristics of vowels, upglides *vs.* inglides, are most clearly perceptible under heavy stress, especially at the end of a phrase or utterance, where they are apt to be prolonged. They are less noticeable before voiceless stops, somewhat more prominent before voiced stops, fricatives, and sonorants (in ascending order). The upglide of free vowels is most striking in word-final position.

In rapid speech, and especially under half-stress, the 'drift' in quality resulting from upglides or inglides may not be observable at all. Hence free and checked vowels of similar quality that are clearly differentiated under heavy stress are less distinct under weaker stress, or even merged in one phonic entity (neutralization).

The unitary interpretation of diphthongal vowels adopted here recommends itself for several reasons.

1) In most dialects diphthongal and monophthongal variants occur side by side under observable (hence statable) conditions, i.e., in certain positions or under certain prosodic conditions. For instance, a speaker may have [ɪ] in *bit*, [ʊ] in *put*, [æ] in *bat*, and [ɑ] in *lot* but [ɪ^{ə}] in *crib*, [ʊ^{ə}] in *good*, [æˑ] in *half*, and [ɑˑ] in *rod*. From a unitary point of view, [ɪ ~ ɪ^{ə}] and [æ ~ æˑ], etc. are positional and/or prosodic allophones of the checked phonemes /ɪ/ and /æ/. Again, some speakers have [e'] in *day*, [o^{ʊ}] in *know*, and [aˑ^{ɛ}] in *nine*, but [e] in *make*, [o] in *coat*, and [ɐɨ] in *twice*; here [e^{ɨ} ~ e, o^{ʊ} ~ o, aˑ^{ɛ} ~ ɐɨ] are best treated as allophones of the free vowels /e, o, ai/.

The binary interpretation of diphthongal segments as vowel plus 'semivowel,' if applied consistently, would have to separate [e^{ɨ}, o^{ʊ}]

from [e, o], [aˑ^{ɛ}] from [ɐɨ], and certainly also [ɪ^{ə}, ʊ^{ə}] from [ɪ, ʊ], and [æˑ, ɑˑ] from [æ, ɑ] in such cases. For, if [e^{+}, o^{ʊ}] are taken as /ey, ow/, the segments [ɪ^{ə}, ʊ^{ə}] cannot be taken as unit phonemes; nor can the segments [æˑ, ɑˑ] be taken as units, if length is treated as phonemic in other 'syllabic nuclei.'

2) The vowels in *eight* and *road* vary regionally as [ɛɨ ~ eɨ ~ e^{+} ~ eˑ ~ e^{ə}] and [ɞʊ ~ o˂ʊ ~ oʊ ~ o^{ʊ} ~ oˑ ~ o^{ə}] but occupy the same position in the system of vowels of the several dialects. All these variants are here taken as regional diaphones of the unit phonemes /e/ and /o/.

In current binary phonemicizations, the variants showing an upglide to [ɪ] and [ʊ] are taken as the sequences /ey/ and /ow/, [eˑ] and [oˑ] as /eh/ and /oh/ or /eˑ/ and /oˑ/, and the variants [e^{ə}] and [o^{ə}] are presumably thrown in with [eˑ] and [oˑ] but could be interpreted as /eə̯/ and /oə̯/. In other words, some dialects are said to have an /h/ or /ˑ/, a phoneme of length, in *eight* and *road*, others a /y/ in *eight* and a /w/ in *road*. Since all speakers of American English distinguish /h/ from /y/ and /w/ before vowels, as in *hell* : *yell* : *well*, it is rather incredible that speakers who are said to have /y/ and /w/ in *eight* and *road* should not detect the posited postvocalic /h/ in speakers of another dialect. If the untenable /h/ is replaced by another 'semivowel,' say /ə̯/ or /x/, this difficulty is not resolved. Moreover, there are dialects in which the vowels exemplified in *eight* and *road* vary positionally as [e^{+} ~ e, o^{ʊ} ~ o] or as [e^{ə} ~ e, o^{ə} ~ o] and must, it seems to us, be taken as the unit phonemes /e/ and /o/.

3) The vowels before an /r/ of the same syllable, or before the derivative unsyllabic /ə̯/ in certain coastal dialects, present a challenge to any plan of phonemicization. They differ phonically from vowels in other positions in most, if not all, of the dialects, vary strikingly from dialect to dialect, and frequently exhibit a wide range of phonic variation not only within the regional dialects but also in the speech of one and the same person. Clearly, the vowels occurring in this position must be treated with reference to a scheme of vowel phonemes based upon the phonic characteristics of the syllabics in other positions.

The unitary interpretation of syllabics adopted here provides an approach for dealing effectively with vowels before tautosyllabic /r ~ ə̯/, although some of the decisions may be somewhat arbitrary because of the instability of certain phones or their peculiar character.

The procedure is as follows. After the phonic character and range of all the phonemes in the major dialects have been determined for other positions, the phones appearing before /r ~ ə̯/ are compared with the allophones of the several phonemes and assigned to phonemes they most closely resemble. One soon discovers that the phonemic contrasts shown in *beat:bit*, *tooth:put*, *eight:set:hat* do not occur before tautosyllabic /r ~ ə̯/ and that in this position some dialects also lack the contrast exhibited in *coat:caught*. Since there is only one high-front, one high-back, and one mid-to-low front vowel before /r ~ ə̯/, one is faced with the problem of assigning the phones occurring in *ear*, *poor* and *care* to /i/ or /ɪ/, to /u/ or /ʊ/, and to /e/ or /ɛ/ or /æ/, respectively. Similarly, in dialects that have one and the same mid-back vowel in *four* and in *forty*, the question arises whether the vowel is that of *coat* or of *caught*. In view of the well-known historical fact that /r/ favors a lowered tongue position of the preceding high and mid vowels, the phones occurring in *ear*, *poor* and *care* are assigned to the /i, u, e/ of *beat*, *tooth*, *eight*, if the tongue position is higher than in the vowels of *bit*, *put*, *set*, otherwise to /ɪ, ʊ, ɛ/; and so forth. Decisions must of course be made independently for each dialect, if not for each idiolect.

The practice adopted in some binary interpretations of positing vowel plus /h/ when the vowel before /r ~ ə̯/ is said to be long is not admissible, if only for the fact that /h/, or whatever other 'semivowel' is posited in its place, does not account for the peculiar allophonic deviations of the vowels in this position.

4) A plausible account of the allophones of phonemes in terms of the articulatory features of adjoining sounds and of prosodic factors is an important matter that no scheme of phonemicization can set aside. Satisfactory handling of this aspect of the phonemes is demanded by sound method in structural linguistics itself and is absolutely required for the understanding of phonemic splits and mergers with which the historian of language is intimately concerned. We believe that the unitary interpretation used in this book does in a large measure account for allophonic variations in realistic terms, whereas the binary approach has signally failed to do so. This failure has repeatedly been pointed out.

1.5 *The stressed vowels*

A systematic comparison of the major dialects of English spoken in the Eastern States shows that they have largely the same system of vowel phonemes, though they differ rather markedly in the phonic character of some of the vowels and in their incidence in the vocabulary. Briefly stated, this is the situation.

1) All dialects have the five checked vowels /ɪ, ᴜ, ɛ, ʌ, æ/, as in *six, wood, ten, sun, bag*. In addition, all dialects except that of Eastern New England and that of Western Pennsylvania have the checked vowel /ɑ/, as in *crop*.

2) All dialects have the nine free vowels /i, u, e, o, ɜ, ɔ, ai, au, ɔi/, as in *three, two, April, know, sermon, law, five, boil, down*. In addition, those dialects in which postvocalic /r/ is not preserved as such have a free low vowel /a/ or /ɒ/, as in *car, garden*.

3) The following vowel phonemes are regionally restricted:

a) The free low vowel /a ~ ɒ/ occurs only in areas in which postvocalic /r/ is not preserved as such, that is, in Eastern New England, Metropolitan New York, the Upper South, and the Lower South. It appears in such words as *car, garden* and *calm, palm, father*, in Eastern New England also in *half, glass*, etc., though without any consistency. In New England this vowel ranges from low-front [a˔] to mid-central [ɑ˔] and will be symbolized by /a/; elsewhere it is low-back or low-central-retracted and will be represented by the symbol /ɒ/. Free /a ~ ɒ/ contrasts with checked /ɑ/, as in *hard* /had ~ hɒd/ vs. *hod* /hɑd/, except in Eastern New England, which lacks checked /ɑ/.

b) A checked mid-back vowel /θ/, as in *coat, stone*, occurs in New England, chiefly along the Atlantic coast. In this area checked /θ/ is in contrast with free /o/, as in *road: rode*; but many New Englanders avoid /θ/ entirely or use it rarely. Relics of /θ/ survive sporadically in Western New England and in Upstate New York.

c) A back-gliding free vowel /iu/, as in *music, new* /miuzɪk, niu/, is current in parts of the North alongside the sequence /ju/ or the vowel /u/. It is sharply recessive. As a decrescendo diphthong it must be treated as a unit phoneme, if the [eɨ, oᴜ, aɨ, aᴜ] of *eight, know, five, down* are so interpreted.

4) As pointed out above, Eastern New England and Western Pennsylvania lack the checked low vowel /ɑ/ which occurs in all other dialect areas. Here the free low-back phoneme /ɒ/ corresponds to two phonemes, the checked /ɑ/ of *crop, lot* and the free /ɔ/ of *law, frost*, of the other dialects.

These relatively minor differences in the vowel system of the dialects of American English produce four somewhat divergent types of organization, none of which is exactly the same as that of Standard British English. In listing the vowels, checked and free vowels of similar quality are placed side by side, sometimes perhaps rather arbitrarily. The brief comments following the lists point out the existence of such 'paired' vowels. The cognitive value of these groupings is by no means clear, but they have a practical bearing on the presentation of differences in the incidence of the vowels in the several dialects, e.g., the incidence of /ɪ ~ i, ʊ ~ u, ɛ ~ e/ before /r ~ ə̯/, of /ʊ ~ u/ in *room*, *root*, etc.

TYPE I: UPSTATE NEW YORK, EASTERN PENNSYLVANIA, AND THE SOUTH MIDLAND

crib : three	ɪ	i		ʊ	u	*wood : tooth*
ten : eight	ɛ	e	ɜ	ʌ	o	*sun : road*
bag	æ		ɑ		ɔ	*law*
five		ai	au		ɔi	*boil*
			thirty			
			crop			
			down			

The checked high-front, high-back, mid-front, and mid-back vowels are paired with phonically similar free vowels. The other vowels are not so paired.

TYPE II: METROPOLITAN NEW YORK, THE UPPER SOUTH, AND THE LOWER SOUTH

crib : three	ɪ	i		ʊ	u	*wood : tooth*
ten : eight	ɛ	e	ɜ	ʌ	o	*sun : road*
bag	æ				ɔ	*law*
				ɑ	ɒ	*crop : car*
five		ai	au		ɔi	*boil*
			thirty			
			down			

The checked high-front, high-back, mid-front, and mid-back vowels are paired with phonically similar free vowels, and the checked low-central vowel with the free low-back vowel. The other vowels are not so paired.

TYPE III: EASTERN NEW ENGLAND

crib : three	ɪ	i		ʊ	u	*wood : tooth*
ten : eight	ɛ	e	ɜ	θ	o	*road : rode*
bag : car	æ	a		ʌ	ɒ	*sun : law, crop*
five		ai	au		ɒi	*boil*
			thirty			
			down			

The six checked vowels /ɪ, ɛ, æ, ʌ, θ, ʊ/ are paired with phonically more or less similar free vowels. The free vowels /ɜ, ai, au, ɒi/ are not so paired; in the speech of those who no longer use /θ/, the free vowel /o/ is also unpaired.

TYPE IV: WESTERN PENNSYLVANIA

crib:three	ɪ	i		ʊ	u	*wood:tooth*
ten:eight	ɛ	e	ɜ	ʌ	o	*sun:road*
bag	æ				ɒ	*law, crop*
five		ai	au		ɒi	*boil*
			thirty			
			down			

The high-front, high-back, mid-front, and mid-back checked vowels are paired with phonically similar free vowels. The other vowels are not so paired.

TYPE V: STANDARD BRITISH ENGLISH

crib:three	ɪ	i			ʊ	u	*wood:tooth*
ten:eight	ɛ	e		ɜ		o	*road*
bag	æ		ʌ	ɑ	ɒ	ɔ	*crop:law*
five		ai		au		ɔi	*boil*
				thirty			
				sun:car			
				down			

The checked vowels /ɪ, ɛ, ʌ, ɒ, ʊ/ are paired with phonically similar free vowels. Checked /æ/ and free /ɜ, o, ai, au, ɔi/ are not so paired.

Inspection of these dialectal vowel systems shows that the differences are largely confined to the low and the raised low vowels. Hence a brief consideration of the origin of these differences may prove helpful. A further reason for outlining the sources of the low vowels at this point is the great diversity in the incidence of the low vowels, as shown in the table given on p. 280.

The low vowels of American English are derived from three vowel phonemes of Early Modern English (EMnE): 1) the short checked vowel /æ/ of *bag*, *glass*, *car*, etc.; 2) the short checked vowel /o/ of *lot*, *fog*, *frost*, etc.; 3) the free diphthongal vowel /au/ of *law*, *daughter*, *salt*, etc. The short checked vowels /æ/ and /o/ had positional allophones in some regional varieties of EMnE (as we must infer from their later history), which are phonemicized in various ways in the several dialects

THE LOW VOWEL PHONEMES AND THEIR INCIDENCE IN THE VOCABULARY

Examples of the Several Historical Types	Standard British English	Eastern New England	Metro-politan New York	Upper South	Lower South	Upstate New York	Eastern Pennsyl-vania	South Midland	Western Pennsyl-vania
hat, bag, ashes	æ	æ	æ	æ	æ	æ	æ	æ	æ
glass, calves, can't	ɒ̈	a	æ	æ	æ	æ	æ	æ	æ
car, father, calm	ɒ̈	a	ɒ̈	ɒ̈	ɒ̈	ɑ	ɑ	ɑ	ɒ
crop, lot, rod	ɒ	ɒ	ɑ	ɑ	ɑ	ɑ	ɑ	ɑ	ɒ
frost, long, fog	ɒ	ɒ	ɔ	ɔ	ɔ	ɔ	ɔ	ɔ	ɒ
law, daughter, salt	ɔ̣	ɒ	ɔ	ɔ	ɔ	ɔ	ɔ	ɔ	ɒ
Number of Contrasts	4	3	4	4	4	3	3	3	2

of American English. Thus, short /æ/ splits into /æ/ and /ɒ̈ ~ a/ in some dialects, but not in others; short /o/ splits into /ɑ/ and /ɔ/ in certain dialects (the latter joining the /ɔ/ derived from EMnE /au/), but not in others; the EMnE sequence /ær/, passing through [ɑr > ɑə̯], develops into a new free vowel phoneme /ɒ̈ ~ a/ in several dialects spoken on the Atlantic seaboard, as in Standard British English, but appears as the sequence /ɑr/, containing the checked vowel /ɑ/, in other dialects of American English.

The highly complicated divergent developments and their results in Standard British English (SBE) and in the chief dialects of the Eastern States can be briefly summarized as follows.

In SBE, 1) the EMnE checked vowel /æ/ remains before stops and nasals, as in *bag*, *man*, etc., and in some other positions. 2) The EMnE sequence /ær/ develops into a free vowel /ɒ̈/, as in *car*, *garden*, whereupon the allophone of /æ/ before certain fricatives, as in *laugh*, *bath*, *glass*, *calves*, and before /n/ plus front consonants, as in *can't*, *dance*, *branch*, is phonemicized as /ɒ̈/, though not consistently. 3) Checked EMnE short /o/ remains /ɒ/ before all consonants, as in *lot*, *fog*, *frost*, etc. 4) EMnE /au/ becomes the free vowel /ɔ/, as in *law*, *daughter*, *salt*. Hence, SBE has two checked low vowels, /æ/ and /ɒ/, and two free low vowels, /ɒ̈/ and /ɔ/.

In the dialect of Eastern New England, 1) EMnE short /æ/ survives as /æ/ in the same positions as in SBE, but to a considerable extent also before fricatives and especially before /n/ plus front consonants. 2) EMnE /ær/ appears as the free vowel /a/, articulated low-front or low-central (whereas the corresponding SBE /ɒ/ is low-central to low-back); and this /a/ occurs also to some extent in *laugh*, *bath*, *glass*, *can't*, *aunt*, and occasionally in *dance*, *France*. 3) EMnE short /o/ and /au/ are completely merged in a free vowel /ɒ/. Thus Eastern New England has only three low vowels, checked /æ/ and free /a/ and /ɒ/.

Metropolitan New York, the Upper South, and the Lower South have the same system of low vowels, although the phonic characteristics of these vowels vary regionally. In these three major dialects, 1) EMnE short /æ/ remains /æ/ in all positions, except before historical /r/, after /w/, and sporadically elsewhere. 2) EMnE /ær/ becomes a free low-back vowel /ɒ/, as in SBE. This vowel occurs also in *father*, *calm* in all three areas, in *pasture*, *master* in parts of the South, in *can't*, *aunt*, *glass*, *after*, etc. only occasionally in Virginia and in Metropolitan New York. 3) EMnE short /o/ splits into /ɑ/ and /ɔ/. Unrounded low-central /ɑ/ appears regularly in *lot*, *crop*, *cob*, etc., rounded /ɔ/ regularly before voiceless fricatives, as in *cough*, *frost*, and before /ŋ/, as in *long*, and usually before /g/, as in *dog*, *fog*. 4) EMnE /au/ appears as /ɔ/, with which the /ɔ/ from earlier short /o/ is merged. These three dialects, therefore, have two checked low vowels, /æ/ and /ɑ/, and two free low vowels, /ɒ/ and /ɔ/.

In three areas—Upstate New York with Western New England, Eastern Pennsylvania, and the South Midland (West Virginia to northernmost Georgia)—three low vowels are current: checked /æ/ and /ɑ/, and free /ɔ/. Here the development is as follows: 1) EMnE /æ/ remains unchanged, except before /r/ and after /w/. 2) /au/ becomes /ɔ/. 3) /o/ splits into /ɑ/ and /ɔ/, and this /ɔ/, as in *cough*, *frost*, *dog*, *long*, is merged with the /ɔ/ derived from EMnE /au/. 4) Earlier /ær/ becomes /ɑr/, the vowel being subsumed under the /ɑ/ from earlier /o/.

In the dialect of Western Pennsylvania, 1) EMnE short /æ/ remains unchanged, except before /r/ and after /w/. 2) EMnE short /o/ and /au/ are completely merged in /ɒ/. 3) The sequence /ær/, as in *car*, *garden*, becomes phonically [ɒr], which in the absence of an /ɑ/ phoneme must be taken as the phoneme sequence /ɒr/; earlier /wæ/, as in *wash*, *water*, appears as /wɒ/. Owing to the merging of EMnE short /o/ and /au/ and the preservation of /r/ after vowels, this dialect has only two low vowels, checked /æ/ and free /ɒ/.

In the brief sketches presented above the terms 'develop' and 'become' are used quite broadly to refer to changes arising either from the rephonemicization of allophones or from dialect mixture. When either one or the other factor is hinted at, the statement must be accepted with proper caution, since we are as yet not in a position to identify the complicated historical changes with finality. Dialect mixture doubtless had a considerable share in these 'developments' both in SBE and in AE, as one may safely infer from the many inconsistencies and from unsettled usage in all varieties of English.

1.6 *Vowels in unstressed and weakly stressed syllables*

1) All dialects of American English have a free vowel /ə/ that occurs only in unstressed syllables. It appears in *sofa* /sofə/, *again* /əgɛn/, etc., in all dialects; in *father* /faðə ~ fɒðə/, *afternoon* /æftənun/, etc., in dialects that lack postvocalic /r/; in *bucket, houses* /bʌkət, hauzəz/, etc., only in certain dialects. In *borrow*, *value*, etc., /ə/ alternates with /o, u/, etc., dialectally or prosodically.

2) Checked /ɪ/, as in *laughing* /læfɪŋ/, occurs frequently in *sausage* /sɔsɪǰ/. etc., in certain dialects also in *bucket, houses* /bʌkɪt, hauzɪz/, etc.

3) Free /i, u, e, o/, as in *foggy*, *value*, *Tuesday*, *borrow* /fɔgi, vælju, tjuzde, bɑro/, occur in all dialects. Although /i, u/ often resemble checked /ɪ, ʊ/ under weak stress, these phones must be regarded as prosodic allophones of free vowels because they occur in free position and are often articulated as upgliding diphthongs. The /u, o/ of *value*, *borrow* alternate dialectally and prosodically with /ə/, the /e/ of *Tuesday* with /i/.

Free /ɜ/ is restricted to dialects that preserve postvocalic /r/. It occurs in *father*, *further*, *afternoon* /fɑðɜ, fɜðɜ, æftɜnun/, etc.

1.7 *The consonants*

All dialects of English spoken in the Eastern States have the same system of consonants, except that the dialects lacking postvocalic /r/ have an additional consonant, /ə̯/, as in *here*, *care*, *four*, *poor* /hiə̯, keə̯, foə̯, puə̯/.

The consonants are:

stops	p	t		č	k	
	b	d		ǰ	g	
fricatives	f	θ	s	š		h
	v	ð	z	ž		
sonorants	m	n	lr		ŋ	
semivowels	w			j	(ə̯)	

The segments preceding the vowel in such words as *chin* /čɪn/ and *gin* /ǰɪn/ are here treated as units, although they exhibit peculiarities in clustering. They enter into clusters with sonorants after syllabics, as do other stops; compare, for instance, *branch*, *mulch* /brænč, mʌlč/ with *bank*, *milk* /bæŋk, mɪlk/, and *singe*, *bulge* /sɪnǰ, bʌlǰ/ with *bend*, *build* /bɛnd, bɪld/. On the other hand, they do not enter into clusters with sonorants and semivowels before vowels, as other stops actually do, as, for instance, in *clean*, *crib*, *cube*, *quit* and *glass*, *green*, *argue*, *guano*. To regard the initial segments of *chin* and *gin* as phonemically complex, i.e., as consisting of a stop plus a fricative, is to recognize a type of cluster unparalleled in English, one that, in addition, exhibits after vowels the sequence stop-fricative, as in *peach* /pitš/ and *edge* /ɛdž/, whereas in other clusters containing a stop and a fricative the sequence is fricative-stop, as in *loft*, *lost*. Neither treatment can do away with a patently peculiar feature of the English consonant system.

21

JAMES SLEDD

(1914–)

The appearance of *Webster's Third New International Dictionary* in 1961 evoked substantial reaction from critics, both favourable and unfavourable. The central issue was whether or not the lexicographer's aim simply to describe usage did not involve a lowering of standards—Fries, amongst others, had already commented on the purist attitude involved (see Essay 15). In this review, Professor Sledd takes issue with a number of the linguistically misorientated criticisms which had been made—such as the introduction of unwise innovations, the omission of expected encyclopedic subject-matter—and makes some perceptive comments about the *Webster* and about dictionaries in general.

'The Lexicographer's Uneasy Chair'

(*College English*, vol. 23, 1962)

'...this latest dictionary to bear the Merriam-Webster label is an intellectual achievement of the very highest order.' Sumner Ives in *Word Study*

'...the anxiously awaited work that was to have crowned cisatlantic linguistic scholarship with a particular glory turns out to be a scandal and a disaster.'
Wilson Follett in the *Atlantic*

'Somebody had goofed.'
Ethel Merman in *Webster's Third New International Dictionary*

But who? Is the goof trademarked, a Merriam-Webster, or is scholarship in Springfield trans-*Atlantic*? The experts will have to answer that question, and thoughtful laymen after using the new dictionary for a long time. This review has more modest aims. Mainly it examines a few issues which less inhibited critics have already raised, suggests some possible limitations of their criticisms, and urges that the serious work of serious scholars must be seriously judged.

Everyone knows that the *Third International* is an entirely new dictionary for use today. In this eighth member of a series which began in 1828, the Merriam Company has invested over $3,500,000, almost three times the cost of the 1934 *New International*, so that the statements in *Webster's Third* are backed by over a century of experience, by the evidence of more than 10,000,000 citations, and by the knowledge and skill of a large permanent staff and more than 200 special consultants. To a reviewer, those facts should be rather sobering.

Some editors, however, and some reviewers have not been restrained from prompt attacks. They have criticized the *Third International* for its failure to include expected encyclopedic matter, for its technique of definition, and especially for its treatment of what is called usage; and they have charged Dr. Gove and his associates with unwise innovations motivated by the desire to destroy all standards of better and worse in the use of English. While insisting upon the responsibility of lexicographers, some of the attackers have not been equally alert to the responsibility of critics.

The question of motives can be dismissed at once. The lexicographers at the Merriam Company, it may safely be assumed, have just one motive: to make the best possible dictionaries. They may have failed, in one respect or another; but such innovations as they actually have made have not been made without the most serious and responsible consideration.

The charge of unwise innovation has two parts: first, that an innovation has been made; and second, that it is unwise. Some of the critics have assumed that the editors of the *Third International* have departed from established lexicographical custom by assuming the role of historians, not lawgivers. One reviewer, indeed, to prove his accusation that the lexicographers had abandoned authority for permissiveness, quoted a part of their statement that 'the standard of English pronunciation...is the usage that now prevails among the educated and cultured people to whom the language is vernacular.' He had not bothered to read precisely the same statement in the 1934 *New International*.

More generally, too many of the unfavorable critics have ignored the whole history of English lexicography since Samuel Johnson: they have hurried to denounce an innovation as unwise before establishing the fact of innovation. Already in the eighteenth century, the ideal of the standard and standardizing dictionary had been sharply questioned. The encyclopedist Ephraim Chambers declared his view that 'the Dictionary-Writer is not supposed to have any hand in the things he relates; he is no more concerned to make the improvements, or establish the significations, than the historian' to fight the battles he describes. Even Johnson said of himself that he did not 'form, but register the language,' that he did not 'teach men how they should think, but relate how they have hitherto expressed their thoughts'; and when Englishmen a century later set out to make the great *Oxford Dictionary*, they assumed from the beginning that the lexicographer is 'an historian' of the language, 'not a critic.' It may be that professional lexicographers have been on the wrong track for two centuries and that in two hours an amateur can set them straight; but in that event the amateur and not the lexicographer would be the innovator. He would do well, before attempting to put his lawgiving theory into practice, to face Johnson's doubts in that magnificent 'Preface' and to ask himself the unanswerable question how rational choice among the resources of a language is possible for the man who does not know what those resources are.

The relation between a dictionary and an encyclopedia is another problem whose history should have been better known to some reviewers. Few lexicographers are likely to solve it either to their own full satisfaction or to the satisfaction of all their readers. From the *Third International*, the objectors miss the gazetteer and the biographical dictionary of the 1934 volume, and they dislike the new decision to restrict the word-list 'to generic words...as distinguished from proper names that are not generic.' Other readers might just as well make opposite complaints. The hairy-nosed wombat and the hickory shuckworm do not greatly interest the average American, who has equally little need to know the incubation period of the ostrich or the gestation period of the elephant, to contemplate the drawing of a milestone marked 'Boston 20 miles,' or to examine a colorplate of fishes which is a slander to the catfish and the brook trout; and the occasional philologist might hope for a dictionary which explains words and leaves to the encyclopedia, as Murray said, the description of things. But who can say that he knows infallibly how such decisions should be made? Murray did not claim infallibility but admitted inconsistency in his omission of *African* and inclusion of *American*. Since man and the universe cannot be put between two covers, some things must be omitted; 'selection is guided by usefulness'; and usefulness can be guessed at but not measured. Readers who can get the use of a Webster's unabridged will have access to an encyclopedia. They should consult it when they need to know about people and places. Meanwhile they may be grateful that the *Third International* has made space for as many quotations as it now includes. A dictionary without quotations is like a table of contents without a book.

There remain, of the critics' favorite subjects, the technique of definition and the matter of usage. The technique of definition is briefly explained in the editor's preface:

> The primary objective of precise, sharp defining has been met through development of a new dictionary style based upon completely analytical one-phrase definitions throughout the book. Since the headword in the definition is intended to be modified only by structural elements restrictive in some degree and essential to each other, the use of commas either to separate or to group has been severely limited, chiefly to units in apposition or in series. The new defining pattern does not provide for a predication which conveys further expository comment...Defining by synonym is carefully avoided by putting all unqualified or undifferentiated terms in small capital letters. Such a term in small capitals should not be considered a definition but a cross-reference to a definition of equivalent meaning that can be substituted for the small capitals.
>
> A large number of verbal illustrations mostly from the mid-twentieth century has been woven into the defining pattern with a view to contributing considerably to the user's interest and understanding by showing a word used in context.

If it is not naively optimistic to expect most critics of a dictionary to agree on anything, general approval may be expected for careful synonymies and for the distinction between a synonym and a definition; and the value of illustrative quotations has been demonstrated by centuries of English lexicography. The objection that not many mid-century authors deserve quotation has already been answered, for it is only another form of the notion that the lexicographer should be a law-giver and not a historian. It would, moreover, be rash to suggest either that many of the quotations are not particularly informative or that identification by the mere names of the authors makes it impossible to check the quotations or to examine them in their contexts: with 10,000,000 quotations to choose from, the editors must know the possibilities of choice more fully than any critic, and precise references would take up much valuable space.

The definitions themselves are another matter. Without advancing any claim to special competence, an ordinary reader may fairly report that he finds some of the definitions extraordinarily clumsy and hard to follow and that as an English teacher he would not encourage his students to follow the new Merriam-Webster model. The one-phrase definitions of nouns in particular may become confusing because in English it is hard to keep track of the relations among a long series of prepositional phrases, participial phrases, and relative clauses; the reader may simply forget what goes with what, if indeed he ever can find out. A less serious criticism is that the new typeface and the long entries unbroken by indentation are bad for middle-aged eyes. Real mistakes, of course, are extremely rare, but a fisherman may be pardoned an objection to the fourth numbered definition of the noun *keeper* as 'a fish large enough to be legally caught.' The crime is not catching but keeping an undersized or oversized fish.

Perhaps such a quibble is itself no keeper, and some criticism of the dictionary's treatment of usage has been equally frivolous. An excellent bad example appeared in *Life*, whose editors compressed a remarkable amount of confusion into a single sentence when they attacked 'Editor Gove' for 'saying that if a word is misused often enough, it becomes acceptable.' Though one can argue how much use and by what speakers is enough, consistency would force *Life's* editors into silence. Their sacred kye are scrawnier than Pharaoh's seven kine, and it is shocking that the influence of such a magazine should force learning to debate with ignorance.

Yet so loud a stridulation of critics cannot simply be ignored. There is a real question whether the *Third International*, though justly called 'the most comprehensive guide to usage currently available,' has recorded usage as precisely as it might have done. Were the editors right to abandon 'the status label *colloquial*'? Have they adequately reported not only what people say and write but also those opinions concerning speech and writing which properly enter into their own definitions of *standard* and of *Standard English*? Those are legitimate questions to ask of a dictionary 'prepared with a constant regard for the needs of the high school and college student' and of the general reader. However diffidently and respectfully, a reviewer must give the best answers that he can.

Several reasons have been offered, by various authorities, for the abandonment of the label *colloquial*. Those reasons are not all alike. It is one thing to say that we cannot know 'whether a word out of context is colloquial or not' (Gove), that lexicographers cannot distinguish the 'many different degrees of standard usage' by status labels but can only suggest them by quotations (Gove), or that 'the bases for discrimination are often too subtle for exact and understandable verbal statement' (Ives); it is quite another thing to argue against marking words *colloquial* because many readers have wrongly concluded that a word so marked is somehow bad (Ives). In a matter to which the editors must have given their best thought, the variety itself of these justifications and the failure to order them in any coherent and inclusive statement is somewhat puzzling; and the impertinent might be tempted to inquire how 200,000 quotations will enable the inexpert reader to do what 10,000,000 quotations did not make possible for the expert lexicographer or how a dictionary can be made at all if nothing can go into it which the ignorant might misinterpret. One reason for the widespread misinterpretation of the policy adopted is surely that the underlying theory has not been clearly explained.

And that is not all. The very defenses of the new policy appear sometimes to refute the contention that finer discriminations are not possible than those in *Webster's Third*. When the newspapers attack the dictionary for listing words like *double-dome* and *finalize* as standard, defenders reply by citing other slangy or colloquial or much reprobated terms from the columns of those same newspapers. What is the force of the attack or the defense unless the intelligent layman can draw precisely that distinction between 'the formal and informal speech and writing of the educated' which the *Third International* refuses to draw for him? If he lacked that ability, both attackers and defenders would be wasting their citations.

Much can be said, of course, about the confusion of styles in modern writing. Perhaps distinctions among styles are now indeed less clear and stable than they were in a less troubled age; perhaps the clumsier writers do ignore the existing distinctions while the sophisticated use them to play sophisticated tunes; perhaps the scrupulously objective lexicographer cannot establish those distinctions from his quotation slips alone. For all that, distinctions do exist. They exist in good writing, and they exist in the linguistic consciousness of the educated. Dr. Gove's definers prove they exist when they give *egghead* as a synonym for *double-dome* but then define *egghead* in impeccably formal terms as 'one with intellectual interests or pretensions' or as 'a highly educated person.' Such opposition between theory and practice strikes even a timid and generally admiring reviewer as rather odd, as though some notion of scientific objectivity should require the scientist to deny that he knows what he knows because he may not know how he knows it.

In the absence, then, of convincing argument to the contrary, a simple reader is left with the uneasy feeling that the abandonment of '*Colloq.*' was a mistake which the introduction of more quotations does not quite rectify and that as a teacher he must now provide foreigners and inexperienced students both with some general principles of linguistic choice and with specific instruction in instances where the new dictionary does not discriminate finely enough among stylistic variants. The dictionary leaves unlabeled many expressions which this teacher would not allow a beginning writer to use in serious exposition or argument except for clearly intended and rather special effects: (*to be caught*) *with one's pants down*, *dollarwise*, *stylewise* (*s.v.* *-wise*), (*to give one*) *the bird*, *dog* 'something inferior of its kind,' *to enthuse*, *to level* 'deal frankly,' *schmaltz*, *chintzy*, *the catbird seat*, *to roll* 'rob,' *to send* 'delight,' *shindig*, *shook-up*, *square* 'an unsophisticated person,' *squirrelly*, *to goof*, and the like. Enforcing such modest niceties will now be more difficult; for classroom lawyers and irate parents will be able to cite the dictionary which the teacher has taught Johnny how to read but which has collapsed the distinction between formal and informal Standard English. Similar difficulties could occur with various mild obscenities, such as *pissed off* and *pisspoor*, which should be marked not only as slang but with some one of the warning labels that the dictionary attaches to the almost quite adequately recorded four-letter words; and the label *slang* itself might well be more freely used with the various synonyms for *drunk*—*stewed*, *stinko*, *stoned*, *tight*, *tanked*, *sozzled*, *potted*, *pie-eyed*, *feeling no pain*, *blind*, *looped*, *squiffed*, *boiled*, *fried*, *high*, etc. Odzooks!

The convenience of a classroom teacher, however, is a rather petty criterion by which to judge a great dictionary, and the tiny handful of evidence here alleged must not be taken as justifying the shrill lament that *Webster's Third* is 'a scandal and a disaster.' The wake has been distinctly premature. Both the dictionary and the language it records are likely to survive the keening critics, whose exaggerations are something of a stumbling block themselves. The mere extent of the information in a dictionary unabridged should fix in a reviewer's mind the salutary knowledge that as no one man can make such a book, so no one man can judge it; but the popular reviews of the *Third International* have merely skimmed its surface and have said little of its technical features or substantial accomplishments. The present discussion will conclude with a few slight remarks on some such matters and with the renewed insistence that longer use and more expert study will be necessary before the dictionary can be definitively judged.

Teachers of elementary composition may be especially interested in the dictionary's three well-filled pages on English punctuation. As several recent grammarians have done, the editors attempt to establish definite relations between pointing and intonation, and they pursue that end with some care and vigor: the theory that punctuation may in part be taught by relating it to pitch-contours and to pauses here receives a better-than-average statement.

Yet the composition teacher may still be sceptical. For one thing, no account of English intonation has deserved or won universal acceptance. The editors themselves thus seem to postulate more than the three 'pauses' allowed in the Trager-Smith phonology, which their description directly or indirectly follows. What is worse is the failure of the proposed relationships between speech and pointing as one moves from dialect to dialect: rules that may hold in one region do not hold in another. For much Southern American speech and for much Southern British, it is simply not the case that 'the rising pause...is usually indicated in writing by a comma'; for many speakers and writers in many areas, an exclamation point may correspond to a *low*-pitched 'terminal stress' as well as to a high one; and a colon may be used in writing not just for 'a fading or sustained pause in speech' but for a 'rising pause' or for no pause at all. The editors have weakened their case by stating it too simply and too strongly.

For the linguistically inclined, Mr. Edwin Artin's extensive 'Guide to Pronunciation' will have a particular attraction. The 'Guide' is just that—a guide; 'not a treatise on phonetics' or a structural dialectologist's systematic account of American pronunciation, but an explanation of the way the editors have used their new alphabet in their transcriptions. Though the forgetful will regret that the key is no longer before them at each opening, and though a stern phonemicist might call the whole system sloppy, the new alphabet is an arguable solution to an extremely complex theoretical and practical problem and a definite improvement over the more complicated yet less accurate and more misleading diacritical key in the *Webster's* of 1934. The objective in devising the alphabet 'was a set of symbols which would represent each speech sound which distinguishes one word from another and each difference in sound which is associated with some large region of the country' (Ives), so that the editors might record both the formal and the informal pronunciations actually heard in cultivated conversation from speakers of the standard dialects in the various regions. The *Third International* can thus do fuller justice than its predecessor did to regional variation and to modes of speech less artificial than the 'formal platform speech' of the earlier work.

Like every competent writer on American pronunciation, Mr. Artin will be criticized as well as praised. He writes, indeed, at a particularly difficult time, when phonological theory is so unsettled that rival groups among the linguists can scarcely communicate with one another. Since pleasing one group of theorists means displeasing its opponents, since it is easily possible to please neither or none, and since Mr. Artin does not include in his 'Guide' the sort of general and historical information which could be found in the corresponding section of the 1934 dictionary, perhaps he will not have so large an audience as Kenyon reached. His readers will be the kind who will argue the results of equating the medial consonants of *tidal* and *title* because in some dialects they are phonetically identical or of distinguishing them because the preceding diphthongs may be of different lengths and because the consonants of *tide* and *titular* clearly differ. Other readers, if they find the 'Guide' hard going, will not risk too much confusion by limiting their study to the table of symbols and to the short section on pronunciation in the 'Explanatory Notes.'

Within the dictionary proper, the word-list first invites examination. Like the addenda to the later editions of the *Second*, the vexing miscellaneous entries at the bottoms of the pages are now gone from *Webster's Third*, either dropped or worked into the main alphabet; numerous obsolete words have disappeared, since the cut-off date has been advanced from 1500 to 1755; and further space for additions has been found by rejecting many no longer useful terms from the rapidly changing and never generally current technical vocabulary with which both the *Second* and the *Third International* are stuffed. This plethora of scientific and technical terms, carefully gathered in an elaborate reading program, is of course no plethora at all but only a comfortable supply for the scientist and technologist, who seem pleased with the dictionary's coverage of their fields; and a general dictionary must make room as well for some regionalisms, for a certain amount of recent slang, and for the new words in general use which so eloquently damn our culture. When all this has been done, it would be unfair to complain that perhaps not enough attention has been paid to the distinctive vocabularies of English-speaking nations other than Britain and the United States.

Beyond the word-list, neither space nor the reviewer's competence will allow him to go. He has few complaints about spelling, the only loud one being against *alright*; as far as a layman's knowledge goes, the etymologies are accurate, and beyond that point they remain clear and comprehensible; the discrimination and the arrangement of senses impose silence on the reader who has not studied them with the same care that went into their making; and the synonymies have already proved their practical value. A sweeping conclusion will not be expected of a review whose thesis is that the prematurity of sweeping conclusions has already been sufficiently exemplified, but a moderately serious examination has made a few things perfectly plain about the *Third International.* As a completely new, independent, responsibly edited, unabridged dictionary, no other work can rival it on precisely its own ground. Its merits are infinitely greater than those of the reviews which have lightly questioned them. Time and the experts will ultimately decide its just rank in the world of English lexicography, whether above, below, or alongside its predecessor; but meanwhile it can usefully fill a place in the libraries of a generation.

22

ANTHONY BURGESS

(1917–)

Anthony Burgess (a *nom de plume* of John Burgess Wilson) was born and went to university in England. He later taught in England, in Malaya, and in Brunei. He has written a number of novels and books of criticism. In *Language Made Plain* he has sought to mediate the findings of modern linguistic research for the common reader. This chapter deals with words both as a level of structure and as integers of communication.

'Words'

(*Language Made Plain*, 1964)

I

For the moment—but only for the moment—it will be safe to assume that we all know what is meant by the word 'word'. I may even consider that my typing fingers know it, defining a word (in a whimsical conceit) as what comes between two spaces. The Greeks saw the word as the minimal unit of speech; to them, too, the atom was the minimal unit of matter. Our own age has learnt to split the atom and also the word. If atoms are divisible into protons, electrons, and neutrons, what are words divisible into?

Words as things uttered split up, as we have already seen, into phonemes, but phonemes do not take *meaning* into account. We do not play on the phonemes of a word as we play on the keys of a piano, content with mere sound; when we utter a word we are concerned with the transmission of meaning. We need an appropriate kind of fission, then—one that is *semantic*, not *phonemic*. Will division into syllables do? Obviously not, for syllables are mechanical and metrical, mere equal ticks of a clock or beats in a bar. If I divide (as for a children's reading primer) the word 'metrical' into 'met-ri-cal', I have learned nothing new about the word: these three syllables are not functional as neutrons, protons, electrons are functional. But if I divide the word as 'metr-; -ic; -al' I have done something rather different.

I have indicated that it is made of the root 'metr-', which refers to measurement and is found in 'metronome' and, in a different phonemic disguise, in 'metre', 'kilometre', and the rest; '-ic', which is an adjectival ending found also in 'toxic', 'psychic', etc., but can sometimes indicate a noun, so that 'metric' itself can be used in a phrase like 'Milton's metric' with full noun status; '-al', which is an unambiguous adjectival ending, as in 'festal', 'vernal', 'partial'. I have split 'metrical' into three contributory forms which (remembering that Greek *morph-* means 'form') I can call *morphemes*.

Let us now take a collocation of words—a phrase or sentence—and attempt a more extended analysis. This will do: 'Jack's father was eating his dinner very quickly.' Here I would suggest the following fission: 1) 'Jack'; 2) '-'s'; 3) 'father'; 4) 'was'; 5) 'eat'; 6) '-ing'; 7) 'hi-'; 8) '-s'; 9) 'dinner'; 10) 'very'; 11) 'quick'; 12) '-ly'—making a total of twelve morphemes. 'Jack' can exist on its own, but the addition of '-'s' (a morpheme denoting possession) turns a proper noun into an adjective. 'Father' cannot be reduced to smaller elements, for, though '-er' is an ending common to four nouns of family relationship, 'fath-' on its own has no more meaning than 'moth-' or 'broth-' or 'sist-'. 'Eat' can be an infinitive or imperative, but the suffix '-ing' makes it into a present participle. 'Hi-' signals an aspect of the singular masculine personal pronoun, but it can have no real meaning until it is completed by the objective ending '-m' or, as here, the '-s' denoting possession. 'Dinner' is indivisible, for 'din' on its own belongs to a very different semantic area, and to use 'din' for 'dinner' (as some facetious people do) or to make a duplicated child's form 'din-din' is merely to use a truncated form of a whole word, implying the prior existence of that word. Finally, 'quick' is an adjective; the morpheme '-ly' turns it into an adverb.

It will be seen from the above that morphemes fall into two classes. There are those which cannot stand on their own but require to be combined with another morpheme before they can mean anything—like '-'s', '-ing', 'hi-', '-ly'. We can call these *bound forms*, or *helper morphemes*. The other morphemes are those which can stand on their own, conveying a meaning, and these can be called *free forms* or *semantemes* ('meaning-forms'). 'Jack', 'father', 'was', 'eat', 'dinner', 'quick' are of this order: these are simple free forms, because they cannot be subdivided into smaller elements. But words like 'Jack's', 'his', 'quickly' *can* be subdivided, each into either *a*) a free form + a bound form or *b*) two bound forms (like 'hi-' and '-s').

I have used the term 'word' so far without attempting a definition, yet the fact that we have been able to analyse words into morphemes shows that we are finding no difficulty in recognising a word. But the time has come for definition, and the great Bloomfield, who may be regarded as the father of modern linguistic theory, suggested that a word was a 'minimum free form', meaning a form unlimited as to the number of bound forms or 'helper morphemes' but strictly limited to one free form only. This would make words of 'John' (one free form), 'John's' (one free form and one bound form), 'its' (the same), 'his' (two bound forms adding up to one free form). It would not, however, make words of compounds like 'penknife', 'manhole-cover' or German *Geheimestaatspolizei* ('Secret-state-police' or 'Gestapo'). There would have to be a new term, such as 'word-compound', to cover these and the following fantastic verb coined by Robert Browning:

> While treading down rose and ranunculus,
> You Tommy-make-room-for-your-uncle us.

But these compounds frequently set into what are, at least phonemically, simple entities—'breakfast' (/brɛkfst/, not 'break fast'); 'cupboard' (/kʌbəd/, not 'cup board'); 'bo's'n', not 'boatswain'. It is difficult to draw the line, and the need for Bloomfield's limited definition is not at all clear: a compound word is still a word, doing a word's job.

Bloomfield also said that a free form could be recognised by its ability to stand as a complete utterance—granted, of course, a context of other words or of pure situation which would make the meaning of the isolated free form quite clear. Thus, we can take words from our sentence 'Jack's father was eating his dinner very quickly' and demonstrate this thesis without too much strain:

'Whose is that cap?' '*Jack's.*'
'*Father!*' (The speaker is calling.)
'She *is* pretty, isn't she?' '*Was.*'
'What's he doing now?' '*Eating.*'
'Whose book will you borrow?' '*His.*'
'Why have you come? What do you want?' '*Dinner.*'
'Ugly, isn't he?' '*Very.*'
'*Quickly!*' (The speaker gives an errand-goer a shove.)

The trouble with this is that a breakdown occurs with the indefinite articles 'a' and 'an' and the definite article 'the'. These can only make complete statements in a context of language, not of life: it is the words themselves that are referred to, not—as with the above examples—what the words stand for. Thus, 'What word did you use then?' '"The".'—'Do you say "a" or "an" before "hotel"?' '"An".'

It seems that, if Bloomfield's thesis is to hold so far, we must regard the articles as bound forms, forms incapable of acting on their own—that is to say, not as words at all. Not all languages possess a definite article, but some that do seem unable to regard it as a separate word. Rumanian has a newspaper called *Timpul* ('The Times'); the original Latin was *Tempus illud*, but now the remains of the *illud* act as an article glued to the end of the noun. The same glueing of an article to the end of a word is found in Aztec—*tomatl*; *chocolatl*; *Quetzlcoatl*; *Popacatapetl*. Arabic glues its article to the front, as in our own Arabic loan-words 'alchemy', 'algebra', 'alcohol', 'apricot' (*al-praecoq*), in *Al-Sultan*, even in the holy name *Allah*. (Note that the great Alexander appears in Arabic as Al-Iskander; the 'Al' is assumed to be an article and removed to leave 'Iskander'—a common Muslim name.) English itself has timidly played with the glue-pot: 'an adder' should be 'a nadder', 'an apron' was once 'a napron', and 'an orange' ought to be, as in Spanish, 'a norange' (*una naranja*).

So, if the articles—'the', 'a', 'an'—are bound forms, they cannot be words; yet we say they *are* words: they have space before and behind; they are defined in dictionaries. Evidently something is wrong somewhere. For that matter, something seems to be wrong with the limitation of 'single-word sentences' to bound forms. If a pupil says, 'I came quick,' and the teacher utters the chiding correction '"-Ly"', then an error of usage is being corrected: the referent of '-ly' is itself. But if a man says, 'It's been ages since I saw you. I'll just run up to the nursery and take a look at your son,' the proud parents can answer: '-s!' (/zzzzz/), meaning 'We've more than one son now!' In other words, that bound form the plural suffix can refer, not to mere accidence (the correct inflection of a word), but to something in the real, external world—'more than one son'.

I suggest that we allow the morpheme in its two forms—the morpheme expressing meaning; the morpheme which merely helps to modify meaning or create larger structures—to rest as our scientific unit. The term 'word' cannot have any *significant* denotation: a word is what my typing fingers think it is—a cluster of symbols or even a single symbol separated by space from other clusters or single symbols. The symbols represent phonemes. The words of connected speech do not even have the frame of silence around them: they are all glued together in a single act of communication. But it is convenient to assume that words have real existence and even to create a science of word-study called *lexicology* (not to be confused with *lexicography*, which is the harmless drudgery of dictionary-making). Not delving too deeply into what a word is, we are able to embrace the single phoneme /ə/ (the indefinite article 'a') or /o/ (French for 'water'—*eau*) as easily as the word-monsters of the so-called agglutinative languages: *nakomajn'-ytamjun'n'ybolamyk*, for instance, which, according to W. J. Entwistle (*Aspects of Language*, 1953), is the Koryat for 'They're always telling lies to us' (Koryat is spoken in Siberia). It appears to be a good language for telegrams.

2

Get ready for two new fearsome technical terms. Looking at words, we soon become aware that they fall into two rough categories—words that mean something when in isolation, like 'apple', 'gramophone', 'tulip'; words that only possess meaning when combined with other words in phrases or sentences—such as 'it', 'and', 'if', 'or'. These are, of course, analogous to the two types of morpheme that can exist within the word itself, like the free form 'eat' and the bound form '-ing' in 'eating'. So in the statement 'The orange is yellow', we can pick out 'orange' and 'yellow' as words which carry meaning if chalked up singly or written in the sky by sky-writing aircraft. These free forms, because they possess independent meaning, are called *auto-semantic* words. 'The' and 'is', on the other hand, mean nothing outside the context of a sentence; they only develop meaning when we make a synthesis of them with words like 'orange' and 'yellow'. We can say that they are *synsemantic*.

But can a word really possess meaning outside a context? Are not perhaps all words really synsemantic? Having read the sentence 'The orange is yellow', you will have a clear enough image of a fruit which is juicy within and yellow without. But if the word 'orange' were suddenly to be written on the sky by an aircraft, would we—without the assistance of other words—really be sure of its meaning? Certain contexts or associations might fix 'orange' as a fruit (oranges are regularly advertised through various media), but the word might merely mean a colour. In Liverpool, 'ORANGE' painted on a wall might have completely different associations—William of Orange, the Orange Lodges, the Battle of the Boyne—and the citrous element would be expunged by the political. Similarly, 'yellow' without a context hovers between the colour and the adjective meaning 'cowardly'. Indeed, one can think of few words that are genuinely autosemantic, and these are not necessarily autosemantic in every language. 'Milk' in English is unambiguous enough, but *leche* in Spanish can be an insult, and *susu* in Malay can mean as much the source of the milk as the milk itself. This is as much as to say that no single thing in the non-linguistic world is capable of preserving the word attached to it from vagueness, imprecision, ambiguity.

Though one may except proper names—words or word-groups signifying some unique natural or human referent: 'the Taj Mahal'; 'William Ewart Gladstone'; '*La Bohème*'; 'the English Channel'; 'Ben Nevis'; 'Brigitte Bardot'; 'Lolita.' Yet these names only strictly come within the field of the lexicologist (and the lexicographer, for that matter) when they start to shed their particular denotation. If a girl is called a 'proper little Lolita', then 'Lolita' is turning into a common noun—a word expressive of a whole class instead of a single fictitious character. Indeed, proper names do not really possess a meaning at all: they are arbitrary signs, mere laundry marks. What does the name 'Theodore' mean? Its *etymology* (etymology deals with word-origin) is Greek, and the Greek words which make up the name mean 'God's gift', but this tells us nothing about the person or persons to whom the name is attached. (Etymology, one may say now, has nothing to do with the meaning of any word. 'Silly' is derived from Anglo-Saxon 'saelig'—'happy, blessed, holy'—but this etymology does not help us to fix the present-day meaning of the word.) 'Theodore', then, means all people called Theodore, taking the widest context; taking the narrowest, it means all the people called Theodore whom we happen to know or know about.

The science of meaning is called *Semantics*, and it deals with language at those points where it is closest to the 'real world'. The phonetician and grammarian tend to lock themselves in their laboratories, but the semantic specialist is close to the very roots of thought and action. George Orwell, in his novel *Nineteen Eighty-four*, saw how it might be possible for semantic control of language to change the whole pattern of a society. 'Newspeak' is the official language of Ingsoc ('English Socialism'), and its limitation of the field of possible linguistic expression aims at making heterodox opinion impossible: political rebellion cannot be conceived in the mind, for the semantic elements of dissidence do not exist. If 'bad' means 'opposed to the principles of Ingsoc', and Big Brother is the eternal personification of these principles, then a statement like 'Big Brother is bad' is absurd; it is like saying 'x = not-x'. In the totalitarian societies of our day we have seen how meaning can be delimited to serve the ends of the Party; but even in free societies we are perpetually bombarded by semantic perversions —mainly from politicians and advertisers, whose interests are furthered by the distortion or delimiting of meaning. 'The pacific uses of the H-Bomb' is as absurd as the Orwellian 'War is Peace'; 'peace offensive' is a phrase I have heard on the radio; 'X is a man's smoke' is a deliberate exploitation of a limited area of connotation; 'It's the ice-cream treat of the TV age' does not really admit of analysis.

Semantics is so big and important a subject that, in the few decades of its acknowledged existence as a science, it has already built up its own vast polyglot library. The book by Ogden and Richards—*The Meaning of Meaning*—states in its title what the basic inquiry of Semantics is; it is an inquiry which may well go on for ever. We all use words; do we know how tentative, complex, and fundamentally dangerous it is to commit even the simplest statement to the air? A friend says to me, 'I like cats'; I say that I understand his meaning. But once I start to analyse I find myself plunging into a world where things seem neither intelligible nor necessary: what is 'I', what is 'like', what is 'cats'? I am drawn into ontology, psychology, physiology, zoology, and I end doubting the existence of everything, including the possibility of language's possessing any sense-potentialities at all.

One thing we can be fairly sure about is that a word—a 'phonemic event'—only exists at all because of some entity that has prior existence in the non-linguistic world. This non-linguistic world may be seen as having two aspects: first, there are the things to which language ultimately refers—'real' events or objects, which we assume have a life of their own; second, there is an area of mind where the speaker and hearer (or writer and reader) meet to agree on some interpretation of the real event or object. Thus, at one end we have the *word*, at the other we have the *referent*, in the middle we have the *sense*. The referent is perhaps a matter for the philosopher; the word is certainly the linguist's concern; the sense interests everybody, from the logician to the literary critic.

Whether the referent of a word really (in the sense of 'demonstrably') exists is no concern of ours. We may talk about the attributes of God even though some would say that God's existence has not been satisfactorily proved. We may talk about the characters of a novel, knowing that these exist only in a very special sense—certainly not as the Albert Memorial or Red Square exists. A hypothesis may have a mental existence and the ginger-and-white cat that sits by me at this moment of writing may have a physical one: to the user of words they inhabit the same area of reference. Ultimately, of course, even the most abstract idea must go back to something in the world of sense, so that the notion of God may derive from tree-spirits, which themselves are an attempt to explain the outward manifestations of a tree's life. I repeat: this is no concern of our present study, though we cannot help being curious about referents. After all, Dr Johnson said in the preface to his Dictionary: 'I am not yet so lost in lexicography, as to forget that words are the daughters of earth, and that things are the sons of heaven.'

A speaker speaks a word; a hearer hears it. If he understands the word he has stepped into the same area of sense as the speaker. The meaning of a word, then, may be thought of as this common area of meeting. But the sense, it goes without saying, depends on the referent, and the nature of the referent has to be defined by the context. Thus, the 'cat' of 'The cat sat on the mat' is different from the 'cat' of 'Bring back the cat for thugs and rapists'. We cannot say that 'cat' is a single word possessing two distinct meanings; there are two words phonemically identical but semantically different: we call these *homonyms*. The 'cat' of the second sentence refers back etymologically—by the grim fancy of 'cat o'nine tails'—to the cat of the hearthrug, but word-origin can never be invoked, as we have already pointed out, in the examination of meanings.

But what makes words less precise than mathematical symbols is their tendency to suggest meanings other than the ones intended in particular limited contexts. The definition of context is often not enough; many words tremble at various frontiers of sense; ambiguity is a vice of words. Ambiguity comes about not merely through homonymity, but through metaphorical extension (which may or may not lie behind homonymity, as with 'cat'), and through the fact that words attempt two opposing jobs—particularisation and generalisation. 'Cat' will describe a new-born kitten and a fully-grown tiger, so that opposite notions (weakness, strength; tame, wild; tiny, huge) are contained in the same word. 'I love fish' can have opposed meanings; Shakespeare makes Henry V say that he loves France so well that he will not part with a single province of it. It is, indeed, only with the poet or imaginative prose-writer that language functions smoothly. Ambiguity ceases to be a vice; its deliberate exploitation is revelled in. There are layers of meaning, all relevant to the context. Homonyms become deliberate puns—not necessarily comic. Lady Macbeth will *gild* the faces of the grooms with blood, 'for it must seem their *guilt*.' 'Die' in *Romeo and Juliet* means what it says, but also means to experience the sexual orgasm. 'Reasons,' to Falstaff, can be plentiful as blackberries ('reasons' = /re:znz/ = 'raisins'). A scientific age like our own tends to worry about this aspect of language. Some readers of a novel of mine were unhappy about the title, *The Worm and the Ring*: they wanted to know what it really meant. It meant, I told them, sexual incapacity, the failure of a marriage because of the moral weakness of the husband, the lowliness of crawling things, and the golden round of heaven, the Wagnerian myth (*Wurm* = dragon). They were dissatisfied: meaning should be mathematical, unambiguous. But this plurality of reference is in the very nature of language, and its management and exploitation is one of the joys of writing.

Words tend not merely to be ambiguous but to be emotional. 'Mother' has a clear dictionary meaning (a *denotation*), but, because of the filial status shared by all men, it is drenched in associations of strong feeling, it has powerful emotional *connotations*. Thus, 'mother' may be attached to a country or a college ('motherland'; *alma mater*) so that appropriate attitudes of loyalty may be induced in citizens or alumni. But the connotations can be wiped out completely in a term like 'mother-of-pearl', which is as cold as 'matrix'. This has much to do with the distribution of emphasis: 'pearl' is the stressed element and the rest of the compound is pronounced weakly: /mʌðərəv 'pɜ:l/. The same process is at work in 'This is the BBC Home Service', where the highly emotive 'home' is given less stress than the following word. As ambiguity may be used by advertisers and demagogues to confuse or deceive, so that emotional connotations of words like 'England', 'children', 'duty' can be exploited in wartime oratory or in bad poetry at any time. Words like these are assured of a 'stock response' in the unwary reader; the bad poet lets emotive associations do his work for him.

It follows from what I have said that the learning of foreign languages involves more than the amassing of denotations, the taking in of primary meanings only. *Fille* and *baiser*, which seem to mean 'girl' and 'to kiss' respectively in French, are notoriously dangerous words to use. *Buang ayer* in Malay means literally 'to throw water' but has taken on a particular gross meaning; *bulan* in the same language can mean primarily 'moon' or 'month' but also, by a natural extension, 'menstruation.' One has to watch context all the time. Meaning resides shadowily in the morpheme, less so in the word, less so again in the phrase or sentence or paragraph; but meaning only comes to its fullest flower in the context of an entire way of life.

3

Everything flows, including language, and one of the difficulties we meet with in the study of meaning is the fact that meanings change. There are various reasons for this—some essentially linguistic, others psychological or historical. *Pas* means 'step' in French, and *ne...pas* means 'not' (literally: 'not a step'). Because *pas* is associated with the negative *ne*, it has taken on a negative meaning of its own, as in *Pas moi* —'not me'. This, the effect of association, is entirely a linguistic cause of semantic change.

But most changes take place because society changes—either in its attitude to life or in its formal institutions. 'Parliament' does not mean for us what it meant in the Middle Ages, because the institution which is the referent of the word has changed radically. Hamlet, talking about actors, refers to the 'humorous man'—not the comedian, but the emotional actor: the old theory of humours (the primary fluids of the body which, according to the proportions of their mixture, determined a man's temperament) has long gone, but left this word behind to take on a different meaning. It is not long since 'atom' meant what it meant to the Greeks—'what could not further be divided'. The word can no longer mean that, but we retain it. Inertia, conservatism will ensure that a word remains in the vocabulary, but change of meaning will be enforced by the non-conservative elements in man himself.

We cannot examine all types of semantic change here, but we can note the tendency of words to move from a wider to a narrower range of meaning. For instance, 'fowl' once meant any kind of bird but now only means a chicken; 'hound' was once any kind of dog but its meaning is (except in a jocular sense) now strictly limited; a deer was once 'beast in general'. All these words retain the older meaning in their modern German form: *Vogel*; *Hund*; *Tier*. 'Meat', once any kind of food, is now restricted to what comes from the butcher, though the older sense is fossilised in 'sweetmeat'. The opposite process—expansion of meaning instead of restriction—is rarer; perhaps the change in meaning of 'bird' (which once meant merely a young bird) is due to the limiting of the meaning of 'fowl'.

Sometimes a limitation of meaning will be associated with a sort of value-judgement, so that 'smelly' refers only to a bad smell. We can call this a pejorative change and note some very peculiar examples. Italian, for instance, derives its word for 'bad'—*cattivo*—from the Latin word for a prisoner, *captivus*. A cretin is, etymologically, a Christian.

A knave was merely a boy (German *Knabe*). A villain once merely lived on a farm in Roman times; he was to become a serf and, finally, a bad man. This kind of social prejudice is matched by xenophobia or hatred or contempt of the foreign, making the Portuguese for 'word'—*palavra*—into 'palaver'. As the *hoc est corpus* of the Mass has become 'hocus pocus', so Mary Magdalene's weeping has become 'maudlin', and the fairings from St Audrey's fair 'tawdry'. Ameliorative changes—in which the worse becomes the better—are far rarer than pejorative ones: one should note 'nice', though—*nescius* ('ignorant') in Latin, and always unfavourable (it could mean either 'lascivious' or 'trivial') in Shakespeare's time.

It is interesting to see what we do with foreign importations in our own day. The *Blitz* of *Blitzkrieg* lost its native meaning of 'lightning' and now carries connotations of wanton destruction and massive bravery. 'Beatnik'—a hybrid of American-Jewish origin—meant a member of a group devoted to pacifism and self-denial but has quickly become as contemptuous a term as 'teddy-boy' (itself an example of pejorative change). Conversely, 'spiv'—which had a brief currency just after the war with a cluster of bad meanings—was taken over by the French as an adjective: *très spiv*, as applied to a garment, meant 'stylish'—a good example of ameliorative change. The Malay word *pĕrang*, meaning 'war', passed into RAF usage with the particularised meaning of an attack, usually a 'wizard' one. Other, more recent, borrowings, like *sputnik*, *espresso*, have kept close to the things originally described; *ombudsman*, like science fiction, provides us with the name before the referent.

English is quick to develop old words to serve new purposes. Often *apocope* is the way (cutting off the body but retaining the head), as in 'pop' ('popular music'), 'trad' ('traditional jazz'). 'Television' quickly became 'telly'—a half-contemptuous, half-affectionate shortening. One of the simplest and most telling of adaptations has been in the field of rocketry, where 'go' is now an adjective meaning 'fully prepared'. The age of brinkmanship and the nymphet is quick to satisfy its semantic needs; it is even looking ahead, in its masochistic way, with the term 'megadeath'. Let us hope its referent stays in the world of real, not metaphorical, nightmare.

STUDY QUESTIONS

1 CHARLES DICKENS

1 Is Dickens right in saying that 'Saxon-English' is made up of 'words that are familiar in every home, and find their way even into the prattle of the nursery' (p. 2)? Use an etymological dictionary to trace the origin of the words in a few of his sentences, and note which parts of speech hold most to 'Saxon-English'.

2 Give examples out of your own experience of 'Latin-English' in 'the affectations of the ignorant, and the tardier literary perceptions of the man of science' (p. 2).

3 'English, in truth, is a sort of broken Dutch' (p. 3). What notions of national reputation influence Dickens' view of linguistic reputation? How does he correlate nation and language, language and style? How far do value-words like 'broken', 'pure', 'broad', 'corrupt', enter into his descriptions?

4 Read Henry Wadsworth Longfellow's account of 'Anglo-Saxon Language and Poetry' in his *Poets and Poetry of Europe* (1845). How does this man of letters' view of our ancient literature compare with Dickens'?

5 Find out more about Richard Chenevix Trench and his place in the history of linguistic study.

2 HENRY SWEET

1 How far does Sweet succeed in his promise to 'observe things as they are without regard to their origin' (p. 9)?

2 Sweet begins his essay with a comparison. What role do comparison and analogy play in his study? Is the role a logical one? Is it an effective one?

3 Is it true that 'the syllables (nai), (pouz) and (praiv) have no meaning whatever by themselves' (p. 12)? Consider such a word as 'position', 'oppose'. Is there a level of linguistic structure that Sweet is overlooking?

4 What relation does Sweet's remark that in 'feet' 'the (iy) is as much part of the word itself as a sign of the plural' (p. 17) bear to the observations of Bloch (p. 231) on 'take'?

5 Sweet relates the verbs 'beat', 'see' and 'fear' as different stages on line from object to subject, from accusative to nominative, from active to passive. Is this distinction really one that should be made in a dictionary and not in a grammar?

3 FITZEDWARD HALL

1 Hall is concerned to relate style and usage. Try paraphrasing two or three sentences from his first paragraph in the simplest possible style. What does your version gain over his? What does it lose? What does it tell you about Hall's style?

2 Are Hall's remarks about the 'golden age' of English in the last few pages consistent with what he says in the beginning of the essay? Can you summarize his views on linguistic development in a way that will be true to both his earlier and his later statement?

3 Using A. G. Kennedy's *Bibliography of Writings on the English Language* (1927) or *Poole's Index to Periodical Literature* (1882–1908), find and read an essay by Hall's contemporary Richard Grant White. Do his views coincide with Hall's?

4 Hall seems to be proposing a 'rational' and learned approach to the study of English usage. How does his approach compare with Sweet's 'logical' one?

5 Almost half of the essay is Hall's treatment of William Cullen Bryant and the English language. Does this part follow naturally from what goes before? What are its motivations? Outline its structure.

6 Hall attacks Bryant for 'violations of idiomatic propriety, with the occasional bad grammar and vulgarity', but most of his essay deals with vocabulary. Why do you think he overlooks pronunciation and grammar?

4 WALT WHITMAN

1 What does Whitman mean by 'slang'? Is it a consistent definition? To what degree would he share the views of Partridge (Essay 14)?

2 See also Whitman's *American Primer* (1904) and the essay by the poet Louis Untermeyer, 'Whitman and the American Language' (*New York Evening Post*, 31 May 1919).

3 How far do Whitman's preoccupations as a poet form his views about language? How far do they control his descriptive vocabulary and his use of similes for language?

4 'Hasty...grotesque...appropriateness...originality...perfect.' What are Whitman's linguistic norms?

5 Compare Whitman's views on American place-names with those of Washington Irving ('Geoffrey Crayon') in 'National Nomenclature' (*Knickerbocker*, vol. 14, 1839, and in his *Collected Works*). Compare his views on 'etymological metaphors' with those of Ralph Waldo Emerson, in 'Language' (*Nature*, 1836).

6 Read the essays by William Dean Howells on American English in *Harper's Weekly* (2 November 1895) and *Harper's New Monthly Magazine* (January 1886), and James Russell Lowell's introduction to the second series of *Bigelow Papers* (1867).

5 J. A. H. MURRAY

1 In what respects is the diagram on p. 60 an over-simplification?

2 Is there any information about words other than that given by the *OED* that you would like to see in a dictionary? (Comparing an entry in the *OED* with the same entry in a dictionary of some other tradition, such as the Webster, will provide some suggestions on this point.)

3 The *OED* orders the senses of a word historically. In what other ways could the senses be ordered?
4 Look up some words in the *OED* and decide how satisfactory you find *a*) the system of phonetic transcription, *b*) the system of grammatical designations.
5 Is historical information about the meaning of words of any value in studying the meaning of words today? Note Burgess' view (p. 299).
6 Use the *OED* to see how frequently it makes use of Dr Johnson's explanations unchanged. Compare entries in Johnson's Dictionary which the *OED* editors have thought it desirable to change. Are the changes always for the better?

6 GEORGE BERNARD SHAW

1 Compare the attitude and analysis in this letter with those in Shaw's *Pygmalion* (1912) and in his Preface to R. A. Wilson's *The Miraculous Birth of Language* (1941).
2 How unambiguous are Shaw's phonetic spellings? What do they reveal about his own pronunciation?
3 What does Shaw mean by his observations on 'get' and 'git'?
4 How do Shaw's social values influence his linguistic opinions?
5 Find English examples of phonetic spelling *a*) 'partly out of date' and *b*) 'partly corrupted by an ignorant academic attempt to make it etymological'.
6 Walter Savage Landor was another English man of letters interested in spelling reform. He wrote in 'Letter to an Author' appended to his *Letters of Pericles and Aspasia* (1836); in *Leigh Hunt's London Journal* (1835); in *Fraser's Magazine* (1856); and in *Athenaeum* (1861). How do his views differ from Shaw's?
7 What limitations on Shaw's project are given in W. A. Craigie, 'Problems of Spelling Reform' (Society for Pure English, Tract LXIII, 1944).

7 ROBERT BRIDGES

1 What does Bridges seem to mean by 'Pure English'?
2 Discuss the syntax, and the literary implications, of the sentence beginning 'Now the history of languages...' (p. 88).
3 How does Bridges' plan differ from earlier plans for a linguistic academy, such as Swift's 'Proposal' (1712)?
4 Are all Bridges' replies to the question 'Is Reform Feasible?' reasonable ones?
5 What examples of 'indisputable defects, and of apparent lines of decay' would you provide for the general conditions described under 'Motives and Aims'? Read *SPE* Tracts I (1919) and III (1920) to see whether they give similar ones.
6 What attitude toward linguistic change does Bridges reveal under 'How the Society Should Work'?

7 Read Rose Macaulay's *Catchwords and Claptrap* and Robert Graves' *Impenetrability, or the Proper Habit of English* (Hogarth Essays, 2nd series, London, both 1926) and compare their views with Bridges'.

8 Read Henry James' 'The Question of our Speech' (*Appleton's Booklovers' Magazine*, vol. 6; also separately, both 1905).

8 A. LLOYD JAMES

1 What concise statement of James' criteria for 'right' and 'wrong' pronunciation is possible?

2 What weight ought this essay to have with those who wish to reform spelling?

3 Read Robert Bridges' essay 'On the Present State of English Pronunciation' in *Essays and Studies*, vol. 1 (1910, reprinted 1913).

4 James says that the history of the English language 'is an epitome of the nation's history'. What does he mean?

5 Here is the Committee's section on the letter *g*. How adequate do you find it today? How accurate? How inclusive?

GALA	gáala.
GARAGE	gárraazh.
GENUINE	last syllable is -in, not -ine.
GEYSER	géezer.
GLACIAL	gláyshial.
GLACIER	gláss-, not gláas-.
GONDOLA	stress on 1st syllable.
GOUGE	the vowel as in *how*, not as in *who*.
GREASY	gréezy, gréesy. Some people use both pronunciations with different meanings: *gréezy* meaning *slippery*, literally and metaphorically, and *gréesy* meaning *covered with grease.*
GUSTATORY	stress on 1st syllable.
GUTTA PERCHA	*ch* as in *church.*
GYNECOLOGY	initial *g* hard as in *go.*
GYRATORY	jýratory.
GYROSCOPE	jýroscope.

9 LOGAN PEARSALL SMITH

1 Running throughout this paper is the notion of 'deficiency' in the English language (cf. also the metaphor of 'restoration' on p. 124). Do you agree with the implications of such a notion? Can a language ever in fact be deficient for the majority of its users? (Compare Sapir's view that 'language is an essentially perfect means of expression and communication among every known people' (p. 131).)

2 Following on from question 1, the author continually implies that the words under discussion are needed by all users of the English language. Is this true, or is only a minority of users involved? What kind of audience does Smith seem to be primarily thinking of? What does he mean by 'the finer purposes of thought' (p. 114)?

3 Is the author's criticism of the vocabulary of science as 'ugly, lifeless, mechanical' (p. 125) either true or relevant? What is the basis for his remark? What aspects of scientific English is he implicitly ignoring? Moreover, is his own quest for precision (p. 125) so very different from the scientist's?

4 Is it the case that the power of forming native compounds 'has become more or less atrophied in our standard English' (p. 122)? Look in *Webster's Third New International Dictionary* for examples of recently formed compounds to test this hypothesis (e.g. under *back-*). What kind of audience is Smith thinking of when he says that 'English compounds...seem uncouth to us at first, and meet with almost universal disapprobation' (p. 122)?

5 Do you agree with the view which underlies the author's statement that 'the word *curiosity* has become limited and degraded in our modern usage' (p. 118)?

6 How many of the words cited as innovations in this paper are now standard?

10 EDWARD SAPIR

1 Why does Sapir lay so much stress on the notion that speech is the primary manifestation of language?

2 What features of human language differentiate it from other systems of communication, such as that of animals?

3 Language's forms 'predetermine for us certain modes of observation and interpretation' (p. 135). This view of the relationship between language and thought is not now generally held. Can you see why? (Read also B. L. Whorf's essay 'Science and Linguistics', *Technology Review*, vol. 42, 1940, for further exposition of this viewpoint.)

4 Examine in detail an area where linguistic nationalism is in evidence (e.g. Wales, Ireland, Belgium, India) in the light of Sapir's remarks.

5 What is the present state of affairs as regards the status of international languages? Which of the two processes referred to in the last two sentences of the article is now more likely to be realized?

6 Compare the account of the popularizer H. G. Wells of 'The Languages of Mankind' in his *The Outline of History* (1919) with the relevant part of Sapir's professional account.

11 LEONARD BLOOMFIELD

1 What evidence do you think would be relevant to ascertain the way words sounded in earlier states of the language?

2 Find further examples of the distinction Bloomfield draws between malapropisms and analogic developments (p. 160).

3 How far would you agree with Bloomfield that the meanings of learnèd words are 'largely abstract and vague' (p. 159)?
4 Bloomfield is aware of the complications caused by the changing nature of pronunciation: what changes can you hear taking place in English at present? (Information about some current alternative pronunciations can be found in Daniel Jones' *English Pronouncing Dictionary*.)
5 In what ways would a systematic description of English morphology help the foreign learner of English?
6 Read O. Jespersen's article, 'Monosyllabism in English', in the *Proceedings of the British Academy*, vol. 14, 1933, and compare the kind of word described there with that discussed by Bloomfield. Can you think of examples of monosyllabic learnèd words in English?

12 EILERT EKWALL

1 How far do Ekwall's notions of the value of place-names agree with those of Whitman (Essay 4)?
2 What studies would each 'particular kind' of information outlined by Ekwall assist? What studies contribute to the elucidation of place-names?
3 What role have place-names to play in the history of a relatively 'young' country like the United States? What testimony, for example, would they give for what Ekwall calls 'changes in the population'?
4 How often in your experience are personal names found in place-names? How often are place-names found in personal names?
5 How often have you noticed place-names which contain a word in a form different from the one you use?

13 I. A. RICHARDS

1 Does Richards regard the separation of words in writing in the same way Sweet does? What does Richards mean to convey by 'grammar takes its name from writing'?
2 Characterize Richards' use of similes for language.
3 A few paragraphs from the end, Richards writes 'That so far from a perceived correspondence...'. Study this sentence carefully and pinpoint its meaning.
4 Richards writes near the end of his essay that 'The meaning of a word on some occasions is quite as much in what it keeps out...as in what it brings in'. Does he mean that 'The cat is on the mat' takes its meaning from excluding 'A dog was under that table', 'Some fireirons were over a cloudburst', and other sentences of like construction?
5 Do you agree with Richards' definition and exemplification of the term 'morpheme'? Is he using Bloomfield's meaning of the term correctly? Is he right in saying that Lewis Carroll employed the concept?

6 Would Richards agree with Burgess (Essay 22)? Read J. R. Firth's article, 'Modes of Meaning' (in *Essays and Studies*, 1951), and compare his theory of meaning with that of Richards.

14 ERIC PARTRIDGE

1 How do you account for the fact that, despite the imposing list of favourable functions that Partridge draws up, slang is still very much condemned by large numbers of educated people?
2 Go through the words Partridge cites and assess how many of them have *a*) become standard, *b*) dropped out of use since he wrote.
3 How far is the author's dichotomy of good slang v. bad slang (p. 190) valid?
4 Test Partridge's arguments by finding examples of slang in your own speech or in that of your friends, and relating them to his list of functions.
5 Do you agree with Partridge's definition of 'illiteracy' as 'merely incorrectness of accidence, syntax, pronunciation' (p. 194)?

15 C. C. FRIES

1 What authorities—apart from grammar books—do people turn to who believe in the kind of 'correctness' Fries is criticizing?
2 Continuing the lines along which Fries argues, do you think there is such a thing as an international Standard English, applicable to the whole of the English-speaking world?
3 Can you see a parallel between the attitudes surrounding the writing of grammars, discussed here, and the attitudes surrounding the writing of dictionaries (see Essay 21)?
4 Find out more about Fries' approach to language description by reading *The Structure of English* (1952). Also read a good review of this book (e.g. by Sledd in *Language*, vol. 31, 1955), and the comments by Lees (Essay 19) to see why Fries' structuralism is no longer regarded as a final solution.
5 How much will Fries have to take account of social differences of class in writing his grammar? (An idea of the kind of differences to be found in vocabulary may be obtained by reading A. S. C. Ross, 'Linguistic Class-indicators in Present-day English', *Neuphilologische Mitteilungen*, vol. 55, 1954.)
6 Compare the aims of the Survey of English Usage, as described in R. Quirk, 'Towards a Description of English Usage' (*Transactions of the Philological Society*, 1960), with those of Fries.

16 GEORGE ORWELL

1 Is Orwell's title a good one?
2 Read Sir Arthur Quiller-Couch's essay 'Jargon' (*On the Art of Writing*, 1928) and compare it with Orwell's.

3 Collect recent examples of prose comparable with the five Orwell gives early in his essay, and analyse them.
4 Comment on Orwell's figures of speech, using his own criteria.
5 How sufficient and helpful are his six 'rules'? What does no. 6 mean?
6 Describe Orwell's dialectic, including his use of classification.

17 BERNARD BLOCH

1 Simplicity of description is an important criterion for Bloch, as for many linguists, but in what does the simplicity of a description consist?
2 Bloch is reluctant to multiply morphemic elements unnecessarily. Has he any alternative, if he wishes to retain the morphemic principle?
3 Read the critique of traditional linguistic analysis made by Lees (p. 252). Could Bloch's article be taken as an example of what Lees is criticizing?
4 Read Nida's critique of certain theoretical issues in Bloch and others in his article 'The Identification of Morphemes' (in *Language*, vol. 24, 1943).
5 Compare Bloch's approach with a more recent account of the verbal system in English, e.g. F. R. Palmer's *The English Verb* (1964).

18 H. L. MENCKEN

1 What are Mencken's views on linguistic change? Take account of those which appear after the first paragraph.
2 'Better on all counts—clearer, more rational,...more charming.' Discuss Mencken's ideas about the nature of language, bearing in mind his profession.
3 How does Mencken use authorities?
4 What is the importance of the question in Mencken's title?
5 Read several of the articles mentioned in Mencken's footnotes. Do they really support his case?
6 Read Marius Bewley's essay, 'Mencken and the American Language', in *Scrutiny*, vol. 15 (1948).
7 Read the following works by Mark Twain on language and on American in particular: 'Concerning the American Language', *The Stolen White Elephant* (1882); the 'Explanatory' note at the beginning and chapter fourteen of *Huckleberry Finn* (1884); 'The Jumping Frog in English, then in French, then clawed back into a Civilized Language once more by Patient, Unremunerated Toil' (1875); 'English as She is Taught' (1887); and 'The Awful German Language' (Appendix to *A Tramp Abroad*, 1880).

19 R. B. LEES

1 Do you agree with Lees' criticisms of the various forms of traditional linguistic analysis?
2 Is the notion of empirical induction altogether incompatible with the view advocated by Lees?
3 Lees objects to traditional techniques of substitution-in-frames for grammatical analysis. In what ways does his own approach avoid these objections?
4 It may be the case that you find some of the sentences generated by Lees unacceptable. Would this be a serious objection to his approach?
5 Read 1.3 of Kurath and McDavid's Introduction (Essay 20). Do you feel that the existence of irregularities of the kind they outline could be incorporated into a grammar of the kind Lees wants?
6 Assess D. L. Bolinger's critique of this article in *Language*, vol. 37 (1961).

20 H. KURATH AND R. I. MCDAVID

1 What does the diagram on p. 270 represent? (An account of its origin will be found in any recent phonetics handbook, but see especially Daniel Jones' *Outline of English Phonetics*, 8th edn., 1956.)
2 How far is a truly phonic record of a person's pronunciation possible?
3 What kind of technique could a linguist use to identify the systematic features in a language he is studying?
4 How far do you feel features of intonation are important dialect-differentiators?
5 Compare the approach of Kurath and McDavid with that of other dialect surveys, such as the *Survey of English Dialects* (ed. H. Orton, and others) or the *Survey of Scottish Dialects* (ed. A. McIntosh).

21 JAMES SLEDD

1 How do you reconcile the notions of dictionary as authority and dictionary as record?
2 What is Sledd referring to when he criticizes the sentence 'if a word is misused often enough, it becomes acceptable' for being confused (p. 288)?
3 What is Sledd getting at when he says 'A dictionary without quotations is like a table of contents without a book' (p. 286)?
4 What other stylistic categories than 'colloquial' do you think ought to be included in a dictionary?
5 A useful selection of articles and reviews about the *Webster* can be found in *Dictionaries and THAT Dictionary*, ed. J. Sledd and W. R. Ebbitt (1962). Assess the arguments of either side.
6 Distinguish between encyclopedic and linguistic information. How much of the former do you think a dictionary ought to include?
7 What *is* the distinction between a synonym and a definition?

22 ANTHONY BURGESS

1 How does Burgess use the concept of meaning in his discussion of the morpheme? What does he mean when he says that '"Hi-"...can have no real meaning until it is completed by the objective ending "-m"'?
2 Burgess, a novelist, employs fictional situations to illustrate and even to test some of his propositions about language. Is this a suitable approach?
3 Near the end of his first section Burgess suggests that the plural suffix 'can refer...to something in the real, external world'. He later says that semantics 'deals with language at those points where it is closest to the "real world"', and that a word 'only exists at all because of some entity...in the non-linguistic world'. Are these three instances really the same way of relating linguistic events to external reality?
4 What assumptions about words do regulations limiting their number (as, for example, rates for sending a telegram) make?
5 Is the English word 'milk' really autosemantic?
6 What clues to his cultural context—his interests, beliefs, experiences, etc.—does Burgess give in the course of his essay?

SELECT INDEX OF LITERARY AND LINGUISTIC TOPICS

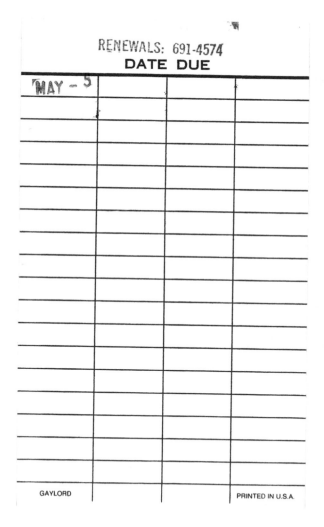